THOMSON

COURSE TECHNOLOGY

Professional ■ Technical ■ Reference

SONAR™ 6
P O W E R !
The Comprehensive Guide

By Scott R. Garrigus

DOWNLOADS
AVAILABLE

Important: Thomson Course Technology PTR cannot provide software support. Please contact the appropriate software manufacturer's technical support line or Web site for assistance.

Thomson Course Technology PTR and the author have attempted throughout this book to distinguish proprietary trademarks from descriptive terms by following the capitalization style used by the manufacturer.

Information contained in this book has been obtained by Thomson Course Technology PTR from sources believed to be reliable. However, because of the possibility of human or mechanical error by our sources, Thomson Course Technology PTR, or others, the Publisher does not guarantee the accuracy, adequacy, or completeness of any information and is not responsible for any errors or omissions or the results obtained from use of such information. Readers should be particularly aware of the fact that the Internet is an ever-changing entity. Some facts may have changed since this book went to press.

Educational facilities, companies, and organizations interested in multiple copies or licensing of this book should contact the Publisher for quantity discount information. Training manuals, CD-ROMs, and portions of this book are also available individually or can be tailored for specific needs.

ISBN-10: 1-59863-307-4

ISBN-13: 978-1-59863-307-8

Library of Congress Catalog Card Number: 2006906792

Printed in the United States of America

07 08 09 10 11 TW 10 9 8 7 6 5 4 3

THOMSON

COURSE TECHNOLOGY

Professional ■ Technical ■ Reference

Thomson Course Technology PTR, a division of Thomson Learning Inc.
25 Thomson Place
Boston, MA 02210
http://www.courseptr.com

Publisher and General Manager, Thomson Course Technology PTR:
Stacy L. Hiquet

Associate Director of Marketing:
Sarah O'Donnell

Manager of Editorial Services:
Heather Talbot

Marketing Manager:
Mark Hughes

Acquisitions Editor:
Orren Merton

Marketing Coordinator:
Adena Flitt

Project Editor and Copy Editor:
Marta Justak

Technical Reviewer:
Ryan Pietras

PTR Editorial Services Coordinator:
Erin Johnson

Interior Layout Tech:
Digital Publishing Solutions

Cover Designers:
Mike Tanamachi
Nancy Goulet

Indexer:
Sharon Shock

Proofreader:
Steve Honeywell

I would like to dedicate this book to Stanley and Stella Berlinski and Richard J. and Yolanda Garrigus, my grandparents. Without their love and support, there is no way I would be where I am today.

 # Acknowledgments

Thanks to all my music technology friends who take the time to visit my Web site and to read my ramblings in the *DigiFreq* newsletter each month. The DigiFreq family is now over 20,000 strong!

Thanks to all the Cakewalk SONAR users whose dedication and support helped to make this book possible.

Thanks to all my friends over at Cakewalk (Steve Thomas, Carl Jacobson, Morten Saether, Jesse Jost, Tom Roussell, Glenn Smith, Dave Malaguti, Ryan Pietras, Alex Westner, Brandon Ryan, and others).

Thanks to Marta Justak, Mark Garvey, Stacy Hiquet, Orren Merton, and the rest of the Thomson Course Technology publishing team.

Thanks to my family, friends, and to God for all that I have.

About the Author

Scott R. Garrigus (www.garrigus.com) has been involved with music and computers since he was 12 years old. After graduating from high school, he went on to earn a B.A. in music performance with an emphasis in sound recording technology at UMass, Lowell. In 1993, he released his first instrumental album on cassette, entitled "Pieces Of Imagination." In 1995, he began his professional writing career when his first article appeared in *Electronic Musician* magazine. In 2000, he authored his first book, *Cakewalk Power!* This was the first book to deal exclusively with the Cakewalk Pro Audio, Guitar Studio, and Home Studio software applications. Since then he has authored a number of other titles including *Sound Forge Power!*, *SONAR Power!*, *SONAR 2 Power!*, *Sound Forge 6 Power!*, *SONAR 3 Power!*, *SONAR 4 Power!*, *SONAR 5 Power!*, and *Sound Forge 8 Power!* Today, Garrigus continues to contribute articles to a number of print and online publications. He also publishes his own music technology e-zine, called *DigiFreq* (www.digifreq.com), which provides free news, reviews, tips, and techniques for music technology and home recording users.

TABLE OF ⨎ Contents

BONUS CHAPTERS AVAILABLE ON WEB SITE

You may find these additional SONAR 6 Power! Chapters 15-18 and Appendices A-B for download at http://www.courseptr.com/downloads. We have included their content and page numbers in this index for your convenience. Please visit our site for further information on SONAR 6.

❈ ❈ ❈

} Introduction

This is the first book on the market that deals exclusively with Cakewalk's SONAR 6. You can find other Cakewalk-related and generic books about using computers to create and record music that might provide a small amount of information about SONAR 6, but none of them provides complete coverage of the product. Of course, SONAR 6 comes with an excellent manual, but like most other manuals, it is meant only as a feature guide.

Instead of simply describing the features of the program and how they work, I'm going to dig deep down into the software and show you exactly how to use the product with step-by-step examples and exercises that will help make your composing and recording sessions run more smoothly. I'll explain all of the features available, and I'll do it in a manner you can understand and use right away.

So why should you listen to me? Well, I've been using SONAR (and its predecessor, Pro Audio) for many years. I've written six Cakewalk-related books before this one—*Cakewalk Power!*, *SONAR Power!*, *SONAR 2 Power!*, *SONAR 3 Power!*, *SONAR 4 Power!*, and *SONAR 5 Power!*. I've also written about Cakewalk products in numerous review articles for magazines such as *Electronic Musician*, *Computer Music*, and *Future Music*. In addition, I've been working with the people at Cakewalk for quite some time now, learning all there is to know about SONAR 6, as well as testing the product during the beta process. And the people at Cakewalk have helped me develop much of the information in this book, making sure that everything is "officially" technically accurate. How's that for a seal of approval? Suffice it to say, I know my way around the product, and now I would like to share that knowledge with you.

I'm going to assume that SONAR 6 is installed on your computer and that you know how to start the program. In addition, you should have at least skimmed through the manual that comes with the software, and you should have all your external audio and MIDI gear set up already. I'm also going to assume that you know how to use your mouse for clicking, dragging, double-clicking, right-clicking, and so on. You also should know how to work with basic Windows features, such as Windows Explorer and the Windows Control Panel. And you should have access to the World Wide Web. Otherwise, all you need is a strong interest in learning how to get the most out of SONAR 6. Just leave the rest up to me, and I promise you'll be working with SONAR 6 like you never have before. You might even have some fun with it, too.

How This Book Is Organized

You'll find that although I've tried to avoid overlapping content between this book and the manual that comes with SONAR 6, in some instances this overlap just can't be avoided. I want to be sure to help you understand all the important features of the program, and doing so means including some basic explanations. For the most part, though, the information included in this book is more "how to" than "this feature does so-and-so."

Chapter 1, "MIDI and Digital Audio Basics," and Chapter 2, "Getting Started with SONAR 6," provide an introduction to computer music and the software. These chapters explain the importance of registration and how to find help, as well as the major features and more obscure parts of the software and how they work together. You'll also find an overview of all the new features included in SONAR 6.

Chapter 3, "Customizing SONAR 6," shows you how to make SONAR 6 work the way you want it to. This chapter explains program preferences and workspace customization, as well as how to find the optimal settings for MIDI and audio functionality.

In Chapter 4, "Working with Projects," you'll learn how to work with projects. This chapter includes step-by-step instructions for opening, closing, and saving existing projects. You'll also learn how to create new projects and make your own project templates.

Chapter 5, "Getting Around in SONAR 6," and Chapter 6, "Recording and Playback," describe how to navigate within SONAR 6 and how to record and play back your projects. You'll find instructions on how to record and play MIDI as well as audio, and you'll learn about recording multiple tracks at once. I'll explain the importance of the Now time and show you how to use the Go menu, search, and markers, as well as the zoom features. After you read these chapters, you'll make your way through SONAR 6 like a pro.

In Chapter 7, "Editing Basics," and Chapter 8, "Exploring the Editing Tools," you're ready to dive into editing. First, I'll explain the basics to you, including tracks and clips, the Event Editor, and Piano Roll. Then you can investigate the editing tools in more detail.

Chapter 9, "Composing with Loops," shows you how to use the looping features and Loop Construction view found in SONAR 6. Using these features, you can compose songs using nothing more than audio sample loops. The looping features add functionality to SONAR 6 similar to what you would find in Sony's ACID software.

Similar to the VST synth features that you find in Steinberg's Cubase software, SONAR 6 gives you access to virtual synthesizer plug-ins. These plug-ins let you compose music with MIDI, using software-based synthesizers rather than the synth in your sound card or your external MIDI keyboard. Chapter 10, "Software Synthesis," explores these features.

Chapter 11, "Exploring Effects," explains one of my favorite parts of SONAR 6 because the things you can do with these tools are amazing. I'll cover both the MIDI and audio effects, and I'll show you how to use them in offline and real-time situations. I'll even share some cool presets I've developed so you can use them in your own recording projects.

Chapter 12, "Mixing It Down," takes a look at mixing. I know that mixing music via software can be confusing sometimes. Nothing beats being able to just grab a fader on a hardware-based mixer, but after you read this chapter, you might find that with all the functionality SONAR 6 provides, mixing is actually easier, and you have more control when you're using an on-screen software mixer.

In Chapter 13, "Surround Sound," I'll discuss one of the most significant features in SONAR 6, surround sound mixing. In this chapter you'll learn how to set up, create, and produce a surround sound mix of your music in SONAR 6. This is a great feature for creating audio for video games and DVD movies.

Finally, in Chapter 14, "Taking Your SONAR 6 Project to CD," I'll show you how to prepare your SONAR 6 project and burn it onto CD.

Bonus Content (Downloadable Chapters)

Starting with *SONAR 6 Power!*, we're trying a little something different. In addition to the printed book, we are offering some additional chapters that are available exclusively for download. This allows us to provide you with more SONAR 6 coverage while keeping the cost of the book at a reasonable price. These additional chapters include:

* Chapter 15: Making Sheet Music
* Chapter 16: Studio Control with StudioWare and Sysx
* Chapter 17: CAL 101
* Chapter 18: Advanced CAL Techniques
* Appendix A: Backing Up Your Project Files
* Appendix B: Producing for Multimedia and the Web

You can download these additional chapters at: www.courseptr.com/downloads.

My hope is that by reading this book, you will learn how to master SONAR 6. If along the way you have a little fun while you're at it, that's all the better.

Conventions Used in This Book

As you begin to read, you'll see that most of the information in this book is solid and useful. It contains very little fluff. I won't bore you with unrelated anecdotes or repetitive data. But to help guide you through all this material, I'll use several different conventions that highlight specific types of information you should keep an eye out for.

> **TIP**
>
> Tips are extra information that you should know related to the topic being discussed. In some cases they include personal experiences or specific techniques not covered elsewhere.

> **CAUTION**
>
> Cautions highlight actions or commands that can make irreversible changes to your files or potentially cause problems in the future. Read them carefully because they might contain important information that can make the difference between keeping your files, software, and hardware safe or losing a huge amount of work.

❄ **NOTE**

Sometimes, you might like to know (but don't necessarily *need* to know) certain points about the current topic. Notes provide additional material to help you avoid problems or shed light on a feature or technology, and they also offer related advice.

1 } MIDI and Digital Audio Basics

If you're anything like me, you want to get started right away learning all about SONAR 6. But if you don't understand the basic concepts and terms associated with computer music, you might have a hard time working your way through this book. To give you a quick overview of the most significant aspects of music technology, this chapter will do the following:

❈ Define MIDI and explain how it works.

❈ Define digital audio and explain how it works.

❈ Explain the differences between MIDI and digital audio.

Of course, this one chapter can't replace an entire book about the subject. If you want to learn more about MIDI and digital audio, plenty of extended resources are available.

❈ **MIDI AND DIGITAL AUDIO RESOURCES**

For more in-depth information about MIDI and digital audio, check out the following resources:

1. *MIDI Power!:*
www.amazon.com/exec/obidos/ASIN/1598630849/compmediaA

2. *Basic MIDI:*
www.amazon.com/exec/obidos/ASIN/1860742629/compmediaA

3. *The MIDI Companion:*
www.amazon.com/exec/obidos/ASIN/0793530776/compmediaA

4. *Basic Digital Recording:*
www.amazon.com/exec/obidos/ASIN/1860742696/compmediaA

5. *Introduction to Digital Audio:*
www.amazon.com/exec/obidos/ASIN/0240516435/compmediaA

What Is MIDI?

MIDI (*Musical Instrument Digital Interface*) is a special kind of computer language that lets electronic musical instruments (such as synthesizer keyboards) "talk" to computers. It works like this: Say you use a synthesizer keyboard as your musical instrument. Every key on the keyboard of your synthesizer has a corresponding electronic switch. When you press a key, its corresponding switch is activated and sends a signal to the computer chip inside your keyboard. The chip then sends the signal to the MIDI interface in your keyboard, which translates the signal into MIDI messages and sends those messages to the MIDI interface in your computer system.

❄ **MIDI INTERFACE**

A MIDI interface is a device that is plugged into your computer, allowing it to understand the MIDI language. Basically, you can think of the interface as a *translator*. When your electronic musical instrument sends out MIDI messages to your computer, the MIDI interface takes those messages and converts them into signals that your computer can understand.

The MIDI messages contain information telling your computer that a key was pressed (called a *Note On* message), which key it was (the name of the note represented by a number), and how hard you hit the key (called the *MIDI velocity*). For example, if you press Middle C on your keyboard, a Note On message is sent to your computer, telling it that you pressed a key. Another message containing the number 60 is sent, telling the computer that you pressed Middle C. And a final message is sent containing a number from 1 to 127 (1 being very soft and 127 being very hard), which tells your computer how hard you hit the key.

Different MIDI messages represent all the performance controls on your keyboard. In addition to each key, MIDI messages represent the modulation wheel, pitch bend wheel, and other features. Your computer can store all the MIDI messages that are sent to it as you play your keyboard. The timing of your performance (how long it takes you to hit one key after another and how long you hold down each key) can be stored as well. Your computer can then send those MIDI messages back to your keyboard with the same timing, so that it seems like you are playing the music, but without touching the keys. The basic concept goes like this: You play a piece of music on your keyboard. Your performance is stored as instructions in your computer. Then those instructions are sent back to your keyboard from the computer, and you hear the piece of music played back exactly the same way you performed it, mistakes and all (see Figure 1.1).

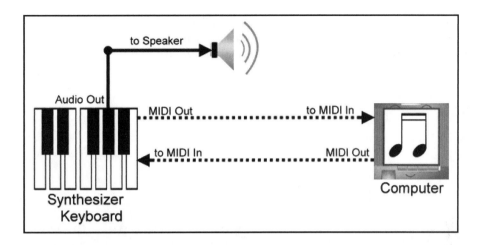

Figure 1.1 This diagram shows how MIDI messages are recorded and played back with a computer.

What Is Digital Audio?

Digital audio is the representation of sound as numbers. Recording sound as digital audio is similar to recording sound using a tape recorder, but slightly different. Suppose that you have a microphone connected to your computer system. When you make a sound (such as singing a tune, playing a musical instrument, or even simply clapping your hands), the microphone "hears" it and converts the sound to an electronic signal. The microphone then sends the signal to the sound card in your computer, which translates the signal into numbers. These numbers are called *samples*.

> ❄ **SOUND CARD**
>
> A sound card is a device that is plugged into your computer, allowing it to understand the electronic signals of any audio device. Basically, you can think of the sound card as a translator. When an audio device (such as a microphone, electronic musical instrument, CD player, or anything else that can output an audio signal) sends out signals to your computer, the sound card takes those signals and converts them into numbers that your computer can understand.

The samples contain information that tells your computer how the recorded signal sounded at certain instances in time. The more samples used to represent the signal, the better the quality of the recorded sound. For example, to make a digital audio recording that has the same quality as audio on a CD, the computer needs to receive 44,100 samples for every second of sound that's recorded. The number of samples received per second is called the *sampling rate*.

The size of each individual sample also makes a difference in the quality of the recorded sound. This size is called the *bit depth*. The more bits used to represent a sample, the better the sound quality. For example, to make a digital audio recording with the same quality as audio on a CD, each sample has to be 16 bits in size.

※ **BINARY NUMERALS**

Computers use binary numerals to represent numbers. These binary numerals are called *bits*, and each bit can represent one of two numbers: 1 or 0. By combining more than one bit, computers can represent larger numbers. For instance, any number from 0 to 255 can be represented with 8 bits. With 16 bits, the range becomes 0 to 65,535.

Your computer can store all the samples that are sent to it. The timing of each sample is stored as well. Then your computer can send those samples back to the sound card with the same timing so that what you hear sounds exactly the same as what was recorded. The basic concept goes like this: Your sound card records an electronic signal from an audio device (such as a microphone or CD player). The sound card converts the signal into numbers called *samples*, which are stored in your computer. Then those samples are sent back to the sound card, which converts them back into an electronic signal. The signal is sent to your speakers (or other audio device), and you hear the sound exactly as it was recorded (see Figure 1.2).

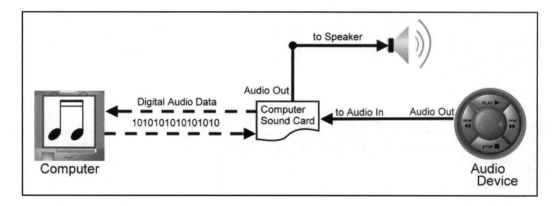

Figure 1.2 This diagram shows how audio is converted into numbers so it can be recorded and played back with a computer.

So What's Really the Difference?

After reading the explanations of MIDI and digital audio, you might still be wondering what the difference is between them. Both processes involve signals being sent to the computer to be recorded, and then the computer sends those signals back out to be played, right?

Well, you have to keep in mind that when you're recording MIDI data, you're not recording actual sound; you are recording only performance instructions. This concept is similar to a musician reading sheet music, with the sheet music representing MIDI data and the musician representing a computer. The musician (or computer) reads the sheet music (or MIDI data) and then stores it in memory. The musician then plays the music back via a musical instrument. Now what if the musician uses a different instrument to play back the music? The musical performance remains the same, but the sound changes. The same thing happens with MIDI data. A synthesizer keyboard can make all kinds of different sounds, but playing the same MIDI data back with the keyboard yields an identical performance, no matter what.

When you're recording digital audio, you *are* recording actual sound. If you record a musical performance as digital audio, you cannot change the sound of that performance, as described earlier. Because of these differences, MIDI and digital audio have their advantages and disadvantages. Because MIDI is recorded as performance data and not actual sound, you can manipulate it much more easily than you can manipulate digital audio. For example, you can easily fix mistakes in your performance by simply changing the pitch of a note. And MIDI data can be translated into standard musical notation, but digital audio can't. On the other hand, MIDI can't be used to record anything that requires actual audio, such as sound effects or vocals. With digital audio, you can record any kind of sound, and you can always be sure that your recording will sound exactly the same every time you play it back. With MIDI, you can't be sure of that because although the MIDI data remains the same, the playback device or sound can be changed.

I hope this description clears up some of the confusion you might have about MIDI and digital audio. You need to be familiar with a number of other related terms, but I will cover them in different areas of the book as I go along. For now, as long as you understand the difference between MIDI and digital audio, I can begin talking about the real reason you bought this book: learning how to use SONAR 6.

2 } Getting Started with SONAR 6

Now that you have a basic understanding of the technology involved in making music with computers, I think you'll find working with SONAR 6 more enjoyable. Ready to get started? This chapter will do the following:

* Tell you how to obtain the latest product update.
* Give you a quick tour of SONAR's major features.
* Briefly cover the new features in SONAR 6.
* Describe a basic studio environment.
* Let you know where to look for help if problems arise.

What Version of SONAR Do You Have?

Even though you're using SONAR 6, it might not be the latest version. Cakewalk is constantly fixing and improving the software. Any problems you experience might easily be remedied with an update. To find out exactly what version you're using, start SONAR, and click Help > About SONAR. A dialog box similar to Figure 2.1 on the next page will appear, displaying your exact version number. You should then check to see whether a more recent update is available.

Getting the Latest Product Update

Although automatically receiving new product updates would be nice, most companies can't afford to send CDs to all their users every time they update their product. That's one of the reasons why the Internet has become such a wonderful tool. Sometimes, the answer to your problem is just a download away. Cakewalk provides a support area on its Web site where you can get the latest updates for SONAR. Just follow these steps to get the updates:

1. Log on to the Internet.
2. Start SONAR and choose Help > SONAR on the Web. This will automatically open your Web browser and take you to the SONAR Owner's Page, as shown in Figure 2.2.

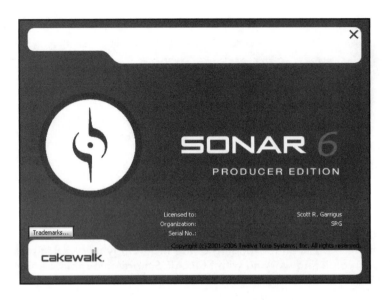

Figure 2.1 The About SONAR dialog box shows the program's current version number.

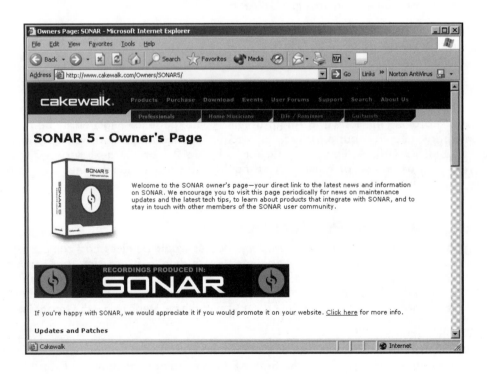

Figure 2.2 You can download SONAR updates from the SONAR Owner's Page.

3. In the section labeled Updates and Patches, click the name of the update you need. If more than one update is available, simply compare your current version to the updates listed and select the appropriate one. For instance, if you have SONAR 5.0, you'll want the update that upgrades version 5.0 to the current version.

4. Click the Download link for the update and follow the instructions to download the update patch.

5. Create a temporary folder on your Windows desktop and download the update file to that folder.

6. Run the file. That's all there is to upgrading—your software is now updated.

❄ **FOUND A BUG?**

Think you've found a bug? Just because a software product is released to the public doesn't mean it's perfect. Improvements are always being made; that's why updates become available. If you have a problem with SONAR on a regular basis and you can reproduce that problem by performing the same steps each time, you might have found a bug in the software. Before you go spreading any rumors, though, first tell some friends about it and see whether they can reproduce the problem on their computer systems. If so, after the bug has occurred in SONAR, choose Help > Cakewalk Problem Reporter to create a report about your PC and current SONAR project. You should then email that report, along with a detailed description of the problem, to Cakewalk using the form on this Web page: www.cakewalk.com/support/email/

The staff might already be aware of the bug and be working on a fix for it. Then again, they might not be aware of it, and although your diligence won't make you famous, you'll feel good to know that you might have saved your fellow SONAR users a lot of frustration.

Taking a Quick Tour of SONAR

Because SONAR is such a powerful application, you can use it for a variety of different tasks: composing music, developing computer game music and sounds, producing compact discs, creating audio for the Web, and even scoring films and videos. SONAR provides a number of features to support all these endeavors and more. As a matter of fact, you can use SONAR as the central piece of equipment in your studio because it controls all your music gear from your computer via on-screen control panels. No matter which way you decide to use SONAR, you'll find plenty of flexibility and power in the tools provided.

Projects

In SONAR, all your music data for a single body of work is organized as a project. A project can be anything from a Top 40 song or a 30-second radio spot to a full-length symphonic score, such as a movie soundtrack. Along with the music data, all of SONAR's settings for a single work are stored in the project. A project is saved on disk as a single file with a .CWP or .CWB file extension. The difference between the two file types is that a work (.CWP) file stores only MIDI data and project settings, whereas a bundle (.CWB) file also includes any audio data within a project.

Tracks, Clips, and Events

The music data within a project is organized into units called *tracks*, *clips*, and *events*. Events, which are the smallest units, consist of single pieces of data, such as one note played on a MIDI keyboard. Clips are groups of events. They can be anything from a simple MIDI melody to an entire vocal performance recorded as audio. Tracks are used to store clips. For example, a pop song project might contain seven tracks of music data—six for the instruments and one for the vocal performance. Each track can contain any number of clips that might represent one long performance or different parts of a performance. SONAR gives you unlimited tracks. The only limitations are the speed of your CPU and hard drive and the amount of memory (RAM) you have in your computer.

Track View

To work with the data in a project, you have to use the views in SONAR. Views are like windows that let you see and manipulate the data in a project in a variety of ways. The most important is the Track view, shown in Figure 2.3

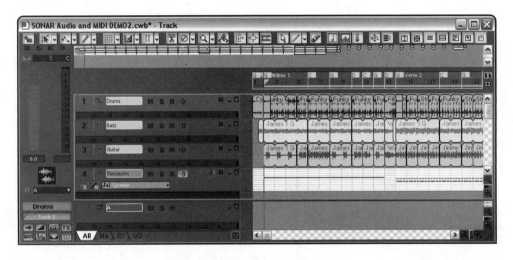

Figure 2.3   The Track view is the main window used to work with a project in SONAR.

In this window, you can see all the tracks that are available in a project. You also can view and edit all the basic track settings, as well as all the clips contained in each track. I'll talk about the Track view extensively in a number of different chapters in the book.

Staff View

In the Staff view, you can work with the MIDI data in your project as standard music notation. By selecting one or more MIDI tracks in the Track view and opening the Staff view, you can see your music just as if it were notes on a printed page, as in Figure 2.4.

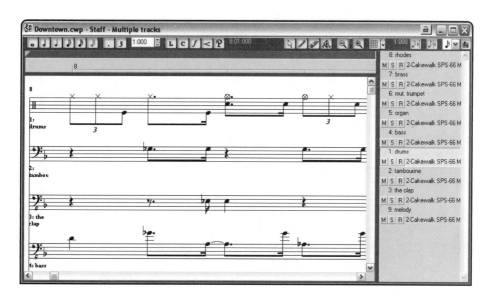

Figure 2.4   In the Staff view, you can see and edit your MIDI data as standard music notation.

Using the Staff view, you also can edit your music notation by adding, changing, or deleting notes. Special notation functions such as dynamics markings, percussion parts, and guitar chord symbols are included, too. You can notate anything from a single one-staff melody to an entire 24-part musical score.

Piano Roll View

Although the Staff view is great for traditional music editing, it doesn't access expressive MIDI data, such as note velocity or pitch bend controller messages. For that data, you can use the Piano Roll view. This view displays notes as they might appear on a player-piano roll, as shown in Figure 2.5.

You can change note pitch and duration by simply dragging the rectangular representations. But more importantly, you can view and edit MIDI controller messages graphically with the mouse instead of having to deal with raw numbers.

Event List View

If you really want precise control over the data in your project, the Event List view is the tool for the job. The Event List view shows individual events in a track (or the entire project) as special keywords and numbers in a list, as shown in Figure 2.6.

Using this view is similar to looking at the raw MIDI data that is recorded from your MIDI keyboard or controller. You can edit the characteristics of single notes and MIDI controller messages by typing in data. You'll probably use the Piano Roll view more often, but it's nice to know the Event List view is available if you need it.

❊ ❊ ❊

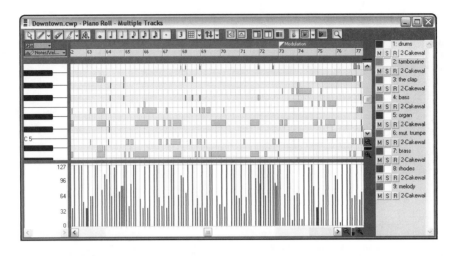

Figure 2.5 The Piano Roll view gives you access to both note and MIDI controller messages.

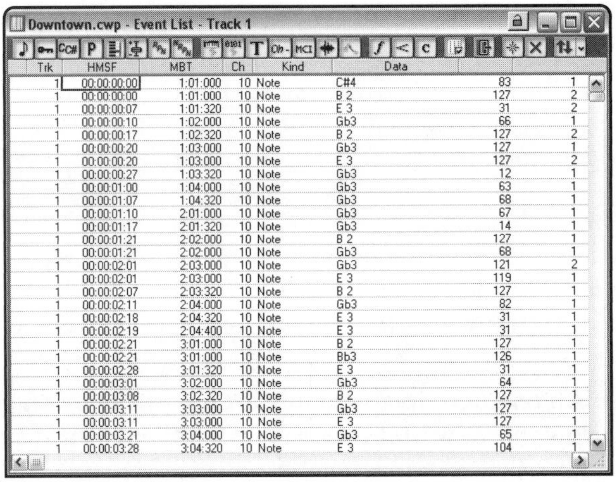

Figure 2.6 For really precise editing tasks, the Event List view gives you access to the individual events in a project.

Loop Construction View

The Loop Construction view gives you an easy way to create your own sample loops. You can use these loops, which are digital audio clips designed to be played over and over, to construct entire songs. When you're working with the Loop Construction view, you'll see the sound wave of your loop (see Figure 2.7).

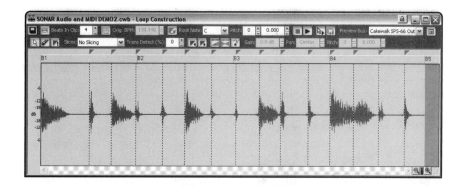

Figure 2.7 The Loop Construction view is a special editing tool for creating sample loops.

Not only does the Loop Construction view allow you to create your own sample loops, but you can also use ACID-compatible loops, like the loops found in Sony's ACID software.

Console View

When you're ready to mix all your MIDI and audio tracks down to a single stereo file, you can use the Console view. This tool is made to look and function like a real recording studio mixing console (see Figure 2.8.)

Figure 2.8 The Console view looks and functions similar to a real recording studio mixing console.

You can use the Console view to adjust the panning and volume for each track in a project. As a matter of fact, you can use the Console view in place of the Track view for adjusting track settings and recording new tracks. And just like on a real mixing console, you can monitor volume levels via on-screen meters, as well as mute and solo individual tracks or groups of tracks.

What's New in SONAR 6?

SONAR 6 introduces many changes in terms of features, some of which were suggested by users. These features include the following:

- **Audio Snap.** The new Audio Snap feature is a collection of tools that manipulates the timing of audio data similar to Pro Tools' Beat Detective, Digital Performer's Beat Detection Engine, and Nuendo's Audio Warp. You can do all kinds of things with Audio Snap, such as align any audio clips to the project tempo, quantize beats within a clip, apply and extract grooves from audio, and more.

- **Automation Enhancements.** SONAR no longer has restrictions for how automation is used. You can now record MIDI, audio, effects, and synth automation during both playback and recording.

- **Enhanced Clip Editing.** SONAR provides some new clip editing enhancements including new clip handles for easier slip editing, new clip lassoing for easier selection, new clip data locking, and the ability to lock clips to specific time for easier video editing and more. There is also a new Fast Zoom feature and mouse wheel support.

- **Superior Control Surface Support.** Those of you using a hardware control surface for mixing and editing will love the new Active Control Technology (ACT) and WAI (Where Am I) Display features. You can now quickly and easily control any plug-in that has the current focus. You can also quickly see what tracks you are controlling.

- **File Versioning.** With the new file versioning feature, you can save and keep track of editing sessions and also easily revert back to any previous sessions.

- **Customization Enhancements.** SONAR now customizes track strips in the Track view, as well as toolbars and menus. This includes plug-in menus. You can also give friendly names to sound card drivers.

- **New Synth Rack.** The Synth Rack has been revamped with a new look and a number of new features. You can now automate synth parameters from the Synth Rack using assignable on-screen controls, and you can determine what track will store the automation data using a simple menu.

- **Redesigned Console View.** Although the layout remains similar, the Console View sports a new look and some new features. Dividers now magnetically snap to strip borders; strips have different colors for easy differentiation; there are new show/hide buttons; and new scroll commands make it easier to traverse a large mix.

- ❋ **Analyst Spectrum Analyzer.** With the new Analyst, you can see a graphic representation of your audio data. You can also record spectrum automation and apply that automation to different effect plug-ins like EQ to match sonic signatures.

Like version 5, SONAR 6 comes in two flavors: SONAR 6 Studio and SONAR 6 Producer. The following new features are only available in SONAR 6 Producer:

- ❋ **VC-64 Vintage Channel Effect.** This is a multi-effect channel strip that provides two equalizers, two compressors, a gate, and a de-esser. The VC-64 provides 10 different internal effect routings, which allow for a large number of sound processing possibilities. You can use this effect on individual tracks or even an entire mix.

- ❋ **Session Drummer 2.** The old Session Drummer is gone and Session Drummer 2 takes its place. Instead of a simple MIDI drum loop generator, Session Drummer is now a full-fledged drum sampler that includes 2GB of custom-designed drum content sampled from seven live kits using multiple mic positions.

A Basic Studio Setup

Over the years, I've built up quite an arsenal of tools that currently reside in my home studio, but you don't need a ton of gizmos and gadgets to produce great music. If I were to scale down my setup to include only the basics, I'd be left with everything I need to compose and record my tunes with SONAR.

Computer

Other than SONAR itself, a basic studio revolves around one main component—your PC. If you already have a PC, be sure to check it against Cakewalk's system requirements for SONAR (www.cakewalk.com/Products/SONAR/System.asp). Your best bet is to check it against the recommended system requirements rather than the minimum because the minimum requirements won't give you very high-quality performance.

If your system matches (or exceeds) the recommended system requirements, you should be all set to run SONAR. If not, then you should seriously consider either upgrading or purchasing a new system. If you decide to go with a new system, you might want to think about building it yourself or picking out the components and having it built for you. It's not that a generic Gateway or Dell PC won't do, but they are not optimized for audio work.

For my last DAW, I purchased a base system (which included the case, motherboard, CPU, memory, etc.) and expanded on it. Recently, I needed to move up to something more powerful and more professional, so I decided to just get a system that was purposely built for audio. I decided to go with a Creation Station from Sweetwater (www.sweetwater.com/creation_station/). Sweetwater is well known for its high quality, high standards, and excellent customer service, and believe me... it's all true. The system I decided upon was their top-of-the-line CSRack Dual 3.4. I needed a system with power and the capability to run 64-bit applications. The CSRack Dual 3.4 does these things and more with flying colors. Here are the system specs with a couple of modifications that I needed (4 GB memory and Win XP 64 added):

- Pentium Dual Core 3.4GHz/800MHz Front Side Bus
- 4 GB DDR2/533
- System drive: Glyph Seagate 80GB SATA 7,200 RPM
- 2x Glyph Seagate 200GB SATA 7,200 RPM "Raid Ready"
- Radeon x300se 1VGA / 1DVI-I Video Card
- DVD+/-RW Burner
- 15-in-1 Multi Card Reader
- 4U Rackmount Case
- Auralex SheetBlok-Plus™ Sound Dampening System
- Windows XP 32 and 64 Professional in a dual-boot configuration

As you can tell, my current PC can easily run SONAR and then some, but you don't need a top-of-the-line system to get good performance. As long as the specifications for your computer land somewhere between SONAR's minimum and recommended system requirements, you shouldn't have any trouble running the software. But if you have the money and decide to get a new PC, by all means get the most powerful system you can afford. You won't be sorry.

> **OPTIMIZE YOUR AUDIO PC**
>
> One of the reasons that many people can get away with using a less powerful system is that they have optimized it for audio work. There are a number of things you can do to your PC that will make it run more efficiently for the purposes of making music. These include making adjustments to the system itself, as well as to the Windows OS. If you'd like more information about how to optimize your audio PC, go to www.digifreq.com/digifreq/article.asp?ID=14 to check out my feature article entitled "Optimize Your Audio PC." Also, go to www.digifreq.com/digifreq/articles.asp for more great articles.

Sound Card

The most important thing to consider when purchasing a sound card for use with SONAR is whether there are WDM or ASIO drivers available for the card. You'll need to get in touch with the manufacturer of the card to verify this. Why is it so important? Because SONAR supports a Microsoft technology called *WDM* (*Windows Driver Model*) and a Steinberg technology called *ASIO* (*Audio Stream Input Output*). If you have a sound card that has WDM or ASIO drivers, SONAR will give you much better performance in terms of audio latency. Basically, latency is a form of audio delay that occurs when a software program such as SONAR can't communicate with your sound card fast enough while processing audio data, which results in an audible delay. This is usually only noticeable with features that use real-time processing. In SONAR, these include input monitoring and real-time soft synth performance.

❋ **RECOMMENDED SOUND CARDS**
For a list of audio cards recommended by Cakewalk, go to www.cakewalk.com/tips/audiohw.asp.

Of course, there are many other things to consider when choosing a particular card. You should look for a PCI-based sound card (one that is installed inside your computer) rather than a USB-based sound card. USB audio interfaces don't really provide enough bandwidth to transfer audio data fast enough for sufficient use. However, with the new USB 2.0 spec, that shouldn't present a problem once manufacturers update their products. You might also want to consider using a FireWire-based sound card. They still aren't as good as a PCI-based card, but they're definitely better than USB 1.0. You should also be aware of the types of connections that sound cards supply. The typical sound card provides a number of different audio inputs and outputs including line level, microphone level, and speaker. Line-level inputs and outputs are used to transfer sound from cassette decks, radios, electronic keyboards, or any other standard audio device. Microphones generate a very low audio level by themselves, so they need a special input of their own, which is connected to an internal preamplifier on the sound card. Speakers also need their own special connector with a built-in amplifier to produce a decent amount of volume. Some high-end sound cards also offer digital inputs and outputs. These special connectors let you attach the sound card directly to compatible devices such as some CD players and DAT (*Digital Audio Tape*) decks. Using these connections gives you the best possible sound because audio signals stay in the digital domain and don't need to be converted into analog signals. In addition, connectors come in a variety of forms. Low-cost cards usually provide the same 1/8-inch jacks used for headphones on boom boxes. For better quality, there are 1/4-inch, RCA, or XLR jacks. Connections can also be balanced or unbalanced. Balanced connections provide shielding to protect the audio signal against RFI (*Radio Frequency Interference*). Unbalanced connections don't provide any type of protection.

If you want to be able to record more than one audio track at once, you'll need a card with multiple audio connections. Most average sound cards internally mix all of their audio sources down to one stereo signal, but higher-end (more expensive) cards let you record each device separately on its own discreet stereo channel. This capability is much more desirable in a music recording studio, but not everyone needs it.

A good quality audio signal is something that everybody desires. During recording, the sampling rate plays a big part in the quality of the audio signal. Suffice it to say, the higher the sampling rate that a sound card can handle, the better the sound quality. The sampling rate of a CD is 44.1 kHz (44,100 samples per second); all sound cards on the market support this. Professional cards can hit 48 kHz or higher.

Bit resolution is also a factor in determining digital sound quality. The more bits you have to represent your signal, the better it will sound. The CD standard is 16 bits, which is supported by all sound cards. Some cards (again, mostly high-end) go up to 20, 22, or even 24 bits.

Two other measurements you need to look for are signal-to-noise ratio and frequency response. As with the other measurements mentioned earlier, the higher the better. Since all electronic devices produce some amount of noise, the signal-to-noise ratio of a sound card tells you how much higher the signal strength is compared to the amount of internal noise made by the sound card. The greater the number, the quieter the card will be. A good signal-to-noise measurement is about 90 dB or higher. Frequency response is actually a range of numbers, which is based on the capabilities of human hearing. The frequency response of human hearing is approximately 20 Hz to 20 kHz. A good sound card will encompass at least that range, maybe even more.

What do I use? I actually have a couple of different interfaces. I have the Mona from Echo Audio, which connects via a PCI card. This is an excellent audio interface that provides excellent built-in preamps. Unfortunately, it is now a discontinued product.

I also use the SONAR Power Studio 660 from Cakewalk (www.cakewalk.com/Products/PowerStudio/default.asp). This is a FireWire based interface that provides two built-in mic/instrument pre-amps, digital I/O, a built-in MIDI interface, and more. I really like this box a lot because I can use it anywhere and not have to fuss with a PCI card installation. You can monitor from either software or hardware, and it provides built-in limiting so you don't overload the input when recording. It also works nicely with SONAR.

MIDI Interface

If you have any external MIDI devices (like a MIDI keyboard), then you'll need a MIDI interface for your computer. If you have a simple setup with only one MIDI keyboard, then you can easily get away with a simple single- or double-port MIDI interface. The best way to go here is to get a USB-based interface. It will be easy to install (just plug it in), and it won't take up an IRQ or PCI slot inside your computer. Also, be sure that the interface has Windows XP compatible drivers (depending on what OS you are using). Bad drivers can cause problems. Other than that, the only major differences between interfaces are the number of ports they provide. If you have many external MIDI devices, it's best to connect each device to its own dedicated MIDI port. I'm currently using the MIDI interface that is built into the Cakewalk SONAR Power Studio 660, which is nice because I don't need two separate devices for audio and MIDI.

Control Surface

While not an absolute necessity, a control surface can save you a lot of time and mouse maneuvers. A control surface is a MIDI device that provides real buttons, knobs, and sliders that can be used to control the different software-based parameters that you normally adjust with your mouse on your computer screen. A control surface can be used for record/playback transport control, editing, and even mixing. One of my favorite devices is the Tranzport from Frontier Design Group (www.amazon.com/exec/obidos/ASIN/B000C179CE/compmediaA/). The Tranzport provides buttons, a jog wheel, and an LCD readout so that you easily control many of your music software parameters. What is unique about this device is that it is wireless. You can actually use it up to 30 feet away from your PC, which makes it extremely easy when you are recording alone in your studio. The only thing it doesn't provide is sliders, so it can't conveniently be used for mixing.

Microphone

If you plan to do any acoustic recording (vocals, acoustic guitar, and so on), you'll need a good microphone. There are literally hundreds of microphones on the market, and entire books have been written on the subject, so I won't go into great detail here. Basically, the microphone you choose depends on the application. I needed a good vocal mic, but not something that was going to put me in the poor house. While I would love to get a Neumann U87 (one of the best), there's no way I could afford one. Luckily, Shure came to my rescue with their KSM27 (www.amazon.com/exec/obidos/ASIN/B0002J1K4Y/compmediaA/). It's a great vocal mic that isn't too expensive. I like the fact that it can also be used for other applications in a pinch. But what's right for me might not be right for you, so I've rounded up a number of online resources for you to educate yourself on the subject of microphones.

- ❋ **Music Technology Article Index:** www.digifreq.com/digifreq/articles.asp
- ❋ **Microphone University:** www.dpamicrophones.com/page.php?PID=1
- ❋ **A Brief Guide to Microphones:** www.audio-technica.com/cms/site/9904525cd25e0d8d/index.html
- ❋ **A Brief Guide to Microphone Selection:** www.audio-technica.com/cms/site/7cadf671dea2c9e0/index.html

Speakers

You also need to be able to hear the music you're recording, so you'll need a good set of speakers (or monitors, as they're called in the professional audio world). Like microphones, there are literally hundreds of different monitors on the market. For home studio purposes, you'll probably want to get yourself a good pair of active nearfield monitors. They're called *active* because they come with a built-in amplifier, which saves you from having to buy an external amp and match it up to your monitors. They're called *nearfield* because you listen to them at a fairly close distance (about four feet). This lets you set up your home studio in just about any space you can find because you don't have to acoustically treat the room, at least not professionally.

CREATING THE RIGHT RECORDING ENVIRONMENT

For some tips about how to set up your home studio space for better recording, go to www.digifreq.com/digifreq/article.asp?ID=36 to check out my feature article entitled "Creating the Right Recording Environment."

There is a wide variety of monitors available, but I'm currently having fun with the V4s from KRK Systems (www.krksys.com). These are a pair of active nearfield monitors that really deliver great sound. I also love the fact that they've been designed for small workstation areas, and they are shielded, which means you can set them close to your computer screen without problems. However, what I like might not be what you like, so I've compiled a number of online resources to help you choose the right monitors for you.

* **Music Technology Article Index:** www.digifreq.com/digifreq/articles.asp
* **Ten Powered Nearfields Reviewed:** www.prorec.com/prorec/articles.nsf/files/0B7FAE7ED3205D3C86256AE100044F41
* **Audio FAQ (Speakers):** www.audioweb.com/AudioFAQ/Default.asp?faq=5
* **eCoustics.com speaker articles:** www.ecoustics.com/Home/Home_Audio/Speakers/Speaker_Articles/

Finding Help When You Need It

Cakewalk provides a number of ways for you to find help when you're having a problem with SONAR. The two most obvious places to look are the user's guide and the SONAR Help file. Actually, these two sources contain basically the same information, but with the Help file, you can perform a search to find something really specific. At the first sign of trouble, you should go through the troubleshooting information. If you can't find an answer to your problem there, you can pay a visit to the Cakewalk Web site.

The support page of the Cakewalk Web site (www.cakewalk.com/Support/SONAR/default.asp) contains a ton of helpful information, including FAQs and technical documents that provide details on a number of Cakewalk-related topics. You can also find great information at the DigiFreq forums (www.digifreq.com/digifreq/discuss/default.asp). I have a special section set up where you can trade tips, advice, and information with other Cakewalk users. Many times, you'll find that someone has had the same problem you're having, and has already found a solution. Isn't sharing great?

> ❄ **FREE MUSIC TECHNOLOGY NEWSLETTER**
>
> Also be sure to sign up for a free subscription to my DigiFreq music technology newsletter. DigiFreq is a monthly email newsletter that teaches you more about music technology. It provides free news, articles, reviews, tips and tutorials for home recording and professional musicians. By applying for your own free subscription, you can learn all about the latest music product releases, read straightforward reviews, explore related Web resources, and have a chance to win free products from brand-name manufacturers. Go to www.digifreq.com/digifreq/ to get your free subscription.

You can also contact Cakewalk Technical Support directly. You can either email your questions using the form on this Web page: www.cakewalk.com/support/email/ or you can call 617-423-9021 (USA). Currently, the hours are Monday through Friday from 10 a.m. to 6 p.m. Eastern time. But remember, in order to receive technical support, you have to be a registered user. If you call or send email, you'll be asked for your serial number. As I said before, remember to send in that registration card! You'll be a much happier camper... er, Cakewalker.

3 } Customizing SONAR 6

Although we all may be SONAR users, that doesn't mean we like to work with the product in exactly the same way. I have my way of doing things, and you probably have your own way. Luckily, SONAR provides a number of settings so you can make the program conform to your way of working. This chapter will do the following:

* Tell you how to organize all the different files associated with SONAR.
* Teach you to customize the program's workspace, including colors, menus, toolbars, window layouts, and key bindings.
* Explain how you can set up all the MIDI parameters.
* Tell you how to find the optimal audio settings.

Organizing Files

As you work with SONAR, you'll deal with many different types of files. These include project files, audio files, StudioWare files, CAL files, and so on. To keep things organized, SONAR specifies different disk locations for storing each file type. Initially, SONAR stores most of the files in the C:\Program Files\Cakewalk\SONAR 6 Producer Edition\Sample Content folder on your hard drive, but that doesn't mean they have to stay there.

Changing File Locations

To specify your own file locations, follow these steps.

1. In SONAR, choose Options > Global to open the Global Options dialog box and then click the Folders tab (see Figure 3.1).
2. In the Project Files parameter, specify where you would like to store all your SONAR projects by typing in a new folder location. This includes .CWP (Work), .CWB (Bundle), and .MID (MIDI) files. When you specify a folder location for this parameter, it affects the location to which the File > Open and File > Save As dialog boxes will initially open.

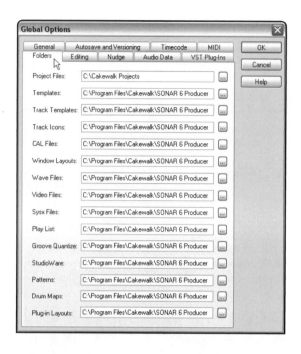

Figure 3.1 Use the Global Options dialog box to specify your file storage locations.

❄ BROWSE FOR FOLDERS

An easier way to specify a folder location is to click the ellipsis button located to the right of each field. This will open the Browse for Folder dialog box, which will let you specify a folder location by navigating through your computer's file directory using your mouse.

Also, if your computer is connected to a network, you can specify a folder location on the network rather than on your computer's hard drive. This can be useful if you want to share your project data with other musicians in your studio.

After you have selected a new file location, click OK.

3. In the Templates parameter, specify where you would like to store all your SONAR project templates (.CWT files).

4. In the Track Templates parameter, specify where you would like to store all your track template (.CWX) files.

5. In the Track Icons field, specify where you would like to store all your track icons (.BMP files).

6. In the CAL Files parameter, specify where you would like to store all your CAL (.CAL) files.

7. In the Window Layouts parameter, specify where you would like to store all your window layouts (.CakewalkWindowLayout files).

8. In the Wave Files parameter, specify where you would like SONAR to look for any external audio files (such as sample loops) for importing into your projects. This includes .WAV, Apple .AIFF, .MPEG, Windows Media, and Next/Sun files. When you specify a folder location for this parameter, it affects the location to which the File > Import Audio dialog box will initially open.

❄ **COPY YOUR LOOPS TO HD**

If you have a large sample loop collection that spans a number of different CDs, it can be cumbersome to try to find the right loop when you have to keep loading and unloading different discs from your CD-ROM drive. Instead, you might want to consider copying all your loops to a folder on your hard drive and then specifying that folder location for the Wave Files parameter. From then on, whenever you need to import an audio loop into a project, you have instant access to all the loops in your collection.

---

9. In the Video Files parameter, specify where you would like SONAR to look for any external video files to import into your projects. This includes .AVI, .MPG, and .MOV files. When you specify a folder location for this parameter, it affects the location to which the File > Import Video File dialog box will initially open.

10. In the Sysx Files parameter, specify where you would like to store all your system-exclusive (.SYX) files. When you specify a folder location for this parameter, it affects the location to which the Load Bank from File and Save Bank to File dialog boxes in the Sysx view will initially open.

11. In the Groove Quantize parameter, specify where you would like to store all your Groove Quantize (.GRV) files. When you specify a folder location for this parameter, it affects the location to which the Open Groove File dialog box from the Groove Quantize function will initially open.

12. In the StudioWare parameter, specify where you would like to store all your StudioWare (.CakewalkStudioWare) files.

13. In the Patterns parameter, specify where you would like SONAR to look for any Pattern files for the Pattern Brush feature. This includes .MID (MIDI) files. When you specify a folder location for this parameter, it affects the patterns that will appear in the Pattern Brush menu in the Piano Roll view.

14. In the Drum Maps parameter, specify where you would like to store all your Drum Map (.MAP) files.

15. In the Plug-In Layouts parameter, specify where you would like to store all your plug-in layout (.PGL) files.

16. When you're finished assigning new folder locations for your files, click OK.

Putting Everything in Its Place

If you've decided to change the location of any of the file types mentioned earlier, be sure to move all your existing files to their new locations, including all the files that ship with SONAR.

1. Open Windows Explorer; then locate and open the C:\Program Files\ Cakewalk\ SONAR 6 Producer Edition folder on your hard drive. You'll find the various folders here containing the files you want to move.

2. SONAR ships with a few sample project files whose filenames end in .CWP and .CWB. These files are located in the Sample Content folder. Move the files to the same folder you specified in the Project Files parameter of the Global Options > Folders dialog box.

3. The templates (.CWT files) included with SONAR are located in the Sample Content folder. Move the files to the same folder you specified in the Templates parameter.

4. The track templates (.CWX files) included with SONAR are located in the Track Templates folder. Move the files to the same folder you specified in the Track Templates parameter.

5. The track icons (.BMP files) included with SONAR are located in the Track Icons folder. Move the files to the same folder you specified in the Track Icons parameter.

6. The CAL (.CAL) files shipped with SONAR are located in the Sample Content folder. Move the files to the same folder you specified in the CAL files parameter.

7. The window layouts (.CakewalkWindowLayout) shipped with SONAR are located in the Sample Content folder. Move the files to the same folder you specified in the Window Layouts parameter.

8. There are no audio sample loops included with SONAR, but if you have some of your own, copy them to the same folder you specified in the Wave Files parameter. This will take up space on your hard drive, but it will also give you quick and easy access to your loops if you ever want to import them into a project.

9. SONAR doesn't include any sample video files, so there are no files to move in this case. But if you have a collection of your own, look for files whose names end in .AVI, .MPG, or .MOV and move them to the same folder you specified in the Video Files parameter.

10. SONAR includes some system-exclusive (.SYX) files, which are located in the C:\Program Files\Cakewalk\SONAR 6 Producer Edition folder. Move those files to the same folder you specified in the Sysx Files parameter.

11. SONAR includes some Groove Quantize (.GRV) files, which are located in the Sample Content folder. Move the files to the same folder you specified in the Groove Quantize parameter.

12. The Sample Content folder also contains a large number of StudioWare (.Cakewalk-StudioWare) files that ship with SONAR. Move these files to the same folder you specified in the StudioWare parameter.

13. SONAR includes some Pattern Brush (.MID) files, which are located in the Pattern Brush Patterns folder. Move the files to the same folder you specified in the Patterns parameter.

14. SONAR ships with Drum Map (.MAP) files, which are located in the Drum Maps folder. Move the files to the same folder you specified in the Drum Maps parameter.

15. SONAR doesn't include any sample plug-in layout files, so there are no files to move in this case. But if you have created any of your own, you can find them in the default location—the Plug-In Menu Layouts folder. Move them to the same folder you specified in the Plug-In Layouts parameter.

That's it—any other files you see in the folder locations I mentioned should be left alone. Do not move them; only move files that have the file extensions I discussed. Of course, you don't really have to move all of SONAR's included sample files, but personally, I really enjoy having all my files properly organized. It makes finding what I need easier, and it makes working with SONAR much more efficient.

Customizing Audio Folders

Although I've already talked about sample loops and audio files that you can import into your projects, SONAR has to deal with additional audio files that represent the audio tracks that you record directly into SONAR. SONAR stores the data for these audio tracks in a special folder on your hard drive. By default, this folder is located at C:\Cakewalk Projects\Audio Data. However, like the other folders I mentioned earlier, you can change the location of this folder if you'd like. One of the main reasons you might want to do so would be if you are using two hard drives in your computer—one for installing all your software and another for storing only your SONAR project files and audio data. This improves SONAR's efficiency during playback and recording tremendously, and I highly recommend it.

If you'd like to change the location of your audio data folder, follow these steps:

1. In SONAR, choose Options > Global > Audio Data to open the Global Options dialog box with the Audio Data tab selected (see Figure 3.2).

2. In the Global Audio Folder parameter, type the new location for your audio data folder. You can also click the ellipsis button to the right of the parameter to browse for a new location instead of typing one.

3. By default, whenever you import an audio file into a project, SONAR will automatically make a copy of that file and place it in your audio data folder. If you don't want SONAR to do this, then deactivate the Always Copy Imported Audio Files option.

4. Click OK.

❋ **ALWAYS COPY IMPORTED AUDIO FILES**

If your audio folder is located on the same hard drive as the audio you are importing, you can save drive space by deactivating the Always Copy Imported Audio Files option. But if your audio folder is located on a different drive (perhaps a second drive), then you should keep this option activated. I recommend this, because if you are using a second hard drive to store your audio data, you don't want SONAR to have to look for your imported audio in a different location on a different drive. This will decrease playback and recording efficiency.

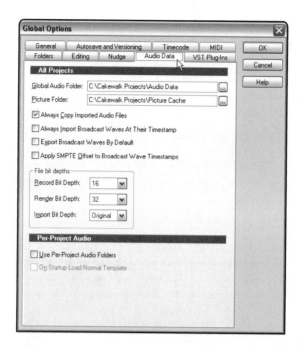

Figure 3.2 Use the Audio Data tab in the Global Options dialog box to change your audio data folder location.

Per-Project Audio Folders

Instead of storing all the audio data from all your projects in the same folder, you can use a different folder for each project if you like. These folders are called per-project audio folders. The advantage of using per-project audio folders is that all the data for each project is stored in its own separate location, which makes it easy to find if you want to access the audio files associated with a project (perhaps for editing in a different software application). To set up SONAR for per-project audio folders, follow these steps:

1. Choose Options > Global > Audio Data to open the Global Options dialog box with the Audio Data tab selected.
2. Activate the Use Per-Project Audio Folders option.
3. Click OK.

Now when you create a new project, you will be able to specify a folder name for it.

The Picture Folder

Whenever you record audio data using SONAR, the program creates temporary picture files for the audio data in your project. These files hold "drawings" of the audio waveforms. Initially, these picture files are stored in the C:\Cakewalk Projects\Picture Cache folder on your hard drive. You can change this location by completing the following steps.

1. Choose Options > Global > Audio Data to open the Global Options dialog box with the Audio Data tab selected.
2. Type a new location for your picture files in the Picture Folder field. You can also click the ellipsis button to the right of the field to browse for a new location instead of typing one.

❋ **DON'T MOVE THE PICTURE FOLDER**

If you are using a second hard drive for your audio data, do *not* put your picture folder on the second hard drive with the audio data. This can decrease SONAR's performance. Instead, keep the picture folder on the same hard drive on which the SONAR software is installed.

---

3. Click OK.

Now SONAR will look for your picture files in the new picture folder location. Don't worry about moving any existing picture files; SONAR will automatically create new ones when you open your projects again. You can just delete the old picture folder and all the files in it.

Customizing the Workspace

Not only can you change the way SONAR handles files, but you also can change the way SONAR looks and responds to your commands. By customizing the SONAR workspace, you can increase your efficiency with the program and make it more comfortable to use. You can adjust the colors, toolbars, menus, window layouts, key bindings, and Track view controls.

Colors

SONAR can change the colors of almost every element on the program screen. Personally, I haven't found the need for making many color changes. The default colors that the program ships with work just fine for me. However, you might find a different set of colors more pleasant to work with, or maybe you can see some colors better than others. Changing the colors SONAR uses is simple—just follow these steps:

1. In SONAR, choose Options > Colors. The Configure Colors dialog box will appear, as shown in Figure 3.3.
2. Using the Color Category list, choose the work area in SONAR for which you would like to change colors.
3. The left side of the dialog box contains a list of all the screen elements you can change. To change the color of an element, select it.
4. Next select how you want that screen element to look by choosing a color from the right side of the dialog box. You can have the color of the element follow the color of some of the default Windows element colors, or you can use a specific color.

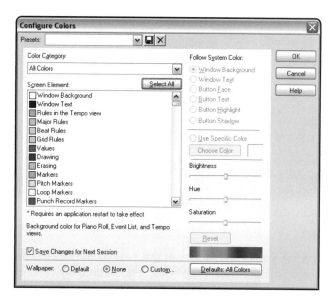

Figure 3.3 In the Configure Colors dialog box, you can change the appearance of SONAR to your liking.

5. You also can change the background wallpaper of the SONAR workspace by choosing one of the options at the bottom of the dialog box. If you choose the Custom option, you can even load your own Windows bitmap (.BMP) file for display. Loading your own file is not particularly useful, but it can be fun.

6. If you want SONAR to use the same color settings every time you run the program, make sure the Save Changes for Next Session option is activated.

7. If you'd like to set up a number of different color schemes, you can save your settings as a preset. Just type a name for the current color settings in the Presets field and click the Save button (the button with the picture of a floppy disk). Then you can change color schemes quickly by simply choosing a preset.

8. When you've finished making your changes, just click the OK button.

Toolbars

To increase your productivity, SONAR provides a number of toolbars for quick access to many of its major functions. Instead of having to hunt through a series of menus, you can simply click a single toolbar button. Toolbars are available for standard file access functions, recording and playback controls, and so on.

SONAR enables you to change the look and position of its toolbars, as well as determine whether or not they are visible. Why wouldn't you want to have all the toolbars on the screen all the time? Because they can clutter up the workspace and get in the way while you're working on a project.

Changing Toolbar Position

Just as with most toolbars in other Windows programs, you can dock the SONAR toolbars at the top, bottom, or sides of the workspace by dragging and dropping them. If you drop a toolbar anywhere within the workspace, it will become a floating window, as shown in Figure 3.4.

Figure 3.4 You can dock toolbars at the top, bottom, or sides of the SONAR workspace. They can also reside anywhere else within the workspace as small floating windows.

Changing Toolbar Appearance

To change the appearance of the toolbars, you need to access the Toolbars dialog box. Just choose Views > Toolbars, and the Toolbars dialog box will appear (see Figure 3.5).

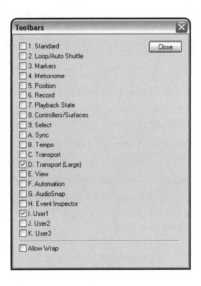

Figure 3.5 Using the Toolbars dialog box, you can change the appearance of SONAR's toolbars.

You can select or deselect each toolbar to determine whether it will be visible. For example, if you remove the check mark in the box next to the Standard selection, the Standard File Functions toolbar will disappear.

HIDE/SHOW ALL TOOLBARS

To quickly hide/show all toolbars, choose Views > Show Toolbars. This will toggle the visibility of all toolbars, which is an easy way to free up more space in the SONAR workspace when you need it and to access toolbars quickly at other times. You can also create a key binding for the Views > Show Toolbars function.

Customizing Toolbars

In addition to docking and changing the visibility of the toolbars, you can also change their configuration. What I mean is that you can change which buttons appear on each of the toolbars, thus customizing them to your own liking. You can even create up to three new toolbars of your own.

NOT ALL FUNCTIONS

Unfortunately, SONAR doesn't allow you to assign all of its functions to a toolbar. You can only use functions that already exist as buttons on other toolbars. For example, you can't create a toolbar that has buttons for the functions under the Process > Audio menu.

Customizing a toolbar is very easy. Follow these steps to customize a toolbar:

1. You can customize one of the standard SONAR toolbars, or you can create a new toolbar with one of the three user toolbars provided by SONAR. Choose Views > Toolbars to display the Toolbars dialog box.

2. Activate the toolbar you want to customize and click Close to make the toolbar, if it isn't already visible.

3. Right-click the toolbar and select Customize from the menu to open the Customize Toolbar dialog box (see Figure 3.6). The Current Toolbar Buttons section shows all the buttons currently assigned to the toolbar. The Available Toolbar Buttons section shows all the buttons that can be assigned to the toolbar.

Figure 3.6 Use the Customize Toolbar dialog box to configure a toolbar to your liking.

4. To assign a button to the toolbar, select a button/function from the Available Toolbar Buttons list and then click Add.

❋ **QUICK FUNCTION FIND**

For a quick way to find a function in the Available Toolbar Buttons list, click the first function in the list to select it. Then press (on your computer keyboard) the first letter of the name of the function you are trying to find. For example, to find the Loop and Auto Shuttle function, press L five times.

5. If you want to delete a button from the toolbar, select the button/function in the Current Toolbar Buttons list and click Remove.
6. To change the position of a button on the toolbar, select the button in the Current Toolbar Buttons list and click Move Up or Move Down to move the button up or down within the list.
7. To set the toolbar back to its default configuration, click Reset.
8. You can also add Separators if you want to group different buttons together. To add a Separator, choose Separator from the Available Toolbar Buttons list and click Add.
9. Click Close.

You now have a customized toolbar. You can also change the toolbar's name, by right-clicking the toolbar and choosing Rename.

Program and Plug-In Menus

Like the toolbars, you can also customize SONAR's program and plug-in menus. This allows you to hide menu commands that you don't use often, as well as organize your effects and soft synth plug-ins for easier access.

Customizing Program Menus

To customize program menu layouts, do the following:

1. Choose Options > Menu Editor to open the Menu Editor dialog box (see Figure 3.7).
2. Use the Menu Layout list to choose the menu layout you would like to edit. If you'd like to create a new menu layout, type a new name into the Menu Layout parameter.
3. The Menu list displays all of the currently available menus. Choose a menu to edit.

❋ **NO NEW MENUS**

Unfortunately, SONAR doesn't allow you to create brand new menus from scratch. Instead, you must select a currently available menu and edit that menu.

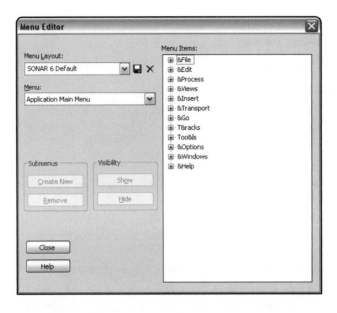

Figure 3.7 Use the Menu Editor dialog box to configure SONAR's program menus to your liking.

4. The Menu Items area displays all of the items available in the currently selected menu. Menu titles and submenus have + buttons next to them, indicating they contain additional menu items. You can show/hide the additional items by clicking the +/- buttons.

5. To create a new submenu, select a menu item and click the Create New button in the Submenus section, or you can right-click a menu item and choose Create Submenu. Doing so creates a new submenu and moves the selected menu item into that submenu.

6. To remove a submenu, select the submenu and click the Remove button in the Submenus section or right-click the submenu and choose Remove Submenu.

7. To move a menu item into or out of an existing submenu, open the submenu and then click and drag the menu item.

8. To show/hide submenus or menu items, select them and click the Show/Hide buttons in the Visibility section. You can also right-click the items and choose Show Item(s) or Hide Item(s). Select multiple items for visibility changes by holding down the Ctrl key.

9. To change the position of a submenu or menu item, simply drag the item up or down in the list.

10. You can also add Separators if you want to group different menu items together. To add/remove a separator, right-click an item and choose Insert Separator or Remove Separator.

11. To rename a submenu or menu item, right-click the item and choose Rename. Then type in a new name. Place the & character in front of the letter in the name that you would

like to use as a keyboard shortcut (hotkey). For example, if you want to name an item CakewalkFX and you want to use the letter C as the hotkey, name the item &CakewalkFX.

12. To automatically generate hotkeys for menu items in the currently selected submenu, right-click the submenu and choose Generate Hotkeys. To verify that there are no duplicate hotkeys in the submenu, right-click the submenu and choose Check Hotkeys.

13. Click Close. SONAR will ask you if you want to save your changes. Click Yes to save, No to exit without saving, or Cancel to make some more changes.

You can now access your new menu layout and others by choosing Options > Menu Layouts > [name of the menu layout].

Customizing Plug-In Menus

In addition to program menus, SONAR customizes plug-in menus. This means that instead of having long, confusing menus listing all your effects and soft synth plug-ins, you can now have organized menus that provide quicker and easier access. You can create and edit menu layouts for MIDI effects, audio effects, and soft synths. The procedure for editing these menus is the same, but the menus are accessed via different areas of SONAR.

To edit or access MIDI effects menu layouts, choose Process > MIDI Fx > Plug-in Layouts > Manage Layouts or choose Process > MIDI Fx > Plug-in Layouts > [name of the menu layout]. To edit or access audio effects menu layouts, choose Process > Audio Fx > Plug-in Layouts > Manage Layouts or choose Process > Audio Fx > Plug-in Layouts > [name of the menu layout]. To edit or access soft synth menu layouts, choose Insert > Soft Synths > Plug-in Layouts > Manage Layouts or choose Insert > Soft Synths > Plug-in Layouts > [name of the menu layout].

To show you how to edit plug-in menu layouts, let me walk you through an example of how I like to organize the audio effects plug-ins that come with SONAR. Instead of one long, list of audio effects, I like to organize my plug-ins by category. Here's how:

1. Choose Process > Audio Fx > Plug-in Layouts > Manage Layouts to open the Cakewalk Plug-in Manager (see Figure 3.8).

2. In the upper right corner of the window (where it says Plug-in Menu Layout), click the New button (the first one from left to right) to create a blank layout. Then type a new name for the layout. For this example, let's call it AudioFX Categories.

3. Use the New Folder button to create the following folders: Chorus, EQ, Delay, Flanger, Compressor, Reverb, Spectrum Analysis, Mastering, Simulation, Pitch, MultiFX, and Surround.

4. To put the folders in alphabetical order, click Sort All.

5. In the Plug-in Categories list, select the DirectX Audio Effects (DX) option.

6. In the Registered Plug-ins list, select the following effects (hold down Ctrl on your computer keyboard to make multiple selections): Cakewalk Chorus, Cakewalk Chorus (Mono), and Cakewalk FxChorus. Select the Chorus folder we created earlier and click Add Plugin to add these effects to the folder.

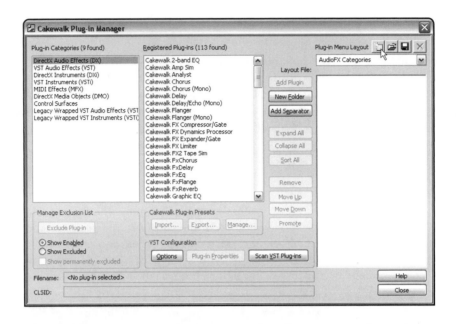

Figure 3.8 Use the Cakewalk Plug-in Manager to configure SONAR's plug-in menus to your liking.

7. Select the following effects and add them to the Compressor folder: Cakewalk FX Compressor/Gate, Cakewalk FX Dynamics Processor, Cakewalk FX Expander/Gate, Cakewalk FX Limiter, Sonitus:fx Compressor, Sonitus:fx Gate, and Sonitus:fx Multiband.

8. Select the following effects and add them to the Delay folder: Cakewalk Delay, Cakewalk Delay/Echo (Mono), Cakewalk FxDelay, and Sonitus:fx Delay.

9. Select the following effects and add them to the EQ folder: Cakewalk 2-band EQ, Cakewalk FxEQ, Cakewalk Parametric EQ, and Sonitus:fx Equalizer.

10. Select the following effects and add them to the Flanger folder: Cakewalk Flanger, Cakewalk Flanger (Mono), and Cakewalk FxFlange.

11. Select the following effects and add them to the Mastering folder: Cakewalk Analyst, Sonitus:fx Compressor, Sonitus:fx Equalizer, and Sonitus:fx Multiband. Also from the VST Audio Effects (VST) plug-in category, add the following effect: Vintage_Channel_VC64.

❄ **MULTIPLE CATEGORIES**

You may have noticed that I added the Sonitus:fx Multiband effect to both the Compressor and Mastering folders. Sonitus:fx Multiband is a compressor effect, but it can also be used for mastering so I like to have it in both categories making it easier to find depending on what I'm doing. You can do this with any of the effects you have installed—add them to multiple folders for easier access and better organization.

12. Back in the DirectX Audio Effects (DX) plug-in category, select the following effects and add them to the MultiFX folder: Cakewalk SpectraFX and Sonitus:fx Modulator.

13. Select the following effects and add them to the Pitch folder: Cakewalk Pitch Shifter and Cakewalk Time/Pitch Stretch 2.

14. Select the following effects and add them to the Reverb folder: Cakewalk FxReverb, Cakewalk Reverb, Cakewalk Reverb (Mono), and Sonitus:fx Reverb. Also from the VST Audio Effects (VST) plug-in category, add the following effect: PerfectSpace.

15. Back in the DirectX Audio Effects (DX) plug-in category, select the following effects and add them to the Simulation folder: Cakewalk Amp Sim, Cakewalk FX2 Tape Sim, and Sonitus:fx Wahwah.

16. Select the following effects and add them to the Spectrum Analysis folder: Cakewalk Analyst.

17. Select the following effects and add them to the Surround folder: Sonitus:fx Surround and Sonitus:fx SurroundComp.

18. Click Collapse All to close all the folders in the menu layout. You can also use the Expand All button to open all folders when working on a layout.

19. Select the Surround folder and click Add Separator to add a separator to the layout.

20. Select the Cakewalk Tuner and Sonitus:fx Phase effects and click Add Plugin to add them to the layout below the separator.

21. If you ever want to remove an item or folder, select it and click Remove.

22. If you want to move items or folders up or down in the list, either drag and drop them or select them and use the Move Up, Move Down, or Promote buttons. Promote moves an item outside of a folder if it resides in one.

23. In the upper right corner of the window, click the Save button (the one with the floppy disk shown it) to save the new menu layout.

24. If you ever want to delete a layout, select it from the drop-down list and click the Delete button (the one with the big red X shown on it).

25. Click Close to close the Cakewalk Plug-in Manager.

If you followed the example, you should now be able to choose Process > Audio Fx > Plug-in Layouts > AudioFX Categories and see a new audio effects menu like the one shown in Figure 3.9. Now you can quickly access all your audio effects by category, and you can add other third-party plug-ins to this layout in addition to the ones the come with SONAR.

Figure 3.9 The AudioFX Categories menu lists all audio effects by category.

Working with Window Layouts

When you're working on a project in SONAR, you need to use many of the views described in Chapter 2. When you save the project, the size and position of the view windows are saved along with it. This capability is nice because you can pick up exactly where you left off the next time you open the project. As you get more experienced with SONAR, you'll probably find that having the views set up in certain configurations helps your recording sessions go more smoothly. For instance, you might like having the Track view positioned at the top of the workspace and the Staff view and the Piano Roll view positioned underneath it, as shown in Figure 3.10.

What if you come up with a few favorite configurations that you'd like to use during different stages of the same project? Or what if you want to use those configurations in a different project? That's where window layouts come in handy. Using window layouts, you can save the current size and position of the View windows as a layout file. Later, you can load the saved layout and apply it to any open project. You can also update, delete, or rename a saved layout by using the Window Layouts dialog box.

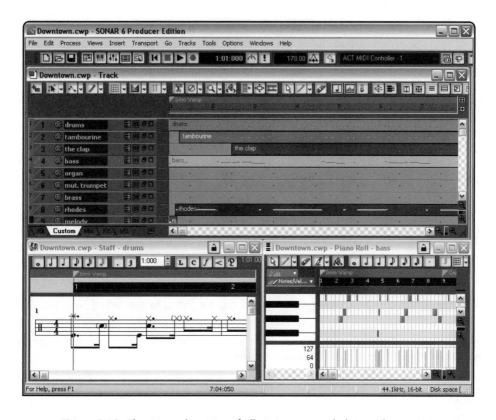

Figure 3.10 The size and position of all views are saved along with a project.

Creating a Layout

Follow these steps to create a window layout:

1. Arrange the views in the workspace in the positions and sizes in which you would like them saved. You also must decide whether you want certain views to be open.

2. Choose Views > Layouts to open the Window Layouts dialog box, as shown in Figure 3.11.

3. Click the Add button and type a name for the new layout in the New Global Layout dialog box that appears.

❋ **USE A DESCRIPTIVE NAME**

I've found that giving a descriptive name to each layout helps me when I want to load them. For example, I include the names of each open view in the name of the layout. If I have the Track, Staff, and Piano Roll views open in the layout, I name it Track-Staff-Piano.

Figure 3.11 You can create new layouts by using the Window Layouts dialog box.

4. Click the OK button, and your new layout will be listed in the Window Layouts dialog box.

5. You can rename or delete a layout in the list. You can also load a layout by selecting it from the list and clicking on the Load button.

6. When you're finished, click the Close button.

Layout Options

The Window Layouts dialog box contains two optional settings that let you control how layouts are loaded. The Close Old Windows before Loading New Ones option determines whether any views you have currently open in the workspace will be closed when you load a new layout. The When Opening a File, Load Its Layout option determines whether SONAR will load the accompanying layout when a project is opened. I like to keep both of these options activated.

Using Key Bindings

Key bindings are one of the most useful customization features that SONAR provides. Like toolbars, they give you quick access to most of SONAR's features. Instead of having to click through a series of menus, you can simply press a key combination on your computer's keyboard. Initially, SONAR ships with a collection of default key bindings, such as for opening and saving a project. These bindings are displayed next to their assigned menu functions, as in the File menu shown in Figure 3.12.

The wonderful thing about key bindings is that if you don't like them, you can change them. You can also create new ones for functions that don't already have default key bindings. You can assign over 600 different key bindings using just about any key combination (the available combinations are listed in SONAR's Key Bindings dialog box).

Figure 3.12 Initially, the key binding for opening a project is Ctrl+O.

Creating Your Own Key Bindings

You can easily create your own key bindings and change existing ones. Here's how:

1. Choose Options > Key Bindings to open the Key Bindings dialog box, as shown in Figure 3.13.

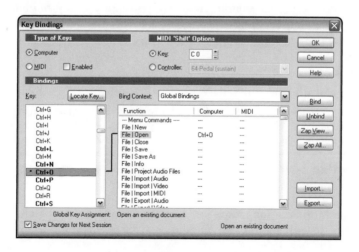

Figure 3.13 You can set key combinations in the Key Bindings dialog box.

2. Using the Bind Context drop-down list, choose the work area in SONAR in which your key binding will be used. For example, if you want the key binding to be accessible in all areas of SONAR, choose Global Bindings, but if you want the key binding only to be accessible in one of the views (like the Track view), choose the appropriate view option.

3. In the Key list under the Bindings section of the dialog box, select the key combination that you want to bind to a function.

❄ QUICK KEY FINDING

Since SONAR provides a very long list of key combinations from which to choose, it can be difficult to find the exact key combination you want by scrolling through the list. To find a key combination quickly, click the Locate Key button. Then press the key combination on your computer keyboard and the combination will be automatically highlighted in the Key list.

4. In the Function list, select the SONAR function that you want to bind to the selected key combination.

5. Click the Bind button. You will see a connection created.

6. As I mentioned before, you can create over 600 key bindings. You can also remove single key bindings using the Unbind button. If you want to get rid of all key bindings, just click the Zap All button. To remove all bindings from a single SONAR view, click the Zap View button.

7. If you would like to share your key bindings with another SONAR user, you can export them by clicking the Export button. Likewise, you can use key bindings from someone else by clicking the Import button.

8. When you're done, click the OK button.

❄ SAVE CHANGES FOR NEXT SESSION

Near the bottom of the Key Bindings dialog box is the Save Changes for Next Session option. When you select it, any key bindings you create will be saved so you can use them every time you run SONAR. If this option is not selected, you will lose any changes you've made when you exit the program. This option is selected by default. I suggest you keep it that way unless, for some reason, you just need a few temporary key bindings during a recording session.

After you've created (or changed) some key bindings, you'll notice the changes in SONAR's menus. As I mentioned earlier, the key bindings are displayed next to their assigned menu functions.

Using MIDI Key Bindings

In addition to creating key bindings using your computer keyboard, you can assign the keys on your MIDI keyboard synthesizer or controller as key bindings to execute functions within SONAR. (Cool, huh?) For example, you could assign the File > New function in SONAR to the Middle C key on your keyboard. Then, when you press Middle C, SONAR would open the New Project File dialog box.

❄ **REMOTE MIDI KEY BINDINGS**

If your studio is set up so that your computer isn't located next to your MIDI keyboard or controller, using MIDI key Bindings is a great way to still have access to SONAR. For example, if you want to be able to start and stop SONAR recording via your MIDI keyboard, you can just assign one MIDI key binding along with the Shift key or controller to the Transport > Play function and another MIDI key binding along with the Shift key or controller to the Transport > Stop function.

You create MIDI key bindings the same way you create computer keyboard bindings. The only difference is that you have to select MIDI as the Type of Keys option in the Key Bindings dialog box and make sure to activate MIDI key bindings by selecting the Enabled option (see Figure 3.14). Also, when you select a key combination in the Key list, you select musical keys rather than computer keyboard keys.

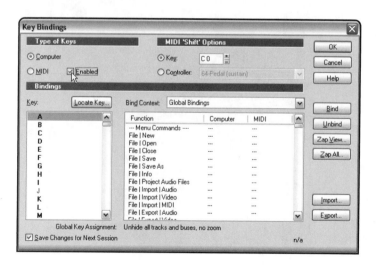

Figure 3.14 You select MIDI as the Type of Keys option to active MIDI key bindings.

In addition, in order to prevent the MIDI key bindings from activating while you're performing, you need to set up a Shift key or controller to turn on and off the MIDI key bindings. Under MIDI Shift Options in the Key Bindings dialog box, you can assign a MIDI key or controller message to act as a sort of on/off switch. When you want to use a MIDI key binding, activate the Shift key or controller first to tell SONAR you're about to use a MIDI key binding.

❄ **WINDOW LAYOUT KEY BINDINGS**

Remember earlier when I talked about window layouts? Normally, you need to choose View > Layouts, select a layout, and click Load just to call up a window layout. For a much quicker way to do this, you can assign key bindings to any or all of the layout files you create. After you've created your window layouts, you will find them listed under the Global Layout Files section of the Function list in the Key Bindings dialog box. Just assign key bindings as described earlier and then you can switch instantly between window layouts at the press of a computer key.

Transforming the Track View

Even though I'll be talking a lot more about the Track view throughout the book (especially in Chapters 7 and 12), I wanted to cover a few of the Track view attributes that SONAR allows you to configure. These include the Track List tabs, the Track List controls (called widgets), and the Time Ruler (see Figure 3.15).

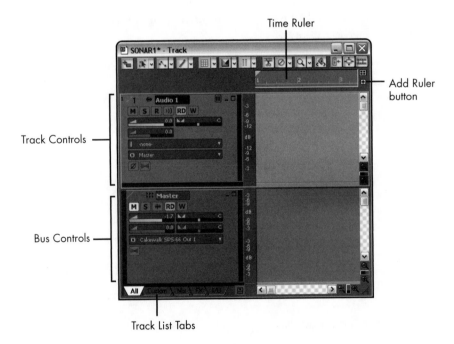

Figure 3.15 You can customize the Track List tabs, widgets, and the Time Ruler.

Customizing the Track List Tabs

Located at the bottom of the Track List section of the Track view, SONAR provides a number of tabs that can be used to hide/show widgets for MIDI, Audio, Synth, and Folder tracks. SONAR comes with a number of predefined tabs. For example, the Mix tab displays widgets that are relevant for mixing a project. However, you can customize these tabs (and even create new ones) to your liking. To customize the tabs, do the following:

1. Right-click a tab and choose Widget Tab Manager to open the Widget Tab Manager dialog box (see Figure 3.16).

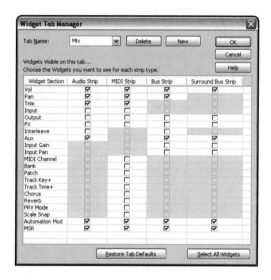

Figure 3.16 Use the Widget Tab Manager to customize the Track List tabs.

2. Choose an existing tab using the Tab Name parameter or create a new tab by clicking New.

3. To delete an existing tab, click Delete.

4. In the Widgets Visible On This Tab table, you'll see five columns. The first column (Widget Section) displays a list of all available widgets. In the second column (Audio Strip), put check marks next to the widgets that you want to be visible in all audio tracks.

5. In the third column (MIDI Strip), put check marks next to the widgets that you want to be visible in all MIDI tracks.

6. In the fourth column (Bus Strip), put check marks next to the widgets that you want to be visible in all buses.

7. In the fifth column (Surround Bus Strip), put check marks next to the widgets that you want to be visible in all surround buses.

8. To set the tab back to its default configuration, click Restore Tab Defaults.

9. To put check marks next to all widgets in all columns, click Select All Widgets.
10. Click OK.

Your new tab is now visible at the bottom of the Track List area.

Customizing the Track List (Controls) Widgets

Other than the track number, name, peak meter indicator and size button located in the top row of each track, all other track controls (widgets) can be moved to different locations. Simply hold down the Alt key on your computer keyboard and drag a widget to a new location. As you drag a widget, you'll see a red outline around the widget, and your mouse will change to reflect the current operation, as shown in Figure 3.17.

Figure 3.17 Alt+click and drag widgets to change their location in the Track List area.

Altering widgets in one track type, alters all tracks of that type. For example, if you change the positions of widgets on an audio track, it affects all audio tracks. To restore the original positions of all widgets, right-click the Track List area of the track type you want to restore and choose Restore Default Widget Order.

Customizing the Time Ruler

By default, the Time Ruler displays the measure numbers in the current project. The Time Ruler format can also be changed to display Hours:Minutes:Seconds:Frames, Samples, or Milliseconds. In addition, rather than showing just one time format, you can set up the Time Ruler to display multiple formats simultaneously. To do this, click the Add Ruler button and choose a format to add. After you've added multiple formats, you can use the Remove Ruler button to remove any formats currently displayed (see Figure 3.18).

Figure 3.18 Customize the Time Ruler to display multiple formats.

Customizing MIDI Settings

Even though SONAR does a good job of setting up all its MIDI options during installation, it's still a good idea to go through them to make sure that everything is the way you want it to be. You might be surprised at how much control you have over how SONAR handles MIDI data. Not only can you designate which MIDI devices the program will use, but you can also determine what types of MIDI data will be recorded and optimize MIDI playback.

Working with MIDI Devices

The first time you run SONAR, it scans your computer system to see whether you have a MIDI interface installed. SONAR prompts you to select the available MIDI *ports* that you want to use, but you can always change your selections later.

❄ **MIDI PORTS**

A MIDI interface is a device that is plugged into your computer, allowing it to understand the MIDI language. Every MIDI interface has at least two connections on it, called *MIDI ports*. One is the MIDI In port, which is used to receive MIDI data; the other is the MIDI Out port, which is used to send MIDI data. Some of the more sophisticated MIDI interfaces on the market have multiple pairs of MIDI ports, which can connect more than one MIDI instrument to your computer.

To see which MIDI ports SONAR is using and to designate the ports you want to use, follow these steps:

1. Choose Options > MIDI Devices to open the MIDI Devices dialog box. This dialog box lists all the input and output MIDI ports you have available (see Figure 3.19).

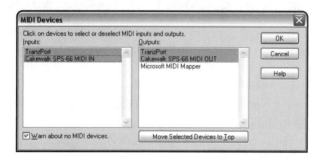

Figure 3.19 The MIDI Devices dialog box lists all the available input and output MIDI ports.

2. Simply select the input and output ports that you want to be able to access for use within SONAR.

3. When you're finished, click the OK button.

All the ports selected here will be available in the Track Properties dialog box.

Setting Global MIDI Options

SONAR provides a number of different MIDI options, some of which are global and some of which are project-oriented. The project-oriented options are saved and loaded along with project files. The global options remain the same no matter which project is currently open.

Filtering Out MIDI Messages

The global MIDI options enable you to select the types of MIDI messages you want to record in SONAR. Sometimes, you might not want certain MIDI data to be included in your recordings. For example, if your MIDI keyboard sends channel aftertouch messages or key aftertouch messages, you might want to filter them out. These types of messages are very resource-intensive and can sometimes bog down your synthesizer with too much data.

✳ **MIDI MESSAGES**

For details on MIDI messages, check out the *Desktop Music Handbook* (www.cakewalk.com/Tips/Desktop.asp).

And for more in-depth information about MIDI, check out the following resources:

1. *MIDI Power!*:

www.amazon.com/exec/obidos/ASIN/1929685661/compmediaA

2. *Basic MIDI*:

www.amazon.com/exec/obidos/ASIN/1860742629/compmediaA

3. *MIDI for the Technophobe*:

www.amazon.com/exec/obidos/ASIN/1860744443/compmediaA

By default, SONAR has notes, controllers, program changes, pitch bend, and system-exclusive messages activated, and it has key aftertouch and channel aftertouch deactivated. If you want to change these settings, you can follow these steps:

1. Choose Options > Global to open the Global Options dialog box.
2. Click the MIDI tab at the top of the dialog box.
3. Under the Record section, select the types of MIDI messages you want to have SONAR record (see Figure 3.20).
4. Click the OK button when you're finished.

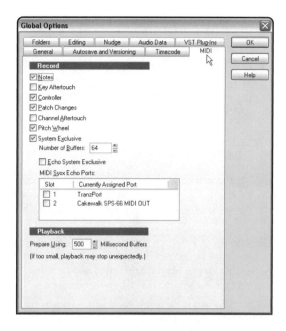

Figure 3.20 You can determine the types of MIDI messages SONAR will record.

Optimizing MIDI Playback

To get smooth and consistent playback of MIDI data, SONAR uses a buffer (a temporary storage area) to hold the data before it gets sent out through the MIDI interface. This buffer keeps the data from getting backed up, which can cause erratic playback or even stop playback altogether. The buffer also helps to control playback latency. Whenever you change a parameter in SONAR while a project is playing, a slight delay occurs between the time you make the adjustment and when you hear the results. That's called *latency*.

The Global Options dialog box contains a setting that adjusts the size of SONAR's MIDI playback buffer. If the buffer is set too low, it can cause erratic playback, and if it is set too high, it can cause noticeable latency. By default, the buffer size is set to 500 milliseconds. This setting should be fine in most cases. However, you might want to experiment to find an even better setting. The trick is to find the lowest setting that doesn't affect playback. I've been able to get away with a setting of 100 most of the time unless I have a lot of MIDI data being played in a project. You can change the buffer size by following these steps:

1. Choose Options > Global to open the Global Options dialog box.
2. Click the MIDI tab at the top of the dialog box.
3. Under the Playback section, type the new buffer size.
4. Click the OK button when you're finished.

Understanding Instrument Definitions

Most MIDI instruments today provide a bank of sounds compatible with the General MIDI standard. At the same time, most instruments also provide additional sounds, as well as other features that aren't defined by General MIDI. Some older MIDI instruments don't support General MIDI at all. To let you work more efficiently with these instruments, SONAR provides instrument definitions.

GENERAL MIDI

Sounds in a MIDI instrument are stored as groups of parameter settings called patches, and patches are stored in groups called *banks*. A MIDI instrument can have up to 16,384 banks of 128 patches each. This means that a MIDI instrument can theoretically contain up to 2,097,152 different sounds, although most don't.

With such a great potential for diversity, MIDI instruments from one manufacturer usually don't provide the same functionality as instruments from another manufacturer. This point is important because MIDI data is ambiguous. The same data can be played back using any MIDI instrument, but that doesn't mean it will sound the same. Different instruments contain different sounds, and they interpret MIDI differently as well.

To remedy the problem, GM (*General MIDI*) was created. GM is a set of rules applied to the MIDI language that standardizes the types of sounds contained in a MIDI instrument (along with their patch numbers) and how different MIDI controller messages are interpreted. Most modern MIDI instruments provide a special bank of GM sounds and a GM operating mode. When you are running in GM mode, different MIDI instruments respond to the same MIDI data in the same way. MIDI data played back on one instrument is guaranteed to sound the same when played on any other instrument.

Using instrument definitions, you can "tell" SONAR all about the features and capabilities provided by each of the MIDI instruments in your studio. This information includes the name of each patch, the range of notes supported by each patch, the supported MIDI controller messages, the supported registered parameter numbers (RPNs) and nonregistered parameter numbers (NRPNs), and the bank select method used. Basically, instrument definitions refer to the patches in your MIDI instruments by name rather than number when you're assigning sounds to tracks in SONAR. The same applies for musical note names and MIDI controller message names.

Setting Up Your Instruments

SONAR includes a number of predefined instrument definitions so you can assign them without having to go through the process of creating your own. You can assign instrument definitions to each of the MIDI ports on your MIDI interface. You can also assign them to the individual MIDI channels (1 through 16).

❀ **MIDI CHANNELS**

The MIDI language provides 16 different channels of performance data over a single MIDI port connection. MIDI instruments can be set to receive MIDI data on a single channel if need be. This means you can control up to 16 different MIDI instruments (each with its own unique sound), even if they are all connected to the same MIDI port on your MIDI interface. In addition, most MIDI instruments are capable of playing more than one sound at a time. This means the instrument is *multitimbral*. If you assign a different sound to each of the 16 MIDI channels, a single MIDI instrument can play 16 different sounds simultaneously.

To assign instrument definitions to each of the MIDI ports and channels in your setup, follow these steps:

1. Choose Options > Instruments to open the Assign Instruments dialog box, as shown in Figure 3.21.

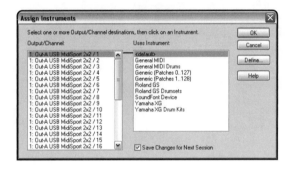

Figure 3.21 You can assign instrument definitions in the Assign Instruments dialog box.

2. From the Output/Channel list, select the MIDI port(s) or MIDI channel(s) to which you want to assign definitions.
3. From the Uses Instrument list, select the instrument definition you want to use. For example, if you're going to use the MIDI instrument that's connected to the selected port in General MIDI mode, choose the General MIDI instrument definition.

❀ **SAVE CHANGES FOR NEXT SESSION**

Near the bottom of the Assign Instruments dialog box is the Save Changes for Next Session option. When you select it, any assignments you create will be saved so that you can use them every time you run SONAR. If this option is not selected, you will lose any changes you make when you exit the program. I suggest you select this option, unless for some reason you change the configuration of your studio for each new recording session.

4. Click the OK button when you're finished.

Now SONAR will know the capabilities of your MIDI instrument(s) and will act appropriately when you access different features, such as editing MIDI controller messages.

Taking the Easy Way Out

If you don't see a specific instrument definition for your MIDI instrument listed in the Assign Instruments dialog box, SONAR can import more definitions. The program ships with a large collection of additional instrument definitions that cover many of the MIDI instruments on the market from manufacturers such as Alesis, E-mu, Ensoniq, General Music, Korg, Kurzweil, Roland, and Yamaha. The instrument definitions are stored in files with .INS extensions. For example, the Yamaha instrument definitions are stored in the file YAMAHA.INS. Importing these files is simple; just follow these steps:

1. Choose Options > Instruments to open the Assign Instruments dialog box.
2. Click the Define button to open the Define Instruments and Names dialog box (see Figure 3.22).

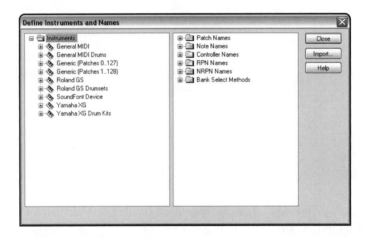

Figure 3.22 The Define Instruments and Names dialog box imports additional instrument definitions.

3. Click the Import button to open the Import Instrument Definitions dialog box and select the .INS file you want to import. For example, if Roland manufactures your MIDI instrument, select the ROLAND.INS file; then click Open.
4. When SONAR displays a list of the instrument definitions contained in that file, select the one(s) you want and click the OK button. Your selections will be listed under Instruments in the Define Instruments and Names dialog box.
5. Click the Close button, and you will see your selections listed under Uses Instrument in the Assign Instruments dialog box. From here you can assign the instrument definitions as described earlier.
6. Click the OK button when you're finished.

If you still can't find an instrument definition for your MIDI instrument from the extensive collection included with SONAR, you can download even more from the Internet. Cakewalk provides a download section on its Web site (www.cakewalk.com/download) where you can pick up additional instrument definition files.

Creating Your Own Instrument Definitions

More than likely, you'll find instrument definitions for all your MIDI equipment either included with SONAR or available for download from the Internet. On the off chance that you don't, SONAR allows you to create your own definitions. This can be a bit complicated because you must have a good knowledge of the MIDI language, and you need to be able to read the MIDI implementation charts that came with your instruments.

❄ **MIDI IMPLEMENTATION CHARTS**

The MIDI language contains more than 100 different messages to convey musical information, and a MIDI instrument isn't required to send or recognize all of them. A MIDI instrument needs to transmit and receive only the messages that are relevant to the features it provides; it can ignore all the other messages. Therefore, manufacturers include MIDI implementation charts with all their products.

A MIDI implementation chart lists all the types of MIDI messages that are transmitted and recognized by its accompanying MIDI instrument. The chart includes the note range of the instrument, the MIDI controller messages it supports, whether it supports system-exclusive messages, and more.

To give you an idea of how to read a simple MIDI implementation chart and how to create a basic instrument definition, I want to go through the process step by step.

1. Choose Options > Instruments to open the Assign Instruments dialog box.
2. Click the Define button to open the Define Instruments and Names dialog box.
3. Take a look at Table 3.1, which shows the MIDI implementation chart for an E-mu PROformance Plus Stereo Piano MIDI instrument.

Table 3.1 E-mu PROformance Plus MIDI Implementation Chart

MIDI Command	Transmitted	Received	Comments
Note On	No	Yes	
Note Off	No	Yes	
Pitch Wheel	No	Yes	
Program Change	No	Yes	0 - 31
Overflow Mode	Yes	Yes	
Channel Pressure	No	No	
Poly Key Pressure	No	No	

MIDI Command	Transmitted	Received	Comments
Control Change	No	Yes	PWH, #1, #7
Sustain Footswitch	No	Yes	#64
Sostenuto Footswitch	No	Yes	#66
Soft Footswitch	No	Yes	#67
Split Footswitch	No	Yes	#70
All Notes Off	No	Yes	
Omni Mode	No	No	
Poly Mode	No	No	
Mono Mode	No	No	
System Exclusives	No	No	

4. **Right-click Instruments on the left side of the Define Instruments and Names dialog box; select Add Instrument from the menu that appears.**

5. **Type a name for the new instrument. For this example, type E-mu PROformance Plus.**

6. **Open the new instrument by double-clicking it to display its data (see Figure 3.23).**

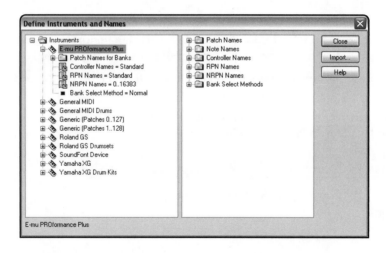

Figure 3.23 This dialog box shows a new instrument definition.

7. **Take a look at what the new instrument contains. SONAR automatically creates the standard settings needed. Because the E-mu PROformance Plus doesn't support bank select messages, RPNs, or NRPNs, you don't need to change them. The PROformance**

supports the standard MIDI controllers, too, so you don't have to change them either. You do need to change the patch names, though.

8. Open the Patch Names for Banks folder in the E-mu PROformance Plus instrument by double-clicking it. You should see General MIDI listed there. Because this instrument doesn't support GM, you need to change that name.

9. To change the General MIDI patch names list, you need to create a new patch names list first, specifically for the PROformance, by right-clicking on the Patch Names folder on the right side of the Define Instruments and Names dialog box.

10. Select Add Patch Names List from the menu that appears and type a name for the new list. In this case, type **E-mu PROformance Plus**.

11. The PROformance manual shows all the patch names for the instrument (numbers 0 to 31). To add those names to the new patch name list, right-click the list and select Add Patch Name from the menu that appears.

12. Type a name for the first patch (in this case, **Dark Grand**) and press the Enter key on your computer keyboard. Because this is just an example, you can leave the list as is, but if you were to add more names to the list, it would look something like Figure 3.24.

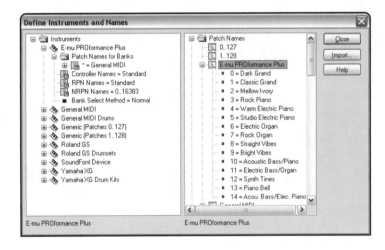

Figure 3.24 This dialog box shows a patch name list for the E-mu PROformance Plus.

13. Drag and drop the E-mu PROformance Plus patch names list into the General MIDI list in the E-mu PROformance Plus instrument definition.

14. In the Bank Number dialog box, enter the number of the bank that you want to use for this set of patch names. Click OK. The patch names list for the instrument will be changed.

15. Click the Close button and then click the OK button to finish.

This set of steps was actually a very simplified demonstration of how to create your own instrument definition. If the controller names need to be changed or if the instrument supports RPNs or NRPNs, you can create and edit those lists in the same way you do a patch name list. It's doubtful that you'll ever need to create your own instrument definitions because SONAR comes with a large number of them and you can download even more from the Internet, but just in case, you can find more details in the SONAR user's guide.

Optimal Audio Settings

When SONAR plays back digital audio on your computer, it puts a lot of stress on the system. Remember when I talked about digital audio in Chapter 1? A CD-quality digital audio recording requires 44,100 numbers (samples) to be processed every second. During playback, most of your computer's processing power is used solely for that purpose. Depending on the power of your system, this processing can make the response of some of SONAR's controls a bit sluggish, particularly the Console view controls. For example, if you adjust the volume of a digital audio track in the Console view during playback, you might experience a slight delay between the time you make the adjustment and the time you hear the results. As I mentioned earlier, this period is called latency, and you'll want as little of it as possible to occur during your sessions.

SONAR provides a number of different advanced settings that enable you to reduce latency. The first time you start the program, it attempts to make some educated guesses about what these settings should be, and although these settings usually work just fine, you still might be able to squeeze better performance out of your computer system. However, adjusting these settings can be tricky and unfortunately, there are no set rules. There are, however, some general guidelines you can follow to optimize your audio settings for the best possible performance.

Adjusting the Buffer Size Slider

One of the most important adjustments you can make is to the Buffer Size slider, and it's pretty simple to do. The lower you set the slider, the lower the latency will be; the higher you set it, the higher the latency will be. It can't be that simple, can it? No, I'm afraid not. By lowering the Buffer Size slider, you also run the risk of making your playback unstable. If you set the Buffer Size slider too low, you might hear dropouts or glitches, or playback might even stop altogether. And the lower you set the Buffer Size slider, the fewer digital audio tracks you can play at the same time.

To find the right setting, you have to experiment with a number of different projects. For projects with only a few digital audio tracks, you might be able to get away with a very low Buffer Size slider setting. For projects with many digital audio tracks, you might have to raise the Buffer Size slider and put up with a bit of latency while you work. The amount of latency also depends on whether you are using ASIO or WDM drivers for your sound card. If you are using ASIO or WDM drivers, SONAR runs much more efficiently, and you should be able to set the Buffer Size slider to a very low value. To set the Buffer Size slider, follow these steps:

1. Choose Options > Audio to open the Audio Options dialog box.
2. Click the General tab. The Buffer Size slider is located in the Mixing Latency section (see Figure 3.25).

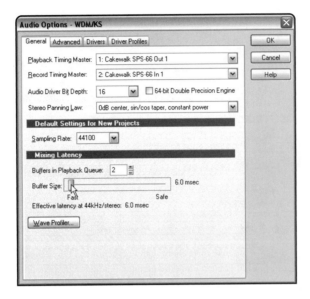

Figure 3.25 In the Audio Options dialog box, you can adjust the Buffer Size slider.

3. Click and drag the Buffer Size slider to the left to lower latency. Drag it to the right to increase latency.

❊ **PRACTICAL LATENCY SLIDER SETTINGS**

A good rule of thumb for setting the Latency slider is this: If you are recording using Input Monitoring or playing soft synths live via your MIDI keyboard, set your latency to a low value—maybe as low as four to six milliseconds when using ASIO or WDM sound card drivers. If you are playing many audio tracks and using a lot of real-time effects while mixing down, then set your latency to a higher value to relieve the strain on your computer system—perhaps a value of around 20 milliseconds (or higher if needed) when you are using ASIO or WDM sound card drivers.

---

4. Click the OK button when you're finished.

Setting Driver Mode

As with MIDI settings, the first time you run SONAR, it scans your computer system to see whether you have a sound card installed. SONAR then automatically chooses the drivers that will be used with your card, but you might get better performance using different drivers. To choose the type of drivers you want to use with SONAR, follow these steps:

1. Choose Options > Audio > Advanced to open the Audio Options dialog box (see Figure 3.26).

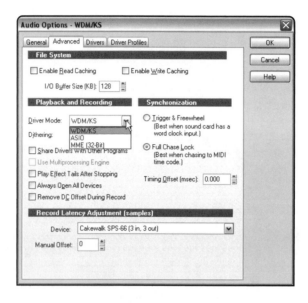

Figure 3.26 Use the Audio Options dialog box to choose your sound card drivers.

2. Under the Playback and Recording section, use the Driver Mode drop-down menu to choose the type of sound card drivers you want to use.

❉ SOUND CARD DRIVERS

MME drivers are an old variety of Windows sound card drivers, and they are provided for the support of older sound cards that might still be in existence. If at all possible, do not choose the MME option for your sound card output because it will provide very poor playback performance. Instead, choose either WDM or ASIO, depending on the type of drivers you have available. As to whether WDM or ASIO is better, that's a tough call. It really depends on the quality of the driver and how well it was programmed, so if you have both available, you'll have to try both to see which provides you with better performance.

3. Click OK.

You need to close SONAR and restart it for your Driver Mode setting to take effect.

ASIO Drivers

If you are using ASIO drivers, you need to open the Audio Options dialog box again and click the ASIO Panel button to make further adjustments after you have restarted SONAR. You might have noticed that the Buffer Size slider might not work in this situation. With ASIO drivers, instead of using the Buffer Size slider to adjust latency, you have to use the ASIO control panel for your sound card. One of my sound cards is the Echo Mona from Echo Audio. The ASIO control panel for the Mona looks like Figure 3.27.

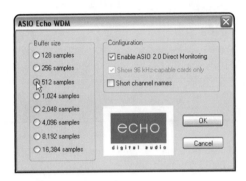

Figure 3.27 Use the ASIO control panel to adjust latency when you are using ASIO drivers.

When you use the ASIO drivers for the Mona, the Buffer Size slider in the Audio Options dialog box doesn't work. Instead, you have to choose a buffer size using the ASIO control panel. To do so, you simply click the ASIO Panel button in the Audio Options dialog box and then choose one of the available options in the Buffer Size section of the ASIO control panel. The lower the buffer size setting, the lower the latency; the higher the setting, the higher the latency. It works just like the Buffer Size slider, except there are set options to choose from instead of an adjustable slider.

Setting Queue Buffers and I/O Buffer Size

Two other settings that affect latency and audio performance are the number of buffers in the playback queue and the I/O (input/output) buffer size. Like the Buffer Size slider, if they are set too low, you can experience dropouts or glitches during playback. Higher settings mean more latency. Again, you need to experiment with the settings. I've found that values between two and four for the number of buffers in the playback queue and around 64 for the I/O buffer size work quite well. If you want to change them, you can follow these steps:

1. Choose Options > Audio to open the Audio Options dialog box.
2. Click the General tab. The Buffers in Playback Queue setting is located in the Mixing Latency section (see Figure 3.28).

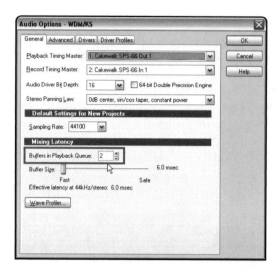

Figure 3.28 In this dialog box, you can adjust the Buffers in Playback Queue setting.

3. Type the new value.
4. Click the Advanced tab. The I/O Buffer Size setting is located in the File System section, as shown in Figure 3.29.

Figure 3.29 In this dialog box, you can adjust the I/O Buffer Size setting.

5. Type the new value.

6. Click the OK button when you're finished.

Read and Write Caching

When your computer sets aside a part of its memory to hold recently read or written information from a disk drive, the process is known as *disk caching*. Windows uses disk caching to help speed up read and write operations to your disk drives. When data is read or written to disk as a continuous stream (as with digital audio), disk caching can actually slow things down.

SONAR has two options that let you enable or disable disk caching while the program is running. By default, SONAR keeps disk caching disabled. If you have a large amount of memory in your computer, disk caching may actually improve performance. If you want to see whether enabling this option makes any difference with your computer system, follow these steps:

1. Choose Options > Audio to open the Audio Options dialog box.

2. Click the Advanced tab. The Enable Read Caching and Enable Write Caching settings are located in the File System section (see Figure 3.30).

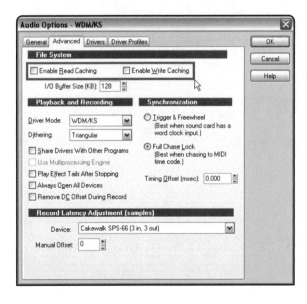

Figure 3.30 In this dialog box, you can adjust the Enable Read Caching and Enable Write Caching settings.

3. Click each setting to activate it.

4. Click the OK button when you're finished.

Understanding DMA and the Wave Profiler

A device that can read your computer's memory directly (without involving the CPU) is said to support DMA (*Direct Memory Access*). A sound card is such a device. SONAR uses the DMA settings of your sound card to ensure that MIDI and digital audio tracks within a project play in synchronization with one another. When you first run SONAR, it scans your sound card to automatically determine the DMA settings. These settings are listed in the Audio Options dialog box under the Driver Profiles tab. Leave these settings alone! In all but the most extreme cases, it won't do you any good to change them. If you're having excessive problems with MIDI and audio playback, you should contact Cakewalk Technical Support.

If you accidentally change the DMA settings (or if you just can't help yourself from seeing what will happen if you do), you can easily have SONAR scan your sound card again to bring back the original settings.

1. Choose Options > Audio to open the Audio Options dialog box.
2. Click the General tab.
3. Click the Wave Profiler button at the bottom of the dialog box. SONAR will scan your sound card and reset its DMA settings.
4. Click the OK button to close the Audio Options dialog box.

✳ IMPROVING AUDIO PERFORMANCE

For more information about optimizing SONAR, be sure to read the SONAR help file section entitled *Improving Audio Performance*.

Also, if you'd like more information about how to optimizeyour audio PC, go to www.digifreq.com/digifreq/article.asp?ID=14 to check out myfeature article entitled "Optimizing your Music & Audio PC."In addition, go to www.digifreq.com/digifreq/articles.aspfor more great articles and go to www.digifreq.com/digifreq/to sign up for my free music technology newsletter.

4 } Working with Projects

A project is SONAR's way of representing a song or any other musical body of work. A project holds all your music data, including MIDI and audio, along with a number of program settings. You can't do anything in SONAR without first creating a new project or opening an existing one. This chapter will do the following:

* Teach you how to open an existing project.
* Explain how to create a new project.
* Show you how to create your own templates.
* Tell you how to save a project.

Opening Projects

Every time you start SONAR, it presents you with the SONAR Quick Start dialog box (see Figure 4.1). In this dialog box, you can open an existing project or a project you recently worked with, or you can create a new one.

If you choose to open an existing project, SONAR displays a standard file selection dialog box so that you can select the project you want to load. If you changed the disk location of

Figure 4.1   The SONAR Quick Start dialog box appears when you start SONAR.

your project files, the dialog box will initially display the contents of the folder specified in the Project Files field of the Global Options > Folders dialog box. Of course, you can examine other disk locations just as you would when you are loading a file in any other Windows application.

By choosing the Open a Recent Project option in the SONAR Quick Start dialog box, you can open a project you've worked with previously. You simply select the project from the drop-down list and then click the folder button next to the list. SONAR keeps track of the last eight projects you've used. When you open a ninth, the project on the bottom of the list is bumped off—not killed or deleted, just removed from the list.

You can also open an existing or recent project using SONAR's standard menu functions. To open an existing project, just choose File > Open. To open a recent project, select the File menu and click the name of the project you want to open in the list on the bottom half of the menu (see Figure 4.2).

Figure 4.2   You can use the File menu to open an existing or recent project.

※ **SHOW THIS AT STARTUP**

Personally, I find it easier to use the standard menu functions to open a project. To keep the SONAR Quick Start dialog box from appearing every time you start SONAR, make sure the Show This at Startup check box at the bottom of the box is not selected (refer to Figure 4.1). You can do the same thing with the Tip of the Day dialog box.

Opening in Safe Mode

If you've used Microsoft Windows for any length of time, you've no doubt come across its notorious Safe Mode, which allows you to start the OS in a somewhat crippled state if you're having trouble booting up your PC. Basically, Safe Mode lets you start Windows with only the bare essentials needed to run the OS. For instance, all unnecessary device drivers are disabled, which enables you to troubleshoot Windows and attempt to find the source of your faulty start-up.

SONAR provides a similar feature (also called *Safe Mode*) for use when opening project files. Like any computer data, project files can become corrupt occasionally, which prevents you from opening them. This corruption can be caused by computer resource limitations or bad audio effect, MIDI effect, or soft synth plug-ins. Using Safe Mode, SONAR loads a project file with only the Track view (in its default layout) open. If you had any other open views in the project, they will not open in Safe Mode. You are also prompted for each and every plug-in that you have assigned to your tracks in the project. This feature lets you determine whether a particular plug-in is preventing you from opening your project. Here is how Safe Mode works:

1. When opening a project using one of the methods described earlier, hold down the Shift key on your computer keyboard. This tells SONAR to open the project in Safe Mode and displays the File Open - Safe Mode dialog box (see Figure 4.3).

Figure 4.3   Use SONAR's Safe Mode to open corrupt project files.

2. If your project contains any plug-ins assigned to your tracks, the Safe Mode dialog box will ask you whether you want to load the plug-ins. You have four choices: Yes, Yes to All, No, and No to All. Choosing Yes will load the currently displayed plug-in. Choosing No will not load the currently displayed plug-in. Choosing Yes to All will close the dialog box and load all plug-ins. Choosing No to All will close the dialog box and open the project without any plug-ins.

3. If you don't choose either Yes to All or No to All, the Safe Mode dialog box will ask you about each individual plug-in contained in the project, and you will have to answer either Yes or No to each one. This method allows you to determine whether a certain plug-in is causing trouble and which plug-in it is.

> ❄ **SAFE SAVING**
>
> If you load a project in Safe Mode with some or all of the plug-ins disabled, be careful when you save the project to disk. You should save the project with a different name so the original file remains intact. If you save the file using the same name, the original file will be overwritten, and all your plug-in assignments will be lost.

Personally, I've found the best way to use Safe Mode is to load a project and individually determine whether or not each plug-in should be loaded. This lets me narrow down the problem to a specific plug-in. I may lose the settings for that troublesome plug-in, but I can keep all the settings for any other plug-ins I have assigned to my tracks in the project.

Finding Missing Audio Files

Another problem that can occur when you are opening projects that contain audio data is that SONAR might be unable to determine the location of the data for that project on your disk. This can happen if you move the location of your Audio Data folder and you forget to specify the new location in the SONAR folder settings. You can also run into this problem if you use individual folders for each project. But if your data gets misplaced, you can use SONAR's Find Missing Audio function.

1. When you open a project in which SONAR cannot find the associated audio data for the audio tracks, the Find Missing Audio dialog box is displayed (see Figure 4.4).

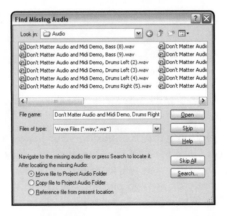

Figure 4.4   Use the Find Missing Audio function to locate misplaced audio data.

2. To locate the missing audio data, you can navigate manually through the folders on your hard drive using the Look In drop-down menu, or you can use the Search feature. The Look In drop-down menu is self-explanatory. To use Search, click the Search button. SONAR will automatically search your entire hard drive for the audio file currently

displayed in the File Name field of the Find Missing Audio dialog box. During the search, the Search for Missing Audio dialog box is shown (see Figure 4.5). If the file is found, select it and click OK. If the file isn't found, click Cancel and search for it manually.

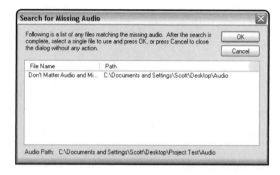

Figure 4.5   Use Search to automatically locate audio files.

3. After you've found the missing file, you can move it to your project's audio data folder, copy it to your project's audio data folder (which also leaves a copy of the file in its current location), or have the project point to the file in its current location. You accomplish these tasks by choosing one of the options in the After Locating the Missing Audio section of the Find Missing Audio dialog box (Move File to Project Audio Folder, Copy File to Project Audio Folder, or Reference File from Present Location, respectively).

4. To finish the operation, click the Open button. If you no longer want to use the file in your project, you can click the Skip button. To discard all audio data for a project, click Skip All.

5. If your project contains data from more than one audio file, you need to repeat steps 2 through 4 for each missing file.

Any files that you couldn't find or just skipped over will be replaced with silence in your project. The clips will still appear in the tracks, but the clips will be empty.

Creating a New Project

To create a new project, you can select the appropriate option in the SONAR Quick Start dialog box, or you can choose File > New from SONAR's menu. Whichever method you use, SONAR displays the New Project File dialog box (see Figure 4.6).

To utilize the dialog box, do the following:

1. By default, SONAR has the per-project audio folders option activated. Per-project audio folders allow you to create a separate disk drive folder for each of your projects. To disable the per-project audio folders option for the current new project you are creating, remove the check mark next to the Store Project Audio in Its Own Folder option.

Figure 4.6 Start a new project by selecting an option from the New Project File dialog box.

2. If you decide to keep the per-project audio folders option activated, type in a name for your new project in the Name field. This name will also be used as the project's folder name.

3. If you want to use a different folder name and location for your project, type a new disk path in the Location field. You can also browse for a new location by clicking the ellipse button located at the right side of the field.

4. The audio for your project is automatically stored in a folder called *Audio* inside the project folder. If you want to use a different folder name and location for the project audio, type a new disk path in the Audio Path field. You can also browse for a new location by clicking the ellipse button located at the right side of the field.

5. Whether or not you use per-project audio folders, you need to choose a template upon which to base your new project. Do this by making a selection in the Template list.

6. Click OK.

After you make your selection, SONAR creates a new project complete with predefined settings that reflect the template you selected.

What's a Template?

A *template* is a special type of file upon which new projects are based. You can think of templates as sort of like predefined projects. Templates contain the settings for all the parameters in a project. They enable you to set up a new project quickly and easily for a particular type of musical session. For example, if you need to record a rock song with guitar, organ, bass, and drums, you could get a head start on your project by using SONAR's Rock Quartet template. You can also use templates to set up SONAR for different kinds of studio configurations or to work with a particular MIDI instrument.

SONAR ships with more than 30 different templates that represent a wide range of recording situations. You can use a template called *Normal* to start a new project totally from scratch. And if you don't find what you need in the templates included with SONAR, you can always create your own.

Creating Your Own Template

Any parameters that are saved in a project can also be saved as a template. To create your own template, you simply follow these steps:

1. Choose File > New and then choose the Blank (No Tracks) template. Choosing this template creates a new, blank project, ready to be filled.

2. Set SONAR's parameters to reflect the type of template you want to create. This includes track configurations.

3. Choose File > Save As to display the Save As dialog box (see Figure 4.7).

Figure 4.7 You can name your new template in the Save As dialog box.

4. Choose Template from the Save as Type menu.

5. If you've created a special folder for storing templates, you can save your new template in that folder by choosing the Template Files option for the Go to Folder parameter.

6. Enter a name for your new template in the File Name field and click Save.

The next time you want to create a new project, your template will be listed along with the other templates in the New Project File dialog box.

❋ **AUTOMATIC TEMPLATE**

If you bypass the SONAR Quick Start dialog box—either by disabling it (as I mentioned earlier) or by clicking on its Close button—SONAR will create a new project automatically every time you start the program. This project is based on the Normal template, which is saved as the NORMAL.CWT file. If you want to have SONAR configured in a particular way every time you run the program, simply create a new template and save it as the NORMAL.CWT file. SONAR will load your special template automatically during startup.

But what parameters do you need to set when you're creating a new template? I'll go through them one at a time.

Track Configuration and Parameters

Before you start recording any MIDI or audio data in SONAR, you have to set up your tracks in the Track view. You need to add tracks and tell SONAR their types (MIDI or audio) by right-clicking in the Track pane of the Track view and choosing either Insert Audio Track or Insert MIDI Track from the menu (see Figure 4.8). Continue doing this until you have all the tracks you need for your template. You can also add Track Folders to your template, which allow you to group different audio and MIDI tracks together.

Figure 4.8 Add new tracks to your template by using the Track pane of the Track view.

In addition to adding new tracks, you also need to set up the accompanying parameters for each track. These parameters include the name, channel, bank, patch, volume, pan, key offset, velocity trim, time offset, input, and output.

ADDITIONAL PARAMETERS

When you look in the Track view, you'll notice there are some additional parameters available for adjustment. These parameters are not usually set up when you create a template, so I will cover them later in the book.

You can change all of these parameters directly in the Track view (see Figure 4.9), but you can also access some of them via the Track Properties dialog box (see Figure 4.10). Because you can change all of the parameters in the Track view, most of the time just using that method is easiest. The only time you might need to use the Track Properties dialog box is if you want to add a descriptive comment to a track, change the colors of a track, or you want to access the Patch browser. (I'll talk more about the Patch browser in a few minutes.) To access the Track Properties dialog box, right-click the number of the track you want to change and choose Track Properties from the menu.

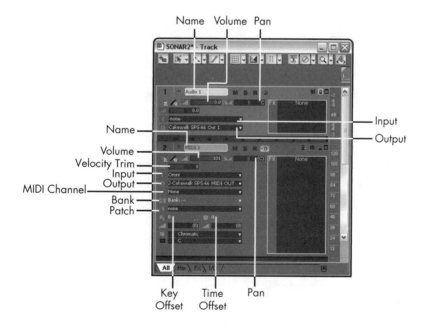

Figure 4.9 You can change all track parameters in the Track view.

Name

To name a track, double-click in its Name field in the Track view and then type the name. Press the Enter key on your computer keyboard when you're done; that's all there is to it. A track name can be anything from a short, simple word like *Drums* to a longer, descriptive phrase such as *Background Vocals (Left Channel)*.

Figure 4.10   Some track parameters are available in the Track Properties dialog box.

MIDI Channel

This parameter is for MIDI tracks only. It tells SONAR what MIDI channel you want it to use to play back the data in a track. To change this parameter, just click the MIDI Channel list and choose a channel.

Bank (Bank)

Also for MIDI tracks only, the Bank parameter tells SONAR which bank of sounds you want to use in your MIDI instrument. To change this parameter, just click the Bank list and choose a bank.

Patch (Patch)

Also for MIDI tracks only, the Patch parameter tells SONAR which patch (or sound) you want to use from the bank in your MIDI instrument. To choose a patch, click the Patch list. If you set up your instrument definitions as described in Chapter 3, you should see the names of the patches for your MIDI instrument in the Patch list.

❋ **THE PATCH BROWSER**

You also can choose patches for a track using the Patch browser. Right-click the number of a MIDI track and choose Track Properties to open the Track Properties dialog box. Then click the Browse Patches button to open the Patch Browser dialog box (see Figure 4.11). You can also simply right-click the Patch parameter of the MIDI track to open the Patch Browser. In the Patch Browser, you will see a list of all the patches available from the instrument definitions you set up earlier. To search for a particular patch, type some text in the Show Patches Containing the Text field. To choose a patch, select it from the list. Then click OK.

Figure 4.11 Use the Patch browser as an alternative for assigning patches to a track.

Volume

The Volume parameter sets the initial loudness of a track. That's basically all there is to it. You can set the volume by clicking and dragging in the Volume parameter. Drag to the left to lower the volume; drag to the right to increase the volume. You can also change the volume numerically by clicking the Volume parameter to highlight it, pressing F2 on your computer keyboard, typing in a new value, and pressing Enter. The value can range from 0 (off) to 127 (maximum) for MIDI tracks and -INF to +6 dB for audio tracks. To set the volume to its default value (0 dB), double-click it.

Pan

The Pan parameter determines where the sound of a track will be heard in the sound field between two stereo speakers. You can make the sound play out of the left speaker, the right speaker, or anywhere in between. That is called *panning*. You can set the pan by clicking and dragging in the Pan parameter. Drag to the left to pan the track to the left; drag to the right to pan the track to the right. You can also change the pan numerically by clicking the Pan parameter to highlight it, pressing F2 on your computer keyboard, typing in a new value, and pressing Enter. The value can range from 100% L (100 percent left) to 100% R (100 percent right). A value of C is dead center. To set the panning to its default value (C), double-click it. Pan works on both MIDI and audio tracks.

Key Offset (Key+)

The Key Offset parameter (which works only with MIDI tracks) lets you transpose the MIDI notes in a track during playback. It doesn't change the data that's actually recorded in the track. If you know you're going to want the notes in a track transposed after they've been recorded, setting up this parameter in your template can be useful. To set the key offset, double-click the Key+ parameter to activate it and then type in a new value and press Enter. The Key+ value can range from -127 to +127, with each number representing a semitone (or half-step). For example, a value of -12 would transpose the notes down an octave; a value of +12 would transpose them up an octave. A value of 0 means no transposition will be applied.

Velocity Trim (Vel+)

The Velocity Trim parameter (which works only with MIDI tracks) is similar to the Key Offset parameter, except instead of transposing MIDI notes during playback, it raises or lowers the MIDI velocity of each note in a track by adding or subtracting a number from -127 to +127. Again, the data that's actually recorded in the track isn't changed. You can set the Velocity Trim by clicking and dragging in the Velocity Trim parameter. Drag left to decrease the value; drag right to increase the value. You can also change the Velocity Trim numerically by clicking on the Velocity Trim parameter to highlight it, pressing F2 on your computer keyboard, typing in a new value, and pressing Enter.

Time Offset (Time+)

When you record a MIDI performance in SONAR, the timing of your performance is recorded along with the notes, and so on. Each MIDI event is "stamped" with an exact start time, which is measured in measures, beats, and clock ticks. The Time Offset parameter is similar to Key Offset and Velocity Trim, except that it adds or subtracts an offset value to the start time of the events in a MIDI track. Just as with Key Offset and Velocity Trim, the data that's actually recorded in the track isn't changed. The offset occurs only during playback, and you can set it back to zero to hear your original performance.

The Time Offset is useful if you want to make a track play a little faster or slower than the rest of the tracks, in case the performance is rushed or late. To change it, just double-click the Time+ parameter to activate it. Then type in the number of clock ticks by which you want the events in the track to be offset and press Enter.

Input (Input)

The Input parameter lets SONAR know where the data for that track will be recorded from—an audio track or a MIDI track. To set the Input for an audio track, choose one of the inputs from your sound card from the Input menu. For example, if you have a Sound Blaster Live! card, your choices would be Left SB Live Wave In, Right SB Live Wave In, or Stereo SB Live Wave In. If you pick either the left or right choices, the track will record audio from either the left or right input on your sound card. If you pick the stereo choice, the track will record audio from both inputs at the same time, making it a stereo audio track.

Setting the Input parameter for a MIDI track is a bit different. Because MIDI can have multiple ports, and each port has 16 different channels, you can choose to record data using any one of those ports/channels. Just make sure your MIDI instrument is set to the same port/channel that you choose as your input, or your performance won't be recorded. You can also use the MIDI Omni setting, which allows SONAR to record data on all 16 channels at the same time. This way, the data from your MIDI instrument will be recorded, regardless of the channel to which it is set. But if you're using multiple instruments, each one set to a different channel, you're better off just setting the correct channel in each of the tracks from the start.

Output (Output To)

The Output parameter tells SONAR which MIDI port or sound card output you want to use to play back the data in a track. If the track is MIDI, you can select a MIDI port from the Output menu. If the track is audio, you can select a sound card output or an audio bus from the Output menu.

 CHANGING MULTIPLE PROPERTIES

You can also change the properties for multiple tracks simultaneously. Just select the tracks you want to adjust by Ctrl-clicking or Shift-clicking the appropriate track numbers in the Track view. Then choose Track > Property > and the property you would like to change.

MIDI Input Presets

When you choose an input for a MIDI track, you might notice a couple of selections in the menu that I didn't mention earlier—the Preset and Manage Presets selections. Normally, when you choose an input for a MIDI track, you are limited to a single port and single channel selection. Using MIDI input presets, you can set up a MIDI track so that it records data from multiple ports and specific multiple channels of your choice. This type of flexibility can come in handy if you have a number of outboard MIDI devices sending MIDI data to SONAR that you would like to have recorded on the same MIDI track, for example.

To set up a MIDI input preset, follow these steps:

1. Click the Input parameter of the MIDI track and choose Manage Presets to open the MIDI Input Presets dialog box (see Figure 4.12).

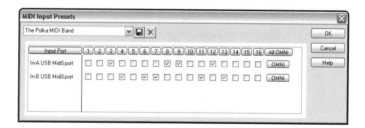

Figure 4.12 Use the MIDI Input Presets dialog box to create your own MIDI port/channel presets.

2. You'll see two lists in the box. In the left list, you will see all the MIDI ports provided by your MIDI interface. In the right list, you'll see all the MIDI channels available for each port. To allow MIDI input on a port/channel, put a check mark under that port/channel. You can activate as many port/channel combinations as you'd like.

3. If you want to allow MIDI input on all the channels of a port, click the OMNI button at the end of the channel list for that port.

4. When you're finished activating ports and channels, type a name for your new preset in the Preset list at the top of the dialog box.

5. Click the Save button (the floppy disk icon) to save your preset.

6. Click OK to close the MIDI Input Presets dialog box.

After you have created your preset(s), they will be listed under the Preset selection in the Input menu for your MIDI track(s).

Timebase

Just like all sequencing software, SONAR uses clock ticks to keep track of the timing of your MIDI performance. Most of the time you see the clock ticks as measures and beats because the program translates them automatically. Hundreds of clock ticks occur for each measure or beat.

The number of clock ticks that happen within a beat are called *pulses per quarter note* (*PPQ*) or the *timebase*. The timebase determines the resolution or accuracy of your MIDI timing data. For example, if you want to use eighth-note septuplets (seven eighth notes per quarter note) in your performance, you have to use a timebase that is divisible by seven (such as 168 PPQ); otherwise, SONAR cannot record the septuplets accurately. By default, SONAR uses a timebase of 960 PPQ, which means every quarter note is represented by 960 clock ticks. You can set the timebase anywhere from 48 to 960 PPQ. To set the timebase, follow these steps:

1. Choose Options > Project to open the Project Options dialog box (see Figure 4.13).

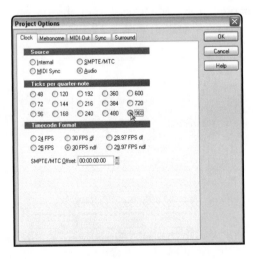

Figure 4.13 You can set the timebase in the Project Options dialog box.

2. Click the Clock tab.

3. Choose the timebase you want to use from the options in the Ticks per quarter-note section.

4. Click the OK button.

System Exclusive Banks

SONAR includes a System Exclusive (Sysx) librarian, which lets you store MIDI System Exclusive messages in up to 256 banks (or storage areas). All the data in the librarian is saved along with a project, which means that each project can hold its own unique library of Sysx data. This capability can be very useful when you're putting together templates for special MIDI recording situations. Because the Sysx librarian is a significant part of SONAR, I will talk about it in more detail in Chapter 16, "Studio Control with StudioWare and SysEx." I just wanted to mention it here so that you know that data contained in the librarian is saved along with your template.

File Information and Comments

SONAR enables you to save description information in a project, including title, subtitle, instructions, author, copyright, keywords, and comments. This information can be useful to remind yourself exactly what the file contains, especially when you're creating a template. To add information to a project, follow these steps:

1. Choose File > Info to open the File Info dialog box (see Figure 4.14).

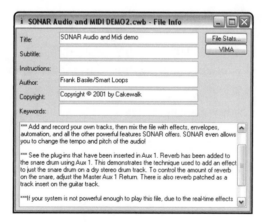

Figure 4.14 You can use the File Info dialog box to add a description to your project or template.

2. Type the appropriate information in each of the fields. By the way, the information you enter in the Title, Subtitle, Instructions, Author, and Copyright fields will appear in the Staff view and on your music notation printouts.

3. Close the File Info dialog box when you're finished.

The information you entered will be included in the project or template file when you save it.

> ✳ **AUTOMATIC FILE INFO**
>
> If you plan to share your project or template files with others, and you want them to follow special in-structions you've included in the File Info dialog box (or you just want to be sure they see your copyright notice), you can display the File Info dialog box automatically when the file is opened. Just save the project or template while the File Info dialog box is still open.

Tempo, Meter, and Key

Every piece of music needs to have a tempo, meter (time signature), and key, so, of course, SONAR sets and saves these parameters within a project or template.

Setting the Tempo

You can set the tempo for your piece by following these steps:

1. Choose Views > Toolbars to make sure the Tempo toolbar is visible (see Figure 4.15).

Figure 4.15 To set the tempo for a project, you need to use the Tempo toolbar.

2. Click the Tempo display in the Tempo toolbar. The Tempo will be highlighted.
3. Type a new value between 8.00 and 1000.00 for the tempo. You can also use the + and - spin controls to adjust the tempo with your mouse.
4. Press the Enter key on your computer keyboard to set the tempo.

Setting the Meter (Time Signature) and Key (Key Signature)

Because a piece of music can have multiple time signatures and key signatures, SONAR will add multiple meters and keys to a project. For the purpose of creating a template, more than likely you'll want to set only the initial meter and key. To do so, follow these steps:

1. Choose Views > Meter/Key to open the Meter/Key view (see Figure 4.16).

Figure 4.16 You can add multiple time and key signatures to a project in the Meter/Key view.

2. Double-click the first meter/key change in the list to open the Meter/Key Signature dialog box (see Figure 4.17). (For this example, there should be only one meter/key change in the dialog box.)

Figure 4.17 In the Meter/Key Signature dialog box, you can edit individual meter/key changes.

3. Enter the Beats Per Measure and the Beat Value you want to use. For example, if your song were in 6/8 time, you would change the Beats Per Measure to 6 and the Beat Value to 8.
4. Choose a key from the Key Signature drop-down menu. For example, if your song is in the key of A, choose 3 Sharps (A).
5. Click OK and then close the Meter/Key view.

Other Parameters

A few other parameters are saved along with projects and templates, including synchronization settings, MIDI echo, metronome, record mode, and punch in/out times. You'll usually set these parameters while you're working on a project (not beforehand), so I'll talk more about them in Chapter 6, "Recording and Playback." For the purpose of creating a template, you can just let these parameters be saved at their default values.

❋ **ADDITIONAL TEMPLATE MATERIAL**

A template can also contain MIDI and audio data, which can be useful if you have some favorite drum grooves or melodic phrases that you like to use frequently in your projects, for example. Simply store these tidbits as clips in one of the tracks, and the MIDI and audio data will be saved along with it when you save the template. Then, whenever you create a new project with that template, the MIDI and audio data will be ready and waiting for you to use.

❋ **THE ULTIMATE TEMPLATE**

When inspiration hits, you don't want to waste your time fiddling with sequencer setup parameters; you want to be able to start your software and get right to work. If you create a template file that contains everything set just the way you like it, you'll have a much better chance of getting that cool lick down before you forget it. For instructions on how to set up the ultimate template, check out my MIDI & Digital Audio Music Sequencer Techniques (Part 2) article over at DigiFreq. Go to: www.digifreq.com/digifreq/article.asp?ID=13 to read the article.

Saving Your Project

When it comes time to save your SONAR project, follow these steps:

1. Choose File > Save As to open the Save As dialog box.
2. Choose the type of project file you want to save from the Save as Type menu.
3. Enter a name for the file in the File Name field.
4. By default, SONAR has the per-project audio folders option activated. Per-project audio folders allow you to create a separate disk drive folder for each of your projects. To disable the per-project audio folders option when saving your project, remove the check mark next to the Copy All Audio with Project option.
5. If you decide to keep the per-project audio folders option activated, type a disc path in the Project Path field to be the storage location for your project. You can also browse for a location by clicking the ellipse button located at the right side of the field.
6. The audio for your project is automatically stored in a folder called *Audio* inside the project folder. If you want to use a different folder name and location for the project audio, type a new disc path in the Audio Path field. You can also browse for a new location by clicking the ellipse button located at the right side of the field.
7. If you would like SONAR to create a separate audio file for each unique clip in your project, activate the Create One File Per Clip option. This can be useful if you want to keep things organized and keep track of all the clips in your project outside of SONAR. It is also useful for editing audio clips outside of SONAR with another audio application.
8. Click Save.

SONAR saves the project according to your settings in the project file type of your choice.

Project File Types

You can save projects as four different types of files: MIDI (.MID), Open Media Format (.OMF), work (.CWP), and bundle (.CWB).

MIDI Files

If you ever need to collaborate on a project with someone who owns a sequencing application other than SONAR, you should save your project as a MIDI (.MID) file. A MIDI file is a standard type of file that you can use to transfer musical data between different music software applications. Most music programs on the market today can load and save MIDI files. The problem with MIDI files, however, is that they can store only MIDI data; they can't hold audio data. None of SONAR's settings are saved within a MIDI file either, so if you're working on a project alone or everyone else in your songwriting group uses SONAR, you don't need to deal with MIDI files. Of course, MIDI files can be useful in other circumstances, such as when you're composing music for multimedia or sharing your music with others via the Internet.

Open Media Format

As with MIDI files, if you ever need to collaborate on a project with someone who owns a sequencing application other than SONAR, you can save your file in the Open Media Format (.OMF). Instead of MIDI data, the Open Media Format only saves the audio data from a project. Why would you need this format? Well, you might want to bring your project into another studio where they don't have SONAR available and hire a recording engineer to mix or master your project. To export your project to OMF, follow these steps:

1. Choose File > Export > OMF to open the Export OMF dialog box (see Figure 4.18).

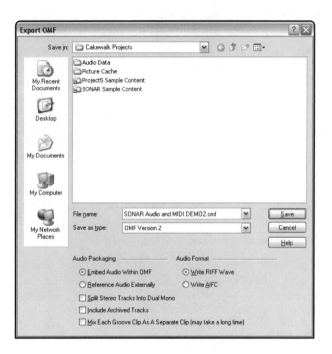

Figure 4.18 Use the Export OMF dialog box to export your project to an OMF file.

2. From the Save In menu, select the folder to which you want to save your OMF file. Then type a name for the file in the File Name box.

3. Choose a file type from the Save as Type menu. Choose OMF Version 1 if you will be importing the OMF file into an application that supports this version. Choose OMF Version 2 if you will be importing the file into an application that supports this version. (Usually, newer applications support Version 2.)

4. In the Audio Format section, choose whether you want the audio data from your project saved in Wave format or AIFC format. Usually, if you are using a Windows-based PC, you should use Wave format. For Macs, AIFC format is the norm.

5. In the Audio Packaging section, choose whether you want to embed the audio data from your project into the OMF file or whether you want the audio data saved as separate audio files. Choose the Embed Audio within OMF or Reference Audio Externally option, respectively.

6. If you want the stereo tracks in your project to be converted into two separate mono tracks, activate the Split Stereo Tracks into Dual Mono option. This option can come in handy if the application you'll use to open the OMF file only supports stereo tracks as two separate mono tracks.

7. If you have any archived tracks in your SONAR project, you can include them in the exported OMF file by activating the Include Archived Tracks option.

8. In SONAR, groove clips contain multiple repetitions of the same audio data over a number of different measures in a track. Normally, when you export a project, the groove clips are simply exported as one clip that contains the groove clip information. However, some applications might not support this type of clip, so you might need to save each repetition of each groove clip as a separate audio clip. To do so, activate the Mix Each Groove Clip as a Separate Clip option. This process can take a long time, depending on the size of your project.

9. Click Save.

If you choose to embed the audio data in the OMF file, you will export only one file. If you chose to reference the audio data externally, you will have one OMF file, along with all the audio files representing the tracks from your original project.

Work Files

If you're working on a project that contains only MIDI data and no audio data, you should save the project as a work (.CWP) file. Work files store all the MIDI data in a project, plus all the parameter settings for the project. Work files do not store audio data.

❄ MANAGING PROJECTS MANUALLY

If you decide to manage your project audio files manually using the per-project audio folders option, you should save your audio projects as work files. In this case, the audio data is stored separately from the project file.

Bundle Files

You can save projects that contain both MIDI and audio data as bundle (.CWB) files, although I recommend saving them as work (.CWP) files and using the Per-Project Audio Folders feature. If you use a bundle file, you can store all the data in a project (MIDI data, audio data, and project parameter settings) in a single file, but this format is best used for archiving completed projects. A single file makes it very easy to keep track of all the data in a project and easy to make a backup of the project for easy recovery in case something goes wrong.

> ❋ **BEWARE OF BUNDLES**
>
> Unfortunately, bundle files have been known to be unstable at times. Since I started writing the SONAR books, I've heard from quite a few users who have had trouble with bundle files becoming corrupt. There hasn't been any explanation as to why this happens, but the best way to avoid the situation is not to use bundle files at all. Instead, use the Per-Project Audio Folders feature and save your project as a Work file in its own folder. Then, to save disk space when archiving your projects, you can use a compression utility to save the folder to a compressed file format such as a ZIP file. Windows XP has built-in support for both creating and opening ZIP files.

Additional Saving Features

Sonar provides some extra save-related features that can help you recover past project versions.

Auto Save Feature

SONAR has an Auto Save feature that automatically saves your data to a special backup file at fixed time intervals or every time a certain number of changes have been made to the project. Using this feature is a great way to keep your data safe in case a power outage occurs or if you make a huge mistake that you can't undo. To activate Auto Save, follow these steps:

1. Select Options > Global to open the Global Options dialog box. Click the Autosave and Versioning tab.
2. For the option Auto-Save Every 0 Minutes or 0 Changes, set either the number of minutes or the number of changes to occur for SONAR to automatically save your project.
3. If you want to disable Auto Save, set both the minute and changes values back to zero.
4. Click OK.

During an automatic save, SONAR saves your project in a special file with a different name. If your project is named myproject.cwp, for example, SONAR automatically saves to a file named "auto save version of myproject.cwp." If you ever need to recover your project, you can just open the special Auto Save file and then save it under the original filename.

File Versioning

As you work on a project, you will save it many different times so that you don't lose your changes during each recording session. There may be times, however, when you wish you could go back to a different version of the same project. One of the most common reasons for this is that you made some major changes to the project that can no longer be undone. In this type of situation, SONAR's File Versioning feature can come in very handy.

When using File Versioning, SONAR will automatically save multiple, successive versions of your project—each with its own date and timestamp. If you ever want to revert to an earlier version of the project, you simply choose the file with the appropriate date/time and your project is instantly returned to a previous state. To activate File Versioning, do the following:

1. Choose Options > Global > Autosave and Versioning.
2. Activate the Enable Versioning of Project Files option.
3. For the Number of Versions to Keep parameter, enter the number of file versions you want SONAR to keep track of while File Versioning is active. You can enter a number as high as 999, but remember that each file version is an actual project file that is saved to disk and takes up space on your hard drive. For a small project, something like five is a reasonable number, but for larger projects that require many changes, you may want to use a number as high as 20 or more. It depends on how far back you may want to revert the project.
4. Click OK.

Now when you edit your project and save it, the current version of the project is saved under the original project name and a previous version (without the edits you made) is saved using the project name plus a timestamp in the filename. The number of timestamped files saved is determined by the Number of Versions to Keep parameter that you set earlier. If you set the parameter to 4, then only four previous project versions are saved. Once SONAR reaches the limit, one of the versions is bumped off the list and deleted.

If you ever want to revert the current project back to a previous state, you need to choose File > Revert. The Revert dialog box shows a list of all the dates and times related to the previous versions of the project. Simply select a date/time and click OK. SONAR loads the data from the timestamped project file, and you are instantly returned to the previous version of the project, which now becomes the current version.

5 } Getting Around in SONAR

To record, play, and edit your music in SONAR, you have to know how to navigate through the data in your project. SONAR includes a number of tools that examine and manipulate your data: these are the Track, Piano Roll, Staff, and Event views. Although each of these views provides a different way to edit your data, they all share some common means of control. In other words, even though your data appears (and is edited) differently in each view, you access the data in a similar manner, no matter which view you use. A little confused? Don't worry, you'll understand exactly what I mean after you finish reading this chapter. This chapter will do the following:

* Explain how to use the Now time.
* Show you how to use the Go menu.
* Describe how to set place marks in your project.
* Teach you how to search for specific music data in your project.

The Now Time

You learned a little about timing in Chapters 1 and 3. Essentially, you learned that in addition to the musical data itself, the timing of your performance is stored during recording. This means that SONAR keeps track of exactly when you play each note on your MIDI keyboard during a performance, and it stores those notes along with a *timestamp* (a timing value) containing the measure, beat, and clock tick when each note occurred.

To give you access to your data in a project, SONAR provides a feature known as the *Now time*. The Now time is essentially a pointer that indicates your current time location within a project. For example, the beginning of a project has a Now time of 1:01:000 (designating measure, beat, and tick), which is the first beat of the first measure. If you want to view the data at the second beat of the tenth measure, for example, you have to set the Now time to 10:02:000. Of course, you can get more precise by specifying clock ticks, such as in a Now time of 5:03:045, which would be the forty-fifth clock tick of the third beat in the fifth measure.

The Now time is also updated in real time, which means it changes constantly during recording or playback of a project. For example, when you play your project, the Now time counts along and shows you the current measure, beat, and tick while you listen to your music.

Show Me the Now Time

You can view the Now time in several different ways. The Now time is displayed numerically in the Position toolbar (see Figure 5.1).

Figure 5.1 You can view the Now time in the Position toolbar.

You can also use the Transport toolbar to view the Now time (see Figure 5.2).

Figure 5.2 The Now time is displayed in the Transport toolbar as well.

On either toolbar, you'll notice that the Now time is shown as measures, beats, and ticks. But each toolbar has an additional numeric display that also displays the Now time—shown as hours, minutes, seconds, and frames (known as SMPTE).

❋ WHAT IS SMPTE?

SMPTE (*Society of Motion Picture and Television Engineers*) is a special timing code used for synchronizing audio and video data, although it can be used for other purposes, too. NASA originally developed the technology because it needed an accurate way to keep track of space mission data. In SONAR, you can use SMPTE to keep track of the timing of your project. SONAR automatically converts the measures, beats, and ticks in a project to the hours, minutes, seconds, and frames format used by SMPTE. The frames parameter comes from the fact that SMPTE is used extensively with video, film, and television.

Video is created by recording a series of still picture frames very quickly. When these frames are played back, you see them as a moving picture. You can use SMPTE to time video data accurately, down to a single frame. Every second of video data usually has 30 frames, but the number depends on the data format.

You'll learn more details about using SMPTE in Chapter 6, "Recording and Playback." For now, just know that you can view and set the Now time of your project either in measures, beats, and ticks or hours, minutes, seconds, and frames.

❊ THE BIG TIME VIEW

If you're like me, and you have some of your MIDI instruments set up in your home studio a fair distance away from your computer, you might have trouble reading the very tiny Now time display on the Position or Transport toolbars.

To remedy this situation, Cakewalk has included the Big Time view in SONAR. Basically, it displays the Now time in large numbers on your computer screen (see Figure 5.3).

To access the Big Time view, choose Views > Big Time. The Big Time view has its own window so you can position it anywhere within the SONAR workspace. You can change the size of the Big Time view by dragging any of its corners, just like you would any window. To toggle the time format between measures, beats, and ticks and SMPTE, just click inside the Big Time view window. You can also change the font and color of the display by right-clicking in the window and then making your selections in the standard Windows Font dialog box.

Figure 5.3   You can use the Big Time view to display the Now time in varying fonts and sizes on your computer screen.

In addition to being displayed numerically, the Now time is displayed graphically in any of SONAR's view windows. In the Track, Piano Roll, and Staff views, the Now time is displayed as a vertical line cursor that extends from the top to the bottom of the view. As the Now time changes (from being set manually or in real time during playback or recording), the cursor in each of the views follows along in perfect sync and indicates graphically the place in the project at which the Now time is pointing currently. To see what I mean, try the following steps:

❊ FAITHFUL MUSIC PROJECT

To follow along with this exercise, please download the Faithful_1.cwp SONAR project file from the SONAR 6 Power book page on my Web site: www.garrigus.com/powerbooks.asp

1. Choose File > Open and load the sample project file that I've created called Faithful_1.cwp (see Figure 5.4).

2. Close the File Info window and then choose Transport > Play or just press the spacebar on your computer keyboard to start playing the project.

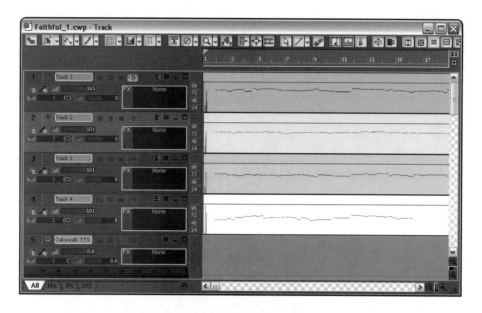

Figure 5.4 This screen shows the Track view for the Faithful_1.cwp sample project.

3. Look at the Track view. See the Now time cursor moving across the track display as the music plays?

4. Click the track number for Track 2 to select it; then choose Views > Piano Roll (or press Alt+5 on your computer keyboard) and look at the Piano Roll view. The same thing is happening, right? Notice the row of numbers just above the place where the Now time cursor is moving. This is the Time Ruler, and every view has one (except the Event view, which I'll talk about shortly). The Time Ruler displays the measure numbers in the current project. By lining up the top of the Now time cursor with the Time Ruler in any of the views, you can get a quick estimate of the current Now time.

❋ **TIME RULER FORMAT**

If you right-click the Time Ruler in the Track view and choose Time Ruler Format, you can change the format of the measurements shown. So instead of keeping track of the Now time in measures, beats, and ticks, you can use hours, minutes, seconds, and frames. The sample's measurement setting comes in handy when you are editing audio data.

You can also display multiple Time Ruler formats simultaneously by clicking the Add Ruler button (shown as a plus sign at the right-end of the Time Ruler) and choosing a format to add. You can also remove displayed formats by clicking the Remove Ruler button (shown as a minus sign at the right-end of the Time Ruler).

5. Choose Views > Event List and look at the Event view. It's different from all the other views because it shows the data as one long list instead of displaying it from left to right. And instead of a vertical line, it shows the Now time cursor as a small red box. While a project plays, the Now time cursor in the Event view moves down the list, and it marks the same place in the project that all the other view cursors do. Everything is synchronized to the Now time.

Setting the Now Time

As you just saw, the Now time changes automatically as a project is played, but you can also set it manually when a project isn't playing. SONAR gives you this capability so you can access different parts of your project for editing.

Numerically

Changing the Now time is easy. If you want to set the Now time to a precise numerical value, you can simply type it in the display on the Position toolbar.

1. If you want to set the Now time using measures, beats, and ticks, click the measures, beats, and ticks display in the Position toolbar. The display will be highlighted, and + and - spin controls will appear next to it (see Figure 5.5).

Figure 5.5 You can change the Now time by clicking on the display to highlight it.

2. Type the measures, beats, and ticks value you want to use and press Enter on your computer keyboard. You can also click the spin controls to change the value.

> ❊ **NOW TIME SHORTCUTS**
>
> If you want to set the Now time quickly to a particular measure or beat, you don't have to enter all the numerical values. For example, to set the Now time to measure two, type **2**. That's it. Or to set the Now time to measure five, beat three, type **5:3** or **5 spacebar 3**. To specify ticks, you must enter something for all the values.

3. If you want to set the Now time using hours, minutes, seconds, and frames, click the SMPTE display in the Position toolbar. The display will be highlighted, and + and - spin controls will appear next to it (see Figure 5.6).

4. Type the hours, minutes, seconds, and frames values you want to use and press Enter on your computer keyboard. You can also click the spin controls to change the values.

Figure 5.6 You can change the Now time by specifying SMPTE time code values, too.

SMPTE SHORTCUTS

Just as with the measures, beats, and ticks, if you want to set the Now time quickly to a particular hour, minute, or second, you don't have to enter all the numerical values. For example, to set the Now time to two minutes, type **0:2**. To set the Now time to five minutes, three seconds, type **0:5:3**. To specify frames, you must enter something for all the values.

Graphically

Remember when I described the Time Rulers in each of the views? Well, you can change the Now time quickly by simply clicking on any of the Time Rulers.

1. Choose File > Open and load the sample project file that I've created called Faithful_1.cwp.

2. Click the Time Ruler in the Track view. See how the Now time changes?

3. Select a track and open the Piano Roll view. Then click the Time Ruler in the Piano Roll view. Same result, right? Depending on where you click the Time Ruler, the Now time changes to the appropriate value within the measure that you click.

SNAP TO GRID

You might notice that when you click the Time Ruler in any of the views, the Now time is automatically set to the first beat of the nearest measure. This is due to SONAR's Snap To Grid feature. Snap To Grid automatically snaps the Now time cursor to the nearest predefined value when you try to set it via a Time Ruler. This feature makes it easy to specify quick and precise settings. Without Snap To Grid, setting the Now time accurately using the Time Ruler can be difficult.

Each view (except Event view) in SONAR has its own separate Snap To Grid, but the feature is set in the same manner, no matter which view you're using. To activate or deactivate Snap To Grid in a view, just click the Snap To Grid button or press N on your computer keyboard (see Figure 5.7). To set a Snap To Grid interval, click the down arrow next to the Snap To Grid button to display the Snap To Grid dialog box (see Figure 5.8); then select any combination of snap methods by choosing Musical Time, Absolute Time, Events, Clips, Markers, or Audio Transients. If you are using the Musical Time or Absolute Time methods, you can choose the Move To or Move By mode, which will snap data to the nearest time or move data by the time amount selected. In addition, the Magnetic Strength option allows you to move data freely until you get within a certain range of the snap settings you have chosen. A Low strength settings provides a minimal amount of pull and allows you to move data more freely, while a High setting snaps data more readily. After you've finished setting the Snap To Grid options, click the Time Ruler, and you'll notice that the Now time cursor will snap according to the settings you've chosen.

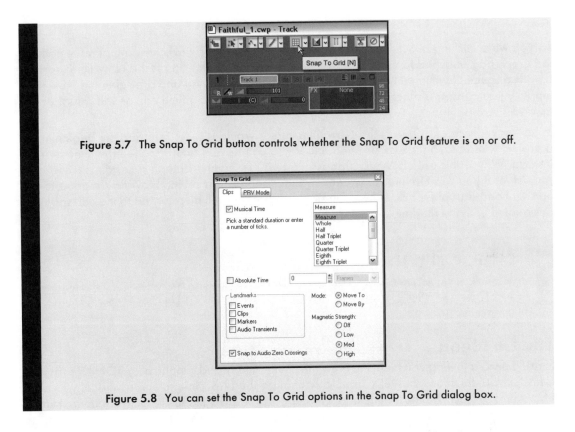

Figure 5.7 The Snap To Grid button controls whether the Snap To Grid feature is on or off.

Figure 5.8 You can set the Snap To Grid options in the Snap To Grid dialog box.

4. As before, the Event view works a little differently. Here, you can click any event in the list, and the Now time will change to the exact timing value of that event.

The Position Slider

Another quick way to set the Now time graphically is to use the Position slider. The slider is part of the Position toolbar (see Figure 5.9). To use the slider, just click and drag it. If you click to the left or right of the slider, the Now Time will update one measure at a time.

Figure 5.9 You can drag the Position slider left or right to decrease or increase the Now time, respectively.

Sticky Now Time

As you were clicking around in the Time Rulers of the various views, you might have noticed the green flag attached to the top of the Now time cursor. This flag is the Now time marker. It adds a special functionality to the Now time cursor. By clicking and dragging the Now time marker, you can set a place in your project to which the Now time cursor will return every time you stop playback.

In earlier versions of SONAR, the Now time cursor would always return to the beginning of a project when playback was stopped. Now you can have it return to the Now time marker instead. Why is this useful? Well, suppose that you're editing data in a certain section of a project, and you want to hear how your changes sound. Just set the Now time marker to the edit spot and start playback. When you stop playback, you'll be returned to the edit spot you designated with the marker.

> ❄ **REWIND TO NOW MARKER**
>
> If you would rather not have the Now time cursor return to the Now time marker when you stop playback, choose Options > Global > General and deactivate the On Stop, Rewind To Now Marker option.

The Go Menu

In addition to allowing you to set the Now time numerically and graphically, SONAR provides a few special functions that let you quickly change the Now time to some musically related points in a project. All these functions are a part of the Go menu. To activate them, simply click the Go menu and choose the appropriate function or press the appropriate key(s) on your computer keyboard (shown in parentheses). The following sections provide explanations for the functions on the Go menu.

Go-Time (F5)

Go-Time changes the Now time numerically by entering measure, beat, and tick values. It works in exactly the same way as the measure, beat, and tick display in the Position toolbar; the only difference is that Go-Time opens a dialog box.

Go-From and Go-Thru (F7 and F8)

When you're editing data in SONAR, you need to select the data that you want to use. This process is the same as in any computer program that lets you work with data. For instance, if you want to delete some text in a word processor, first you select the data to highlight it and then you delete it.

If you have some data currently selected in your project, you can set the Now time to the time that corresponds to the beginning (called the *From time*) or the end (called the *Thru time*) of the selection using the Go-From and Go-Thru functions, respectively.

Go-Beginning and Go-End (Ctrl+Home and Ctrl+End)

The Go-Beginning and Go-End functions are pretty self-explanatory. Simply put, they set the Now time to correspond to the beginning or the end of a project, respectively.

Go-Previous Measure and Go-Next Measure (Ctrl+PgUp and Ctrl+PgDn)

As with Go-Beginning and Go-End, Go-Previous Measure and Go-Next Measure are self-explanatory. They let you set the Now time to correspond to the first beat of the previous measure or the first beat of the next measure relative to the current Now time. In other words, if the Now time is set at 5:01:000 (beat one of measure five), selecting Go-Previous Measure changes it to 4:01:000 (beat one of measure four) and selecting Go-Next Measure changes it to 6:01:000 (beat one of measure six).

❋ **GO-PREVIOUS MEASURE QUIRK**

If the Now time is set to something like 5:01:050, Go-Previous Measure actually changes it to the first beat of the current measure, which, in this case, would be 5:01:000. I'm not sure why, but that's how it works.

Go-Previous Marker and Go-Next Marker (Ctrl+Shift+PgUp and Ctrl+Shift+PgDn)

The Go-Previous Marker and Go-Next Marker functions work in a similar manner to the Go-Previous Measure and Go-Next Measure functions. Go-Previous Marker and Go-Next Marker set the Now time to correspond to the closest previous marker or next marker relative to the current Now time. Of course, because I haven't told you about markers yet, you're probably wondering what I mean. So let's talk about markers, shall we?

Markers, Oh My!

All the methods for setting the Now time that I've described so far have been based on numbers or predefined musical designations, such as measures, beats, or the beginning and ending of a project. These methods are all fine when you already have the music for your project written out so you know exactly where everything occurs ahead of time, but what if you're creating a song from scratch by recording the parts on the fly? In a case like that, being able to put names on certain locations within a project would be very helpful, and that's exactly what markers do.

Using markers, you can assign a name to any exact point in time (in either measures, beats, and ticks or SMPTE) in a project. They're great for designating the places where the verses and choruses start and end within a song. And they make it easy for you to jump to any point in a project that you specify by name.

Make Your Mark(ers)

Creating markers is a simple process. Essentially, you just need to set the Now time to the measure, beat, and tick at which you want to place the marker in the project, activate the Marker dialog box, and type in a name. Activating the Marker dialog box is the key here because you can do so in a number of different ways. To create a marker, just follow these steps:

1. Set the Now time to the measure, beat, and tick or the SMPTE time at which you want to place the marker in the project. You can set the Now time either numerically or graphically.

2. Choose Insert > Marker to open the Marker dialog box (see Figure 5.10). You can also open the Marker dialog box by pressing F11 on your computer keyboard; holding the Ctrl key and clicking just above the Time Ruler (the Marker section) in the Track, Staff, or Piano Roll views; right-clicking on a Time Ruler; clicking on the Insert Marker button on the Markers toolbar; or clicking on the Insert Marker button in the Markers view.

Figure 5.10 You can create a marker using the Marker dialog box.

3. Type a name for the marker in the Name field.

4. If you want the marker to be assigned to a measure/beat/tick value, you don't need to do anything more. The measure/beat/tick time of the marker is shown in the Time field in the middle of the Marker dialog box.

5. If you want the marker to be assigned to an SMPTE time, activate the Lock to SMPTE (Real World) Time option.

> ❈ **LOCK TO SMPTE TIME**
>
> If you use the Lock To SMPTE (Real World) Time value, your marker will be assigned an exact hour/minute/second/frame value. It will retain that value no matter what. Even if you change the tempo of the project, the marker will keep the same time value, although its measure/beat/tick location might change because of the tempo. This feature is especially handy when you're putting music and sound to video because you need to have cues that always happen at an exact moment in the project.
>
> By leaving a marker assigned to a measure/beat/tick value, you can be sure that it will always occur at that measure, beat, and tick even if you change the tempo of the project.

6. Click OK.

When you're finished, your marker (with its name) will be added to the marker section, just above the Time Ruler in the Track, Staff, and Piano Roll views.

> ✽ **REAL-TIME MARKERS**
>
> Usually, you add markers to a project while no real-time activity is going on, but you can also add them while a project is playing. Simply press the F11 key on your computer keyboard, and SONAR will create a marker at the current Now time. The new marker will be assigned a temporary name automatically; you can change this name later.

Editing the Markers

Editing existing markers is just as easy as creating new ones. You can change their names and times, make copies of them, and delete them.

Changing Marker Names

To change the name of a marker, follow these steps:

1. Right-click the marker in the Marker section of the Time Ruler in one of the views to open the Marker dialog box. Alternatively, choose Views > Markers to open the Markers view (see Figure 5.11) and double-click the marker in the list to open the Marker dialog box.

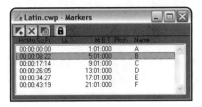

Figure 5.11 The Markers view displays a list of all the markers in a project.

2. Type a new name for the marker.
3. Click OK.

Changing Marker Time

Follow these steps to change the time value of a marker numerically:

1. Right-click the marker in the Marker section of the Time Ruler in one of the views to open the Marker dialog box. Alternatively, choose Views > Markers to open the Markers view and double-click the marker in the list to open the Marker dialog box.
2. Type a new measure/beat/tick value for the marker. If you want to use an SMPTE value, activate the Lock to SMPTE (Real World) Time option and then type a new hour/minute/second/frame value for the marker.
3. Click OK.

You can also change the time value of a marker graphically by simply dragging the marker within the Marker section of the Time Ruler in one of the views. Drag the marker to the left to decrease its time value or drag it to the right to increase its time value. Simple, no?

Making a Copy of a Marker

To make a copy of a marker, follow these steps:

1. Hold down the Ctrl key.
2. Click and drag a marker in the Marker section of the Time Ruler in one of the views to a new time location.
3. Release the mouse button and then the Ctrl key. SONAR will display the Marker dialog box.
4. Enter a name for the marker. You can also change the time by typing a new value, if you want. The time value is initially set to the time for the location on the Time Ruler to which you dragged the marker.
5. Click OK.

Deleting a Marker

You can delete a marker in one of two ways—either directly in the Track, Staff, or Piano Roll views or via the Markers view. Here's the exact procedure:

1a. If you want to use the Track, Staff, or Piano Roll views, click and hold the left mouse button on the marker you want to delete.

or

1b. If you want to use the Markers view, choose View > Markers to open the Markers view. Then select the marker you want to delete from the list.

2. Press the Delete key.

Navigating with Markers

Of course, what good would creating markers do if you couldn't use them to navigate through the data in your project? What's more, all you need to do is select the name of a marker, and the Now time will be set automatically to the exact time of that marker. You can jump to a specific marker in a project in two different ways—either by using the Markers view or the Markers toolbar.

Using the Markers View

To jump to a specific marker using the Markers view, follow these steps:

1. Choose Views > Markers to open the Markers view.
2. Select the marker to which you want to jump from the list. SONAR will set the Now time to correspond to that marker, and the Track, Staff, Piano Roll, and Event views will jump to that time.

Using the Markers Toolbar

To jump to a specific marker using the Markers toolbar, just select the marker from the list (see Figure 5.12).

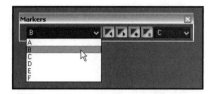

Figure 5.12 Using the Markers toolbar, you can set the Now time to any marker by simply selecting a name from the list.

SONAR will set the Now time to correspond to that marker, and the Track, Staff, Piano Roll, and Event views will jump to that time.

> ❅ **QUICK MARKER LIST**
>
> One other quick way to jump to a specific marker in a project is to select the Now time in the Position toolbar and then press the F5 key on your computer keyboard to bring up a list of all the markers in the current project. Select a marker from the list and click OK. The Now time will be set automatically to the time corresponding to that marker.

Where, Oh Where?

Until now, I have been describing how to navigate through the data in a project by somehow specifying the Now time, with the result being that you go to a specific point in the project. Well, what happens when you don't know the exact position to which you want to move in a project? For instance, out of all the data in all the tracks in your project, suppose that you need to set the Now time to the first occurrence of the note Middle C? Instead of playing the project and trying to listen for the note or looking through each and every track manually, you can use SONAR's Go-Search function.

Go-Search examines all the data in your project automatically and finds any MIDI events that have certain attributes that you specify. Upon finding the first event of the specified type, Go-Search sets the Now time to correspond to that event. This function is very useful for finding significant points within a project and placing markers there or for precision editing tasks. In the meantime, you can find specific MIDI events using the Go-Search function.

1. Choose Go > Beginning to set the Now time to the beginning of the project. If you don't take this step, Go-Search will start looking at your data at the current Now time, not at the beginning of the project. This means, for example, that if the Now time is currently

set to 10:01:000, Go-Search does not look at any of the data contained in the first nine measures.

2. Choose Go > Search to open the Event Filter - Search dialog box (see Figure 5.13).

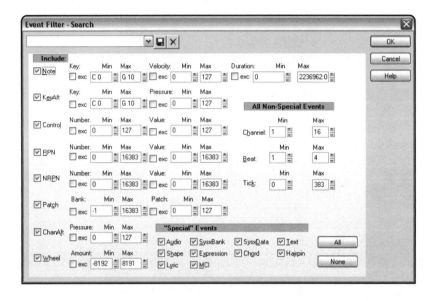

Figure 5.13 In the Event Filter - Search dialog box, you specify the criteria for your search.

3. Select the criteria for your search. Don't let all the settings in the Event Filter - Search dialog box intimidate you; they aren't very complicated to use. Basically, all you need to do is select the types of MIDI events you want to include in your search. For instance, if you want to look for MIDI note and pitch wheel events (but nothing else), deselect all the event types, except for Note and Wheel.

※ **DESELECT ALL EVENT TYPES**

By the way, whenever you open the Event Filter - Search dialog box, it automatically has all event types selected. To deselect all event types quickly, click the None button. The All button performs the exact opposite operation.

After you select all your event types, you need to set the ranges for each of the parameters. For example, suppose that you want to look for any MIDI note events between the pitches of C5 and G7 and with a velocity between 50 and 80. To do so, simply set the Note Key Minimum parameter to C5, the Note Key Maximum parameter to G7, the Note Velocity Minimum parameter to 50, and the Note Velocity Maximum parameter to 80. You can also specify a range of durations (note length) if you want. Each event type has its own unique set of parameter ranges: Key Aftertouch has key and pressure parameters; Patch Change has bank and patch number parameters; and so on. You can also set up searches that are a little more complicated by excluding ranges of parameters. If you select the Exclude (exc) option next to any of the parameter range settings, the search excludes event types with that specific parameter range. For example, if you want to search for MIDI note events that do not fall within the range of C5 and G7, you set up the Minimum and Maximum parameters, as in the earlier example, and you activate the Key Exclude option.

Using the Event Filter - Search dialog box, you can specify special events, too, such as Audio, SysxData, Text, and Chord events. These special events don't include any additional parameter settings, though, so Go-Search simply finds any events of that kind within the data of your project. Finally, you can choose to set a range of MIDI channels, beats, or ticks to search. These are called *non-special events*.

❊ **SAVING PRESETS**

Because setting these search criteria every time you need to find specific data in a project can be tedious, it would be nice if you could save the settings for future use. Well, you can. Just type a name in the Preset box at the top of the Event Filter - Search dialog box and click the Save button (the button with the little disk icon on it). All your current search criteria settings will be saved under that name. The next time you use Go-Search, you can simply select the name from the Preset drop-down list, and all your previous settings will be loaded. You can save as many presets as you want, and if you ever want to delete one, just select it from the list and click the Delete button (the button with the red X on it).

---

4. Click OK.

SONAR will search through the data in your project, find the first event that falls under the search parameters that you specified, and then set the Now time to correspond to that event. If you want to apply that same search again to find the next event with the same criteria, choose Go > Search Next (or press F3 on your computer keyboard). SONAR will continue the search (beginning at the current Now time), find the next event that falls under the search parameters you specified, set the Now time to correspond to that event, and so on. Here's another fact you should be aware of—if you first select some of the data in your project, the search will be conducted only on that selected data, not all the data in the project.

The Go-Search Challenge

So do you think you now have a good understanding of how the Go-Search function works? To test you on what you've learned, I've put together a little search challenge. First, read the challenge, and then see whether you can set up the Event Filter - Search dialog box options appropriately. When you think you've got it, take a look at the answer to see how you did.

A Simple Search

Find the first MIDI note event in the project that falls between the pitches of F4 and D7 and that has a velocity between 40 and 70. Also, restrict the search to MIDI Channel 2 only.

Here's the answer:

1. Choose Go > Beginning to set the Now time to the beginning of the project.
2. Choose Go > Search to open the Event Filter - Search dialog box.
3. Click the None button to clear all settings.
4. Select the MIDI note event type.
5. Set the Note Key Minimum parameter to F4.
6. Set the Note Key Maximum parameter to D7.
7. Set the Note Velocity Minimum parameter to 40.
8. Set the Note Velocity Maximum parameter to 70.
9. Set the Non-Special Event Channel Minimum parameter to 2.
10. Set the Non-Special Event Channel Maximum parameter to 2.
11. Click OK.

Did you get it right? If so, congratulations! I threw that MIDI channel restriction in there to make it a little more confusing. Setting both the minimum and maximum Channel parameters to the same number restricts the search to that MIDI channel. In this case, it was 2. If you didn't get the settings quite right, don't worry. With a little practice, you'll easily master this feature.

6 Recording and Playback

Being able to record and play your music with SONAR turns your computer into a full-fledged recording studio. Without these features, SONAR would just be a glorified music data editor/ processor. If you're going to memorize one chapter in the book, this should be it. You'll probably use the recording and playback features of SONAR most often. Therefore, I'm going to devote separate sections of the chapter to each way you can possibly record data in SONAR. This chapter will do the following:

* Review the parameters that need to be set prior to recording.
* Show you how to record and play MIDI tracks.
* Show you how to record and play audio tracks.
* Demonstrate how you can record multiple tracks at once.
* Demonstrate how to record new tracks automatically using looping.
* Teach you how to correct mistakes using punch in and punch out.
* Explain how to record MIDI one note at a time.
* Show you how to use importing instead of recording.
* Explain what synchronization is and how you can use it.

Preliminary Parameters
In Chapter 4, you learned about a number of parameters you could save to define a project template. Some of those parameters were related to recording, including track parameters, timebase, tempo, meter, and key. I'll mention those parameters throughout this chapter, but I won't go into detail about how to change them.

The Track Inspector
Setting the parameters for individual tracks can be cumbersome sometimes, because you have to widen the track parameter display before you can access the parameters for a track. To

make setting track parameters easier, SONAR provides the Track Inspector. You can use the Track Inspector for both audio and MIDI tracks. Basically, the Track Inspector is a replica of the track modules provided in the Console view. To activate the Track Inspector in the Track view, press the I key on your computer keyboard.

When you make a MIDI track active in the Track view, the Track Inspector displays the parameters for a MIDI track as they pertain to the active track (see Figure 6.1).

Figure 6.1 Access MIDI track parameters easily with the Track Inspector.

When you make an audio track active in the Track view, the Track Inspector displays the parameters for an audio track as they pertain to the active track (see Figure 6.2).

This means that you can keep the track parameters in the Track pane hidden but still have easy access to them simply by making the appropriate track active.

In the meantime, in addition to these track parameters, you need to be aware of a few other parameters before you do any recording in SONAR. I didn't describe them in Chapter 4 because you usually set those parameters while you're working on a project, not before, when you're creating a template.

Figure 6.2 Access audio track parameters easily with the Track Inspector.

Metronome

If you've ever taken music lessons, you know what a *metronome* is. It's a device that makes a sound for each beat in each measure of a piece of music. You simply set the tempo you want, and the metronome sounds each beat accurately and precisely. You use this device to help you play in time with the correct rhythm. In SONAR, the metronome feature helps you keep the right time so that your music data is stored at the right measure and beat within the project.

The metronome feature in SONAR is electronic (of course), and it's a bit more sophisticated than what you might find in a handheld unit. First, the tempo for the metronome is the same as the tempo setting for the project, so when you set the project tempo, you're also setting the metronome tempo. Normally, you would just have to turn the metronome on and off, but in SONAR, you need to set several other parameters before you use the metronome feature. You can access these parameters by selecting Options > Project to open the Project Options dialog box and then clicking on the Metronome tab (see Figure 6.3).

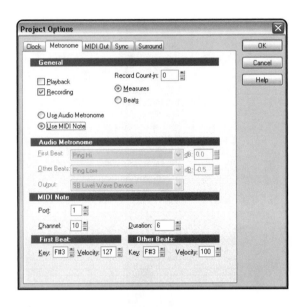

Figure 6.3 In the Project Options – Metronome dialog box, you can access the metronome parameters.

General

In the General section of the Project Options – Metronome dialog box, you can determine whether the metronome will sound during playback, recording, or both by activating the Playback and Recording options. You also can select whether the metronome will use your computer's sound card or one of your MIDI instruments for its sound by activating the Use Audio Metronome or Use MIDI Note options. You have to activate one of them; otherwise, the metronome won't make any sound at all.

Count-In

Using the Count-In option in the General section, you can get the feel of the tempo before SONAR starts recording your performance. Depending on how you set it, the metronome will sound a number of beats or measures before recording begins. For example, if your project is set for a 4/4 meter, and you set the Count-In option to 1 Measure, the metronome will sound four beats before SONAR begins recording.

Audio Metronome

If you choose the Use Audio Metronome option in the General section, the settings in the Audio Metronome section determine which sound card output will be used for the metronome sound, as well as the type of sound the metronome will use when it plays. To choose a sound for the first beat of every metronome tick, use the First Beat drop-down list. There is also a dB setting located to the right of the list that determines how loud each first beat will be. To choose a sound for all other metronome ticks, use the Other Beats drop-down list. There is also a dB setting for this parameter. Normally, you'll want to have the First Beat parameter set a little louder than the Other Beats parameter, so that the first metronome tick is accented.

> ❊ **METRONOME SOUNDS**
>
> SONAR ships with 38 different sounds that you can use for the audio metronome. If you would like to use some of your own sounds for the audio metronome, you can do so by adding audio files to SONAR's metronome folder located at: C:\Program Files\Cakewalk\SONAR 6 Producer Edition\Metronome.
>
> Just copy the audio file representing your sound to this folder. The file must be a WAV file, using the PCM (no compression) format, 16-bit, 44.1 kHz sample rate. The name that you give to the file is what will show up in the First Beat and Other Beats lists.

After choosing metronome sounds, use the Output list to choose the sound card output you would like to use for the audio metronome.

MIDI Note

If you select the Use MIDI Note option in the General section, the settings in the MIDI Note section determine which MIDI instrument is used to make the metronome sound and which note is used for the first beat and remaining beats of each measure. The settings are reasonably self-explanatory. In the Port and Channel fields, you can set the MIDI port and channel that your MIDI instrument uses. Duration determines how long each metronome "beep" will sound. The duration is measured in ticks, so if you use a timebase of 120 ticks per quarter note, a duration of 15 would be equivalent to a thirty-second note.

You can set the pitch (Key) and loudness (Velocity) of the first beat and remaining beats in each measure by using the First Beat and Other Beats options. If you want the first beat of each measure to be accented, you should set the velocity a little higher in the First Beat Velocity option. For example, you could set it to 127 and set the Other Beats Velocity to 110. Also, if your MIDI instrument is General MIDI-compatible, and you set the Channel option to 10, you can use a percussion instrument for the metronome sound. I like to use a rimshot sound.

MIDI Echo

Some MIDI instruments do not provide any way for you to play them except by sending them MIDI messages. These instruments are called *modules*. To play a module, you need to trigger the module's sounds by playing another instrument, such as a MIDI keyboard. If you connect the MIDI Out from the MIDI keyboard to the MIDI In of the module, you can play the sounds in the module by performing on the keyboard.

But what if you want to record your performance using SONAR? In that case, you would have to connect the MIDI Out from the keyboard to the MIDI In on your computer. This means that you would no longer be sending MIDI messages from the keyboard to the module, so how would you hear your performance? You could connect the MIDI Out from your computer to the MIDI In of the module, but the MIDI messages from the keyboard would still go directly to the computer and not the module. To remedy this situation, SONAR includes a feature called *MIDI echo*.

Basically, MIDI echo takes the MIDI messages from your computer's MIDI input(s) and sends them back out to your computer's MIDI output(s). You can control the MIDI channels *from* which the data is echoed and the ports and channels *to* which it is echoed.

The Input Echo Button

Each MIDI track in a project provides an Input Echo button. This button is located right next to the Mute, Solo, and Record buttons on a track's property bar (see Figure 6.4).

Figure 6.4 The Input Echo button controls MIDI echo for a MIDI track.

The Input Echo button provides three states – On, Off, and Auto-Thru. By default, the Input Echo button is set to Off. When Input Echo is set to Off, MIDI data coming into a MIDI track (via the MIDI port/channel that is set using its Input parameter) is not echoed to the MIDI port that is set using its Output parameter. However, if you make a MIDI track the active track (by clicking on its number), Input Echo is set automatically to Auto-Thru, which means that any MIDI data coming into the MIDI port/channel set in that track's Input parameter is echoed automatically to the MIDI port set in that track's Output parameter.

> ❀ **DISABLE AUTO-THRU**
>
> If you would rather not have Auto-Thru active so your MIDI track doesn't enable MIDI echo automatically when the track is activated, you can disable the Auto-Thru feature by choosing Options > Global and deactivating the Always Echo Current MIDI Track option.

By clicking on the Input Echo button, you can change its state. If you click the button to turn it on, it will become highlighted. When the Input Echo for a MIDI track is turned on, it means that any MIDI data coming into the MIDI port/channel set in that track's Input parameter is echoed to the MIDI port set in that track's Output parameter.

Echo Applications

So what can you do with MIDI input echoing? The most basic application allows you to hear the sounds you are playing on your MIDI module or software synth, as I described earlier.

But you can also use input echoing for some more sophisticated applications, such as recording multiple MIDI performances at the same time or layering sounds of multiple synths from one MIDI performance.

Recording Multiple Performances

Suppose that you're in a situation where you need to record the performances of more than one MIDI musician at the same time, and each musician is using a different synth. This means that each one will want to hear his or her individual performance during recording. Accomplishing this is actually quite easy with SONAR's Input Echo feature.

Depending on the number of musicians you need to record, you would create a MIDI track in your project to represent each musician. Then set the Input parameter for each MIDI track to correspond to the MIDI port/channel each musician is using for his or her MIDI device. Next, you would set the Output parameter for each MIDI track to the MIDI port that is being used for each musician's synthesizer. Finally, you would set the Input Echo button to On for each of the MIDI tracks. Each musician's individual performance would be recorded to a separate MIDI track and during recording, each musician would be able to hear his or her performance in real time.

Layering Multiple Synths

Creating new synthesizer sounds requires knowledge of synth programming, and not everyone has the time or patience to try programming his own sounds. But there's an easier way to experiment with new synth sounds; you can combine (or layer) the sounds from multiple synths to create an entirely new sound. SONAR's Input Echo feature makes this very easy to do; here's an example of how you can accomplish it:

1. Choose File > New and select the Blank template from the New Project File dialog box.
2. Choose Insert > Soft Synths > DreamStation.
3. In the Insert Soft Synth Options dialog box, activate the MIDI Source, First Synth Audio Output, and Synth Property Page options. Leave all the other options deactivated.
4. Assign a sound to the DreamStation synth using the Preset list at the top of the DreamStation window.
5. Repeat steps 2, 3, and 4 to set up one more software synth.
6. Set the Input parameters for both of the MIDI tracks you just created to the same MIDI port and channel that you are using for your MIDI keyboard.
7. Set the Input Echo buttons on both MIDI tracks to On.
8. Play your MIDI keyboard.

Isn't that cool? When you play on your MIDI keyboard, you should hear the sounds from both of the software synths playing at the same time. They are effectively layered together, creating a new sound from the combination of both. Of course, you can take this even further and continue to layer more synths, creating a huge ensemble of sound. In the meantime, experiment and have fun.

Sampling Rate and Bit Depth

SONAR lets you set the sampling rate and bit depth used for the audio data that you record. Depending on the sophistication of your sound card, you can set the sampling rate up to 192,000 Hz and the bit depth up to 64-bit.

So what settings should you use? Well, the higher the sampling rate and bit depth, the better the quality of your recorded audio. Higher settings also put more strain on your computer system, however, and the data takes up more memory and hard disk space. Additionally, if your input signal is already bad (if you use a low-end microphone to record your vocals, for instance), higher settings won't make it sound any better.

In my opinion, if your computer has enough power, memory, and hard disk space, you should use the highest settings your sound card will support. Using these settings will ensure that you get the best-quality recording. The only problem to watch out for is if you plan to put your music on CD. In that case, the audio needs to have a sampling rate of 44,100 Hz and a bit depth of 16-bit.

❋ **CHANGE THE AUDIO FORMAT**

To store music on a CD, the audio data must have a sampling rate of 44,100 Hz and a bit depth of 16. These values cannot be higher or lower; they must be exact. Of course, you can start by recording your audio with different settings. For example, if your computer has a limited amount of memory or hard disk space, you might want to use smaller values; however, I wouldn't recommend this unless it's absolutely necessary because lower values mean lower-quality audio. You also can record using higher values, which actually improves the quality of your audio data. When it comes time to put the audio on CD, however, you must convert the sampling rate and bit depth to the values I mentioned.

SONAR provides a Change Audio Format feature that converts the bit depth of the audio in your project. Simply choose Tools > Change Audio Format to access it. A better option is to keep your project audio at the higher bit rate and simply do the conversion when you export the audio as a stereo file for burning to CD. SONAR's Export Audio feature converts both bit depth and sampling rate. To access this feature, choose File > Export > Audio.

❋ **DVD AUDIO**

If you plan to put your music onto either the DVD-A (DVD Audio) or DVD-V (DVD Video) formats, you should be sure to use high settings for the bit depth and sampling rate of your project. If you plan to use DVD-A, then you should use a bit depth of 24 and a sampling rate of 192,000. If you plan to use DVD-V, then you should use a bit depth of 24 and a sampling rate of 96,000. Of course, you will also need to have a sound card that supports these settings. It's also a good idea to use these settings if you plan to create a surround sound project, since that's what publishing to DVD is all about.

To access the sampling rate for a project, choose Options > Audio to open the Audio Options dialog box and then click the General tab (see Figure 6.5).

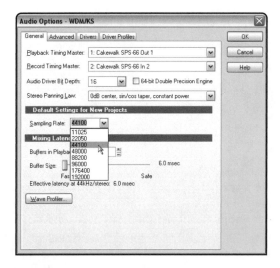

Figure 6.5 In the Audio Options dialog box, you can access the sampling rate parameter.

In the Default Settings for New Projects section, you can make your selection from the Sampling Rate list.

To access the bit depth parameter, choose Options > Global to open the Global Options dialog box and then click the Audio Data tab (see Figure 6.6).

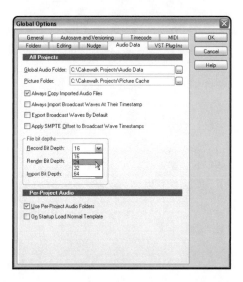

Figure 6.6 In the Global Options dialog box, you can access the bit depth parameter.

In the File Bit Depths section, you can make your selection from the Record Bit Depth list.

 MULTIPLE BIT DEPTHS

A SONAR project can store multiple bit depth audio data. This means that you can record one piece of audio at one bit depth and another piece of audio using a different bit depth, if you'd like. Simply change the Record Bit Depth parameter before you start recording.

Input Monitoring

When you record an audio track, you usually want to listen to your performance as it's being recorded. In the past, due to the limitations of sound card drivers, you could listen only to the "dry" version of your performance. This meant that you would have to listen to your performance without any effects applied. With the input monitoring feature in SONAR, you can listen to your performance with effects applied as it is being recorded. This can be especially useful, for example, when you are recording vocals, when it's customary to let the singer hear a little echo or reverberation during his or her performance. If you're not sure what I'm talking about, don't worry.

Similar to MIDI tracks, audio tracks provide an Input Echo button. This button can be turned on or off, and it activates or deactivates the input monitoring feature (see Figure 6.7).

Figure 6.7   Use the Input Echo button to turn input monitoring on or off for an audio track.

 MONITOR ON ALL TRACKS

You can easily activate or deactivate input monitoring on all audio tracks at once using the Playback State toolbar. Make the toolbar visible by choosing Views > Toolbars > Playback State. Then use the Input Echo button on the toolbar to adjust input monitoring.

 WATCH OUT FOR FEEDBACK

Input Monitoring might cause a feedback loop between your sound card inputs and outputs. For example, this happens when the signal coming out of a speaker is fed back into a microphone and the sound keeps looping and building up into a very loud signal. This feedback looping can damage your speakers. To be safe, you might want to turn down the volume on your speaker system before you activate input monitoring. If you hear feedback, deactivate input monitoring.

For a possible solution to your feedback problem, check the Windows Mixer settings for your sound card. Some sound cards have a monitoring feature that should be turned off when you are using input monitoring. For instance, if you have a Sound Blaster Live! card, open the Record Controls in the Windows Mixer and make sure that you are not using the What U Hear option as your recording input.

Record Mode

When you record MIDI or audio data into an empty track, SONAR simply places that data into the track within a new clip. When you record data in a track that already contains data, what happens to that existing data?

SONAR provides two different recording modes. (Actually there are three, but I'll talk about Auto Punch in the "Punch Recording" section of this chapter.) Both of these modes provide a different means of dealing with existing data. The Sound on Sound mode mixes the new data with the existing data. For example, if you record a vocal part into a track that already contains music, you hear both the vocal and the music when you play back that track. The Overwrite mode replaces the existing data with the new data. So in this example, the music is erased, and the vocal takes its place. When you try to play the track, you hear only the vocal.

Keep in mind that you need to deal with recording modes only when you're recording data into a track that already contains data. More than likely, you won't be doing that very often because SONAR records an unlimited number of tracks, and you can easily place each part of your song on a separate track. If you do need to set the recording mode, just select Transport > Record Options to open the Record Options dialog box (see Figure 6.8).

Figure 6.8 In the Record Options dialog box, you can set the recording mode.

In the Recording Mode section, select either Sound on Sound or Overwrite and click OK.

> ❋ **TRACK LAYERS**
>
> If you choose the Sound on Sound recording mode, SONAR will place each recording that you do on the same track in separate clips. This means that if you record to the same track more than once, each recording will be put in a different clip, even if those recordings overlap. In order to work with overlapping clips in the same track, you can activate the Create New Layer on Overlap option in the Record Mode dialog box so that each overlapping clip will be put on a separate track layer. Then to access those layers, you can activate the Show Layers option by right-clicking the track number and choosing Layers > Show Layers from the menu. Do this before you start recording.
>
> The Show Layers option easily accesses and edits overlapping clips in the same track.

MIDI Track Recording and Playback

Believe it or not, you now have the knowledge you need to start recording in SONAR. Nothing is very complicated about the process, but you should follow a number of steps to make sure everything occurs smoothly. Here and in the following sections, I'll show you step-by-step how to record MIDI tracks, audio tracks, and multiple tracks at the same time. First, you'll tackle MIDI tracks. To get started, follow these steps:

1. Create a new project or open an existing one. If you use a template to create a new project, you might be able to skip some of the following steps, but you probably should run through them anyway, just in case.

2. Set the meter and key signature for the project. The default settings are 4/4 and the key of C Major.

3. Set the metronome and tempo parameters. The default tempo for a new project is 100 beats per minute.

4. Set the timebase for the project. The default setting is 960 PPQ (pulses per quarter note). More often than not, you won't have to change this setting.

5. Set the recording mode. Unless you plan to record data to a track that already contains data, you can skip this step. The default recording mode is Sound on Sound.

6. Add a new MIDI track to the Track view and adjust the track's properties.

7. Arm the track for recording to let SONAR know that you want to record data on the track. Right after (or underneath) the name parameter in the Track view, you'll see three buttons labeled M, S, and R. Click the R button to arm the track for recording (see Figure 6.9).

8. Set the Now time to the point in the project where you would like the recording to begin. Most of the time it will be the very beginning of the project, but SONAR provides flexibility to let you record data to a track starting at any measure, beat, or tick within a project.

9. Select Transport > Record to start recording. (You can also press the R key on your computer keyboard or click the Record button on the Transport toolbar.) If you set a

Figure 6.9 You arm a track for recording by clicking on its associated R button in the Track view.

Count-In, the metronome will first count the number of beats you entered, and then SONAR will begin recording.

10. Perform the material you want to record.

11. After you finish performing, select Transport > Stop to stop recording. (You also can press the spacebar on your computer keyboard or click the Stop button in the Transport toolbar.) SONAR will create a new clip in the track containing the MIDI data you just recorded (see Figure 6.10).

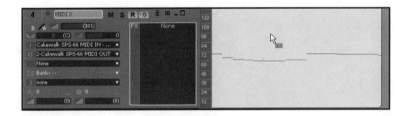

Figure 6.10 After you've finished recording, SONAR will create a new clip in the track representing the MIDI data.

12. Listen to your performance by setting the Now time back to its original position and selecting Transport > Play. (Alternatively, you can press the spacebar on your computer keyboard or click the Play button on the Transport toolbar.) If you don't like the performance, you can erase it by selecting Edit > Undo Recording. Then go back to step 8 and try recording again.

❈ **UNDO HISTORY**

SONAR provides an Undo feature that reverses any action you take while working on a project. You're probably familiar with this feature because it is included in most applications that manipulate data, such as word processing software and so on. SONAR goes a bit further by providing an Undo History feature. This feature logs every step you take while working on a project and undoes each step all the way back to the beginning of your current session. The Undo History is not saved, though, so as soon as you close a project, you lose the ability to undo any changes.

To access the Undo History feature, select Edit > History to open the Undo History dialog box (see Figure 6.11). You will see a list of all the tasks you've done during the current session. To go back to a certain point in the session, select a task in the list and click OK. SONAR will undo any tasks performed after the task you selected. The Maximum Undo Levels parameter determines how many tasks SONAR will log in the Undo History list. You can set this parameter higher if you'd like. Remember, though, that the more tasks SONAR keeps track of, the more memory and hard disk space it needs.

Figure 6.11 Using the Undo History dialog box, you can reverse your actions.

EDIT MIDI DATA

If you find that your performance is good for the most part, except for a few trouble spots, you might want to try fixing the mistakes by editing the MIDI notes rather than using Undo and then performing the entire thing all over again.

13. After you've recorded a performance you like, disarm the track by clicking on its R button again. By disarming the track, you won't accidentally record over the data while you're recording any additional tracks.

14. Go back to step 6 and record any additional tracks you want to add to the project. While you're recording the new tracks, you will hear the previously recorded tracks being played back. Because you can hear these tracks, you might want to turn off the metronome and just follow the music of the previous tracks as you perform the material for the new ones.

SAVE YOUR PROJECT

Be sure to save your project after each successful track recording. This step isn't mandatory, but it's a good precautionary measure because you never know when your computer might crash on you. Rather than lose that really great performance you just recorded, quickly select File > Save (or press Ctrl+S on your computer keyboard), so that you can rest easy in knowing that your data is safe.

Audio Track Recording and Playback

Recording audio tracks in SONAR is very similar to recording MIDI tracks, but because the nature of the data is different, you need to take a few additional steps. Here's the step-by-step process for recording audio tracks:

1. Follow steps 1 through 5 of the previous MIDI Track Recording and Playback section since they are the same.
2. Set the sampling rate and the file bit depth for the project.
3. Add a new audio track to the Track view and adjust the track's properties.
4. If you want to hear effects added to your performance while you're recording, activate Input Monitoring for the audio track by clicking on its Input Echo button. Then add effects to your track by right-clicking on the Fx bin (located in the Track pane along with all the other track parameters) and choosing Audio FX > Cakewalk > [*the effect you would like to add*].

❋ **TUNING YOUR INSTRUMENT**

If the audio track you are about to record is for an instrument like the guitar, you may want to check the tuning before going further. SONAR provides a built-in electronic tuner that is very easy to use. Simply right-click in the Fx bin of the track you are about to record. Then choose Audio FX > Cakewalk > Tuner from the menu. This will add the Tuner to the Fx bin and open the Cakewalk Tuner window. To activate the Tuner, click the track's Input Echo button to turn input monitoring on for that track. Then just play your instrument. You'll notice the musical note readings displayed as you play in the Cakewalk Tuner window. If you would like to hear your instrument through the track output via your sound card as you play, activate the Output Monitor button in the Cakewalk Tuner window. It's the only button available there, so you can't miss it. After you've finished tuning your instrument, right-click the Tuner listing in the Fx bin of the track and choose Delete from the menu to remove the Tuner before you start recording.

---

5. Arm the track for recording to let SONAR know that you want to record data on the track. Right after (or underneath) the name parameter in the Track view, you'll see three buttons labeled M, S, and R. Click the R button to arm the track for recording.
6. After you arm the track, you'll notice the meter (shown to the right of or underneath the Fx bin) light up (see Figure 6.12). This meter displays the level of the audio input for your sound card in decibels.

Figure 6.12 Each audio track has a meter showing its input signal level in decibels.

7. Set the audio input level for your sound card so that it's not too loud but also not too soft. To do so, you have to use the software mixer that came with your sound card. On the Windows taskbar, you should see a small speaker icon. Double-click the speaker icon to open your sound card mixer. Then select Options > Properties to open the sound card mixer's Properties dialog box. In the Adjust Volume For section, select Recording, make sure all boxes below it are checked, and click OK to display the recording controls for your sound card mixer (see Figure 6.13).

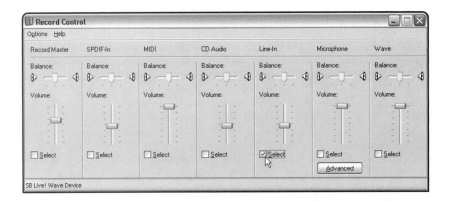

Figure 6.13 You use your sound card mixer to adjust the input levels for your sound card.

8. For the set of controls labeled Line-In, either activate the Select option or deactivate the Mute option (depending on your mixer configuration). This option tells your sound card that you want to record audio using its line-input connection. If you want to use a different connection (such as a microphone or internal CD player), you need to use the set of controls associated with that connection.

9. When you have access to the input level controls for your sound card, begin your performance, playing at the loudest level at which you plan to record. As you play, the
meter for the track will light up, displaying the sound level of your performance. You
should adjust the input level so that when you play the loudest part of your performance,
the meter does *not* turn red. If it turns red, you have overloaded the input, and if you
record at that level, your audio signal will be distorted. When you play the loudest part
of your performance, if the meter lights up anywhere between -6dB and -3dB, then you
have a good input level setting.

10. After you finish setting your input level, close the sound card mixer. Next, set the Now
time to the point in the project where you would like the recording to begin. Most of the
time, it will be at the very beginning of the project, but SONAR provides flexibility to let
you record data to a track starting at any measure, beat, or tick in a project.

11. Select Transport > Record (or press R) to start recording. If you set a Count-In, the
metronome will count the number of beats you entered, and then SONAR will begin
recording.

12. Perform the material you want to record.

13. After you finish performing, select Transport > Stop (or press the spacebar) to stop
recording. SONAR will create a new clip in the track containing the audio data you just
recorded (see Figure 6.14).

Figure 6.14 After you've finished recording, SONAR will create a new clip in the track representing the
audio data.

14. Listen to your performance by setting the Now time back to its original position and
starting playback. If you don't like the performance, erase it by selecting Edit > Undo
Recording. Then go back to step 14 and try recording again.

15. After you've recorded a performance you like, disarm the track by clicking on its R button
again. By disarming the track, you won't accidentally record over the data while you're
recording any additional tracks.

16. Go back to step 7 and record any additional tracks you want to add to the project. While
you're recording the new tracks, you will hear the previously recorded tracks playing
back. Therefore, you might want to turn off the metronome and just follow the music of
the previous tracks as you perform the material for the new ones.

> ❋ **RECORDING REMOTELY**
>
> If you have your home studio set up in a single room containing all your equipment (including your computer) and you are recording audio tracks using a microphone, the microphone will pick up the background noise made by your electronic devices (including the fan inside your computer). To remedy this situation, you might want to set up your microphone and one of your MIDI instruments in a different room, while keeping them connected to your computer via longer cables. Then you can set up some MIDI key bindings, so that you can control SONAR remotely. That way, when you record the audio from your microphone, it won't pick up all that background noise.

Multiple Track Recording and Playback

If you have more than one MIDI input on your MIDI interface or more than one audio input on your sound card, you can record to multiple tracks simultaneously. Recording multiple tracks works well when you need to record an entire band of musicians. Instead of having each musician play individually (which can sometimes ruin the "groove"), you can record everyone's part at once (which usually makes the song flow much better).

To record multiple tracks, just follow the same instructions I outlined earlier for recording MIDI and audio tracks. The only difference is that you must set up and arm more than one track. When you start recording, the MIDI or audio data for each musician will be recorded to separate tracks simultaneously.

> ❋ **BASIC SOUND CARD**
>
> Even if you're using a basic sound card to record audio, you can still record two different audio tracks at once because your sound card has a stereo input. This means that you can use the left and right audio channels separately to record two individual tracks. When you set up the tracks prior to recording, just select the input for one track to be the left audio channel of your sound card and the input for the other track to be the right audio channel of your sound card. You also might need a special audio cable. Most basic sound cards provide only one stereo input connection at a 1/8-inch size. The cable you will need is called a Y-adapter audio cable with a stereo 1/8-inch mini plug to phono plugs (or connections). You should be able to find the cable at your local Radio Shack.

Loop Recording

If you plan to add a vocal track or an instrumental track (such as a guitar solo) to your project—something that might require more than one try to get right—you might want to use *loop recording* instead of recording and undoing a single track over and over again manually. Loop recording records several tracks, one right after the other, without having to stop between each one. Here's how it works:

1. If you want to record MIDI tracks, follow steps 1 through 7 in the "MIDI Track Recording and Playback" section presented earlier in this chapter. If you want to record audio tracks, follow steps 1 through 13 in the "Audio Track Recording and Playback" section.

2. Set the Now time to the point in the project at which you want looping to begin. Then select Transport > Loop and Auto Shuttle to open the Loop/Auto Shuttle dialog box (see Figure 6.15). Click the Loop Start parameter and then press F5 on your computer keyboard to bring up the Markers dialog box. Select the marker named Now from the list and click OK to set the start time at which the looping will begin.

Figure 6.15 In the Loop/Auto Shuttle dialog box, you can set the loop recording parameters for SONAR.

3. Type an end time for the loop using measure, beat, and tick values. Then activate the Stop at the End Time and Rewind to Start and Loop Continuously options and click OK. Setting these options tells SONAR that when you start recording, it will begin at the loop start time, continue to the loop end time, and then loop back to the start time to cycle through the loop over and over again, until you stop it.

❋ **SET LOOP POINTS QUICKLY**

For a quick way to set the start and end times, just click and drag in the Time Ruler of the Track view to make a data selection; then right-click the Time Ruler and choose Loop > Set Loop Points from the menu.

❋ **THE LOOP TOOLBAR**

You also can use the Loop toolbar to set the parameters for looping.

4. Select Transport > Record Options to open the Record Options dialog box. In the Loop Recording section, select either Store Takes in a Single Track or Store Takes in Separate Tracks. The first option stores each performance in the same track but in different clips stacked on top of each other. The second option stores each performance in a different track, but automatically setting the same track parameters as the one you began with. The option I like to use depends on the amount of flexibility I need. For example, if I'm trying to record the perfect vocal track and want to piece it together from a number of different takes, then I'll choose the Store Takes in a Single Track option and use the track layers and comping features after I'm done recording. If I want to record multiple takes but use each take separately and apply different effects, then I'll choose the Store Takes

in Separate Tracks option. For this example, choose the Store Takes in Separate Tracks option.

❄ TRACK LAYERS

If you choose the Store Takes in a Single Track option, SONAR will place each recording that you do on the same track in separate clips. This means that if you record to the same track more than once, each recording will be put in a different clip, even if those recordings overlap. In order to work with overlapping clips in the same track, you can activate the Create New Layer on Overlap option in the Record Mode dialog box, so that each overlapping clip will be put on a separate track layer. Then to access those layers, you can activate the Show Layers option by right-clicking the track number and choosing Layers > Show Layers from the menu. Do this before you start recording.

The Show Layers option easily accesses and edits overlapping clips in the same track (see Chapter 7, "Editing Basics" for more information).

---

5. Select Transport > Record (or press R) to start recording. If you set a Count-In, the metronome will count the number of beats you entered, and then SONAR will begin recording.
6. Perform the material you want to record until you get a good take.
7. After you finish performing, select Transport > Stop (or press the spacebar) to stop recording. SONAR will create a new track containing the data you just recorded for every loop you cycled through (see Figure 6.16).

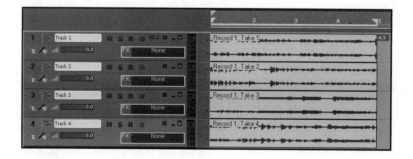

Figure 6.16 For every loop you record, SONAR creates a new track containing each individual performance.

8. Each track (except for the original one) is disarmed. To listen to any of your performances, turn off looping by selecting Transport > Loop and Auto Shuttle to open the Loop/Auto Shuttle dialog box. Deactivate the Stop at the End Time option and click OK. Set the Now time back to its original position and select Transport > Play (or press the spacebar) to start playback. To listen to one of the recorded tracks, solo it by clicking the S button next to its name parameter in the Track view.

9. After you've found a performance that you like and want to keep, delete the others by clicking the appropriate track number on the left side of the Track view to select a track and then selecting Track > Delete. If you want to select more than one track, hold down the Ctrl key while you're selecting track numbers.

❄ **ARCHIVE TRACKS**

Instead of deleting all the extra tracks you created during looping, you might want to keep them for later use. You can do so by using SONAR's Archive feature. By archiving tracks, you store them within the current project, but they become invisible to SONAR. This means that when you play your project, the archived tracks will not play. As a matter of fact, archiving tracks helps increase SONAR's performance because it doesn't process the tracks at all when they are archived. To archive a track, right-click its track number and select MSR > Archive. You'll notice that the track's Mute button turns into an A (Archive) button. This change in the button name shows that the track is archived. You can still make changes to the track (and the data in it), but SONAR will not play it.

Punch Recording

When you make a mistake while recording MIDI data, it's usually no big deal because you can make corrections easily (such as changing the pitch of a note) with SONAR's various editing tools. But what about when you're recording audio? Sure, you can edit the data by cutting and pasting sections or processing it with effects, but you can't edit the pitch of a single note or make any other precision corrections like you can with MIDI data. With audio, you have to record your performance all over again. Using SONAR's punch recording feature, you have to re-record only the part of the performance you messed up, leaving the good parts alone.

Using punch recording, you can set up SONAR to start and stop recording automatically at precise times during a project. You therefore can record over certain parts of your performance without having to redo the entire thing. Punching is very similar to regular audio track recording, but with a few differences. Here is the step-by-step procedure:

1. Suppose that you want to correct some mistakes on an audio track you just recorded. To get started, make sure the track is still armed for recording (its R button is red).

2. Activate punch recording by selecting Transport > Record Options to open the Record Options dialog box (see Figure 6.17). In the Recording Mode section, select Auto Punch. You can also choose whether you want the punch to overwrite the existing data or be blended with the existing data by choosing the Overwrite or Sound on Sound modes, respectively. Then, in the Punch In Time field, type the measure, beat, and tick at which you want SONAR to begin recording. In the Punch Out Time field, type the measure, beat, and tick at which you want SONAR to stop recording. The section of the track that falls between the Punch In Time and the Punch Out Time should contain the part of your performance in which you made the mistakes. In addition, if you use the Sound on Sound

recording mode, you can decide whether or not you want to hear previous takes by using the Mute Previous Takes option.

Figure 6.17 You use the Record Options dialog box to set the recording mode to Auto Punch and to set the Punch In and Punch Out Times.

SET PUNCH POINTS QUICKLY

For a quick way to set the Punch In and Out Times, just click and drag in the Time Ruler of the Track view to make a data selection; then right-click the Time Ruler and choose Set Punch Points from the menu.

3. Set the Now time to the point in the project before the Punch In Time where you want playback to begin. You might want to start from the very beginning of the project or just a few measures before the Punch In Time. However long it takes you to get into the groove of the performance is how far ahead of the Punch In Time you should set the Now time.

4. Select Transport > Record (or press R) to start recording. If you set a Count-In, the metronome will count the number of beats you entered, and then SONAR will begin playback.

5. Play along with the existing material, exactly as you did before when you first recorded the track. When SONAR reaches the Punch In Time, it will automatically start recording the new part of your performance.

6. When the Now time has passed the Punch Out Time, SONAR will stop recording, and you can select Transport > Stop (or press the spacebar) to stop SONAR. SONAR will replace any existing material between the Punch In Time and the Punch Out Time with the new material you just played. As long as you didn't make any mistakes this time, your track will be fixed.

7. Listen to your performance by setting the Now time back to its original position and selecting Transport > Play (or press the spacebar) to start playback. If you don't like the performance, you can erase it by selecting Edit > Undo Recording. Then go back to step 3 and try recording again.

Step Recording

Even though you might be an accomplished musician, more than likely you have one main instrument you're good at playing. If that instrument is the keyboard, that skill puts you ahead of some other musicians because the keyboard is one of the easiest instruments to use to record a MIDI performance. You can use other MIDI instruments, such as MIDI woodwind instruments, MIDI drums, and MIDI guitars, but those instruments tend to be very expensive. And if you learn to play a wind instrument or the drums or a guitar, you probably have a real instrument of that kind, not a MIDI one. This puts you at a bit of a disadvantage when you're trying to record MIDI tracks. However, SONAR provides a feature called *step recording* that records a MIDI track one note at a time without having to worry about the timing of your performance.

In other words, you select the type of note you want to enter (such as a quarter note or a sixteenth note) and then you press one or more keys on your MIDI keyboard. SONAR records those notes into the track with the timing you selected. You can also enter the measure, beat, and tick at which you want the notes to occur. Here's how the step recording feature works:

1. Create a new project or open an existing one. If you use a template to create a new project, you might be able to skip some of the following steps, but you probably should run through them anyway, just in case.
2. Set the meter and key signature for the project. The default settings are 4/4 and the key of C Major.
3. Set the tempo parameter. The default tempo for a new project is 100 beats per minute.
4. Set the timebase for the project. The default setting is 960 PPQ (pulses per quarter note). More often than not, you won't have to change this setting.
5. Step Recording always uses the Sound on Sound (Blend) record mode, so you do not need to set this parameter.
6. Add a new MIDI track to the Track view and adjust the track's properties. Then select the track by clicking on its number. You can also just use an existing MIDI track. You do not need to arm the MIDI track for recording. Step recording adds data to the track whether the track is armed or not.
7. Select Transport > Step Record (or press Shift + F4) to open the Step Record window (see Figure 6.18). To activate step recording, click the Activate Step Record button so that it turns red (or press Shift + R). There is also a Basic/Advanced button, which allows you to switch between the Basic and Advanced modes of the Step Record window. The Basic mode simply provides fewer parameters and a smaller window. It might come in handy when you don't need access to all the parameters and would like the window to

take up less space on the screen. I'll be talking about the Advanced mode here, which covers the parameters for both modes.

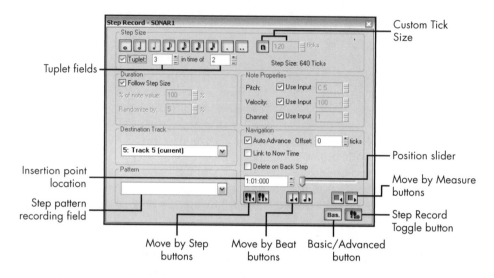

Figure 6.18 Using the Step Record window, you can record MIDI data to a track without having to worry about the timing of your performance.

8. In the Step Size section, choose the size of the note you want to record by clicking on the appropriate button. For example, if you want to record a quarter note, click the button with the picture of a quarter note on it. You can also record dotted notes by activating the one of the dotted buttons. And you can record tuplets by activating the Tuplet option and entering values for the type of tuplet you want to record. In addition, you can set a custom step size by activating the Custom Ticks Step Value button and entering the number of ticks you want to use.

❄ **NUMBER KEYPAD SHORTCUTS**

You can use the Num Pad on your computer keyboard to activate most of the features in the Step Record window. Just hover your mouse over a button or parameter to see what Num Pad key to press. Also, be sure that your Num Lock button on your Num Pad is activated.

---

9. In the Duration section, you can set the length of the note, independent of the step size. More often than not, you'll want the duration to be the same as the step size. To make things easier, you can activate the Follow Step Size option, so that both values will be the same, and you won't have to bother selecting a duration. If you don't activate the Follow Step Size option, you can have the duration be a percentage of the step size.

For example, if you have a step size of a quarter note and you'd like the duration to be half of that (or an eighth note duration), set the % Of Note Value parameter to 50%. In addition, you can randomize the duration by entering a value for the Randomize By parameter. This can be useful if you want to keep your step-recorded music from sounding too "robotic" in nature.

10. In the Destination Track section, you can choose the track to which you want to record your MIDI data. This should already be set to the track you chose earlier in step 6, but you can switch to another track at any time.

11. In the Note Properties section, you can set how the pitch, velocity, and channel of each note will be recorded. If you want any of the parameters to use the data values that are received from your MIDI keyboard, just activate the Use Input option for each parameter. If you want to set any of the parameters to a permanent value, no matter what you play on your MIDI keyboard, deactivate the Use Input option and enter a value for the parameter. All recorded notes will then use the exact values that you enter.

12. In the Navigation section, set the Insertion Point location (the point in the track to which you'd like to record notes) by entering a value into the Insertion Point field or moving the Position slider. If you want the Now Time to correspond to the Insertion Point location, activate the Link to Now Time option. I like to use this option most of the time because I usually use the Now Time to keep track of where I am in a project, whether it is recording or editing data. But the Insertion Point location gives you the flexibility to record data independently of the Now Time, so that it's really up to you about how you like to work in SONAR.

13. To record a note, press a key on your MIDI instrument. For example, if you want to record a Middle C to the track, press Middle C on your MIDI instrument. You can press more than one key at a time if you want to record a chord. For example, if you want to record a C Major chord, press the C, E, and G keys on your MIDI instrument at the same time.

14. SONAR will record the data to the track (as well as display it in the Track, Staff, Piano Roll, and Event List views) and (if the Auto Advance option in the Navigation section is activated, which it is by default) will move the Insertion Point location forward by the step size amount (which is a quarter note in this example). If the Auto Advance option isn't activated, you have to click one of the Move buttons to move the Insertion Point location manually. Also, if you want to record a rest instead of a note, you have to click one of the Move buttons. This way, SONAR will move the Insertion Point location ahead by the step size amount without recording anything. You can also use the Move buttons to move the Insertion Point location backwards, in case you want to record more data at a previous point in the track. If you want previous data to automatically be deleted when you move backwards, activate the Delete on Back Step option.

RECORD PATTERNS

If you need to record many repeating patterns, you might want to use the Pattern option in the Step Record dialog box. In the Pattern box, you can enter a pattern of beats that SONAR will follow automatically, so that you don't have to click the Move buttons at all, even for rests. For example, if you need to record a pattern with notes on the first two beats, a rest on the third beat, and another note on the fourth beat, you enter 12.4 (the period represents a rest) in the Pattern box. Now when you start to record the pattern, you simply press keys on your MIDI instrument for beats 1 and 2, SONAR advances past beat 3 because it is a rest, and then you press another key for beat 4. Then you keep repeating the same routine over and over again until you get to the point in your music where you no longer need to repeat the same rhythmic pattern. I know this process sounds a bit complicated, but if you play with it for a while, you'll get the hang of it. To stop using the Pattern option, just select the text in the Pattern box and delete it. The Pattern drop-down list will store 10 of your previously entered patterns for quick selection.

15. You can keep the Step Record dialog box open while you tend to other tasks. If you'd like to do something else before you finish using the Step Record feature, just click the Activate Step Record button (or press Shift + R) to turn off step recording. Then click the button or press the keys again when you're ready to do some more step recording.

16. When you're finished recording, click the Activate Step Record button (or press Shift + R) to turn off step recording. Alternatively, you can just close the Step Record window.

17. Listen to your performance by setting the Now time back to its original position and selecting Transport > Play (or press the spacebar) to start playback. If you don't like the performance, you can erase it by selecting Edit > Undo Recording. Then go back to step 7 and try recording again.

 TRY THE STAFF VIEW

As an alternative to the step-recording feature, you might want to try using the Staff view. With the Staff view, you still can enter your MIDI data one note at a time without worrying about performance timing. Plus, the Staff view allows you to enter and edit your data using standard music notation.

Importing

One other way you can get MIDI and audio data into a project is to import it rather than record it. SONAR imports data from audio files, MIDI files, and other project files. Why would you want to import files? Well, you might have a great drum track in a project or a MIDI file that you want to use in another project. You also might want to use sample loops for some of the material in your audio tracks. Importing material is actually very easy.

Importing from SONAR Project Files

Importing data from a project or a MIDI file into another project is just a matter of copying and pasting, as shown in the following steps. To get started, just follow these steps:

1. Open the project file from which you want to copy data.
2. In the Track view, select the clips you want to copy. You also can select an entire track or a number of whole tracks to copy.
3. Select Edit > Copy to open the Copy dialog box (see Figure 6.19). Make sure the Events in Tracks option is activated and then click OK.

Figure 6.19 Using the Copy dialog box, you can copy data within a project or from one project into another.

4. Open the project into which you want to paste the data.
5. In the Track view, select the track where you want to start pasting the data. If you copied more than one track, the first copied track will be pasted to the selected track, and the other copied tracks will be pasted to consecutive tracks after the selected one.
6. Set the Now time to the point in the track at which you want the data to be pasted.
7. Select Edit > Paste to open the Paste dialog box (see Figure 6.20). You don't have to change any of the parameters here. Click OK.

Figure 6.20 The Paste dialog box takes any previously copied data and places it where you specify.

SONAR will copy the data you selected from the first project and place a copy of it into the second project in the tracks and at the Now time you specify. In addition to reusing your own material, you can share material with a friend this way.

Importing MIDI Files and Project5 Patterns

SONAR also imports data directly from a MIDI file or Project5 pattern. For those of you who own Cakewalk's other sequencing software called *Project5*, you can now use your Project5 patterns (which are basically MIDI files in a special format) within SONAR. To import a MIDI file or Project5 pattern into your existing SONAR project, do the following:

1. Select the MIDI track into which you want to import the MIDI file or Project5 pattern.
2. Set the Now time to the point in the track that the file should be placed.
3. Choose File > Import > MIDI to open the Import MIDI dialog box.
4. Select the type of file you want to import using the Files of Type parameter.
5. Choose a MIDI file or Project5 pattern you want to import.
6. If you want to listen to the file before you import it, click the Play button.
7. Click Open.

SONAR will import the file and insert it into the track you selected at the Now time you specified.

Importing Audio Files

You learned about audio files in Chapter 3. SONAR imports WAV, Apple AIFF, MPEG, Windows Media, and Next/Sun audio files. This is important because at some time you might want to record some audio using another program, and you might want to use that data in one of your SONAR projects. Doing so is really simple; just follow these steps:

1. Select the track into which you want to import the audio file.
2. Set the Now time to the point in the track that the file should be placed.
3. Select File > Import > Audio to open the Import Audio dialog box.
4. Choose the audio files you want to import.

 IMPORT MULTIPLE FILES

You can import more than one audio file at a time by holding down the Ctrl key while selecting your files.

5. If you want to listen to the file before you import it, click the Play button. This function will not work if you select multiple files.
6. If the file is a stereo audio file, you can have either the left and right channels merged into one track, or you can split between two different tracks (starting with the one you selected). To have the file split, activate the Import as Mono Tracks option.
7. If you want the audio file to be copied to the same location as all the other audio files in your project, keep the Copy Audio to Project Folder option activated. Most of the time, you will want to have this option activated because it keeps things more organized. Also, if you have your audio located on a second hard drive, this will increase SONAR's

performance because it doesn't have to look on a different drive when playing the imported audio in your project.

8. If you want to convert the bit depth of the audio file during import, use the Bit Depth parameter to choose a value. If you set the parameter to Original, the audio file will be imported using its original bit depth.

9. Click Open.

SONAR will import the files and insert them into the tracks you selected at the Now time you specify.

SAMPLE RATE CONVERSION

If the sampling rate of the audio file you are importing is different from your project's sampling rate, SONAR will automatically convert the sampling rate of the audio file to match the sampling rate of the project.

Synchronization

One other aspect related to recording that you should know about is *synchronization*. This subject is fairly complicated and a bit beyond the scope of this book, but you might need to utilize synchronization in two somewhat popular situations. I'll cover a few of the basics and explain how to use synchronization in those two particular situations.

Synchronization Basics

All music is based on time. Without time, there is no music. To record and play music data, SONAR needs a timing reference. It uses this reference to determine the exact measure, beat, and tick at which an event should be stored during recording or at which it should be played. When you work with SONAR alone, it uses one of two different clock sources as its reference—either the clock built into your computer (internal) or the clock built into your sound card (audio). By default, SONAR uses the internal clock as its timing reference. Because the internal clock cannot be used if you have audio data in your project, SONAR automatically changes the clock to audio when a track's source is set to an audio input or when an audio file is inserted into the project. So the built-in clock on your sound card provides the timing for all the data you record into a project, and SONAR keeps all the tracks synchronized during playback. This is internal synchronization.

Sometimes, though, you might need to synchronize SONAR externally with another piece of equipment. For example, if you have a drum machine (a special type of MIDI instrument that plays only drum sounds) containing some special songs that you programmed into it, you might want to have the data in your current SONAR project play along with the data contained in the drum machine. You would have to synchronize SONAR to the drum machine. In this situation, the drum machine would be known as the *master device*, and SONAR would be the *slave device*. The master would send messages to the slave, telling it when to start and stop playback and what tempo to use so that they could stay in sync with one another. To accomplish this, you need to use what is called *MIDI Sync.*

MIDI Sync

MIDI Sync is a special set of MIDI messages that synchronizes MIDI devices to one another. These messages include Start (which tells a slave device to start playback at the beginning of the song), Stop (which tells a slave device to stop playback), Continue (which tells a slave device to continue playback from the current location in the song—the Now time in SONAR), Song Position Pointer or SPP (which tells a slave device to jump to a specific time position in the song—the Now time in SONAR), and Clock (a steady pulse of ticks sent to the slave device, telling it the speed of the current tempo of the song).

To synchronize SONAR with an external MIDI device using MIDI Sync, follow these steps:

1. Configure your drum machine (or other MIDI device you want to use as the master) to transmit MIDI Sync messages. You'll have to refer to the user guide for the device for information on how to do so.

2. In SONAR, open the project you want to synchronize. Select Options > Project to open the Project Options dialog box and then click the Clock tab (see Figure 6.21).

Figure 6.21 Using the Project Options dialog box, you can configure SONAR for synchronization.

3. In the Source section, click the MIDI Sync option and then click OK.

4. Follow the steps outlined earlier for recording or playing MIDI tracks. However, when you activate recording or playback, SONAR won't respond right away. Instead, it will display a message that says "Waiting for MIDI Sync."

5. After you see this message, start playback on your master device. It will send a Start message to SONAR, and both the device and SONAR will play through the song in sync with one another. In the case of the drum machine, you will hear it play its sounds in time with the music being played by SONAR.

6. To stop playback, don't use the commands in SONAR; instead, stop playback from the master device. It will send SONAR a Stop message, and SONAR will stop at the same time automatically.

While working with SONAR via MIDI Sync, just remember to start, stop, and navigate through the project using the master device instead of SONAR. Otherwise, all the other steps for recording and playback are the same.

SMPTE/MIDI Time Code

You might need to use synchronization when you're composing music to video. Here, though, the synchronization method is different, because a VCR is not a MIDI device, so MIDI Sync won't work. Instead, you have to use SMPTE/MIDI Time Code. You learned a little about SMPTE in Chapter 5, so you know it is a timing reference that counts hours, minutes, seconds, and frames (as in video frames). But you really didn't learn how it works.

SYNC TO A TAPE DECK

In addition to video, SMPTE/MIDI Time Code is used often to synchronize a sequencer to an external multitrack tape recorder or DAT (*Digital Audio Tape*) deck. The procedure for doing so is the same.

SMPTE is a complex audio signal that is recorded onto a tape track (or, in the case of video, onto one of the stereo audio tracks) using a time code generator. This signal represents the absolute amount of time over the length of the tape in hours, minutes, seconds, and frames. A sequencer (such as SONAR) reading the code can be synchronized to any exact moment along the length of the entire tape recording. In this case, the VCR would be the master, and SONAR would be the slave. When you play the tape in the VCR, SONAR will play the current project in sync to the exact hour, minute, second, and frame.

Reading the time code from tape requires an SMPTE converter, which translates the SMPTE code into MTC (*MIDI Time Code*). The MIDI Time Code is read by the MIDI interface and sent to the sequencer (SONAR). MIDI Time Code is the equivalent of SMPTE, except it exists as special MIDI messages rather than an audio signal. As SONAR receives MTC, it calculates the exact measure, beat, and tick that correspond to the exact time reading. This means you can start playback anywhere along the tape, and SONAR will begin playing or recording MIDI or audio data at precisely the right point in the current project in perfect sync.

As an example, suppose that you need to compose some music to video. This video could be your own or a video from a client. To synchronize SONAR to the video, you need to follow these steps:

1. If the video is your own, you need to add SMPTE Time Code to it using an SMPTE generator. This process is called *striping*. I won't go into the details of doing that here. You'll need to purchase a SMPTE generator and read the instructions in the included manual on how to stripe SMPTE to tape. If the video is from a client, he will probably stripe the tape before sending it to you.

> ❋ **SMPTE CONVERTER**
>
> You also need an SMPTE converter to read the time code from the tape. If you have a professional MIDI interface attached to your computer, it might provide SMPTE generating and converting capabilities. Check the user manual to make sure. You might be able to save yourself some money.

2. In SONAR, open the project you want to synchronize. Then select Options > Project to open the Project Options dialog box and click the Clock tab.
3. In the SMPTE/MTC Format section, you need to select a frame rate for the time code. If you're composing music to your own video, just use the default selection, 30 FPS ndf (Frames Per Second – Non-Drop Frame). If you're composing music for a client, he should let you know the frame rate you need to use.

> ❋ **FRAME RATES**
>
> Different types of video material use different tape speeds for recording. The frame rate corresponds to the number of frames per second used to record the video to tape. For film, 24 frames per second is used. For video, several different rates are used, depending on whether the video is recorded in color or black-and-white, and so on. For more information about frame rates, you should consult the user guide for your SMPTE generating/reading device.

4. You might also need to enter a SMPTE/MTC Offset in hours, minutes, seconds, and frames. Whether you need to enter an offset depends on whether the video material starts at the very beginning of the time code stripe, which is a value of 00:00:00:00.

> ❋ **SMPTE OFFSET**
>
> When you stripe a tape with SMPTE, the time code always starts with a value of 00 hours, 00 minutes, 00 seconds, and 00 frames. However, the actual video material on the tape may start a bit later, say at 00 hours, 01 minutes, 20 seconds, 00 frames. If that's the case (your client should let you know this fact), you need to enter an offset of 00:01:20:00 into SONAR, so SONAR will begin playing the project at that time rather than at the initial time code value.

5. After you finish entering the settings, click OK.

6. Now you can follow the steps outlined earlier for recording or playing MIDI or audio tracks. However, when you activate recording or playback, SONAR won't respond right away. Instead, it will display a message saying "Waiting for 30 Frame" (or whatever frame rate you selected).

7. After you see this message, start playback on your master device. (In this case, start the tape playing in the VCR.) It will then send SMPTE code to SONAR, and both the device and SONAR will play through the song in sync. In the case of the VCR, you will see it play the video in time with the music that is being played by SONAR.

8. To stop playback, don't use the commands in SONAR; instead, stop playback from the master device.

A little confused? Well, as I said, synchronization is a complicated subject. You'll find a little more information in the SONAR Help files, but it isn't any easier to understand than the information I've provided here. Your best bet is to experiment as much as possible with synchronization and get a good beginner book on audio recording. Knowing how to utilize synchronization is worthwhile, in case a situation that requires it arises.

7 Editing Basics

After you've finished recording all your tracks, it's time to do some editing. Actually, if you're like me, you might end up doing some editing during the recording process. This is especially true for MIDI tracks because it's so easy to fix the pitch or timing of a note quickly if you happen to make a mistake or two. You'll do most of your editing after the fact, though, and SONAR provides a number of different tools to get the job done. This chapter will do the following:

※ Show you how to deal with tracks and clips in the Track view.

※ Describe editing MIDI note and controller messages in the Piano Roll view.

※ Explain creating and editing drum tracks in the Piano Roll view.

※ Teach you how to edit audio data in the Track view.

※ Describe editing individual events in the Event List view.

※ Show you how to change the tempo via the Tempo view.

> ※ **BACK UP YOUR PROJECT**
>
> Before you do any kind of editing to your recently recorded material, I suggest you make a backup of your project file. That way, if you totally mess things up during the editing process, you'll still have your raw recorded tracks. Take a look at Appendix A, "Backing Up Your Project Files," for more information.

Arranging with the Track View

Since the first part of the editing process deals with arranging the material in your project, it's logical to start with arranging. Basically, this step involves rearranging the tracks and clips in your project so they provide a better representation of the song you're trying to create. For example, after listening to the project a few times, you might find that the guitar part in the second verse sounds better in the first verse, or you might want the vocal to come in a little earlier during the chorus. You can accomplish these feats by manipulating your tracks and clips.

Dealing with Tracks

You already learned how to work with the Track view in terms of setting up track properties, navigating within SONAR, and recording new tracks. Manipulating includes selecting, sorting, inserting, and otherwise changing your original data.

Scrolling

The Track view consists of two areas: The Track pane (on the left) shows the track properties and the Clips pane (on the right) shows the track data. The Clips pane contains scroll bars (see Figure 7.1). These scroll bars work the same as scroll bars in any standard Windows application. You either click the arrows to move the display, or you click and drag the scroll bars to move the display.

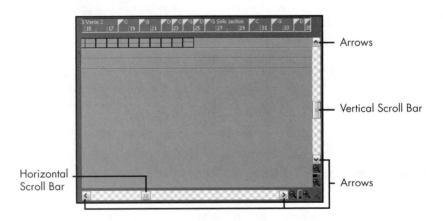

Figure 7.1 Using the scroll bars, you can access additional information that doesn't fit on the screen.

The horizontal scroll bar displays all the data in all the tracks. As you scroll to the right, the measure numbers on the Time Ruler increase. Scrolling doesn't change the Now time, though. The vertical scroll bar affects both the Track and Clips pane areas. As you move the bar up or down, the different tracks in the project are displayed, starting from 1 (at the top of the list).

In addition to the Track view, scroll bars are available in all the other views. In the Piano Roll view, you can scroll horizontally to display the data in a track similar to the clips in the Track view. You also can scroll vertically to display different MIDI note ranges. The Event List view is the oddball because it only lets you scroll vertically to display all the events in a track as one long list.

Zooming

The Track view (as well as other views, except the Event List view) also provides zooming functions. Using these functions, you can magnify the data in a track, in case you want to do some really precise editing. If you take a look at the bottom-right corner of the Track view (see Figure 7.2), you'll notice two sets of buttons (one along the bottom and one along the side) that have little pictures of magnifying glasses on them.

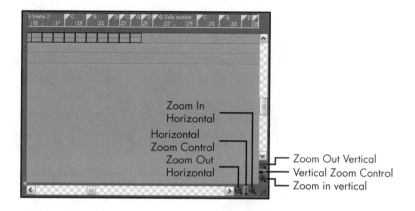

Figure 7.2 The zoom features reside in the bottom-right corner of the view.

Using the buttons along the bottom, you can magnify the track data horizontally. When you click the Zoom In button (the button with the magnifying glass with a + sign on it), the clips will grow larger horizontally and give you a more detailed look at the data they contain. Clicking the Zoom Out button does the opposite. The same buttons along the side of the Track view perform the same functions, except they affect the display vertically. You'll also notice that as you zoom in vertically, the track parameters will be shown beneath each track in the Track pane. In addition, you'll notice a little control button between each set of zoom buttons. These control buttons show you the current level of magnification.

❅ **ZOOM METER**

Click and hold the mouse on any Zoom control button, and a Zoom meter will pop up. You can use the meter to set the Zoom level by dragging your mouse (see Figure 7.3).

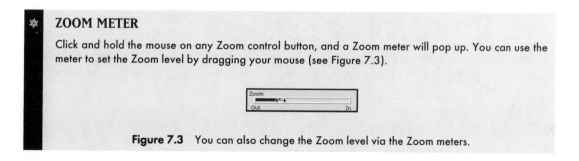

Figure 7.3 You can also change the Zoom level via the Zoom meters.

The Zoom Tool

In addition to the aforementioned zoom features, SONAR provides the Zoom tool. You can use this tool to select a range of data and zoom in on that selection. To use it, simply follow these steps:

1. Either press and hold the Z key or click the Zoom tool button (see Figure 7.4).

Figure 7.4 Activate the Zoom tool by clicking the Zoom tool button.

2. Move your mouse pointer within the Clips pane, and it will turn into a magnifying glass.
3. Click and drag anywhere within the area to select some data (see Figure 7.5).

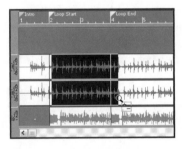

Figure 7.5 You simply click and drag to make a selection with the Zoom tool.

4. Release the mouse button. SONAR will zoom in on the selection (both horizontally and vertically, depending on how you drag the mouse), and your mouse pointer will return to normal.

❋ **QUICKLY UN-ZOOM**

To quickly undo the view change you made by using the Zoom tool, press the U key. You can also redo the same zoom action by pressing Shift + U.

❋❋❋

You have to hold down the Z key or click the Zoom tool button every time you want to use it.

The Fast Zoom Feature

If you have a mouse wheel, SONAR also provides the Fast Zoom feature. Normally, if you use the mouse wheel, it scrolls the current view vertically up or down. But using certain keyboard shortcuts, you can use the mouse wheel for quick and easy zooming, as follows:

- ❅ **1x Zoom In or Out.** To zoom in or out normally using the mouse wheel, hold down the Alt key and move the mouse wheel forward (zoom in) or backward (zoom out).
- ❅ **2x Zoom In or Out.** To zoom in or out with increased magnification, hold down the Alt+Shift keys.
- ❅ **Track Scale Zoom.** To adjust the track scale (zoom the data inside of clips), hover your mouse over the track you want to adjust and hold down the Alt+Ctrl keys. This feature only works in the Track view.

You can also adjust the behavior of the Fast Zoom feature by doing the following:

1. Click the down arrow next to the Zoom tool in the Track view toolbar and choose Fast Zoom Options to open the Fast Zoom dialog box.
2. In the Zoom Factor section, you can set the magnification for horizontal and vertical zooming. A setting of 1 will magnify the data by a factor of 1 every time you move the mouse wheel. A setting of 2 will magnify by a factor of 2 and so on.
3. In the Zoom In section, you can specify where the zoom will be centered. So as you zoom in, the center of the zoomed display will be located according to these settings. The most intuitive setting is At Cursor, which will center the zoom at the position of your mouse cursor. You can, however, change this so that horizontally, the zoom will be centered at the current Now Time and vertically at the currently active track.
4. The Zoom Out section options work the same as the Zoom In section options, except the Zoom Out options specify where the zoom will be centered when zooming out.
5. Set the Simultaneous Horizontal and Vertical Zoom option. Activating this option will zoom the data both horizontally and vertically at the same time. You'll probably want to keep this option activated most of the time. If you turn it off, the Alt and Alt+Shift shortcuts will only zoom vertically and the Alt+Ctrl will zoom horizontally. The Track Scale Zoom feature is not available when this option is turned off.

The Project Navigator

In addition to scrolling and zooming using the various features previously described, SONAR provides the Project Navigator. This is the pane located at the top of the Track view (see Figure 7.6). If you don't see this pane that means the Project Navigator is not activated. To toggle the Project Navigator on or off, press D.

❅ **PROJECT NAVIGATOR VIEW**

You can also display the Project Navigator as a separate view. Choose Views > Navigator to open the Project Navigator view.

Figure 7.6   The Project Navigator is located at the top of the Track view.

The Project Navigator provides a bird's-eye view of all the data in a project. You'll notice many rectangular shapes shown in the Navigator. These shapes represent the tracks and clips in the current project. The green rectangle represents the data that is currently visible in the Track view.

Scrolling

To scroll through a project (either horizontally or vertically), simply position your mouse anywhere inside the green rectangle and click/drag your mouse horizontally or vertically. If you drag horizontally past the left or right sides of the Track view, the Navigator will continue to scroll until you reach the beginning or end of the project. If you drag vertically past the top of the Track view or the bottom of the Navigator, scrolling will continue until you are displaying track 1 or the last track in the project.

 LEFT-CLICK SCROLLING

To move quickly through a project, just left-click anywhere within the Project Navigator pane. You can also deactivate the left-click zoom option by right-clicking in the Project Navigator pane and choosing Left Click Positions Rectangle.

Zooming

In addition to clicking inside the green rectangle, you can click any of its nodes (small squares around its perimeter) to change the current zoom level. Click and drag the top and bottom nodes to zoom in or out vertically. Click and drag the left or right nodes to zoom in or out horizontally. Click and drag any of the corner nodes to zoom vertically and horizontally at the same time.

❋ **PROJECT NAVIGATOR OPTIONS**

To quickly set one of six horizontal zoom levels, right-click anywhere within the Project Navigator pane and choose Horz Zoom Level 1 through 5. The sixth option (Horz Zoom To Project) will fit all the data in the current project into the current size of the pane.

In addition, you can set the vertical size of the data shown in the pane by choosing one of three Track Height options: Short, Medium, or Tall. Track Height just changes the displayed size of the data, not the zoom level.

Selecting

To manipulate your tracks for editing, you have to select them first. To select a single track, click the track number of the track you want to select. Sometimes you might want to have multiple tracks selected at one time. You also might need a quick way to select all the tracks in your project. Or after going through the trouble of selecting a number of tracks, you might want to deselect one or two, while keeping the others selected. You accomplish these tasks as follows:

- ❋ To select more than one track, hold down the Ctrl key as you click the track numbers.
- ❋ To select all tracks in a project, select Edit > Select > All or press Ctrl+A.
- ❋ To deselect all tracks in a project, select Edit > Select > None or press Ctrl+Shift+A.
- ❋ To deselect a track while keeping others selected, hold down the Ctrl key as you click the track number.

By the way, all these procedures also work in the other views; the only difference is the items being selected. Just remember that to select a single item, you simply click it. To select more than one item, you hold down the Ctrl key as you click. To select all or none of the items, you choose Edit > Select. Some special selection features are also available, but I'll talk about them later in this chapter and in Chapter 8, "Exploring the Editing Tools."

Sorting Tracks

You can change the order in which the tracks appear in a couple of different ways. Being able to sort the tracks can be useful if you want to keep related tracks together in the track list. For instance, you might want to keep all the percussion tracks or all the vocal tracks together. It's easier to work on your song when the tracks are grouped together in this way.

Clicking and Dragging

The easiest way to move a track within a list is simply to drag it to a new location. Just move your mouse pointer over the little icon next to the name of the track you want to move (see Figure 7.7); then click and drag it up or down anywhere in the list. When you release your mouse button, the track will move to the new location and take on a new track number.

Using the Track Sort Function

You also can use the Track Sort function to sort tracks in the list, based on the track properties. You use this function as follows:

Figure 7.7 Click and drag a track icon to move the track within the track list.

1. Choose Tracks > Sort to open the Sort Tracks dialog box (see Figure 7.8).

Figure 7.8 Using the Sort Tracks dialog box, you can rearrange the tracks in the Track view.

2. In the Sort By section, select the track property by which you want to sort the tracks.
3. In the Order section, select whether you want the tracks to be sorted in ascending or descending order.
4. Click OK.

SONAR will sort the tracks, according to the settings you specified. Remember, the track numbers for the tracks will also be changed because the tracks have moved to new locations in the list. However, each track maintains its parameter settings and data.

Track Folders

In addition to sorting tracks, you can organize them into groups called *Track Folders*. A Track Folder acts like a container that can hold any number of other tracks—MIDI, audio, etc. (see Figure 7.9). Track Folders organize your tracks into groups for easier access, such as all vocals in one Track Folder and all percussion in another Track Folder, and so on.

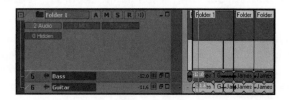

Figure 7.9 Use Track Folders to organize your various MIDI and audio tracks into groups.

Creating Track Folders

To create a Track Folder, use one of the following methods:

❋ Right-click in the Tracks pane and choose Insert Track Folder.

❋ Choose Insert > Track Folder from SONAR's main menu.

❋ Right-click an existing track and choose Move To Folder > New Track Folder.

Adding and Removing Tracks

To add or remove tracks to/from a Folder Track, use one of the following methods:

❋ To add a track to a Track Folder, drag and drop the track onto the Track Folder. You can also right-click the track and choose Move to Folder > [Name of the existing Track Folder].

❋ To remove a track from a Track Folder, drag and drop the track outside the Track Folder. You can also right-click the track and choose Remove from Folder.

Editing Track Folders

In addition to their organizational power, Track Folders provide composite editing power, which means that you can apply global editing to all the tracks in a Track Folder simply by applying the editing to the Track Folder itself. Just remember that when I talk about editing single tracks, those editing features can also be used on Track Folders. In the meantime, here are some of the things you can do to control Track Folders, along with all the tracks within them:

❋ To select a Track Folder and all the tracks it contains, click the Track Folder number area.

❋ To show or hide all the tracks in a Track Folder, click the Track Folder's plus/minus icon.

❋ To archive all the tracks in a Track Folder, click the Track Folder's A button.

❋ To mute all the tracks in a Track Folder, click the Track Folder's M button.

❋ To solo all the tracks in a Track Folder, click the Track Folder's S button.

❋ To enable recording for all the tracks in a Track Folder, click the Track Folder's R button.

❋ To enable Input Monitoring for all the tracks in a Track Folder, click the Track Folder's Input Echo button.

❋ **FOLDER TRACK DESCRIPTIONS**

You can add text notes to a Track Folder to label it with information about what is in the folder, what edits you've done to the folder, and so on. To do this, double-click the Track Folder note area and type in your text (see Figure 7.10).

Figure 7.10   Add text notes to your Track Folders by using the note area.

❄ **USING QUICK GROUPS**

Using the Quick Groups feature, you can group all track parameters in a Track Folder and then make parameter changes to all tracks in the folder simultaneously. For example, all track volume parameters can be grouped. Then by changing one track volume, they all change. Check out the Quick Groups section of Chapter 12, "Mixing it Down" for more information.

Track Icons

In addition to Track Folders, SONAR provides the Track Icons feature to help with the organization of tracks. Track Icons identify the contents of a track. Basically, this feature assigns a picture to each track in a project. This picture can be of anything you like, but SONAR provides a number of helpful Track Icons, such as pictures of musical instruments and other musical symbols. For example, you could assign a guitar picture to all your guitar tracks so that with a quick glance at the screen, you would know what type of data is contained in those tracks.

Showing/Hiding Track Icons

You have the option to show or hide Track Icons with a quick click of the mouse. Icons are displayed in the Track view, Console view, and the Track Inspector. Icons are also shown in the Synth Rack view, which I'll talk about in Chapter 10, "Software Synthesis." You can control whether icons are shown in each individual area or in all the areas at once.

To show/hide Track Icons in all the areas, choose Options > Icons > Show Icons. To show/ hide Track Icons in each area, choose Options > Icons > [*name of the area*] > Show Icons.

Track Icon Settings

You can also control the size of Track Icons in each area by choosing Options > Icons > [*name of the area*] > Large Icons or Small Icons.

The Track view provides some additional settings that determine whether or not standard or custom icons are shown and where they are shown. Choose Options > Icons > Track View > and one of the following: Show In Header, Show Custom In Header, or Show In Strip.

Loading Track Icons

If you want to change a Track Icon for a specific track, right-click the Track Icon and choose Load Track Icon from the menu to display the Open dialog box (see Figure 7.11).

Figure 7.11 Choose a new Track Icon by using the Open dialog box.

Select a Track Icon and click Open to assign that icon to the track. If you decide you don't like that icon, you can load another one or go back to using the default icon by right-clicking the icon and choosing Reset Track Icon from the menu.

Creating Track Icons

If you have a bit of a graphic artist in you, SONAR allows you to create your own Track Icons. It doesn't provide any tools for this purpose, so you'll need to get your hands on some graphics software. Simply create a graphic image that is 128 by 128 pixels square in size and save it as a BMP file (the standards Windows graphic file format). Put the file in your C:\Program Files\Cakewalk\SONAR 6 Producer Edition\Track Icons folder, and it will be available for you to use within SONAR.

Inserting Tracks

If you ever need to insert a new track between two existing tracks in the list, you can do so by following these steps:

1. Right-click the track number of the track above which you want to insert a new track.
2. From the menu, select Insert Audio Track or Insert MIDI Track, depending on the type of track you need.

SONAR will move the current track down one location in the list and insert a new track at the location on which you clicked. For example, if you right-click track 2 and select Insert MIDI Track, SONAR will move track 2 (and all the tracks below it) down by one and insert a new MIDI track at number 2 in the list.

Inserting Multiple Tracks

To save time, you can also insert more than one track simultaneously by doing the following:

1. Choose Insert > Multiple Tracks to open the Insert Tracks dialog box (see Figure 7.12).

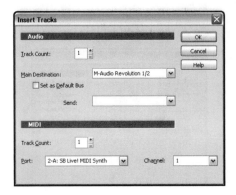

Figure 7.12   Use the Insert Tracks dialog box to insert multiple tracks simultaneously.

2. In the Audio section, set the Track Count parameter to the number of audio tracks you would like to insert. Set the parameter to zero if you don't want to insert any audio tracks.

3. Set the Main Destination parameter. This parameter determines the Output setting for the new tracks.

4. If you want all new tracks that you insert in your project to use the same Output setting (as designated by the Main Destination parameter), activate the Set as Default Bus option.

5. To add a send to the new tracks, select an output for that send using the Send list.

6. In the MIDI section, set the Track Count parameter to the number of MIDI tracks you would like to insert. Set the parameter to zero if you don't want to insert any MIDI tracks.

7. Set the Port and Channel parameters. These parameters determine the Port and Channel parameter settings for the new MIDI tracks.

8. Click OK.

SONAR inserts the new tracks as specified by your settings in the Insert Tracks dialog box. These new tracks are always added to the end of the track list, so if you want them positioned differently in the list, you will need to move them manually.

Track Templates

In addition to the previous track inserting methods, SONAR provides Track Templates. The Track Templates feature allows you to insert a group of tracks along with their corresponding settings. This feature makes it easy for you to create and reuse your favorite track configurations.

To create your own Track Template, simply insert some tracks into your project. Then set their parameters—this includes all track parameters, as well as inserted effects and their settings, along with the Mute, Solo, and Record button settings. Select the tracks and choose File > Export > Track Template to open the Export Track Template dialog box. Type in a name for the template and click Save.

To use an existing Track Template, simply choose Insert > Insert From Track Template > [name of the Track Template]. You can also right-click in the Tracks pane of the Track view and choose Insert From Track Template > [name of the Track Template] from the menu. SONAR ships with a number of predefined Track Templates to give you an idea of how to use this feature.

> ❋ **TRACK TEMPLATE FILTER**
>
> When inserting a Track Template, you may not want to include all of the track parameter settings defined in the template. To filter out the settings you don't want to use, choose Insert > Insert From Track Template > Import Filter to open the Track Template Import Options dialog box (see Figure 7.13). In this dialog box, put check marks next to the parameter types that you would like to have included when you insert a Track Template. Click OK. These settings will remain in effect for every inserted Track Template until you change the settings again.

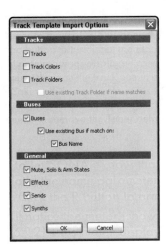

Figure 7.13   Filter out Track Template parameters with the Track Template Import Options dialog box.

Cloning Tracks

If you ever need to make an exact copy of any tracks in your project (including events, properties, effects, and sends), you can do the following:

1. Select the track(s) you want to copy.
2. Choose Tracks > Clone to open the Clone Track(s) dialog box (see Figure 7.14).

Figure 7.14 You can copy entire tracks in your project by using the Clone Track(s) dialog box.

> ❊ **CLONE A TRACK**
>
> For a quicker method, just right-click the track(s) you want to copy and choose Clone Track(s) to open the Clone Track(s) dialog box.

3. You can choose to copy the events within the track(s), the track properties, the effects assigned to the track(s), the bus sends, or all of the above. Simply activate the appropriate options. There is also an option for preserving linked clips.

4. You can also choose how many copies of the track(s) you want to make by entering a number in the Repetitions field.

5. To designate the number of the first copied track, enter a number in the Starting Track field. Your first copied track will use this number, and all other copies will be consecutively numbered after this one.

6. Click OK.

SONAR will make a copy (or copies) of the tracks you selected, according to the parameter settings you specified. If you want to move the tracks to a new location in the list, you can do so by using the methods explained earlier in the Sorting Tracks section of this chapter.

Erasing Tracks

Getting rid of tracks you no longer need is very easy. Simply select the track and choose Tracks > Delete. Alternatively, you can right-click the track and choose Delete Track from the menu. But SONAR also provides another erasing function that's a little more flexible. Instead of erasing the track entirely, it allows you to delete all the data in the track while keeping the track properties intact. To do so, just select the track and then choose Tracks > Wipe. Nothing could be easier.

Hiding Tracks

If you press the M key while you are working in the Track view, you can access the Track Manager. Using the Track Manager, you can hide tracks in the Track view. To hide or unhide tracks, follow these steps:

1. Press the M key to open the Track Manager (see Figure 7.15). You will see a list of all the tracks in the Track view.

Figure 7.15 Use the Track Manager to hide tracks in the Track view.

2. To hide an individual track, click to remove the check mark next to that track in the list and then click OK.

3. To hide a group of tracks (such as all the audio tracks, MIDI tracks, muted tracks, or archived tracks), click the appropriate button—Audio, MIDI, Muted, Archived—to select the appropriate group. Then press the spacebar to remove the check marks. Finally, click OK.

You can make tracks reappear by doing the opposite of the preceding procedures. These changes to the Track view are in appearance only; they don't affect what you hear during playback. For example, if you hide an audio track that outputs data during playback, you'll hear that data, even if you hide the track. Hiding tracks can come in handy when you want to work only on a certain group of tracks, and you don't want to be distracted or overwhelmed by the number of controls being displayed.

> ❋ **HIDE TRACK**
>
> You can hide a single track by right-clicking its track number and choosing Hide Track. To make the track visible again, you need to use the Track Manager.

The View Options Menu

In addition to all of the features I've already described, SONAR provides some predefined options for zooming and the appearance of tracks. These options are available from the Zoom tool menu, which you can access by clicking the small down arrow button located to the right of the Zoom tool button in the Track view toolbar (see Figure 7.16).

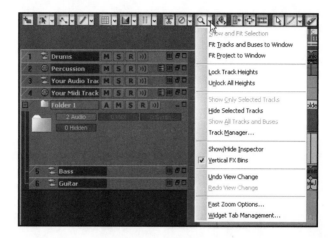

Figure 7.16   Use the Zoom tools menu for additional zooming and track appearance options.

Each of the selections in the Zoom tools menu has a different function. They work as follows:

* **Show and Fit Selection.** Makes the data in the selected tracks fit within the current dimensions of the Track view and shows only the selected tracks. All other tracks will be hidden. This also works if you simply select some data within a track (or tracks).

* **Fit Tracks and Buses to Window.** Sets the vertical zoom to make all the tracks fill the current dimensions of the Track view vertically.

* **Fit Project to Window.** Sets both the vertical and horizontal zoom functions to make all the tracks fill the current dimensions of the Track view both vertically and horizontally.

* **Lock Track Heights.** Permanently sets the vertical zoom of the selected tracks. This means that if you use any of the zoom functions, they will not alter any locked tracks. The tracks will stay at their current vertical zoom level.

* **Unlock All Heights.** Unlocks any locked tracks so they will respond to the zoom functions again.

* **Show Only Selected Tracks.** Keeps all currently selected tracks visible and hides any unselected tracks.

* **Hide Selected Tracks.** The opposite of the Show Only Selected Tracks option, choosing this option hides all currently selected tracks and keeps all unselected tracks visible.

* **Show All Tracks and Buses.** Makes all tracks in the project visible.

* **Track Manager.** Gives you access to the Track Manager dialog box.
* **Show/Hide Inspector.** Toggles the visibility of the Track Inspector.
* **Vertical FX Bins.** Toggles whether or not the FX parameter for each track is displayed vertically or horizontally.
* **Undo View Change.** Undoes the last view change you made to the Track view.
* **Redo View Change.** Redoes the last view change you undid using the Undo View Change option.

Dealing with Clips

Unless you insert, copy, or erase tracks in your project, you're not actually doing any kind of data manipulation. If you move a track in the track list or sort the tracks, that doesn't change the data within them. To make changes to the data in your project, you have to manipulate the clips within the tracks.

Clip Properties

For organizational purposes, SONAR allows you to change the way clips are displayed. To change the properties, you can right-click a clip and select Clip Properties to open the Clip Properties dialog box (see Figure 7.17). Here, you can assign a name to the clip (which doesn't have to be the same name as the track in which the clip resides) and also set the color of the clip.

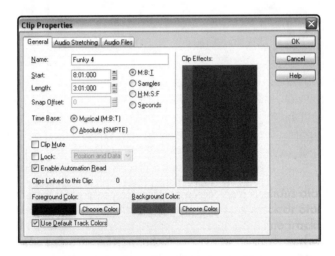

Figure 7.17 To change the name or color of a clip, you use the Clip Properties dialog box.

The name and the color of a clip don't affect the data within your project, but you also can change the start time of the clip in this dialog box. The start time is the position within the project at which the clip begins. If you enter a new start time for the clip, the clip is moved to the new time within the track, and during playback SONAR will play the clip at the new time. This move *does* change the data in your project. In addition, you can mute the clip so that it will not produce any sound during playback by activating the Clip Mute option. You may have noticed the FX bin, which adds effects to an individual clip.

The Clip Properties dialog box also allows you to lock clip positions and the data within a clip. To lock a clip, activate the Lock option and choose the clip attributes you would like to lock from the Lock menu. If you choose Position and Data, then both the position of the clip in the project and data within the clip cannot be changed until you unlock it. The Lock option can help you keep from making accidental changes to your data.

View Options

You can change whether the names you assign to clips will be displayed and whether clips will be displayed with a graphical representation of the data they contain. In other words, if a clip contains audio data, it shows a drawing of what the sound wave for the audio data might look like. For MIDI data, the clip shows a mini piano roll display.

To change these options, just right-click anywhere in the Clips pane and select View Options to display the Clip View Options dialog box (see Figure 7.18). Activate the appropriate options (Display Clip Names and Display Clip Contents) and click OK.

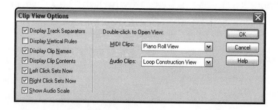

Figure 7.18   Using the Clip View Options dialog box, you can show or hide clip names and contents.

Using the Clip View Options dialog box, you can specify whether left-clicking or right-clicking will change the Now time (using the Left Click Sets Now or Right Click Sets Now options), whether to display vertical rule lines for the Time Ruler (using the Display Vertical Rules option), whether to display track separators (using the Display Track Separators option), and which views open automatically when you double-click a MIDI or audio clip. Another option chooses whether or not to display the Audio Scale.

Selecting Clips

You select clips the same way you select tracks. To select a single clip, click it. To select more than one clip, hold down the Ctrl key while you click the clips you want to select.

There is one additional selection method that doesn't apply to tracks—selecting only a portion of a clip. This procedure is known as *working with partial clips*. This capability is useful when you want to split a clip into smaller clips or combine one clip with another clip to make a larger clip (see "Splitting and Combining Clips").

To select only part of a clip, hold down the Alt key and drag your mouse pointer across the clip to select a part of it. You also can drag across several clips (or even over several tracks) to make a partial selection of multiple clips.

SNAP TO GRID

When you're making selections or moving data, the start and end times of your selections or data are affected by the Snap to Grid.

CLIP PREVIEW

You can preview your selected data by pressing Shift+spacebar.

Splitting and Combining Clips

Using partial selections, you can combine and split clips into new smaller or larger clips. Combining clips is very easy. Just select the clips you want to combine and choose Edit > Bounce to Clip(s). SONAR will create one new clip from the old selected ones.

The Bounce to Track(s) Function

The problem with the Bounce to Clip(s) function is that it works only on clips that are on the same track. If you want to combine clips from different tracks, you have to use the Bounce to Track(s) function as follows:

ONLY AUDIO TRACKS

The Bounce to Track(s) function also has a limitation: It works only with audio tracks, unless you are using software synthesizers. In that case, it will also work with MIDI tracks.

1. Select the clips you want to combine.
2. Choose Edit > Bounce to Track(s) to open the Bounce to Track(s) dialog box (see Figure 7.19).
3. Because you are combining clips from multiple tracks into one clip, the new clip has to reside on a single track. In the Destination drop-down list, choose the track on which you want your new combined clip to reside.
4. The Bounce to Track(s) function lets you determine the format of your new clip. In the Channel Format list, choose the format you want to use. Choose Stereo to create a single stereo track from your combined clips. Choose Split Mono to create two new tracks, each holding the left and right stereo channels of your new audio data, respectively. Choose Mono to create a single mono track from your combined clips.

Figure 7.19 Use the Bounce to Track(s) function to combine clips from multiple tracks.

5. In the Source Buses/Tracks section, select the buses that you want SONAR to use when combining your clips.

6. In the Source Category field, choose how you want SONAR to deal with the output from each bus. Select the Buses option for situations in which you have each track assigned to a different output bus and you want the combined clips from each track to be put on a separate new track. Choose the Main Outputs option for situations in which you have each track assigned to a different physical sound card output and you want the combined clips from each track to be put on a separate new track. Choose the Entire Mix option to combine all the clips from the selected tracks onto one new track. Choose the Tracks option to create a new track for each selected track in the Source Buses/Track section.

7. In the Mix Enables section, activate the automation and effects options you want to include in the new clip from the clips being combined. Usually, you should keep all these options activated.

8. If you want to save your settings as a preset for quicker bouncing the next time you use this feature, type in a name for the preset in the Preset field. Then click the Save button (the button with the floppy disk shown on it).

9. Click OK.

SONAR will combine all your clips, according to your settings in the dialog box.

The Split Function

SONAR enables you to split clips using its Split function. It works like this:

1. Set the Now Time at the point where you want the split to occur.

2. Choose Edit > Split to open the Split Clips dialog box (see Figure 7.20).

Figure 7.20 Using the Split Clips dialog box, you can split clips into new, smaller clips in a variety of ways.

3. Choose the split option you want to use. The Split at Time option splits a clip at a certain measure, beat, or tick. The Split at Selection option splits a clip at both ends of a selected data area. The Split Repeatedly option splits a clip into a bunch of smaller clips instead of just two new smaller ones. Just enter the measure at which you want the first split to occur and the number of measures at which you want each consecutive split to occur after that. For example, if you have a clip that begins at measure 2 and ends at measure 7, and you want to create three two-bar clips out of it, enter 2 for the starting measure and 2 for the split interval. The Split at Each Marker option lets you split clips according to the markers you set up in the Track view. Finally, the Split When Silent for at Least option lets you split clips at any place within them where silence occurs. You can set the interval of silence that SONAR has to look for by entering a number of measures.

4. If you are splitting MIDI clips, you have the option of having them split nondestructively, which means that any data (such as note durations) that extends beyond the split point isn't deleted; only the appearance of the clips is changed. To do this, activate the Use Non-Destructive Cropping When Splitting MIDI Clips option. More than likely, you usually will want to have this option activated.

5. Click OK.

The Split Tool

In addition to the Split function, you can split clips graphically with your mouse by using the Split tool. To access the Split tool in the Track view, press C.

Using the Split tool, you can split long audio and MIDI clips into shorter ones by clicking and dragging with your mouse. To use the Split tool, simply follow these steps:

1. Press C to access the Split tool.

2. Move your mouse pointer within the Clips pane, and it will turn into a pointer with a pair of scissors attached to it.

3. Click and drag anywhere within the Clips pane to select some data (see Figure 7.21). You can make a selection over multiple clips and multiple tracks simultaneously if you want.

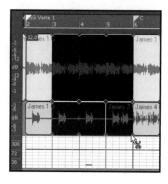

Figure 7.21   You just click and drag to make a selection with the Split tool.

4. Release the mouse button. SONAR will split all the selected clips, according to the boundaries of the selection.

5. When you are finished using the Split tool, be sure to activate the Select tool (press T) so that you don't accidentally split some clips by mistake when you're just trying to make a selection.

Moving and Copying Clips

You can change the arrangement of your data by moving and copying clips to new locations, either within the same tracks or into other tracks. One way to move a clip is to use the Clip Properties dialog box and enter a new start time for the clip. You also can move a clip by simply clicking and dragging it to a new location with your mouse. As long as the track you're dragging the clip into doesn't contain any other existing clips, you don't have to worry, because SONAR simply will move the clip to its new location.

However, if the track contains existing data, SONAR will ask how you want the data to be handled by displaying the Drag and Drop Options dialog box (see Figure 7.22). Then you have to choose one of three options: Blend Old and New, Replace Old with New, or Slide Over Old to Make Room.

❄ **ASK THIS EVERY TIME**

If you have the Ask This Every Time option activated in the Drag and Drop Options dialog box, SONAR will open the box every time you drag data, even if there is no existing data in the track to which you're dragging. If you don't want this to happen, deactivate the Ask This Every Time option.

Figure 7.22 If you move a clip within a track that contains existing material, SONAR will display the Drag and Drop Options dialog box.

If you choose the Blend Old and New option, the clip you're moving simply will overlap any existing clips. This means that the clips remain separate, but they overlap so that during playback the data in the overlapping sections will play simultaneously. If you choose the Replace Old with New option, the overlapping portion of the clip you are moving will replace (which means it will erase and take the place of) the portion of the clip being overlapped. If you choose the Slide Over Old to Make Room option, the start times of any existing clips will be changed to make room for the new clip. During playback, the new clip will play at the time it was placed at, and the existing clips will play a little later, depending on how much their start times had to be changed.

If you would rather copy a clip instead of moving it, you can use SONAR's Copy, Cut, and Paste functions. Actually, using the Cut function is the same as moving a clip. If you use the Copy function, you can keep the original clip in its place and put a copy of it in the new location. This procedure works as follows:

1. Select the clip(s) you want to copy.
2. Choose Edit > Copy (or Ctrl + C) to open the Copy dialog box (see Figure 7.23).

Figure 7.23 To copy clips, you use the Copy dialog box.

3. Choose the type(s) of data you want to copy. Usually, you should choose the Events in Tracks option.

4. Click OK.

5. Click the number of the track into which you want to copy the clips.

6. Set the Now time to the point in the track at which you want to place the clips.

7. Choose Edit > Paste (or Ctrl + V) to open the Paste dialog box and then click the Advanced button to open the advanced Paste dialog box (see Figure 7.24).

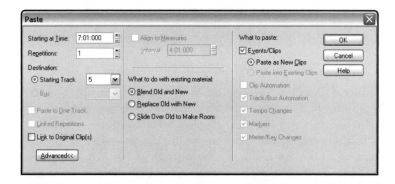

Figure 7.24 The advanced Paste dialog box provides many different options for copying data in SONAR.

8. Choose the options you want to use. Most of these options are self-explanatory. Setting the Starting at Time option is the same as setting the Now time in step 6. Setting the Destination: Starting Track option is the same as setting the track in step 5. The Repetitions option simply lets you create more than one copy of the clip if you want. I've already talked about the What to Do with Existing Material options. The Paste as New Clips option creates a new clip and then follows the overlapping rules that you chose with the What to Do with Existing Material options. The Paste into Existing Clips option merges the clip that you are copying with any existing clips that it overlaps. Material from both clips is merged into one.

9. Click OK.

If some of these options sound a little confusing, just experiment with them a bit. Make an extra backup of your project and then use it to go wild with the copying and pasting functions. Try every possible combination, and soon you'll get the hang of using them.

❈ **QUICK CLIP COPY**

You can copy a clip quickly by holding down the Ctrl key and clicking and dragging the clip to a new location. A copy of the clip will be made and placed at the new location.

Linked Clips

You might have noticed a few other options in the Paste dialog boxes, namely the Linked Repetitions and Link to Original Clip(s) options. These options deal with a special feature in SONAR called *linked clips*. Using this feature, you can link copies of a clip to each other so that any changes you make to one clip will affect the other clips that are linked to it. This way, you can easily create repeating patterns and later make changes to the patterns.

For example, you might have a cool drum pattern in a clip that takes up one measure, and you want to repeat that pattern through the first eight measures of your song. You can copy the clip and then paste it (setting the Repetitions to 7 and activating the Linked Repetitions and Link to Original Clips options). SONAR will copy your clip and paste seven identical, linked copies of it. If you make any changes to one of the clips, these changes affect them all. For instance, you can change the snare drum from sounding on beat 2 to sounding on beat 3 in one of the clips, and the change will happen in all of them. Linked clips are a fun, cool, and timesaving feature.

If you ever want to unlink linked clips, just follow these steps:

1. Select the clips you want to unlink. You don't have to unlink all linked clips in a group. For example, if you have four linked clips, you can select two of them to unlink, and the two that you leave unselected will remain linked.

2. Right-click one of the selected clips and choose Unlink to open the Unlink Clips dialog box.

3. Choose an unlink option. The New Linked Group option unlinks the selected clips from the other clips, but keeps them linked to each other. The Independent, Not Linked at All option totally unlinks the clips from any others.

4. Click OK.

Linked clips are shown with dotted outlines in the Clips pane of the Track view. When you unlink them, they appear as normal clips again.

Erasing Clips

Deleting any clips that you no longer need is an easy process. Simply follow these steps:

1. Select the clips you want to delete.

2. Choose Edit > Delete to open the Delete dialog box (see Figure 7.25).

3. Make sure the Events in Tracks option is activated.

4. If you want SONAR to remove the space that's created when you delete the clips, activate the Delete Hole option. SONAR will move any other existing clips in the track backward (toward the beginning of the project) by the amount of time opened when you delete the clips.

5. If you activate the Shift by Whole Measures option as well, the existing clips will be moved back only to the nearest whole measure.

6. Click OK.

Figure 7.25 In the Delete dialog box, you can determine the type of data you want to erase.

Inserting Space

Instead of manipulating existing data, you might need to introduce silent parts into your project. You can do so by using SONAR's Insert > Time/Measures feature. This feature inserts blank space in the form of measures, ticks, seconds, or frames. You can insert the space either into the whole project or into selected tracks. It works like this:

1. Choose Edit > Select > None (or Ctrl + Shift + A) to clear any currently selected data in the project.
2. If you want to insert space into the whole project, skip to step 3. Otherwise, select the tracks into which you want to insert space.
3. Set the Now time to the point in the tracks or project at which you want the space inserted.
4. Choose Insert > Time/Measures to open the Insert Time/Measures dialog box (see Figure 7.26).

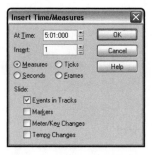

Figure 7.26 Using the Insert Time/Measures dialog box, you can insert blank space into selected tracks or the entire project.

5. The At Time field reflects the current Now time. Type a new time here or make adjustments if you want.
6. For the Insert field, type the number of units of blank space you want inserted.

7. Select the type of unit you want inserted. You can choose to insert measures, ticks, seconds, or frames.

8. In the Slide section, choose the types of data that will be affected by the insert process. The types of data you select will be moved to make room for the new blank space. Of course, you'll almost always want to have the Events in Tracks option activated. When you're inserting space into selected tracks, the Events in Tracks option is usually the only one you want to have activated. However, when you're inserting space into the entire project, more than likely you'll want to have all the options activated.

9. Click OK.

SONAR will insert the number of measures, ticks, seconds, or frames you typed into the Insert parameter at the Now time you specified. It also will move the types of data you selected by sliding the data forward in time (toward the end of the project). For instance, if you inserted a measure of blank space in the entire project at measure 2, then all the data in all the tracks starting at measure 2 will be shifted forward by one measure. Whatever data was in measure 2 will be in measure 3, any data that was in measure 3 will be in measure 4, and so on.

Slip Editing

Up until now, all of the editing functions I've described in this chapter work by making permanent changes to the MIDI and audio data in your clips and tracks. This is called *destructive processing* because it "destroys" the original data by modifying (or overwriting) it according to any editing you apply.

❉ **UNDO FUNCTION**

As you know, you can remove any destructive processing done to your data by using SONAR's Undo function. You also can load a saved copy of your project containing the original data. However, neither of these restoration methods is as convenient as using nondestructive processing.

In contrast to destructive processing, SONAR also includes some editing functions (called *slip editing* functions) that provide *nondestructive* processing. The slip editing functions are nondestructive because they don't apply any permanent changes to your data. Instead, they are applied only during playback and let you hear the results while leaving your original data intact.

You can use the slip editing functions to crop the beginning or end of a clip, shift the contents of a clip, or shift-crop the beginning or end of a clip. Slip editing can be done on multiple clips at once by selecting the clips first.

Cropping a Clip

To crop the beginning or end of a clip, follow these steps:

1. If you want to crop the beginning of a clip, position your mouse over the left end of the clip until the cursor turns into a square and a clip handle is displayed (see Figure 7.27).

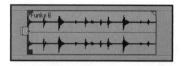

Figure 7.27   Position your mouse over the left end of the clip to crop the beginning.

2. Click and drag your mouse to the right so that the clip changes length, as shown in Figure 7.28.

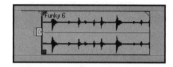

Figure 7.28   Click and drag to the right to shorten the clip from the beginning.

3. If you want to crop the end of a clip, follow steps 1 and 2 but adjust the right end of the clip rather than the left end, so it looks like Figure 7.29.

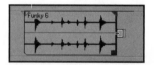

Figure 7.29   Click and drag the right end of the clip to crop the end.

When you crop a clip, the data that is cropped is not deleted. Instead, the data is masked so you will not hear it during playback. So if you crop the first two beats in a one-measure clip, those first two beats will not sound during playback. And if you crop the last two beats in a one-measure clip, those last two beats will not sound during playback.

❋ **REPOSITION YOUR CLIPS**

When you crop a clip, the length of the clip is altered. The space where the cropped data used to be will be filled with silence during playback. You might need to make some adjustments to the positions of your clips within your tracks.

❋ **PERMANENT CHANGES**

If you ever want to apply your cropping changes to a clip permanently, choose Edit > Apply Trimming.

Shifting a Clip

Instead of cropping a clip (and thus changing its length), you can shift the data inside the clip without changing the clip's length. To shift a clip, follow these steps:

1. Press and hold the Alt+Shift keys.
2. Position your mouse over the middle of the clip until the cursor turns into a square (see Figure 7.30).

Figure 7.30   To shift a clip, position your mouse in the middle of it.

3. Click and drag to the left to shift the data in the clip toward the beginning of the clip.
4. Click and drag to the right to shift the data in the clip toward the end of the clip.

When you shift a clip, the data in the beginning or the end of the clip is cropped, but the length of the clip is not altered, as shown in Figure 7.31.

Figure 7.31   Shifting a clip crops the data but doesn't alter the length of the clip.

Shift-Cropping a Clip

Shift-cropping is a combination of the aforementioned functions. When you shift-crop a clip, the data in the clip is shifted, and the length of the clip is altered. To shift-crop a clip, follow these steps:

1. Press and hold the Alt+Shift keys.
2. Position your mouse over the left or right end of the clip (depending on whether you want to shift-crop the beginning or end of the clip) until the cursor turns into a square.
3. Click and drag to the left or right to alter the length of the clip and shift the data inside the clip at the same time.

The slip editing functions can be a very powerful alternative to cutting and pasting. Since the data from the clips isn't deleted, you can edit the clips at any time to specify the portions of their data that will sound during playback. For example, if you have a clip that contains a vocal phrase, and the first word in the phrase isn't quite right, you can crop it. But later on, if you decide that the word actually sounded good, just uncrop it, and your data will restored, just like magic. SONAR also provides additional nondestructive editing with envelopes.

SRGAudio Editing

Although SONAR provides separate views for precise editing of MIDI data, it doesn't provide a dedicated view for editing audio data. Instead, the Track view doubles as an audio editor. To edit audio in the Track view, you simply use all of the functions described previously in this chapter to edit any audio clips in your tracks. There are some other more sophisticated functions available for editing audio data that I'll describe in Chapter 8, "Exploring the Editing Tools."

There are, however, a few things that you should keep in mind while editing audio in the Track view. The following sections will describe these things.

Audio Waveforms

When examining audio clips, you'll notice that they display the audio waveforms corresponding to the audio data inside them.

❋ AUDIO WAVEFORMS

An *audio waveform* is a graphical representation of sound. Let me try to explain using the cup and string analogy. Remember when you were a kid, and you set up your own intercom system between your bedroom and your tree house using nothing but a couple of paper cups and a long piece of string? You poked a hole in the bottom of each cup and then tied one end of the string to one cup and the other end of the string to the other cup. Your friend would be in the tree house with one of the cups, and you would be in your bedroom with the other. As you talked into your cup, your friend could hear you by putting his cup to his ear, and vice versa.

Why did it work? Well, when you talked into the cup, the sound of your voice vibrated the bottom of the cup, making it act like a microphone. This movement, in turn, vibrated the string up and down, and the string carried the vibrations to the other cup. This movement made the bottom of that cup vibrate so that it acted like a speaker, thus letting your friend hear what you said. If it were possible for you to freeze the string while it was in motion and then zoom in on it so you could see the vibrations, it would look similar to the audio waveform shown in Figure 7.32.

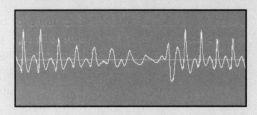

Figure 7.32   An audio waveform is similar to a vibrating string if you could freeze and zoom in on the string to observe the vibrations.

As you can see, a waveform shows up and down movements just like a vibrating string. A line, called the *zero axis,* runs horizontally through the center of the waveform. The zero axis represents the point in a waveform at which there are no vibrations or there is no sound, so the value of the audio data at the zero axis is the number zero (also known as zero *amplitude).* When a waveform moves above or below the zero axis, vibrations occur, and thus there is sound. The amplitude value of a waveform in these places depends on how high above or how low below the zero axis the waveform is at a certain point in time (shown on the Time Ruler).

Snap to Zero Crossing

Another thing to keep in mind is that you need to make sure to edit your audio data at zero crossings in the waveform to avoid noisy pops or clicks. You can do so by activating the Snap to Audio Zero Crossings feature, which you access via the Snap to Grid dialog box. Just open the Snap to Grid dialog box by clicking on the Snap to Grid Options button in the Track view toolbar (see Figure 7.33). Then put a check mark next to the Snap to Audio Zero Crossings option.

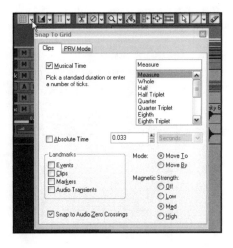

Figure 7.33   Use the Snap to Grid Options button to access the Snap to Grid dialog box.

The Snap to Audio Zero Crossings feature (when activated) makes sure that, when you make a selection or perform an edit, your selections or edits fall on zero crossings in the audio waveform.

❋ **ZERO CROSSING**

Remember the description of the zero axis? Well, any point in an audio waveform that lands on the zero axis is called a *zero crossing.* It's called that because as the waveform moves up and down, it crosses over the zero axis.

Why is it important that your selections and edits line up with zero crossings? A zero crossing is a point in the audio waveform at which no sound is being made, so it provides a perfect spot at which to edit the waveform—for example, when you're cutting and pasting pieces of audio. If you edit an audio waveform at a point where it's either above or below the zero axis, you might introduce glitches, which can come in the form of audible pops and clicks. You get these glitches because you cut at a moment when sound is being produced. You also get them because when you're pasting pieces of audio together, you cannot guarantee that the ends of each waveform will line up perfectly (except, of course, if they both are at zero crossings).

Audio Scaling

Lastly, SONAR provides some special zooming features when you are working with audio tracks. These are the audio scaling features, and they allow you to zoom in on the audio waveforms shown inside the clips in your audio tracks. Audio scaling measures the amplitude of your audio data, and it comes in handy for doing very precise audio editing.

When you are working with audio tracks, you'll notice some numbers displayed along the left side of the Clips pane in the Track view (see Figure 7.34). These numbers represent the Audio Scale, which displays a measurement of the amplitude of the audio data in your audio tracks.

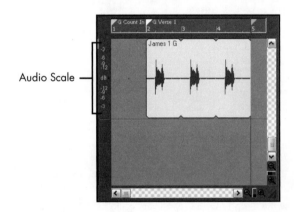

Figure 7.34 Use the Audio Scale to measure the amplitude of your audio.

The measurement can be shown in decibels, as a percentage, or as a zoom factor. To change the measurement display, right-click anywhere in the Audio Scale area and choose an option (see Figure 7.35).

To change the Audio Scale factor for a single audio track, just left-click and hold your mouse on the Audio Scale of the track. Then drag your mouse up or down to change the Audio Scale factor. You'll notice that the audio waveform display for the track changes as you move your mouse. So you can zoom in and out of the audio waveform, but it doesn't affect the Track

Figure 7.35 Change the Audio Scale measurement display by right-clicking it.

view zooming. To return the Audio Scale factor to its default value, double-click inside the Audio Scale area.

You also can change the audio scaling factor for all audio tracks at once by using the Zoom Out Vertical, Zoom In Vertical, and Vertical Zoom Control functions. To use them for audio scaling, just hold down the Ctrl key while you manipulate the functions with your mouse.

Layer Management and Comping

Back in Chapter 6, I discussed the Sound on Sound recording mode to record multiple takes into the same track. I also showed you that by right-clicking on that track and choosing Layers > Show Layers, you could see those multiple takes displayed in separate lanes within the same track. This feature gives you easy access for editing those takes.

Working with Layers

You can work with layers similar to the way you work with separate tracks. Follow these steps to work with track layers:

1. In addition to the method I mentioned earlier, you can show layers in a track by right-clicking inside the Audio Scale and choosing Show Layers. Once the layers in a track are shown, you can apply a number of other layer functions.

2. If you have more than one layer in a track, you will notice that the Audio Scale area is replaced by Mute and Solo buttons for each layer. These buttons mute and solo each layer within a track independent of the Mute and Solo functions used for the entire track.

3. To insert a new layer into a track, right-click the Audio Scale and choose Insert Layer. You can copy clips into the new layer and arrange them just like clips in a track.

4. To delete a layer, right-click the Audio Scale (making sure your mouse is aligned with the layer you want to delete) and choose Delete Layer.

5. To select a layer for processing with any of SONAR's processing functions, right-click the Audio Scale (making sure your mouse is aligned with the layer you want to select) and choose Select Layer.

6. After you've finished working with the layers in a track, you can "clean up" the layers by moving clips to the least number of layers needed. For example, you may have a number of layers with clips that are positioned in different places within the track, but that do not overlap. These clips can be moved to occupy the least number of layers by right-clicking the Audio Scale and choosing Rebuild Layers.

7. In addition, if you have a number of empty layers that you no longer need, instead of having to delete each layer one at a time, you can right-click the Audio Scale and choose Compact Layers to delete all empty layers with one action.

Besides normal editing tasks, layers are extremely useful for *comping*. Comping consists of recording multiple takes of the same performance and then piecing together the best parts of each take to get the best performance possible. In addition to multilane tracks, SONAR provides additional features to make comping a quick and easy process.

Clip Muting

In order to put together a composite track, you need to gather all the good parts of each take. You can do this in two ways. The first way is by muting selected parts of each take. Using muting, you can "turn off" any of the bad parts of each take and leave all the good parts alone. SONAR does this by using the Mute Tool:

1. Press K to activate the Mute tool in the Track view.

2. To mute part of a clip, position the mouse in the lower half of the clip. Then click and drag over the region of the clip you want to mute (see Figure 7.36). The part of the clip you've muted will show the audio waveform as an outline rather than a filled-in waveform.

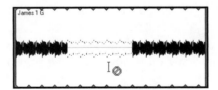

Figure 7.36 Click and drag inside the lower part of a clip to mute the data.

3. To unmute part of a clip, position the mouse in the upper half of the clip. Then click and drag over the region you want to unmute (see Figure 7.37).

4. You can also use the Mute tool to mute an entire clip. Just hold down the Alt key and click on a clip to mute it (see Figure 7.38). Hold down the Alt key and click on the clip again to unmute it.

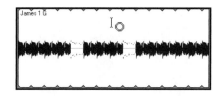

Figure 7.37 Click and drag inside the upper part of a clip to unmute the data.

Figure 7.38 A muted clip is displayed in a grayed-out color with a red, slashed circle shown in the upper-left corner.

> ❋ **MUTING ENTIRE CLIPS QUICKLY**
>
> You can also mute/unmute entire clips in two additional ways. Right-click on the clip and choose Clip Mute/Unmute, or when using the Select tool, click on the clip to select it and then press the Q key.

Clip Isolating

The second way to create a composite track is to use clip isolating. This means that instead of muting all the bad parts in each take, you solo all the good parts. This method can be much easier and faster if you are working with a large number of clips. To isolate (solo) the good parts in a clip, do the following:

1. Press K to activate the Mute tool in the Track view.

2. To isolate part of a clip, hold down the Ctrl key and drag through the part of the clip you would like to isolate. By doing so, this keeps the part of the clip you selected, and it mutes the same part of any clips that are in different lanes but occupy the same time region (see Figure 7.39).

3. You can de-isolate part of a clip by using the same method used to unmute part of a clip. Just click and drag the Mute tool in the upper part of the clip that you want to de-isolate (unmute), as shown in Figure 7.40.

4. You can also isolate an entire clip. Just hold down the Ctrl+Alt keys and simply click on a clip to isolate it (see Figure 7.41). Hold down the Alt key and click on the muted clip to de-isolate (unmute) it.

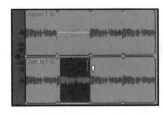

Figure 7.39 Isolate part of a clip by using the Mute tool and the Ctrl key.

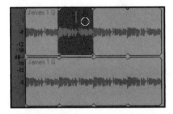

Figure 7.40 De-isolate part of a clip simply by unmuting it as described previously.

Figure 7.41 Use the Ctrl+Alt keys to isolate an entire clip.

Whichever method you choose, the comping tools in SONAR piece together the perfect composite track. And once you've muted or isolated all the parts you want, you can either leave the track as it is for future editing, or you can select the track and use the Bounce to Track(s) feature to mix all your edits down to a new, clean track.

Using the Piano Roll View

By manipulating the tracks and clips in your project, you can change the overall structure, but to fix single-note mistakes and make smaller changes, you need to do some precision editing. You do so by selecting individual or multiple tracks or clips in the Track view and then using the View menu to open the data within one of the other available views. For editing MIDI data, that would be the Piano Roll view. (You also can edit MIDI data as standard music notation in the Staff view)

Using the Piano Roll view (see Figure 7.42), you can add, edit, and delete MIDI note and controller data within your MIDI tracks. Looking somewhat like a player-piano roll, the Piano Roll view represents notes as colored shapes on a grid display with the pitches of the notes designated by an on-screen music keyboard.

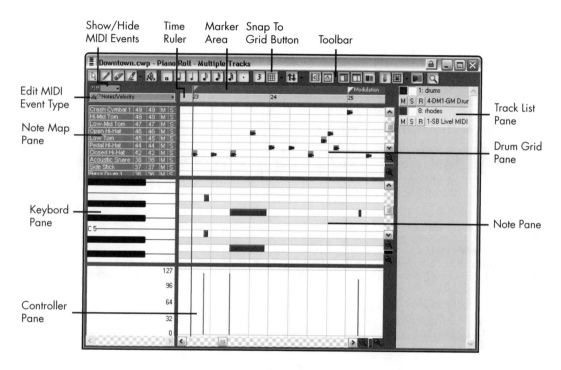

Figure 7.42   The Piano Roll view resembles the old player-piano rolls used in the late 1800s and early 1900s.

More precisely, the Piano Roll view consists of seven major sections: the toolbar (containing all the view's related controls), the Drum Grid pane (displaying the drum notes in the currently selected track), the Note Map pane (displaying the drum instruments represented by the note shown in the Drum Grid pane), the Note pane (displaying the melodic notes in the currently selected track), the Keyboard pane (displaying the pitch values of the notes shown in the Note pane), the Controllers pane (displaying the MIDI controller data in the currently selected track), and the Track List pane (showing a list of all the tracks currently being displayed; the Piano Roll view can display the data from more than one track at one time).

You'll also notice that the Piano Roll view has scroll bars and zoom tools just like the Track view. These tools work the same way as they do in the Track view. In addition, a Snap to Grid function is represented by the Snap to Grid button in the toolbar. Other similarities are the Marker area and the Time Ruler, which are located just above the Drum Grid pane.

Basically, you can use the Piano Roll view to edit and view the data in the MIDI tracks of your project in more detail.

You can open the Piano Roll view in three different ways.

* In the Track view, select the tracks you want to edit and choose View > Piano Roll or press Alt + 5.
* In the Track view, right-click a track or clip and choose View > Piano Roll.
* In the Track view, double-click a MIDI clip in the Clips pane.

Whichever method you choose, SONAR will open the Piano Roll view and display the data from the track(s) you selected.

Working with Multiple Tracks

If you select more than one track to be displayed at one time, the Piano Roll view will show the data from each track by using a unique color. For example, the notes and controllers from one track might be shown as yellow, and the data from another track might be shown as blue.

> ❄ **CHANGE TRACK COLORS**
>
> The one exception to the use of track colors is that tracks with numbers ending in the same digit (that is, 1, 11, 21, and so on) must all share the same color. There's no way around this. However, you can change the color used by each number group by using the Colors dialog box, which you access by selecting Options > Colors.

Each track also is listed in the Track pane with a set of individual controls (see Figure 7.43).

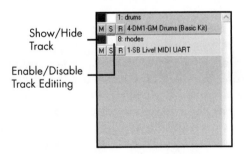

Show/Hide Track

Enable/Disable Track Editiing

Figure 7.43 The data from multiple tracks is shown with different colors, and each track is listed in the Track pane.

The Track Pane

When you open the Piano Roll view, the names and numbers of the tracks you selected are listed in the Track pane. For convenience, the associated Mute, Solo, and Record buttons for each track are provided as well. Plus, you'll notice two other controls available for each track in the list.

❋ **Enable/Disable Track Editing.** The white button next to each track in the Track pane is the Enable/Disable Track Editing button. This button determines whether you can edit the notes for its associated track. When the button is white, the notes appear in color in the Drum Grid and Note panes, and they can be edited. When the button is gray, the notes appear gray in the Drum Grid and Note panes, and they cannot be edited. Clicking on the button toggles this function on and off.

❋ **Show/Hide Track.** The button to the left of the Track Editing button is the Show/Hide Track button. This button determines whether the notes for its associated track will be displayed in the Drum Grid and Note panes. When the button is in color (the same color as the notes for that track), the notes are shown in the Drum Grid and Note panes. When the button is white, the notes are not shown in the Drum Grid and Note panes. Clicking on the Show/Hide Track button toggles it on and off.

The Track Tools

In addition to the Track pane controls, six other track-related controls are located on the toolbar (see Figure 7.44):

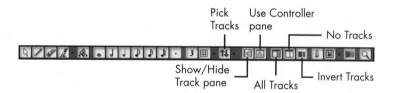

Figure 7.44 Use the track controls via the Piano Roll toolbar to manipulate your displayed tracks.

❋ **Pick Tracks.** While you have the Piano Roll view open, you might want to add or remove some of the tracks in the Track pane. Instead of having to close the Piano Roll view, select other tracks in the Track view, and then open the Piano Roll view again, you can use the Pick Tracks feature.

Clicking the Pick Tracks button opens the Pick Tracks dialog box. This box displays a list of all the tracks in your project. You can select one or more tracks from the list. (Hold down the Ctrl key to select multiple tracks.) After you click the OK button, the tracks that you selected will be listed in the Track pane.

❋ **Show/Hide Track Pane.** Clicking this button toggles between having the Track pane open or closed.

❋ **Use Controller Pane.** Clicking this button toggles between having the Controller pane open or closed.

❋ **All Tracks.** This button is the exact opposite of the No Tracks button. Clicking the All Tracks button turns on the Show/Hide Track buttons for each track in the Track pane.

* **No Tracks.** Clicking this button turns off the Show/Hide Track buttons for each track in the Track pane. No matter what state each Show/Hide Track button is in (either on or off), the No Track button turns them all off.

* **Invert Tracks.** Clicking this button toggles the Show/Hide Track buttons for each of the tracks in the Track pane. If one track has its Show/Hide Track button on and another track has its button off, clicking the Invert Tracks button turns off the first track's Show/ Hide button and turns on the second track's Show/Hide button. It toggles the current state of each Show/Hide Track button.

CHANGE TRACK ORDER

If you have two or more tracks that contain the same notes, those notes overlap one another in the Drum Grid and Note panes. The order of the tracks in the Track pane determines which track's notes are on top. For example, if track 4 is listed above track 2 in the Track pane, the data from track 4 overlaps the data from track 2 in the Note pane. If you want to change this order (meaning you want the data from track 2 to overlap the data from track 4), you can click and drag the track listing in the Track pane to a new position in the list.

Dealing with Notes

When you open a melodic MIDI track in the Piano Roll view, the notes in that track are displayed in the Note pane. Each note is represented by a colored rectangle. The horizontal location of a note designates its start time when you line up the left side of the rectangle with the numbers in the Time Ruler, and the vertical location of a note designates its pitch when you line up the whole rectangle with the keys in the Keyboard pane. The length of the rectangle designates the duration of the note (for instance, quarter note, eighth note, and so on).

You can add new notes to a track or edit the existing ones by using the tools represented by the first five buttons in the toolbar, from left to right on the left side of the Piano Roll view (see Figure 7.45).

Figure 7.45 Add and edit notes using the tools represented by the first five toolbar buttons.

Melodic Scales

Before you begin adding or editing notes to a track, you might want to set the melodic scale for that track. SONAR provides a Snap to Scale feature that, when activated, will automatically force all added or edited notes to conform to the melodic scale of your choice. This feature can make it much easier to add and edit notes in a track when you know you'll be composing using a certain melodic scale. To activate the Snap to Scale feature for a track, right-click the track in the Track pane and choose Enable/Disable Snap to Scale.

Setting the Scale

After you've enabled the Snap to Scale feature, you'll want to set the scale to be used for the track being edited. Follow these steps to set the scale:

1. Right-click the track in the Track pane and choose Root Note > [*name of musical note*] to set the root note for the scale. This allows you to choose the beginning note and musical key for the scale. For example, if your song is being composed in the key of C, choose C as the root note.

2. Right-click the track in the Track pane and choose Scales > [*type of scale*] > [*name of scale*] to set the scale for the track. For example, if your song is being composed in the key of C Major, choose Diatonic Scales > Ionian (Major) as the scale.

3. In addition to the root name and type of scale, you need to set the Snap Settings for the track. The Snap Settings determine how non-scale notes are handled. To set the Snap Settings, right-click the track in the Track pane and choose Snap Settings to open the Snap Scale Settings dialog box (see Figure 7.46).

Figure 7.46 Use the Snap Scale Settings dialog box to determine how non-scale notes are handled.

4. Choose one of the options in the dialog box. Choose Adjust to Next, Higher Note so that any non-scale notes are moved to the next higher note in the chosen scale. Choose Adjust to Previous, Lower Note so that any non-scale notes are moved to the previous lower note in the chosen scale. Choose Adjust to Nearest Note so that any non-scale notes are moved to the note closest in pitch in the chosen scale.

5. Click OK.

❋ **MULTIPLE TRACK SCALES**

You can also set up the Snap to Scale feature for multiple tracks simultaneously by selecting the tracks in the Track view and then using the Track > Snap to Scale functions from SONAR's main menu.

Create Your Own Scales

Even though SONAR ships with a large collection of scales from which you can choose, SONAR also allows you to create your own scales for use with the Snap to Scale feature. To create your own scale, do the following:

1. Right-click a track in the Track pane and choose Scale Manager or choose Track > Snap to Scale > Scale Manager from SONAR's main menu to open the Scale Manager dialog box (see Figure 7.47).

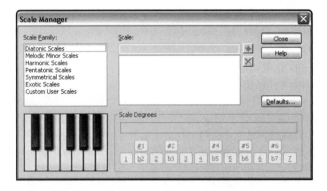

Figure 7.47 Use the Scale Manager to create your own scales for the Snap to Scale feature.

2. In the Scale Family section, select the scale category in which you would like your new scale to be listed.

3. In the Scale section, type a name for your new scale and then click the Create New Scale button (the one with the yellow star shown on it), as shown in Figure 7.48.

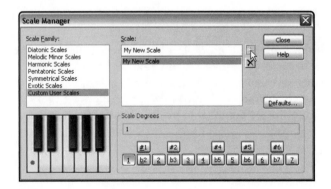

Figure 7.48 Click the Create New Scale button to create a new scale.

4. To add or remove degrees to or from the scale, either click the keys in the Keyboard display or click the buttons in the Scale Degrees section (see Figure 7.49).

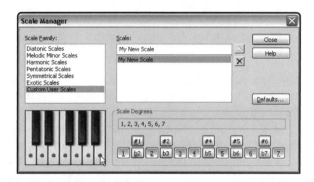

Figure 7.49 Click the Keyboard keys or Scale Degree buttons to add or remove degrees for the scale.

5. If you don't like your scale and want to delete it, just click the Delete Scale button (the one with the big red X shown on it).

6. If you edit one of the default scales included with SONAR and you want to put it back to the way it was, click the Defaults button to open the Scale Defaults dialog box. Choose one of the options and click OK. The Restore Current Scale option restores the default scale with which you are currently working. The Restore Any Missing Scales option restores any default scales you may have deleted. The Restore All Factory Scales option restores all default scales to their original configurations.

7. When finished, click the Close button in the Close button in the Scales manager dialog box.

Now when you go to set the scale for a track, your new scale will be listed under your chosen category in the Scales menu.

❋ **QUICK SNAP TO SCALE OVERIDE**

In the following sections, I'll be talking about how to add and edit notes. If you have the Snap to Scale feature activated while adding or editing notes, your notes will be automatically moved to conform to your chosen scale. However, if you are working with a particular note that you do not want altered, you can temporarily bypass the Snap to Scale feature by holding down both mouse buttons as you edit the note.

Selecting Notes

Using the Select tool, you can select notes for further manipulation, such as deleting, copying, moving, and so on. Essentially, you select notes the same way you select clips in the Track view. To select a single note, click it. To select more than one note, hold down the Ctrl key while clicking the notes you want to select. You know the rest.

One additional selection method involves the Keyboard pane. To select all the notes of a certain pitch, you can click one of the keys in the Keyboard pane. You can also drag your mouse pointer across several keys to select the notes of a number of different pitches.

Editing

After you've made a selection, you can copy, cut, paste, move, and delete the notes the same way you do with clips in the Track view. You can also edit notes individually by using the Draw tool. Using this tool, you can add and edit the notes in the Note pane.

To change the start time of a note, drag simply the left edge of its rectangle left or right. This action moves it to a different horizontal location along the Time Ruler. To change the pitch of a note, drag the middle of its rectangle up or down. This action moves it to a different vertical location along the Keyboard pane. To change the duration of a note, drag the right edge of its rectangle left or right. This action changes the length of the rectangle and thus the duration of the note.

Sometimes you might want to make more precise changes to a note. There are two ways to do this. The first method is to use the Select tool to select the note and then use the Time, Pitch, Vel (Velocity), Dur (Duration), and Chn (MIDI Channel) parameters in the Event Inspector toolbar to change those characteristics of the note.

> ✳ **EVENT INSPECTOR**
>
> The Event Inspector toolbar is no longer a part of the Piano Roll view. The Event Inspector is now a global toolbar that can be accessed from any view. It acts just like any other toolbar. If it is not active, choose Views > Toolbars to make the Event Inspector visible.

You can also use the Note Properties dialog box to edit a note. Right-click a note to open the Note Properties dialog box (see Figure 7.50).

Figure 7.50 In the Note Properties dialog box, you can make precise changes to a note in the Piano Roll view.

In the Note Properties dialog box, you can make precise changes to the start time, pitch, velocity, duration, and MIDI channel of an individual note by typing numerical values.

Drawing (or Adding) Notes

In addition to editing, the Draw tool adds notes to a track by literally drawing them in. To do so, just follow these steps:

1. Select the Draw tool by clicking its toolbar button or by pressing D.
2. Select a duration for the new notes. If you look a little further over in the toolbar, you'll notice a number of buttons with note values shown on them (see Figure 7.51). Clicking these buttons determines the duration for your new notes. For example, if you click the Quarter Note button, the duration will be set to a quarter note. You'll also see two additional buttons—one representing a dotted note and another representing a triplet note. So if you want your notes to be dotted or triplets, click one of those buttons as well.

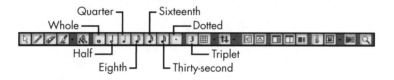

Figure 7.51 Use the duration toolbar buttons to choose a duration for your new notes.

3. Click inside the Note pane at the point at which you want to place the new notes. Remember, the horizontal position of the note determines its start time, and the vertical position of the note determines its pitch.

Erasing Notes

Although you can select and delete notes, the Piano Roll view also includes an Auto Erase tool for added convenience. To use it, select the Auto Erase tool and then click any notes in the Note pane that you want to delete. You can also click and drag the Erase tool over a number of notes to erase them all at once.

❋ **QUICK DRAW ERASE**

You also can use the Draw tool to erase notes. Just left-click the note you want to erase, and while holding down the left mouse button, press the Delete key.

Scrubbing

When you're editing the data in a track, the procedure usually involves making your edits and then playing back the project to hear how the changes sound. However, playing back very small sections can be a bit difficult, especially when you're working with a fast tempo. To remedy this situation, SONAR provides a Scrub tool.

Using the Scrub tool, you can drag your mouse pointer over the data in the Piano Roll view and hear what it sounds like. To use the Scrub tool, simply select it by clicking its button on the toolbar or by pressing the B key. Then click and drag your mouse pointer over the data in the Drum Grid or Note panes. Dragging left to right plays the data forward (what would normally happen during playback), and dragging right to left enables you to hear the data played in reverse. This capability can be useful for testing very short (one or two measure) sections.

❋ **EDIT DATA WHILE LOOPING**

Instead of using the Scrub tool, you might want to try a more useful technique for hearing what your changes sound like. Did you know that you could edit the data in your project as it's being played back? Of course, it's a bit difficult to edit anything while SONAR is scrolling the display as the project plays. I like to work on a small section of a project at a time. I set up a section of the project to loop over and over, and as SONAR is playing the data, I make any changes I think might be needed. Because the data is being played back while I edit, I can instantly hear what the changes sound like. This procedure is much easier than going back and forth, making changes, and manually starting and stopping playback. By the way, you can use any of the views to edit your data while SONAR is playing a project. This tip is not just for the Piano Roll view.

Dealing with Drum Tracks

Because drum tracks are a bit different from regular MIDI tracks, SONAR provides some special features for dealing with drum tracks. What do I mean by different? Well, notes in a drum track usually represent a number of different percussion instruments grouped in the same track. Each note pitch in a drum track represents a different instrument. It used to be that if you wanted to work easily with each specific instrument, you had to split a drum track into many different tracks—one track for each note pitch. This allowed you to mute and solo different instruments, as well as do other things that you couldn't do when all the drum notes were grouped together on the same track.

With SONAR's new drum-specific features, you no longer have to go through the trouble of creating separate tracks for each drum instrument. You also have the flexibility of specifying different MIDI channels and MIDI ports for each instrument (among other things) using drum maps.

Using Drum Maps

A drum map defines your drum instruments for SONAR, thus "telling" SONAR how each note pitch in a drum track should be handled. Each note pitch defined in a drum map can have its own instrument name, MIDI channel, MIDI port, velocity offset, and velocity scale.

Assigning Drum Maps

The easiest way to explain drum maps is to show you how to assign a drum map to a MIDI track and explain the results. I'll use an example to help clarify things a bit:

1. Choose File > Open and select the demo project file included with SONAR named Downtown.cwp. Then click Open to load the project.

2. Close the Auto-Send Sysx and File Info windows. You won't need them.

3. Select track 1 (drums) by clicking its number and then choose View > Piano Roll to open the track in the Piano Roll view. This is what a drum track looks like without a drum map assigned to it. You can see the notes in the track, but you don't know what percussion instruments they represent. And you can't easily work with each individual instrument because there is no way to mute or solo a specific group of note pitches. In addition, all the notes in the track have to share the same MIDI port and channel specified by the parameters in track 1. To get beyond these limitations, you need to assign a drum map to track 1.

4. Close the Piano Roll view, and in the Track view expand track 1 (drums), so you have access to its Output parameter. Then click on the Output parameter to display the Output menu (see Figure 7.52).

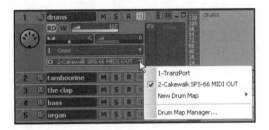

Figure 7.52   Use a track's Output parameter to assign a drum map to the track.

5. Highlight the New Drum Map option and then choose GM Drums (Complete Kit) from the extended menu. This assigns the GM Drums (Complete Kit) drum map to track 1. SONAR ships with a number of predefined drum maps, as you can see from the list.

6. Select track 1 by clicking its number and choose View > Piano Roll to open the track in the Piano Roll view again. Also, choose Edit > Select > None to get rid of the selection.

This time the track data looks a bit different, right? Instead of the Note pane, the Drum Grid pane is shown, and instead of rectangles, there are triangles representing the notes, even though these are the same notes as before.

More important is what is shown in the Note Map pane. Each row in the Note Map pane represents a different percussion instrument. By lining up the notes in the Drum Grid pane with the rows in the Note Map pane, you can see what instrument the notes represent. And even though all these note pitches (instruments) reside on the same MIDI track, each instrument can be muted or soloed individually using the M and S buttons next to each instrument name in the Note Map pane. This makes working with drum tracks much easier.

Creating Drum Maps

However, there might be times when the predefined drum maps included with SONAR don't provide what you need. In that case, you'll need to create a drum map of your own. To do that, you need to use the Drum Map Manager (see Figure 7.53), which you can access by choosing Options > Drum Map Manager.

Figure 7.53 Use the Drum Map Manager to create and manage your drum maps.

The Drum Map Manager is divided into three sections. The first section (Drum Maps Used in Current Project) lists all the drum maps being used in the current project. It allows you to delete existing drum maps or create new ones. The second section (Map Settings) shows all the parameter settings for the selected drum map. It also allows you to define each instrument in the drum map by specifying note pitches, instrument names, MIDI channels, MIDI out ports, velocity offsets, and velocity scales. The third section lists all the MIDI output port and channel pairs that are used by the selected drum map. It also lets you specify a MIDI bank and patch for each port/channel combination.

To create a drum map of your own, follow these steps:

1. With a project already open in SONAR, choose Options > Drum Map Manager to open the Drum Map Manager.

2. Click the New button in the first section (Drum Maps Used in Current Project) of the window to create a blank drum map. Don't worry about naming or saving it yet; you'll do that later.

3. Click the New button in the second section (Map Settings) of the window to create a new instrument mapping complete with default parameter settings, as shown in Figure 7.54.

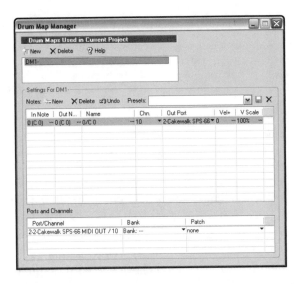

Figure 7.54 New instrument mappings initially contain default parameter settings.

4. Double-click the In Note parameter for the new instrument mapping and enter a number (from 0 to 127) to specify the source pitch for this instrument. I'll explain what I mean by source pitch in a moment.

❄ **NOTE PITCHES**

Note pitches in MIDI are represented by a range of numbers (0 to 127). These numbers represent the note pitches C0 (pitch/octave) to C8, with the number 60 (C4) being middle C. Unfortunately, you have to enter numbers for note values in the Drum Map Manager. There is no way to enter the pitch/octave of a note directly. However, after you enter a number, the pitch/octave of the note is displayed.

5. Double-click the Out Note parameter for the new instrument mapping and enter a number (from 0 to 127) to specify the destination pitch for this instrument.

❄ **HOW DRUM MAPS WORK**

A drum map is sort of like a MIDI data processor. After you assign a drum map to a MIDI track, SONAR passes all the data in that MIDI track through the drum map for processing during playback. As SONAR reads each note from the MIDI track, it compares the pitch of the note to all of the source pitches (In Note parameters) in the drum map. If it finds a match, it converts the incoming note to the destination pitch (Out

Note parameter) of the matching source pitch. For example, if you set up an instrument mapping in your drum map with an In Note pitch of C4 and an Out Note pitch of D5, any incoming notes that have a pitch of C4 will be converted to a pitch of D5.

Why is this useful? Well, more often than not, the In Note and Out Note parameters for an instrument mapping will be the same. But there might be times when you have a MIDI drum track that was recorded using a MIDI percussion synth other than what you have in your studio. This means that the drum sounds in your MIDI percussion device will be different and are probably triggered with different pitches. Using a drum map, you can map the pitches from the MIDI track to the different pitches used by your MIDI percussion device. This saves you the work of having to rewrite all the note pitches in the MIDI track.

6. Double-click the Name parameter for the new instrument mapping and enter a name for the instrument. For example, if you are creating your own General MIDI drum map and you enter 56 for both the In Note and Out Note parameters, that means you are creating an instrument mapping for a cowbell sound because the number 56 represents a cowbell in General MIDI. So for the name, you would enter something like Cowbell.

7. Double-click the Chn (channel) parameter and enter a MIDI channel for the instrument. This should be the same MIDI channel that your MIDI percussion synth is using to play the particular instrument sound.

8. Double-click the Out Port parameter and choose a MIDI output port for the instrument. This should be the same MIDI output port that your MIDI percussion synth is using to play the particular instrument sound.

9. If you find that this instrument sound in your MIDI track is too loud or soft, you can add an offset to the MIDI velocity of the notes for that instrument sound. Just double-click the Vel+ parameter and enter a number from -127 to +127. This number will be subtracted or added to the MIDI velocity value of each incoming note for that instrument sound.

10. You also can adjust the loudness of an instrument sound using the V Scale parameter. Instead of having to designate a set value to be added to or subtracted from the MIDI velocity values of the incoming notes, you can apply a velocity scale. Double-click the V Scale parameter and enter a value from 10% to 200%. A value of 100% means there is no change. A value less than 100% means the velocity values will be decreased. A value greater than 100% means the velocity values will be increased.

11. Repeat steps 3 through 10 to create as many instrument mappings in the drum map as you need. If you make a mistake, you can use the Undo button to remove your last change. To delete an instrument mapping, click the Delete button.

12. In the third section (Ports and Channels) of the window, you can set the bank and patch parameters for each MIDI port/channel combination used in the drum map. Basically, this is where you designate the drum set sounds that each MIDI percussion synth connected to your computer system should use. Your MIDI percussion synths should allow you to choose from a number of different drum sets.

13. To save your drum map, type a name in the Presets parameter and click the Save button (located just to the right of the Presets parameter, showing a picture of a computer disk).

When you go to assign a drum map to a MIDI track, you'll see your new drum map listed there along with all the others.

Composing Drum Tracks

After you've assigned a drum map to a MIDI track, you can start composing the percussion parts for your project. By opening the track in the Piano Roll view, you can use the Note Map pane and the Drum Grid pane to add, edit, and delete drum notes. Most of the procedures that I described earlier in the "Dealing with Notes" section can be applied here. But there are a few differences of which you need to be aware. Instead of just describing these differences, I'd like to walk you through the procedure I use to compose my own drum patterns. Here is how it goes:

1. Choose File > New and select the Blank template to create a new project.
2. Right-click in the Track List pane of the Track view and choose Insert MIDI Track to create a new MIDI track for the project.
3. Assign a drum map to the MIDI track. For this example, use the GM Drums (Complete Kit) drum map. You'll need to use a synth that has a General MIDI-compatible mode. Most modern synths have this capability.
4. If you need to set a bank and patch for your synth, choose Options > Drum Map Manager. In the third section (Ports and Channels) of the window, set a bank and patch for single port/channel listing there. Close the Drum Map Manager.

❋ **USE A SOFTWARE SYNTH**

You can also use a software synth to play the sounds for your drum track. Follow these directions to set up one:

1. Choose Insert > Soft Synths > Cakewalk TTS-1.
2. In the Insert Soft Synth Options dialog box, deactivate the MIDI Source option and activate the First Synth Audio Output option. Make sure that all other options are deactivated and click OK.
3. Choose Options > Drum Map Manager to open the Drum Map Manager.
4. While holding down the Ctrl + Shift keys, double-click one of the Out Port parameters in the Map Settings list and choose Cakewalk TTS-1 from the menu.
5. Close the Drum Map Manager.

Now the Cakewalk TTS-1 software synth will play any notes you add to your MIDI drum track. If you need to change the sound card output for the TTS-1, expand track 2 in the Track view and change its Output parameter.

5. I like to create my drum tracks by composing small sections at a time, and I also like to hear my music as I'm composing it. SONAR allows me to do this by using its playback looping features. Suppose that you want to create a one-measure drum pattern starting at the very beginning of the project and going to the beginning of measure 2. To set up

a playback loop for this example, just choose Transport > Loop and Auto Shuttle. Set the Loop Start parameter to 1:01:000 and the Loop End parameter to 2:01:000. Activate the Stop at the End Time and Loop Continuously options; then click OK.

6. To continue with the drum composing exercise, choose View > Piano Roll to open the MIDI drum track in the Piano Roll view. You'll be presented with the Note Map pane filled with all the instruments available in the drum map you assigned to track 1, as well as a blank Drum Grid pane. Scroll down the window vertically until you can see the last instrument (Acoustic Bass Drum) in the Note Map pane. You might also want to increase the horizontal zoom of the window a bit so the first measure of the track fills the window.

7. The best way to start composing a drum pattern is to lay down a solid beat foundation. That means creating a kick drum part. You'll see in the list that you've got two kick drum sounds available to you: Bass Drum 1 and Acoustic Bass Drum. To audition an instrument, just click its name in the list. Personally, I like the Acoustic Bass Drum, so I'll use that for this exercise. For the kick drum part of the pattern, lay down a basic four-quarter note beat. To do that, activate the Draw tool and choose the quarter-note duration, using the Quarter Note button on the toolbar. Then place a note at each of the four beats in the first measure of the track, as shown in Figure 7.55.

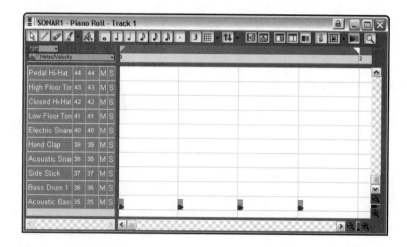

Figure 7.55 Start a drum pattern with a solid kick drum beat foundation.

❄ SNAP TO GRID

If you have a hard time placing the notes exactly on the beats, activate the Snap to Grid function by clicking the Snap to Grid button. Then click the drop-down arrow to the right of the Snap to Grid button to set the function to a musical time interval that you want to use (in this case, a quarter note).

You can have SONAR display a visual grid over the Drum Grid pane to help you place notes by clicking the Show/Hide Grid button (see Figure 7.56). I also like to click the down arrow button to the right of the

Show/Hide Grid button and choose the Follow Snap Settings option. This makes the visual grid use the same resolution settings as the Snap to Grid function, so if you change the Snap to Grid resolution, the visual grid will change along with it.

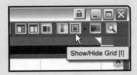

Figure 7.56 Use the Show/Hide Grid button to display a visual grid to help with note placement.

8. Choose Transport > Play (or press the spacebar) to start playback and listen to the drum pattern so far. It sounds good, but now you need to add accompanying instruments to emphasize the beat, like a snare drum part. There are two snare drum instruments available in the list: Electric Snare and Acoustic Snare. I think you should go with the Acoustic Snare sound for this example, so place a quarter note at beats 2 and 4 in the pattern for the Acoustic Snare instrument (see Figure 7.57). You should hear both the kick and snare instruments playing.

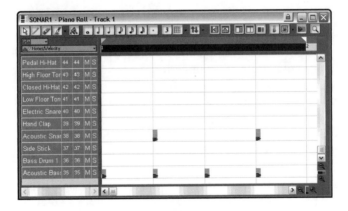

Figure 7.57 Add some acoustic snare to the drum pattern.

❊ **FIX MISTAKES**

Remember that if you make any mistakes, you can use the same editing techniques I talked about earlier to fix things. If you need to delete a note, you can use the Auto Erase tool or the Draw tool. If you place a note on the wrong beat, just use the Select tool to click and drag the note right or left along the grid. Or if you place a note in the wrong instrument row, just use the Select tool to click and drag the note up or down to the correct instrument row.

9. Now let's spice up the pattern a bit with a closed hi-hat rhythm. Instead of quarter notes, however, use sixteenth notes. Change the Snap to Grid to a sixteenth-note resolution and then place notes at every sixteenth note line on the grid using the Closed Hi-Hat instrument, as shown in Figure 7.58.

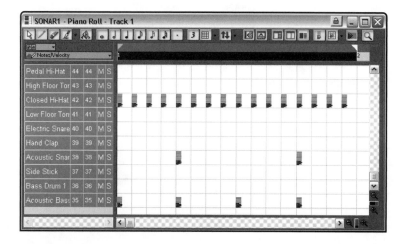

Figure 7.58 Add a rhythmic closed hi-hat part to the drum pattern.

10. The closed hi-hat part is missing something. Usually, a part like this will emphasize each beat in a pattern by playing each sixteenth note that falls on a beat a little louder than the rest. To make this happen, you need to adjust the velocity of these four notes using the Show Velocity Tails feature. By default, this feature is already activated, but to turn it on or off, just press the Y key on your computer keyboard.

11. You'll notice some vertical lines attached to each of the notes in the pattern. These lines represent the MIDI velocity for each note. To adjust the velocity of a note, use the Draw tool and just hover your mouse over the lines of a note until your mouse turns into a pointer with some vertical lines attached to it. Then click and drag your mouse up to increase the note's velocity or down to decrease the note's velocity. For this example, increase the velocity of the four closed hi-hat notes that reside right on each beat of the pattern to 127.

❋ **EVENT INSPECTOR**

Instead of using the Show Velocity Tails feature to change the velocity of each note graphically, you can make changes more precisely by selecting notes with the Select tool and then entering a new value in the Vel parameter of the Event Inspector toolbar.

12. Your new drum pattern sounds pretty good, no? I know it's basic, but I mainly wanted to show you how to use all the tools at your disposal. To create more patterns, just repeat steps 4 through 11. In step 5 just change the loop points to cover the next measure in the track (or several measures if you want to create longer drum patterns).

✿ **AUDITION DRUM INSTRUMENTS**

If you ever want to audition the entire drum track, you'll need to disable looping playback and then enable it again to continue working on your current drum pattern. A quick way to do this is to set up a key binding for the Loop On/Off function.

Also remember that as you're listening to your drum patterns, you can mute and solo individual instruments by using the M and S buttons next to each instrument in the Note Map pane. And for quick access to the drum map parameter settings for an individual instrument, just double-click the instrument.

The Pattern Brush

If you're not inclined to compose your own drum parts, then you'll really enjoy SONAR's Pattern Brush tool. Also found in the Piano Roll view (see Figure 7.59) the Pattern Brush tool creates drum parts by painting in whole drum patterns that have already been composed for you.

Figure 7.59   Access the Pattern Brush tool in the Piano Roll view.

Composing with the Pattern Brush

To compose drum parts using the Pattern Brush tool, follow these steps:

1. Set up a MIDI drum track as I explained in the "Composing Drum Tracks" section.
2. Click the down arrow to the right of the Pattern Brush button in the Piano Roll view toolbar. The first four options in the menu adjust how the Pattern Brush will work. The Velocity option specifies an exact MIDI velocity to which all your notes will be set. The Note Duration option makes all your notes use the duration specified in the Piano Roll view toolbar. Personally, I don't use those settings very much because you can achieve the same thing using the Draw tool. The Use Pattern Velocities and Use Pattern Polyphony options tell SONAR to use the MIDI velocities and rhythms from the predefined patterns, which you can choose from the remaining menu selections. So basically, you'll almost always want to have those options activated. Activate them after you've chosen a pattern, as described in the next step.

3. The lower part of the Pattern Brush menu chooses predefined drum patterns you can use to compose your drum tracks. In this example, choose Kick+Snare Patterns (D-F) > Funky 1 for your first pattern.

4. Choose the Pattern Brush tool by clicking the Pattern Brush button on the toolbar. Then click and drag your mouse from left to right over the first measure in your drum track. It doesn't matter at what vertical location you drag; the drum notes are placed automatically with the correct instruments at the correct rhythmic locations (see Figure 7.60).

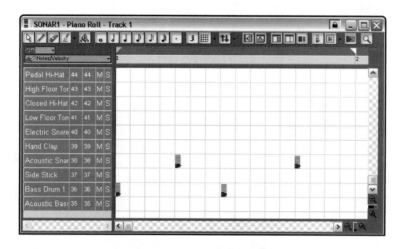

Figure 7.60 Just click and drag the Pattern Brush to create a drum part automatically.

5. Now add another instrument to the drum part by choosing a different Pattern Brush pattern. This time, try the Dumbec, Egg Shaker, Finger Bongos, and Guiro Patterns > Egg Shaker 1 pattern. Click and drag the Pattern Brush. You'll notice that this adds a Maracas instrument to the drum part.

6. Let's add one more final touch. Choose Conga Patterns > Congas 1 for the Pattern Brush pattern, and paint the instrument into the drum part (see Figure 7.61).

7. The drum part sounds pretty good, but it could use a few adjustments. The Open Hi Conga and Mute Hi Conga instruments are a bit low in volume. Double-click each instrument and set the Vel+ parameters to 36 and 45, respectively. You'll see that this is where the Vel+ and V Scale settings can come in handy.

8. You can't really hear the Mute Hi Conga instrument because it sounds at the same time as the snare drum. To fix this, activate the Select tool and drag both notes for that instrument to the left by one-sixteenth note. Just because you are using predefined patterns, that doesn't mean you can't make changes to them. Many times you'll find that you come up with something even better.

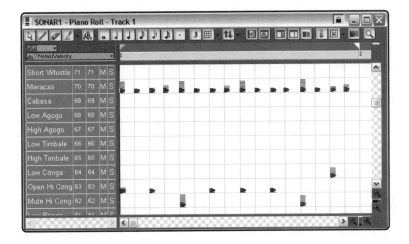

Figure 7.61 Add a conga instrument to the drum part.

You can keep adding more instruments to the drum part or add more drum parts (measures) to the drum track. The process is really intuitive. Don't be afraid to experiment. If something doesn't sound good, change it. Choose Edit > Undo and try a different pattern. Or make small adjustments like I showed you earlier. I guarantee you'll have a lot of fun with the Pattern Brush while creating your own drum tracks.

Creating Pattern Brush Patterns

After you've created some of your own drum patterns, you might want to save them for future use in other projects. You can do this by converting them into patterns that can be used with the Pattern Brush. Follow these steps to do so:

1. After you've finished creating a drum pattern, close the Piano Roll view and switch to the Track view.

2. You'll notice a clip in the Clips pane of the Track view that represents the drum pattern you just created (see Figure 7.62). Click the clip to select it and then choose Edit > Copy. Make sure the Events in Tracks option is activated in the Copy dialog box and then click OK.

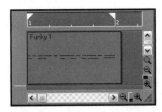

Figure 7.62 A clip in the Track view represents your newly created drum pattern.

3. Choose File > New. Then select the Pattern Brush Template and click OK. Also, close the File Info window. In the Track view of this new project, you'll see a single MIDI track with a bunch of markers placed in it. Each marker is there to represent a different pattern. You can put as many patterns in a Pattern Brush file as you'd like, but the last marker in the file always has to be an END marker.

4. Set the Now time to the beginning of the project.

5. Choose Edit > Paste, leave the Paste dialog box settings as they are, and click OK. Your drum pattern will be pasted in the place of the first pattern in the project.

6. You can add more patterns if you want, but for now just delete the rest of the pattern markers and move the END marker to the beginning of measure 2 (2:01:000), as shown in Figure 7.63. You can also change the name of the first pattern marker to something that describes the pattern. This name will be displayed later in the Pattern Brush menu.

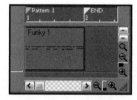

Figure 7.63 Paste your drum patterns in a new file with markers.

7. Choose File > Save As. Set the Save as Type parameter to MIDI Format 0. Type a name for the file. Also be sure to save the file in the same folder location as specified in the Patterns parameter of the Global Options > Folders dialog box. Initially, SONAR has this location set to the C:\Program Files\Cakewalk\SONAR 6 Producer Edition\Pattern Brush Patterns folder. Click Save.

Now your new Pattern Brush patterns will be displayed in the Pattern Brush menu for you to use in future projects.

Dealing with Controllers

When you open a MIDI track in the Piano Roll view, in addition to the notes in the Drum Grid and Note panes, SONAR will display the MIDI controller data for that track in the Controller pane (see Figure 7.64).

You can also have the MIDI controller data displayed as an overlay in the Note pane, if you'd rather work that way, by simply clicking the Use Controller Pane button to close the Controller pane (see Figure 7.65).

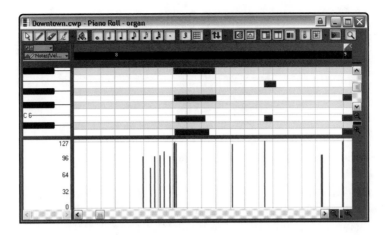

Figure 7.64 MIDI controller data for a track is displayed in the Controller pane when you open the Piano Roll view.

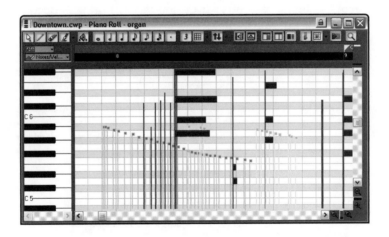

Figure 7.65 Close the Controller pane to have MIDI controller data displayed in the Note pane.

Because there are many different types of MIDI controller messages, SONAR allows you to control the type of data being displayed by using the Show/Hide MIDI Events button (see Figure 7.66). Click the left side of the button to activate or deactivate it. This will show or hide all MIDI controller data. To show or hide individual MIDI controllers, click the right side of the button and choose a controller type from the menu. You can also choose to show or hide notes or their velocities by choosing Show Notes or Velocity. The Show Clip Outlines option will display outlines of the clips that contain the MIDI notes you are editing. Finally, the Display All Continuous Events option will show all MIDI controller data for all listed tracks.

Figure 7.66   Use the Show/Hide MIDI Events button to determine what MIDI controllers will be visible.

Each controller is represented by a colored line that runs from the bottom of the Controller pane or Note pane toward the top. The height of the line designates the value of the controller, according to the ruler on the left side of the Controller pane. Unfortunately, the Note pane doesn't provide a ruler. This ruler gives you a reference for determining the value of a controller; it usually runs from 0 to 127, starting at the bottom of the Controller pane and going all the way to the top. The values can be different according to the type of controller being edited. The horizontal location of a controller designates its start time according to the Time Ruler at the top of the Piano Roll view.

❋ PITCH WHEEL

In one instance, the controllers in the Controller pane and the ruler values appear differently. If you select the pitch wheel event type for editing, you'll notice that, instead of starting at the bottom of the Controllers pane, the controllers start at the center and extend either up or down (see Figure 7.67). They do so because values for the pitch wheel range from -8192 to 0 to +8191, which you can see in the ruler values. Other than that, pitch wheel events are handled exactly the same as any other types.

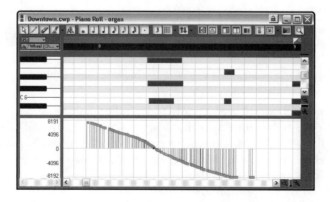

Figure 7.67   The pitch wheel is the one exception to the way controllers are displayed in the Controllers pane.

Working with Controllers

Adding, editing, and deleting controllers is similar to doing the same with notes, but with some exceptions. Here are the steps for working with controllers:

1. Click the Edit MIDI Event Type menu and choose New Value Type (see Figure 7.68).

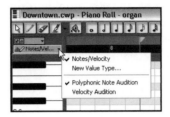

Figure 7.68 The Edit MIDI Event Type menu determines the type of data you are currently adding or editing.

2. In the MIDI Event Type dialog box, choose the kind of MIDI controller you would like to add or edit, including the Type, Value, and MIDI Channel (see Figure 7.69). For example, to edit modulation on MIDI channel 1, choose Type: Control, Value: Modulation, and Channel: Channel 1.

Figure 7.69 Use the MIDI Event Type dialog box to choose the type of MIDI controller you would like to add or edit.

3. Use the Draw tool to add MIDI controller data to the Controller pane or Note pane. You can click your left mouse button once to add a single controller event, or you can click and hold your left mouse button and drag over an area to create a series of controller events.

❊ **THE DRAW LINE TOOL**

Older versions of SONAR included another drawing tool called the *Draw Line tool*. This tool is no longer included in the Piano Roll view toolbar, but it's still a part of SONAR. The Draw Line tool creates a smooth series of controllers starting at one value and smoothly increasing or decreasing to another value. To use the Draw Line tool, activate the Draw tool. Then hold down the Shift key and click and hold your mouse at the controller value you want to begin with. Now drag your mouse to a different location. You'll see a line appear as you drag. When you release your mouse button, SONAR will add a smooth series of controllers from the first point to the second point.

❊ ❊ ❊

4. If you want to erase any controller events, use the Auto Erase tool. To erase a single controller event, click the small square at the top of the event. To erase multiple events at once, click and hold the left mouse button and then drag your mouse over the events you want to erase.

5. To edit controller events, use the Select tool. To edit a single controller event, click the small square at the top of the event. While holding down your mouse button, move up or down to change the value of the controller. Move left or right to change the position of the controller. To edit multiple events, click and drag your mouse over the events to select them. Then use any of SONAR's editing functions to edit those events, just like you would with notes.

6. To listen to the data, select the Scrub tool and click and drag your mouse over the events you want to hear.

7. To work with a different controller, go through steps 1 through 5 again.

8. If you want to go back to editing a controller that you've already created, use the Edit MIDI Event Type Menu to select the controller.

9. When you're finished editing controllers, you can go back to working with notes by clicking the Edit MIDI Event Type menu and choosing Notes/Velocity.

Inserting Controllers

SONAR provides one other way to add a smooth series of controller values to your tracks—the Insert Series of Controllers function. I find using the Draw Line tool in the Piano Roll view much more intuitive, but if you need to add controllers over a very long span of time, the Insert Series of Controllers function can be useful. To use it, just follow these steps:

1. Select the track to which you want to add the controller values. You can do so either in the Piano Roll view or the Track view.

2. Select Insert > Controllers to open the Insert Series of Controllers dialog box (see Figure 7.70).

3. In the Insert section, choose the type of controller you want to add, the number of the controller (if appropriate), and the MIDI channel you want the controller to use.

4. In the Value Range section, type numbers for the Begin and End parameters. These numbers determine the values of the controller over the range of the series. For example, if you're using a volume controller type, you can have an instrument get louder over time by typing a smaller value for Begin and a larger value for End. If you want the instrument to get softer over time, you type a larger value for Begin and a smaller value for End.

5. In the Time Range section, type the measure, beat, and tick values for the location in the project where you want the series of controllers to be inserted.

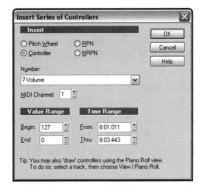

Figure 7.70   Using the Insert Series of Controllers dialog box, you can add a series of controllers that change smoothly from one value to another.

✳ **TIME RANGE SELECTION**

You can set the Time Range parameters before you open the Insert Series of Controllers dialog box by dragging your mouse pointer over the Time Ruler in either the Piano Roll view or the Track view. This action sets up a selection within the project that is used automatically to set the From and Thru values of the Time Range parameters.

Bank/Patch Change

The one type of data that the Piano Roll view doesn't allow you to manipulate is the bank/patch change. This type of event is useful when you want the sound of your MIDI instrument to change automatically during playback of your project. SONAR provides an Insert Bank/Patch Change function that you can use if you need it.

Using the Insert Bank/Patch Change function is very simple. You just follow these steps:

1. Click the number of the track in the Track pane into which you want to insert the bank/patch change.
2. Set the Now time to the measure, beat, and tick at which you want the bank/patch change to occur.
3. Choose Insert > Bank/Patch Change to open the Bank/Patch Change dialog box.
4. Choose a bank select method, bank, and patch from the appropriate lists.
5. Click OK.

SONAR will insert a bank/patch change event in the track at the Now time you specified. By the way, you can insert (and also edit) bank/patch change events by using the Event List view.

The Inline Piano Roll View

In addition to the Piano Roll view, SONAR edits MIDI note and controller data from within the Track view with the Inline Piano Roll view feature. Basically, this is like having the Piano Roll view integrated into the Track view. So why would you still need the Piano Roll view? Well, one reason is that the Piano Roll view allows you to edit data from multiple tracks simultaneously within the same display. In the Track view, the Inline Piano Roll view feature is limited to each individual track. Other than that, both the Piano Roll view and the Inline Piano Roll view work in almost exactly the same way with only minor differences—one of which is where to access the associated parameters, as shown in Figure 7.71.

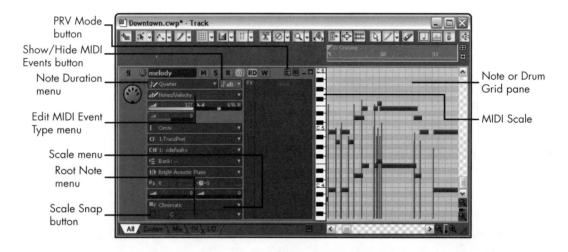

Figure 7.71 The Inline Piano Roll view parameters are accessed differently from the Piano Roll view.

Here are the steps needed to use the Inline Piano Roll view feature:

1. In the Track view toolbar, you'll see the Inline Piano Roll tools (see Figure 7.72). This section of the toolbar is used to access the Select, Draw, and Auto Erase tools (the same tools from the Piano Roll view), plus some other features.

2. To activate the Inline Piano Roll view feature for a single MIDI track, click the PRV Mode button for the corresponding track. To activate the feature for all MIDI tracks, either click the PRV Mode toolbar button or choose Tracks > Inline PRV > PRV mode. You'll notice that the Clips pane turns into the Note pane or Drum Grid pane, depending on the type of track you are editing.

3. The MIDI Scale (shown to the left of the Note pane) doubles as the Keyboard pane, Note Map pane, and Controller ruler. Right-click inside the MIDI Scale and choose Notes (to edit melodic and drum tracks) or 7Bit Values (to edit controllers).

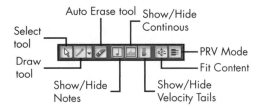

Figure 7.72 Use the Inline Piano Roll section of the Track view toolbar to access the MIDI note and controller editing tools.

4. The MIDI Scale is also used for zooming. Right-click the MIDI Scale and choose Fit Content from the menu to fit that track's content into the current display. To fit the content for all tracks, either click the Fit Content toolbar button or choose Tracks > Inline PRV > Fit Content. In addition, you can left-click and drag up or down within the MIDI Scale to change the zoom factor for the track.

5. To set a melodic scale for the current track, click the Scale Snap button to activate it. Then use the Root Note and Scale menus to choose a scale.

6. If you want to add or edit notes, click the Edit MIDI Event Type menu and choose Notes/ Velocity. Then click the Note Duration menu to choose the duration for the notes you want to add. To add or edit notes, click the Draw Tool, Select Tool, or Auto Erase toolbar buttons. You can add, edit, and select notes using the same procedures as you would in the Piano Roll view. One exception is when selecting notes using the MIDI Scale. With the Select tool activated, hold down the Shift key on your computer keyboard and then click a note in the MIDI Scale to select all notes of the same pitch. You can also drag your mouse to select a range of pitches.

7. If you want to add or edit controllers, click the Edit MIDI Event Type menu and choose New Value Type to set the type of controller with which you would like to work. To add or edit controllers, click the Draw Tool, Select Tool, or Auto Erase toolbar buttons. You can add, edit, and select controllers using the same procedures as you would in the Piano Roll view.

8. When working with both note and controller data or multiple controllers, use the Show/ Hide MIDI Events button to determine what types of events will be visible. This allows you to temporarily hide some events that may be overlapping and causing difficulty when editing.

You can keep the Inline Piano Roll feature activated as you work with your project and easily switch back to the regular Clips pane with a quick click of the PRV Mode button or menu.

Using the Event List View

For the most precise data editing (meaning individual events and their properties), you have to use the Event List view (see Figure 7.73). Using this view, you can add, edit, and delete any kind of event in any track within the entire project. The Event List view doesn't resemble any of the other views; instead of providing a graphical representation of your data, it provides a numerical representation, which you can edit and view. The Event List view displays events as one long list of columns and rows (similar to a spreadsheet). Each row holds the data for a single event, and columns separate the event's different properties.

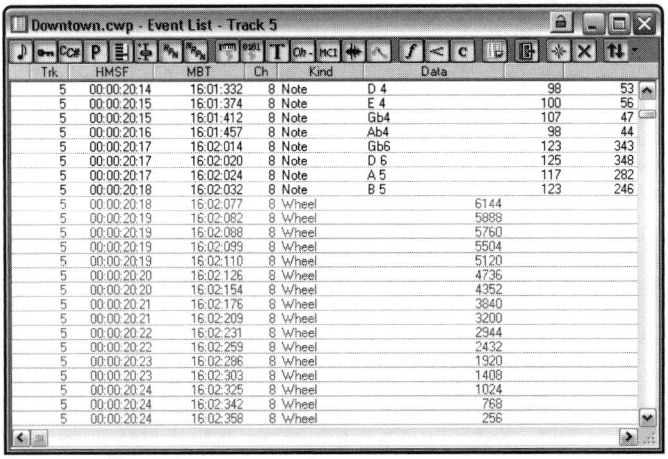

Figure 7.73 You can use the Event List view to edit events numerically using a spreadsheet-like format.

You can use the first column in the list to select events. The second column (titled *Trk*) shows the track number in which an event is stored. The third column (titled *HMSF*) shows the start time of an event in hours, minutes, seconds, and frames. The fourth column (titled *MBT*) also shows the start time of an event, but as measures, beats, and ticks. If an event is a MIDI event, the fifth column (titled *Ch*) shows the MIDI channel to which that event is assigned. The sixth column (titled *Kind*) shows the type of data an event holds (for example, a MIDI note event). The seventh column (titled *Data*) actually spans the seventh, eighth, and ninth columns (the last three), and these columns hold the data values associated with each event. For instance, for a MIDI note event, the seventh column would hold the pitch, the eighth column would hold the velocity, and the ninth column would hold the duration for the note.

Because the Event List view doesn't have any graphical data to contend with, it doesn't provide any Snap to Grid, Zoom, Time Ruler, or Marker features. It does scroll the list up and down and left and right so you can access all the events shown. It also provides a toolbar full of buttons. One button that you'll recognize, though, is the Pick Tracks button. Just as with the other views, the Event List view displays the data from multiple tracks at once.

Opening the View

You open the Event List view via the Track view. You simply select one or more tracks and then select Views > Event List or right-click one of the selected tracks and choose Views > Event List.

Filtering Events

There are many different types of events available in SONAR, and sometimes having to wade through them all in the Event List view can get a bit confusing, especially when you're displaying the data from multiple tracks. To help you deal with the problem, the Event List view filters each of the event types from being displayed. This filtering does not affect the data at all; it just helps unclutter the list display if that's what you need.

The first 18 buttons on the toolbar represent different event types. Initially, all these buttons are set so that all event types are shown in the list when you open the Event List view. By clicking a button, you can filter out its associated event type from the list. You can click as many of the buttons as you want to filter out multiple types of events. Clicking a button again turns off its associated event type filter, so the events can be shown in the list again. To see the type of event with which each button is associated, just hover your mouse pointer over a button until the pop-up text appears, showing the name of the event type.

The Event Manager

If you find it easier to deal with the event types by name rather than by using the buttons, you can use the Event Manager. Press V to open the Event Manager dialog box (see Figure 7.74).

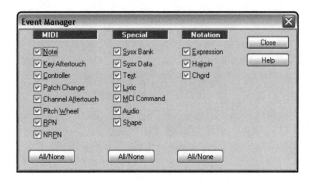

Figure 7.74   You can use the Event Manager dialog box to filter event types by name.

Initially, all the event types are activated so they will be displayed in the list. To filter out a certain type, just click it to remove its check mark. You can also use the All/None buttons to quickly activate or deactivate groups of event types. Click the Close button when you're done.

EVENT TYPE LIST

You can also filter out event types by simply right-clicking anywhere in the Event List and then selecting an event type from the list.

Editing Events

If you've ever used a spreadsheet application, you'll be right at home with editing events in the Event List view. To navigate through the list, use the arrow keys on your computer keyboard. These keys move a small rectangular cursor through the list. This cursor represents the Now time. As you move the cursor up and down through the list, the Now time changes to reflect the time of the event upon which the cursor is positioned. You also can move the cursor (which I'll call the Now time cursor from this point on) left and right to access the different event parameters.

Changing Event Parameters

To change an event parameter, just position the Now time cursor over the parameter, type a new value, and then press the Enter key to accept the new value.

 MOUSE EDITING

You also can increase or decrease the value of an event parameter by double-clicking it and then clicking the little plus or minus buttons, respectively.

You can change the start time in the HMSF or MBT columns, the MIDI channel, the type of event, and most or all of the values in the data columns, depending on the type of event you're editing. The only thing you can't change is the track number of an event.

Changing the type of an event via the parameter in the Kind column is a bit different from changing the values of the other parameters. Instead of typing a new value, you either must press the Enter key or double-click the parameter. This action opens the Kind of Event dialog box (see Figure 7.75). The Kind of Event dialog box displays a list of all the event types available. Select the type of event you want to use and then click OK.

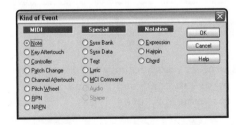

Figure 7.75 *You use the Kind of Event dialog box to change the type of an event.*

Selecting Events

If you ever need to copy, cut, or paste events in the Event List view, you have to select them first. To select a single event, click in the first column of the row representing the event. You also can select more than one event by dragging your mouse pointer in the first column of the list. If you want to remove a selection, click or drag a second time.

Inserting Events

You can add new events to the list by using the Insert function. It works as follows:

1. Position the Now time cursor at the point in the list at which you want to insert a new event.

 POSITION THE NOW TIME CURSOR

Setting the position of the Now time cursor in the Event List view isn't very intuitive. Because the list gives you such a specific close-up look at your data, it's sometimes hard to tell where in your project the Now time cursor is pointing. You might find it easier to use one of the other views (such as the Track view or the Piano Roll view) to position the Now time cursor. That way, you get a graphical representation of your project and a better feel for the placement of the cursor. Then you can simply switch to the Event view, and the cursor will be positioned exactly at the point where you want to insert the new event (or at least very close to it).

2. Press the Insert key or click the Insert Event button in the toolbar (the one with the star shown on it). SONAR will create a new event in the list, using the same parameter values as the event upon which the Now time was positioned.

3. Edit the event parameters.

 EVENT KIND HELP

When you're changing the type of event using the Kind parameter, the values in the Data columns change according to the type of event you choose. For a list of all the types of events available, along with all their associated parameters, look in the SONAR Help file under Editing MIDI Events and Controllers > The Event List View > Event List Buttons and Overview.

Special Events

There are two types of events in SONAR that you can access only via the Event List view. You can't manipulate them in any of the other views. The first one, called a *text event*, adds notes to the data in your project. I'm not talking about musical notes; I'm talking about text notes. (You know, like those little sticky notes you have plastered all over your studio.) Text events can act as little reminders to yourself in case you need to keep track of some kind of special information in certain parts of your project. I haven't had a lot of use for text events, but it's nice to know they're available if I need them.

The other type of special event is called the *MCI Command event*, or the *Windows Media Control Interface (MCI) Command event*. You can use the MCI Command event to control the multimedia-related hardware and software in your computer system. For example, by setting the type of an event to MCI Command and setting the event's Data parameter to PLAY CDAUDIO, you can make the audio CD inside your CD-ROM drive start to play. You also can use MCI Command events to play audio files, video files, and more. But the problem is that you can't synchronize any of these files to the music in your project, so you can't really use these events for too many things. In addition, the subject of MCI commands can be complex and is well beyond the scope of this chapter. If you want to find more information, take a look at http://msdn.microsoft.com and do a search for the term *MCI*.

Deleting Events

Erasing events from the list is as easy as it gets. Just move the Now time cursor to the row of the event you want to remove and click the Delete Event button on the toolbar (the one with the big red X on it). Alternatively, you can press the Delete key.

If you want to delete more than one event, select the events you want to remove and then select Edit > Delete to open the Delete dialog box. The parameters in this dialog box work the same way as I described them in the Track view section of this chapter.

Playing

If you want to quickly preview the event you're currently editing, you can have SONAR play back that single event by holding down the Ctrl+Shift keys and then pressing the spacebar. If you continue holding the Ctrl+Shift keys, each press of the spacebar will scroll down through the list and play each event. This capability is especially useful for testing MIDI note events.

PRINT THE EVENT LIST

You can print a hard copy reference of the Event List if you have a printer connected to your computer system. While the Event List view is open, just select File > Print to print a copy of the list. You also can preview the list before you print it by choosing File > Print Preview.

Using the Tempo View

You learned how to set the initial tempo for a project by using the Tempo toolbar in Chapter 4. But in addition to the initial project tempo, you also can have the tempo change automatically during playback. To allow you to specify tempo changes in a project, SONAR provides the Tempo view (see Figure 7.76). The Tempo view has some similarities to the Piano Roll view in that it displays a graphical representation of the data you need to manipulate—in this case, tempo. The Tempo view shows the tempo as a line graph with the horizontal axis denoting time (via the Time Ruler) and the vertical axis denoting tempo value.

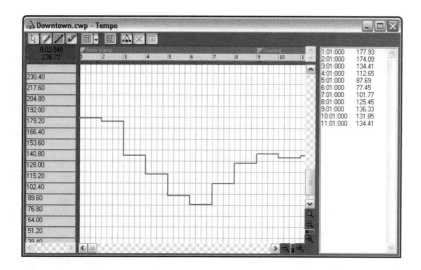

Figure 7.76 The Tempo view displays the tempo in a project as a line graph.

More precisely, the Tempo view consists of three major sections: the toolbar (located at the top of the view, containing all the view's related controls), the Tempo pane (located in the main part of the view, displaying all the tempo changes in the project as a line graph), and the Tempo Change pane (located at the right of the view, showing a list of all the tempo changes within the project). Because tempo affects the entire project, no track selection tools are available here.

Because the Tempo view shows tempo changes graphically, it has scroll bars and zoom tools just like in the Piano Roll view. And these tools work the same way here. In addition, this view provides a Snap to Grid function, which is represented by the Grid button on the toolbar. The Tempo view also contains a marker area and a Time Ruler located just above the Tempo pane. Along the left of the Tempo pane are the tempo measurements, which show the value of the tempo changes displayed in the line graph.

Opening the View

To open the Tempo view, choose Views > Tempo. You don't need to select a track, clip, or anything else. For a new project (or a project that doesn't contain any tempo changes), the Tempo view will display a straight horizontal line located vertically on the graph at the tempo measurement value that corresponds to the current tempo setting for the project. For instance, if your project has a main tempo of 100, then the line is shown at a tempo measurement of 100 on the graph. In addition to the horizontal line, a single entry in the Tempo Change pane shows the measure, beat, and tick at which the tempo event occurs, along with the tempo value itself. In this example, it is 1:01:000 for the measure, beat, and tick, and 100 for the tempo value.

Editing Tempo Changes

Just as you can edit controller messages graphically in the Piano Roll view, you can use the Tempo view to edit tempo changes. Also, the Tempo view provides Select, Draw, Draw Line, and Erase tools. All these tools work the same way they do in the Piano Roll view. You can use the Select tool to select individual changes and groups of tempo changes by clicking and dragging. Using the Draw tool, you can literally draw in tempo changes on the line graph in the Tempo pane. The Draw Line tool enables you to create smooth tempo changes from one value to another by clicking and dragging. Using the Erase tool, you can erase single and multiple tempo changes by clicking and dragging. As you draw and erase within the Tempo pane, the line graph will change its shape accordingly to display how the tempo will change over time as the project plays. An increase in the tempo (*accelerando*, in musical terms) is shown as an incline in the line graph, and a decrease in tempo (*ritardando*, in musical terms) is shown as a decline in the line graph.

The Tempo Change Pane

As I mentioned earlier, tempo changes also are listed numerically in the Tempo Change pane. Luckily, you can edit them there, too. I find it easier and more accurate to add and edit tempo changes via the Tempo Change pane than to draw them in.

Inserting Tempo Changes

To add a new tempo change to the list, follow these steps:

1. Set the Now time to the measure, beat, and tick at which you want the tempo change to occur.

2. Click the Insert Tempo button on the toolbar (the one with the plus sign on it) or press the Insert key to open the Tempo dialog box (see Figure 7.77).

Figure 7.77 In the Tempo dialog box, you can add and edit tempo events.

3. Enter a value for the Tempo parameter. You can also tap out a tempo by clicking the Click Here to Tap Tempo button. When you click repeatedly on the button, SONAR will measure the time between each click and calculate the tempo at which you're clicking. It will then enter the value into the Tempo parameter automatically.

> **❈ TAP THE SPACEBAR**
>
> Instead of using your mouse to click the Click Here to Tap Tempo button, you might find it easier (and more accurate) to use the spacebar. Click the button with your mouse once to highlight it, and then use your spacebar to tap out a tempo value.

4. Make sure the Insert a New Tempo option is activated.

5. You shouldn't have to enter a value for the Starting at Time parameter because you set the Now time earlier. However, you can change it here if you want.

6. Click OK.

SONAR will add the new tempo change and display it in the Tempo Change pane, as well as on the graph in the Tempo pane.

Deleting and Editing Tempo Changes

You can edit or remove a tempo change from the list by using the appropriate toolbar buttons. First, select the tempo change you want to edit or delete by clicking it in the list. If you want to delete the tempo change, click the Delete Tempo button on the toolbar (the one with the big red X on it) or press the Delete key. If you want to edit the tempo change, click the Tempo Properties button on the toolbar (the very last button at the right end of the toolbar) or press P. This action will open the Tempo dialog box. Make any changes necessary, as per the same settings I described for inserting a new tempo change.

Using the Tempo Commands

In addition to the Tempo view (and the Tempo toolbar), SONAR provides two other tempo-related functions. The Insert Tempo Change function works the same as adding a new tempo change in the Tempo Change pane in the Tempo view. However, you can use this function from any of the other views. To access it, just choose Insert > Tempo Change to open the Tempo dialog box (which you learned about earlier).

SONAR also provides a function that inserts a series of tempos so you can have the tempo change smoothly from one value to another over time. Using it is similar to using the Draw Line tool in the Tempo view, but here you specify your values numerically. You use this function as follows:

1. Choose Insert > Series of Tempos to open the Insert Series of Tempos dialog box (see Figure 7.78).

2. In the Tempo Range section, enter a beginning and an ending value for the range of tempos to be inserted.

3. In the Time Range section, enter a beginning and an ending value for the range of time in your project in which you want the tempo changes to occur.

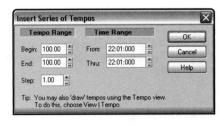

Figure 7.78 You can change the tempo smoothly from one value to another by using the Insert Series of Tempos dialog box.

TIME RANGE SELECTION

If you make a selection by dragging your mouse pointer in the Time Ruler of the Track view, for instance, before you select Insert > Series of Tempos, the Time Range values in the Insert Series of Tempos dialog box will be set according to your selection. This shortcut makes it easier to see where in your Project the tempo changes will be inserted.

4. For the Step parameter, enter a beat and tick value for how often you want a tempo change to be inserted within the Time Range you specified. For example, if you enter a value of 1.00, then the Insert Series of Tempos function will insert a new tempo change at every beat within the Time Range you specified.

5. Click OK.

SONAR will insert a smooth series of tempo changes, starting and ending with the Tempo Range values you specified within the time range you specified. Any existing tempo changes are overwritten.

8 Exploring the Editing Tools

In Chapter 7, you learned about some of the essential editing features found in SONAR, including all the views (and the tools they provide), as well as how to manipulate your data via copy, cut, paste, move, delete, and other functions. Although these features provide a lot of power, you might be asking yourself, "Is that all there is?" Not likely! In addition to its fundamental tools, SONAR provides a full arsenal of sophisticated editing features. Some can be used to process audio data, some to process MIDI data, and some to process both kinds of data. One aspect they all have in common, however, is that they can be accessed in more than one view (similar to the copy, cut, and paste functions). As you learned previously, for MIDI data, you'll use the Track, Piano Roll, Staff, and Event views, and for audio data, you'll use the Track view.

This chapter will do the following:

- ❈ Explain advanced data selection.
- ❈ Show you how to change the loudness of audio clips.
- ❈ Describe equalization.
- ❈ Explain quantization.
- ❈ Cover transposition.
- ❈ Show you how to use various advanced timing features.

Advanced Data Selection

You can select the data in your project in each of the views by using some basic clicking and dragging techniques. SONAR also provides some more sophisticated data selection features that enable you to use time, as well as individual event properties, for more precise editing.

Selecting a Range of Data by Time

If you ever need to select a range of data in a project that is based on time rather than data that is neatly tucked away in individual clips, you can choose Edit > Select > By Time to do so. For example, suppose that you need to copy the data in Track 8 that falls between the range of 4:2:010 (measure, beat, tick) and 13:3:050. But what if that data is stored in multiple clips within that range, and the clips don't neatly start and end at the beginning and ending times you specified? That's the kind of situation for which this feature is useful. It works like this:

1. Choose Edit > Select > By Time to open the Select by Time dialog box (see Figure 8.1).

Figure 8.1   You can use the Select by Time dialog box to define a time range within your project in which data will be selected for editing.

2. Type the beginning (From) and ending (Thru) measure, beat, and tick values to define the range of time you want to select. Then click OK. You use this dialog box to select a range of time within your project, but it doesn't select any actual data. For that, you need to select the tracks you want to edit.

❋ **RANGE SELECTION USING MARKERS**

While editing either the From or Thru parameter in the Select by Time dialog box, press the F5 key on your computer keyboard. This will open the Markers dialog box. Here you can select a predefined time to use for either of the parameters.

3. In the Track view, select the tracks that contain the data you want to edit.

❋ **USE THE TIME RULER**

You also can make time selections in any of the views by simply clicking and dragging on the Time Ruler or by Alt-dragging within a clip. However, by choosing Edit > Select > By Time, you can make more precise selections because you can enter the exact numerical values for the measures, beats, and ticks that define the range.

Selecting a Range of Data by Filter

For really precise editing tasks, you can choose Edit > Select > By Filter. Using this approach, you can refine a selection that you've already made with any of the other methods discussed previously. For instance, if you select some clips or tracks in the Track view, you can choose Edit > Select > By Filter to zero in (so to speak) your selection even further on the individual events within those clips and tracks based on their event properties.

Suppose that you have a MIDI track in which you want to change all the notes with a pitch of C4 to C5. You can easily select only those notes by choosing Edit > Select > By Filter, and then you can change their pitch by using the Transpose feature. All the C4 pitches are then changed to C5, but none of the other notes in the track are affected. This feature works as follows:

1. Select the clips, tracks, or set of events you want to use as your initial selection. You can select clips and tracks in the Track view or a group of events in the Piano Roll view, Event view, or Staff view.

2. Choose Edit > Select > By Filter to open the Event Filter - Select Some dialog box (see Figure 8.2).

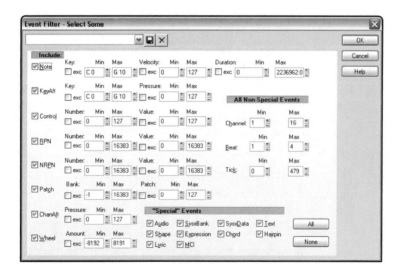

Figure 8.2   You can use the Event Filter - Select Some dialog box to set the criteria for the type of data you want to have selected.

3. Does this dialog box look familiar? The Event Filter - Select Some dialog box is the same as Chapter 5's Event Filter - Search dialog box. The same information about how to use all the options applies here, so go ahead and set the options as you want.

> ❄ **SAVE A SELECT PRESET**
>
> As with the Event Filter - Search dialog box, the Event Filter - Select Some dialog box saves presets for instant access to your favorite settings. By the way, presets are also available in many of the features that you'll learn about later in this chapter.

4. Click OK.

SONAR will search through the data in your initial selection, find the events that fall under the filter parameters you specified, and then select those events, leaving any other events alone. If you want to refine your selection even further, just choose Edit > Select > By Filter again on the previous selection results.

Some Selection Applications

I've had many people ask me how to go about deleting specific notes or data within a MIDI track, while at the same time leaving other data in the track alone. Here's an example of how you can do that:

1. Select the clips, tracks, or set of events you want to use as your initial selection. You can select clips and tracks in the Track view or a group of events in the Piano Roll view, Event view, or Staff view.
2. Choose Edit > Select > By Filter to open the Event Filter - Select Some dialog box.
3. Click the None button to deactivate all the available options.
4. Activate the options for the type of data you want to delete. For example, if you want to delete all notes with the value of C5 within a track, activate the Note option. Then set the Key Min and Key Max parameters to C5. Leave all the other parameters as they are.
5. Click OK. This selects all the notes with a value of C5 in your initial selection.
6. Choose Edit > Delete to open the Delete dialog box.
7. Set the appropriate options. For this example, just make sure the Events in Tracks option is activated so the selected notes will be deleted.
8. Click OK.

SONAR will delete all the selected data from your initial selection. In this case, all the notes with a value of C5 have been deleted. You can use this procedure for any other kinds of specific data deletions as well. You also can use it to manipulate selected data in other ways. For example, instead of deleting all the C5 notes, maybe you want to transpose them. In that case, instead of using the Delete function, you would use the Transpose function by choosing Process > Transpose in step 6 of the preceding steps.

Advanced Audio Editing

Using the cut, copy, paste, and slip editing tools in the Track view, you can manipulate the data in your audio tracks in a variety of ways. SONAR also provides a number of advanced features you can use to adjust the volume, get rid of DC offset, and even reverse the data within audio clips. You access all these features by choosing Process > Audio.

Removing DC Offset

Depending on the quality of your sound card, your audio may not get recorded as accurately as it should. Many times (especially with less expensive sound cards, such as the Sound Blaster), an electrical mismatch may occur between a sound card and the input device. When this happens, an excess of current is added to the incoming signal, and the resulting audio waveform is offset from the zero axis. This is known as *DC offset*. To remove DC offset from existing audio data, do the following:

1. Select the audio data from which you want to remove the DC offset. If you want to process all the audio in your project, choose Edit > Select > All (or press Ctrl + A).

2. Choose Process > Audio > Remove DC Offset to open the Remove DC Offset dialog box (see Figure 8.3).

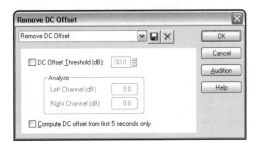

Figure 8.3 Remove DC offset from audio data via the Remove DC Offset dialog box.

3. To have SONAR automatically detect and remove any DC offset in your audio data, leave the DC Offset Threshold parameter deactivated.

4. If you don't want SONAR to process the audio below a certain volume level, activate the DC Offset Threshold parameter and enter a value (in Decibels). Anything below that value will not be processed.

5. If you are processing a lot of audio data, activate the Compute DC Offset from First 5 Seconds Only option. This instructs SONAR to look only at the first five seconds of audio data when determining how much DC offset it contains.

❄ **DC OFFSET STATS**

To manually find out the amount of DC offset in your audio data, click the Audition button in the Remove DC Offset dialog box. Then click the Stop button. The Analyze section of the dialog box will display the amount of DC offset present.

❄ **ACCURATE OFFSET DETECTION**

Activating the Compute DC Offset from First 5 Seconds Only option usually provides accurate results. However, if your audio data starts off with a long period of silence or the volume of the data is gradually faded in, you should deactivate this option. In these circumstances, with the option activated, SONAR does not accurately detect the amount of DC offset.

6. Click OK.

The DC offset in your audio data is removed.

❄ **ALWAYS REMOVE DC OFFSET**

If you have existing audio data and are not sure whether it contains DC offset, you should always process the data with the Remove DC Offset function before you do any other kind of editing or processing. If you don't, editing and processing can introduce noise and other anomalies into your data.

❄ **REMOVE DURING RECORDING**

In addition to removing DC offset from existing data, SONAR can remove DC offset during recording. Choose Options > Audio > Advanced. Then activate the Remove DC Offset During Recording option. Click OK. SONAR will now use the settings from the Remove DC Offset dialog box to remove DC offset from any audio data that you record.

Adjusting Audio Volume

If you ever need to adjust the volume of an audio clip, you can use a number of different SONAR features to increase or decrease the volume of your data.

The Gain Feature

Using the Gain feature, you can increase or decrease the volume of audio data by an amount that you specify. You can also use this feature to convert stereo audio into mono audio and even swap the channels of stereo audio. Here is how the Gain feature works:

1. Choose Process > Audio > Gain to open the Gain dialog box (see Figure 8.4).
2. In the New Left Channel section, adjust the From Left and From Right parameters. These parameters determine the amount of left/right original audio that will be added to the

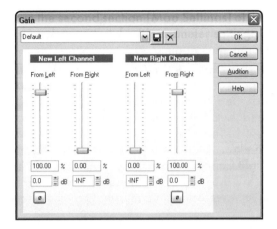

Figure 8.4 Use the Gain feature to change the volume, phase, and stereo interleave of audio data.

left channel processed audio. If you simply want to change the volume of the audio, adjust the From Left parameter to either boost or cut the volume and set the From Right parameter to 0.00%. If you want to convert stereo audio to mono, set both the From Left and From Right parameters to 100%. If you want to swap stereo channels, set the From Left parameter to 0.00% and the From Right parameter to 100%.

3. In the New Right Channel section, adjust the From Left and From Right parameters. These parameters determine the amount of left/right original audio that will be added to the right channel processed audio. If you simply want to change the volume of the audio, set the From Left parameter to 0.00% and adjust the From Right parameter to either boost or cut the volume. If you want to convert stereo audio to mono, set both the From Left and From Right parameters to 100%. If you want to swap stereo channels, set the From Left parameter to 100% and the From Right parameter to 0.00%.

❄ **CLIPPING AND DISTORTION**

Be careful not to set the input level too high during the recording process because it could overload the input and cause your audio to be distorted. Well, when you're raising the volume of audio data, you also have to be careful not to raise it too high because it can cause *clipping*. Clipping occurs when SONAR attempts to raise the amplitude of audio data higher than 100 percent. The top and bottom of the waveform become clipped, and the audio sounds distorted when you play it. So be careful when using the Gain feature. Be sure to keep an eye on the amplitude levels of your audio waveforms and remember to listen to your audio data right after you increase its volume to see whether it sounds okay. If you hear distortion, use Undo to remove the volume change.

4. Click the Audition button to hear how your audio will sound before you have SONAR make any actual changes to the data. If you don't like what you hear, click Stop and adjust the previous parameters again.

5. After adjusting the levels in the New Left Channel and New Right Channel sections, click the Audition button again. This time, listen to determine if the audio sounds "hollow." This usually happens due to phase cancellation, which occurs when one audio waveform increases in volume and the other decreases in volume at exactly the same time with the same amount. Because of this phenomenon, they cancel each other out, making the mixed audio sound hollow. If this occurs, try activating the Invert Left Channel Phase option or the Invert Right Channel Phase option, but not both. You can do so by clicking the buttons located below the New Left Channel and New Right Channel sections. These options invert the audio waveform and can usually fix the phase cancellation problem.

6. Click OK.

The Normalize Feature

Like the Gain feature, the Normalize feature also raises the volume of audio, but in a different way. Instead of simply increasing the volume, Normalize first scans the audio waveform to find its highest amplitude level. It subtracts that amplitude level from the maximum level, which is 100 percent (or a maximum level that you set). Normalize then takes that value and uses it to increase the volume of the audio data. So when all is said and done, the highest amplitude in the waveform is 100 percent (or a maximum level that you set), and all the other amplitude values are increased.

In other words, if an audio waveform has its highest amplitude value at 80 percent, and you set a normalize level of 100 percent, Normalize subtracts that value from 100 percent to get 20 percent. It then increases the volume of the audio data by 20 percent, so the highest amplitude value is 100 percent and all the other amplitude values are 20 percent higher. Basically, you can use Normalize to raise the volume of audio data to the highest it can be without causing any clipping.

To use Normalize, do the following:

1. Select the audio data that you want to normalize.

2. Choose Process > Audio > Normalize to open the Normalize dialog box (see Figure 8.5).

3. Adjust the Normalize level parameter, which sets the highest amplitude level to where you want your audio to be normalized. More often than not, you want to set this to 100%, but if you plan to do any additional editing or processing to your data, you should set this parameter to a lower level, such as 50% or –6 dB, because additional processing can raise the amplitude and cause clipping.

4. Click the Audition button to hear how your audio will sound before you have SONAR make any actual changes to the data.

5. Click OK.

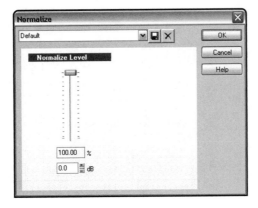

Figure 8.5 You can normalize the amplitude of your audio data using the Normalize feature.

The Fade Features

If you want to get a little more creative with your volume changes, you can build much more complex volume changes by using the Fade/Envelope feature as follows:

> ❈ **FADE-IN AND FADE-OUT**
>
> A *fade-in* is a gradual and smooth increase from a low volume (loudness) to a higher volume. This increase in volume is also called a *crescendo* in musical terms. A *fade-out* is the exact opposite—a gradual and smooth decrease from a higher volume to a lower volume. In musical terms, this decrease in volume is called a *decrescendo*.

1. Select the audio data to which you want to apply the fade. Then choose Process > Audio > Fade/Envelope to open the Fade/Envelope dialog box (see Figure 8.6). The dialog box displays a graph. The left side of the graph displays amplitude values, 0 to 100 percent from bottom to top. Inside the graph is a line, which represents the fade that will be applied to your selected audio data. If you look at the line from left to right, the left end of the line represents the beginning of your audio data selection, and the right end of the line represents the end of your audio data selection. When you open the dialog box, the line runs from the bottom left to the top right of the graph. If you leave it this way, a straight linear fade-in will be applied to your audio data because, as you look at the graph, the left end of the line is set at 0 percent, and the right end of the line is set at 100 percent. Therefore, the volume of the audio data would begin at 0 percent and fade all the way up to 100 percent.

2. You can change the shape of the fade line in one of two ways. You can select one of the six available presets from the drop-down list at the top of the dialog box. You can

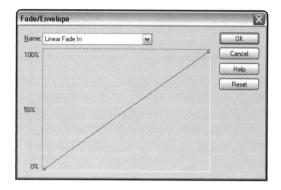

Figure 8.6 You can use the Fade/Envelope dialog box to apply fades to your audio data.

change the fade line graphically by clicking and dragging the small squares at the ends of the line. These squares are called *nodes*.

3. If you want to create some really complex fades, you can add more nodes by clicking anywhere on the fade line. The more nodes you add, the more flexibility you'll have in changing the shape of the line (see Figure 8.7).

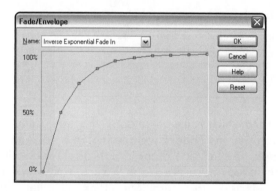

Figure 8.7 You can create some really complex fades by adding more nodes.

4. After you've finished setting up the graph the way you want it, click OK.

In addition to the Fade/Envelope feature (which allows you to apply destructive fades to your data), SONAR applies nondestructive fades. To apply a fade nondestructively, follow these steps:

1. If you want to create a fade-in for an audio clip, position your mouse in the upper-left corner of the clip until the shape of the mouse changes to a triangle. Then click and drag the mouse toward the right end of the clip to define the fade, as shown in Figure 8.8.

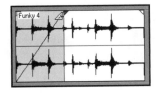

Figure 8.8 Apply a nondestructive fade-in to a clip by clicking in the upper-left corner of the clip and dragging toward the right.

2. If you want to create a fade-out for an audio clip, position your mouse in the upper-right corner of the clip until the shape of the mouse changes to a triangle. Then click and drag the mouse toward the left end of the clip to define the fade.

3. You also can define the shape of a fade if you would rather not use the straight linear process. SONAR provides three choices: Linear, Slow Curve, and Fast Curve. To change the type of fade, position your mouse on the fade line at the top of the clip so the shape of the mouse changes to a triangle. Then right-click and choose a fade type (see Figure 8.9).

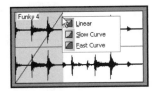

Figure 8.9 Change the fade type by right-clicking at the top of the fade line.

❋ **SET THE DEFAULT FADE TYPE**

If you use a particular type of fade most often, you can set the default fade types. Just click the small down arrow next to the Enable/Disable Automatic Crossfades button to reveal a menu, which will let you choose the default types for fade-in, fade-out, and crossfades (see Figure 8.10).

Figure 8.10 Set the default fade type by using the Enable/Disable Automatic Crossfades menu.

> ❄ **COMPLEX FADES WITH ENVELOPES**
>
> The nondestructive fade feature doesn't define complex fades by adding nodes as you can with the Fade/ Envelope feature, but you can apply nondestructive complex fades or volume changes to a clip (or an entire track) using envelopes.

You can also create nondestructive fades or edit existing nondestructive fades for multiple clips using the Fade Selected Clips feature. To use this feature, do the following:

1. Select the clips to which you want to apply fades. If the clips do not already contain fades, new ones will be created. If the clips already contain fades, the existing fades will be edited according to your specifications.

2. Choose Process > Fade Selected Clips to open the Fade Selected Clips dialog box (see Figure 8.11).

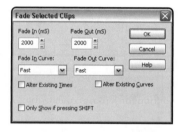

Figure 8.11   Use the Fade Selected Clips feature to create or edit fades for multiple clips.

3. Set the Fade In parameter. This parameter determines the length of the fade-in in milliseconds. Most of the time, you'll probably want the fade to last for a certain number of seconds. In order to do this, just enter a multiple of 1000 for each second. For example, for a two-second fade-in, type the value 2000.

4. Set the Fade Out parameter. This parameter determines the length of the fade-out in milliseconds.

5. Choose a Fade-In Curve and a Fade-Out Curve. You have three types of fades to choose from: Linear, Slow, and Fast.

6. If you are editing existing fades in your clips, you need to activate the Alter Existing Times and Alter Existing Curves options. If you are creating new fades for your clips, these options do not need to be activated.

7. You can use the same dialog box settings over again without having to open the dialog box. Simply activate the Only Show if Pressing Shift option. Now the dialog box will only open if you hold down the Shift key on your computer keyboard when you choose Process > Fade Selected Clips.

8. Click OK.

❄ ❄ ❄

All fades in the selected clips are set to the same values that you set in the dialog box.

Crossfades

A *crossfade* is a special kind of fade that you can apply only to overlapping audio clips. This kind of fade can come in handy when you want to make a smooth transition from one style of music to another or from one instrument to another. It is especially useful when you're composing to video; you can change smoothly from one type of background music to another as the scene changes. It has many other types of creative uses as well.

When you apply a crossfade to two overlapping audio clips, it works like this: During playback, as the Now time reaches the point at which the two audio clips overlap, the first audio clip fades out, and the second audio clip fades in at the same time. You can apply a crossfade as follows:

1. Select the two overlapping audio clips to which you want to apply the crossfade. The two audio clips you select don't have to reside on the same track; they only have to overlap in time.

2. Choose Process > Audio > Crossfade to open the Crossfade dialog box (see Figure 8.12).

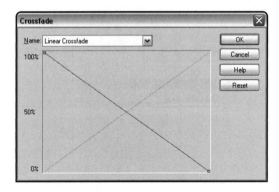

Figure 8.12 You can apply a crossfade to two overlapping audio clips by using the Crossfade dialog box.

3. Notice that the Crossfade dialog box looks almost exactly the same as the Fade/Envelope dialog box. It works almost exactly the same, too. You can choose from three preset fades, and you can manipulate the fade line with your mouse by adding, clicking, and dragging nodes. The only difference here is that an additional line appears on the graph. The gray line represents the second selected audio clip, and you can't manipulate it directly. As you make changes to the purple line, the gray line mimics it. This feature ensures that the volumes of both audio clips are synchronized, and it provides a perfectly smooth crossfade. So go ahead and make your changes as discussed earlier.

4. Click OK.

In addition to the Crossfade feature (which allows you to apply destructive crossfades to your data), SONAR applies nondestructive crossfades. To apply a crossfade nondestructively, follow these steps:

1. Activate the Enable/Disable Automatic Crossfades button located in the Track view toolbar. (Or press the X key.)
2. Click and drag one audio clip so it overlaps another audio clip. Both clips must reside on the same track.
3. In the Drag and Drop Options dialog box, choose the Blend Old and New option.
4. Click OK. SONAR will overlap the clips and automatically apply a perfect crossfade to the overlapping sections (see Figure 8.13).

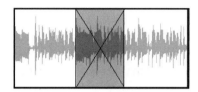

Figure 8.13   SONAR automatically applies a crossfade to the overlapping sections of the clips.

5. As with fades, you can define the shape of a crossfade, if you would rather not use the straight linear process. SONAR provides nine different choices. To change the type of crossfade, position your mouse in the crossfade area, and then right-click and choose a crossfade type.

SET THE DEFAULT CROSSFADE

If you use a particular type of crossfade more often, you can set the default crossfade type. Just click the small down arrow next to the Enable/Disable Automatic Crossfades button in the Track view toolbar to reveal a menu, which will let you choose the default crossfade type. This is also how you define the default fade-in and fade-out types.

Getting Rid of Silence

When you record an audio track in SONAR, even though there might be pauses in your performance (such as between musical phrases), your sound card still picks up a signal from your microphone or instrument, and that data is recorded. Although you might think that the data is just recorded silence, in actuality it contains a very minute amount of noise that might come from your sound card itself or the microphone or instrument connected there. More often than not, you can't really hear this noise because it's masked by the other music data in your project. And even during quiet passages, if you have only one or two audio tracks playing, the noise is probably still inaudible. With a large number of audio tracks, however, the noise can add up.

In addition, during playback SONAR still processes those silent passages, even though they don't contain any actual music. These passages take up valuable computer processing power and disk space. To remedy this problem, SONAR provides the Remove Silence feature. This feature automatically detects sections of silence in audio clips, according to a loudness threshold that you set. Then, by first splitting long audio clips into shorter ones, it removes the resulting clips containing only silence. Thus, SONAR doesn't process that extra data during playback, and it doesn't save it to disk when you save your project.

To detect silent passages in audio, the Remove Silence feature uses a digital noise gate. Depending on the parameter settings you specify, this noise gate opens up when the Remove Silence feature comes upon a section in your audio that has an amplitude level greater than the one you set. It identifies this part of the audio as acceptable sound and lets it pass through. When the level of audio dips below a certain amplitude level that you set, the noise gate identifies that part of the audio as silence, and it closes to stop it from passing through. At that point, the Remove Silence feature splits the audio clip with one new clip containing just the music and another new clip containing just the noise. This process happens over and over until the entire initial audio clip is finished being scanned.

You use this feature by following these steps:

1. Select the audio data you want to scan for silence.

2. Choose Process > Audio > Remove Silence to open the Remove Silence dialog box (see Figure 8.14).

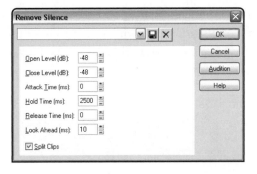

Figure 8.14 You can use the Remove Silence feature to clean up your audio tracks and make them more manageable.

3. Type a value in the Open Level field. This parameter determines how loud the audio data has to be to make the noise gate open, thus identifying the data as acceptable sound.

4. Type a value in the Close Level field. This parameter determines how soft the data has to be to make the noise gate close, thus identifying the data as silence.

5. Type a value in the Attack Time field. This parameter determines how quickly (in milliseconds) the noise gate will open to the amplitude set in the Open Level parameter. If the beginning of your audio data starts off soft (such as with a fade-in) and its amplitude is below the Open Level setting, it could get cut off by the noise gate. For example, the beginnings of the words in a vocal part might be cut. To prevent this problem, you can set the Attack Time parameter so the noise gate takes this kind of situation into consideration.

6. Type a value in the Hold Time field. This parameter determines how long the noise gate will remain open even when the amplitude level of the audio dips below the Close Level. This parameter is useful when the level of your audio goes up and down very quickly, which could make the noise gate react when it's not supposed to (such as during quick percussion parts). By setting a Hold Time, you can make sure that musical passages containing quick sounds don't get cut by mistake.

7. Type a value in the Release Time field. This parameter is the same as the Attack Time parameter, but in reverse. It determines how quickly the noise gate will close after the amplitude of the audio reaches the Close Level. This feature is useful if your audio data gradually gets softer at the end, such as with a fade-out.

8. Type a value in the Look Ahead field. This parameter determines how long (in milliseconds) the amplitude of the audio must stay above the Open Level before the noise gate will open. Basically, this setting lets you fine-tune the way the noise gate determines whether the audio being scanned is acceptable sound or silence.

9. If you want SONAR to delete the audio clips that contain only silence, activate the Split Clips option. Otherwise, the silent portions of the audio won't be deleted. They will be reduced to vacant space, but your clips will remain as they are.

10. You can save your settings as a preset, and you can use the Audition feature to hear the results of your settings if you want.

11. Click OK.

❈ **SPLIT THE AUDIO CLIPS**

Unless the musical passages and silent passages of your audio are separated pretty neatly, it can be difficult to get the right settings for the Release Time feature to perform accurately. You might find it easier and more precise if you simply split the audio clips by hand using the Split function. The process is a bit more time-consuming, though.

Playing It Backward

Assuming you're old enough to remember vinyl recordings, did you ever take a record and play it backward to see whether your favorite band had left some satanic messages in their songs or perhaps a recipe for their favorite lentil soup? Well, guess what? You can do the same thing with your audio data. SONAR lets you flip the data in an audio clip so that it plays in reverse.

This feature doesn't have much practical use, but combined with some other processing, it can render some cool effects. To use it, simply select the audio clip you want to change and choose Process > Audio > Reverse. Now the data in that clip will play backward.

> ❄ **REVERSE A TRACK**
>
> If you want to reverse the data in an entire track, make sure to combine all the audio clips in the track into one large audio clip first. If you don't, the data in each separate clip will be reversed, which is not the same as reversing the entire track. Try it, and you'll hear what I mean.

The Process Menu

Up until now, I've talked about editing features that pertain strictly to audio data. The rest of SONAR's editing features are more diverse in their uses, meaning some can be used with MIDI data, some with audio data, and some with both. The one aspect they all have in common is that they are accessed via the Process menu. Because of their diversity, I'll go through each feature, explaining what it does and how and why you would want to use it. I'll also let you know the kinds of data with which each feature works.

Deglitch

Occasionally, you might find that while you're playing your MIDI instrument, some unintended notes get recorded along with the legitimate musical material. This is especially true for people who play a MIDI guitar. The strings on a MIDI guitar can easily trigger notes when they're not supposed to. To help with this problem, SONAR provides the Deglitch feature. Using this feature, you can filter out any notes from your MIDI data that don't fall within the correct pitch, velocity, and duration range for the music you're recording. It works like this:

1. Select the MIDI data from which you want to filter any unwanted notes.

2. Choose Process > Deglitch to open the Deglitch dialog box (see Figure 8.15).

3. If you want to filter out notes by pitch, activate the Pitch option. In the Notes Higher Than field, type the maximum note value allowed in your material. For example, if the highest note in your MIDI data should be C5, then you should set the Notes Higher Than parameter to C5. If the Deglitch feature finds any notes in the data that have a pitch higher than C5, it will delete them.

4. If you want to filter out notes by velocity, activate the Velocity option. In the Notes Softer Than field, type the minimum velocity value allowed in your material. For example, if the lowest velocity in your MIDI data should be 15, then you should set the Notes Softer Than parameter to 15. If the Deglitch feature finds any notes in the data that have a velocity lower than 15, it will delete them.

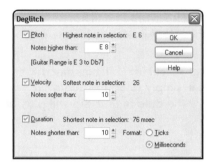

Figure 8.15 Using the Deglitch feature, you can filter out any unintended notes from your MIDI data by specifying acceptable pitch, velocity, and duration ranges.

5. If you want to filter out notes by duration, activate the Duration option. In the Notes Shorter Than field, type the minimum duration value allowed in your material. Also, be sure to specify whether the duration should be measured in ticks or milliseconds by choosing either the Ticks option or the Milliseconds option for the Format parameter. For example, if the lowest duration in your MIDI data should be 20 ticks, then you should set the Notes Shorter Than parameter to 20 and the Format parameter to Ticks. If the Deglitch feature finds any notes in the data that have durations lower than 20 ticks, it will delete them.

6. Click OK.

By the way, you can scan for pitch, velocity, and duration all at once by having all the options activated if you want.

Slide

Remember back in Chapter 7, when I described how to move clips in the Track view by dragging and dropping them or by using the Clip Properties dialog box to change their start times? Well, the Slide feature performs the same function. You can use it to move clips backward or forward within a track. So why does SONAR provide the same functionality more than once? Because the Slide feature has a few differences. Instead of just working with clips, you can use it with any kind of selected data from a group of MIDI notes to single events. And instead of having to specify an exact Start time (as in the Clips Properties dialog box), you can move data by any number of measures, ticks, seconds, or frames. In addition, the Slide feature doesn't give you the option of blending with, replacing, or sliding over existing events in a track. It simply moves the selected data so that it overlaps with any existing data. You use it as follows:

1. Using the appropriate view, select the MIDI data or audio clips you want to move.
2. Choose Process > Slide to open the Slide dialog box (see Figure 8.16).

Figure 8.16 You can use the Slide feature to move any kind of data, not just clips.

3. If you want to move events, be sure the Events in Tracks option under the Slide parameter is activated. If you want to move any markers that happen to fall within the same time range as the selected data, activate the Markers option.
4. For the By parameter, type the number of units by which you want to move the selected data. If you want to move the data backward in time, enter a negative number. If you want to move the data forward in time, enter a positive number.
5. Choose the type of unit by which you want to move the selected data by activating the appropriate option. You can select Measures, Ticks, Seconds, or Frames.
6. Click OK.

Nudge

In addition to the Slide feature, SONAR provides the Nudge feature. It works almost exactly the same as the Slide feature, except that the Nudge feature can be accessed with quick and simple keystrokes, and you can configure up to three different Nudge key bindings.

To use the Nudge feature, you simply select some data and choose Process > Nudge > Left 1 through 3 or Right 1 through 3. Or you can just press one of the appropriate numeric keypad numbers on your computer keyboard. (You can see the keypad numbers shown next to each Nudge option in the menu.)

> ❄ **NUM LOCK**
>
> In order to access the Nudge feature using the numeric keypad, you must have the Num Lock key activated on your computer keyboard.

There is also a unique ability that the Nudge feature provides—it nudges data up or down into different tracks. The Slide feature can't do this. You simply select a clip in a track and choose Process > Nudge > Up or Down. This will move the clip up or down to the adjacent track.

In addition, you can configure each of the three left and right Nudge options by choosing Process > Nudge > Settings to open the Global Options Nudge dialog box (see Figure 8.17).

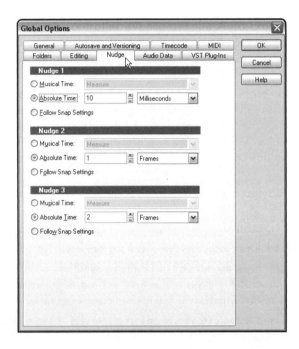

Figure 8.17   Use the Global Options Nudge dialog box to configure the Nudge feature.

In the dialog box, you'll see the three Nudge options listed, which correspond to the Left 1/Right 1, Left 2/Right 2, and Left 3/Right 3. Each can be set to move data by a specific musical time, an absolute time, or to follow the Snap to Grid settings. After you've finished configuring the options, click OK. Now you can nudge your data quickly with a click of the mouse or a press of a key.

Quantize

Even though you might be a great musician, you're bound to make mistakes occasionally when playing your instrument, especially when it comes to timing. No one I know can play in perfect time during every performance, and having to listen to a metronome while you play can be distracting. Instead of playing notes at the same time as the metronome sounds, you'll more than likely play some of them either a little ahead or a little behind the beat. You might even hold some notes a little longer than you're supposed to. Usually, if these timing errors are slight enough, they'll make your performance sound more human than anything else. But if the mistakes are obvious enough to stand out, they can make your performance sound sloppy. At this point, the Quantize feature comes in handy. It can help you correct some of the timing mistakes you make.

To understand how to use the Quantize feature, you first have to know how it works. The Quantize feature scans the MIDI events in your selected data one by one, and it changes the start time of each event so that it is equal to the nearest rhythmic value you specify (using

226
❋ ❋ ❋

the Resolution parameter). If you want all the events in your data to be moved to the nearest sixteenth note, you can set the Resolution parameter to Sixteenth. The Quantize feature uses this value to set up an imaginary (for lack of a better word) time grid over your data. In this case, the grid is divided into sixteenth notes.

During the scanning process, the Quantize feature moves an imaginary pointer along the grid, one division at a time. Centered around the pointer is an imaginary window, for which you can set the size using the Window parameter. As the Quantize feature moves its pointer and window along the grid, it looks to see whether any of your events are in the vicinity. Any events that fall within the window have their start times changed so they line up with the current position of the pointer. Any events that fall outside the window are left alone. This procedure continues until the Quantize feature comes to the end of the data you selected.

1. Select the data you want to quantize. It can be anything from all the data in your project to a single track or clip or a selected group of events.

2. Choose Process > Quantize to open the Quantize dialog box (see Figure 8.18).

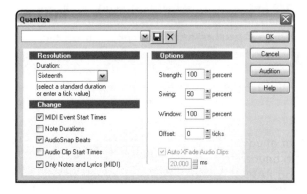

Figure 8.18   The Quantize dialog box provides a number of parameters you can set to determine exactly how you want your data to be corrected.

3. In the Resolution section, set the Resolution parameter. This parameter determines the rhythmic value that will be used to set up the imaginary grid and the nearest rhythmic value to which the events in your data will be aligned. It's best to set this parameter to the smallest note value found in your data. For instance, your data might contain quarter notes, eighth notes, and sixteenth notes. Because the smallest note value in your data is the sixteenth note, set the Resolution parameter to Sixteenth.

4. In the Change section, activate the appropriate options for the types of events and the event properties you want to have quantized. You'll almost always want to activate the MIDI Event Start Times option. Along with the start times of events, you can also quantize the durations of MIDI note events by activating the Note Durations option. Usually, you'll activate this option as well. If you don't, the ends of some notes may overlap the

227
✳ ✳ ✳

beginnings of others, which might not sound good. You might not want to quantize the start times of events, but only the durations if you want to create a staccato (separated notes) feel to your music. When activated, the Only Notes and Lyrics option quantizes only MIDI note and lyric events and leaves any other events (such as MIDI controller events) alone. Usually, you'll want to keep this option activated; otherwise, the Quantize feature will move controller events to the nearest grid point, which can actually screw up their timing.

5. You can also quantize audio in two different ways. One way involves SONAR's AudioSnap feature and the AudioSnap Beats option. The other way involves simply moving the start of entire audio clips. For this method, activate the Audio Clip Start Times option. Also, when quantizing the start time of audio clips, you may find that some audio clips become overlapped. To handle these clips more gracefully, you can apply a cross-fade between the clips by activating the Auto XFade Audio Clips option and entering the number of milliseconds to control the crossfade time.

6. In the Options section, set the Strength parameter. Quantizing your data so that all the events are aligned in perfect time with the grid can make your performance sound mechanical (as if it is being played by a machine). So instead of having the Quantize feature move an event to the exact current pointer position on the grid during the scanning process, you can have it move the event only slightly toward the pointer, thus taking the sloppiness out of the performance but keeping the "human" feel. You can do so by setting a percentage for the Strength parameter. A value of 100 percent means that all events will be moved to the exact grid point. A value of 50 percent means that the events will be moved only halfway toward the grid point.

7. Set the Window parameter. This parameter tells SONAR how close to the current grid point an event has to be in order to be quantized. If the event falls inside the window, it is quantized. If it falls outside the window, it isn't. You set the Window parameter by using a percentage. A value of 100 percent means the window extends halfway before and halfway after the current pointer position on the grid. Basically, all events get moved; if they don't fall inside the window at the current pointer position, they will fall inside at the next position. A value of 50 percent means the window extends only one-quarter of the way before and after the current pointer position, meaning only half of the events in your selection will be processed.

8. Set the Offset parameter. This parameter is an extra setting thrown in to make the Quantize feature even more flexible (and complicated) than it already is. When the Quantize feature sets up its imaginary grid over your selected data, the grid is perfectly aligned to the measures and beats in your project. So if your data selection started at the beginning of your project, the grid would be set up starting at 1:01:000 (measure, beat, and tick). If you enter a value for the Offset parameter (in ticks), the grid will be offset by the number of ticks you enter. For example, if you enter an Offset of +3, the grid will be set up starting at 1:01:003 instead of 1:01:000. This means that if the current event being scanned was initially supposed to be moved to 1:01:000, it would be moved to 1:01:003 instead. Basically, you can use this parameter to offset

the selected data from the other data in your project, in case you want to create some slight timing variations, and so on. It works similarly to the Time Offset parameter in the Track view.

9. Set the Swing parameter. You might use this parameter to work on a song that has a "swing" feel to it, similar to a waltz, where the first in a pair of notes is played longer than the second. It's difficult to explain, but essentially the Swing parameter distorts the grid by making the space between the grid points uneven. If you leave the parameter set at 50 percent, it doesn't have any effect. If you set it to something like 66 percent, the space between the first two points in the grid becomes twice as much as the space between the second and third points. This pattern of long space, short space is repeated throughout the length of the grid, and your data is aligned according to the uneven grid points.

10. Click the Audition button to hear how the quantized data will sound. Go back and make any parameter changes you think might be necessary.

11. If you want to use the same settings again later, save them as a preset.

12. Click OK.

SONAR provides additional quantizing features with the Quantize MIDI effect.

The Groove Quantize Feature

Not only can you use quantizing to correct the timing of your performances, but you can also use it to add a bit of a creative flair. The Groove Quantize feature works almost the same as the Quantize feature, but it's slightly more sophisticated. Instead of using a fixed grid (meaning you can set the grid to use only straight rhythmic values, such as sixteenth notes), it uses a grid with rhythmic values that are based on an existing rhythmic pattern called a groove pattern. This groove pattern can contain any kind of musical rhythm, even one taken from an existing piece of music.

Basically, the Groove Quantize feature works by imposing the timing, duration, and velocity values of one set of events onto another set. For example, suppose that you record a melody that comes out sounding a bit too mechanical, but your friend slams out this really kickin' MIDI bass line that has the exact feel you want. You can copy the bass clip data and use it as a groove pattern to groove quantize the melody clip data. By doing so, you impose the timing, duration, and velocity values (depending on your parameter settings) from the bass line onto the melody. Thus, the melody will have the same rhythm as the bass line, but keep its original pitches.

The preceding example is just one of the many uses for the Groove Quantize feature. Just like the Quantize feature, the Groove Quantize feature provides Strength parameters to give you control of how much influence a groove pattern has over the data you're quantizing. You can define via percentages how much the timing, duration, and velocity values of the events will be affected; you can use this feature for all kinds of editing tasks. You can correct off-tempo tracks, add complex beat accents to each measure of a tune, synchronize rhythm and solo tracks, align tracks with bad timing to one with good timing, and steal the feeling from tracks.

As a matter of fact, groove quantizing has become so popular that companies now sell groove pattern files; you can steal the feeling from tracks that have been recorded by professional keyboard, drum, and guitar players. It's almost like having Steve Vai play on your latest tune! Just look in any copy of *Electronic Musician* or *Keyboard* magazine, and you'll see advertisements for these types of products. Naturally, you need to know how to use the Groove Quantize feature before you can use these groove pattern files, so let me tell you how.

1. If you want to grab the timing, duration, and velocity values from existing data, first select and copy that data so that it is placed onto the clipboard. Otherwise, you can use one of the groove patterns that comes included with SONAR.

2. Select the data you want to groove quantize.

3. Choose Process > Groove Quantize to open the Groove Quantize dialog box (see Figure 8.19).

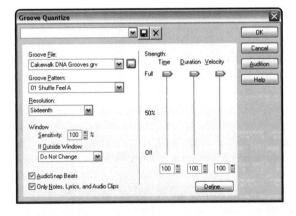

Figure 8.19 The Groove Quantize dialog box provides a number of parameters you can set to determine exactly how you want your data to be groove quantized.

4. Set the Groove File parameter. If you're grabbing the values from existing data, as explained previously, then select Clipboard from the list and skip to step 6. Otherwise, choose an existing groove file. SONAR ships with only one groove file (Cakewalk DNA Grooves.grv), so unless you've created your own groove files, choose the Cakewalk DNA Grooves.grv file. If you have other groove files available, you can load them by clicking the small button to the right of the Groove File parameter to bring up the Open Groove File dialog box. Just select a file and click Open.

5. Set the Groove Pattern parameter. Each groove file can contain any number of groove patterns. For example, the groove file that comes with SONAR contains 12 different groove patterns. Choose the groove pattern you want to use.

6. The rest of the parameters for the Groove Quantize feature are the same as for the Quantize feature. You need to set the Resolution parameter; the AudioSnap Beats option; the Only Notes, Lyrics, and Audio option; and the Window parameter. The Window Sensitivity parameter is the same as the Window parameter for the Quantize feature, but one additional Window parameter is available here. You can choose the If Outside Window parameter to have Groove Quantize change events, even if they fall outside the window. If you select Do Not Change, then events outside the window are left alone (just as with the Quantize feature). If you select Quantize to Resolution, any events outside the window are moved to the nearest grid point, as specified by the Resolution parameter. If you select Move to Nearest, then the Window Sensitivity parameter is ignored, and all events outside the window are moved to the nearest grid point, as defined by the groove pattern. If you select Scale Time, SONAR looks at the events located right before and after the current event being scanned (as long as they are within the window), and it sets their relative timing so that they're the same. The Scale Time parameter is very difficult to explain, so you should try it out to hear what kind of effect it has on your music.

7. You also need to set the Strength parameters. They work the same as with the Quantize feature, but instead of just having one parameter to affect the timing of events, three Strength parameters are provided to give you control over how the Groove Quantize feature will affect the time, duration, and velocity of each event. If you want the events to have the same timing, duration, and velocity as their counterparts in the groove pattern, then set all these parameters to 100 percent. Otherwise, you can make the events take on only some of the feel of the events in the groove pattern by adjusting the percentages of these parameters.

8. Click the Audition button to hear how the quantized data will sound. Go back and make any parameter changes you think might be necessary.

9. If you want to use the same settings again later, then save them as a preset.

10. Click OK.

SONAR will quantize the selected data so the timing, duration, and velocity of the events will sound exactly or somewhat like those in the groove pattern you used (depending on your parameter settings). By the way, if the groove pattern is shorter than the material you are quantizing, the Groove Quantize feature will loop through the groove pattern as many times as necessary to get to the end of your selected data. For example, if you use a groove pattern that is only one measure long, but your selected data is three measures, then the timing, duration, and velocity values of the groove pattern will be repeated over each of those three measures.

Saving Groove Patterns

If you create your own groove pattern by grabbing the timing, duration, and velocity values from existing data, you can save it for later use as follows:

1. After you've gone through steps 1 through 4 in the preceding example, and you've set the Groove File parameter to Clipboard, click the Define button at the bottom of the Groove Quantize dialog box to open the Define Groove dialog box (see Figure 8.20).

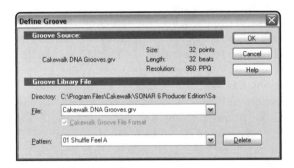

Figure 8.20   Using the Define Groove dialog box, you can save your own groove patterns and groove files.

2. In the Groove Library File section, select an existing groove file via the File parameter. You can also type a new name to create your own new groove file.

❈ GROOVE FILE FORMATS

SONAR supports two types of groove files. One type is the DNA groove file, which contains only timing data, but is compatible with other sequencing software. The groove files being sold by other companies are usually in this file format. SONAR also has its own proprietary groove file format that stores timing, duration, and velocity data. Unless you really need to share your groove files with others who don't own SONAR, I suggest you save your files in the SONAR format because it provides more flexibility. To do so, be sure to activate the Cakewalk Groove File Format option in the Define Groove dialog box.

3. If you want to replace an existing groove pattern in the current groove file, just select one from the Pattern list. If you want to save your groove pattern under a new name, type the name in the Pattern parameter.

❈ DELETE EXISTING PATTERNS

You can delete existing groove patterns in the current groove file. Just select the groove pattern you want to delete from the Pattern list and click the Delete button. SONAR will ask you to confirm the deletion process.

4. Click OK. If you're replacing an existing groove pattern, SONAR will ask you to confirm the replacement process.

SONAR will save your new groove pattern inside the groove file you selected (or created) under the name you specified.

GROOVE QUANTIZE APPLICATIONS

For examples of some cool applications for the Groove Quantize feature, look at the SONAR Help in the Editing MIDI Events and Controllers > Changing the Time of a Recording > Quantizing section.

The Interpolate Feature

Throughout this book, I've mentioned the name SONAR quite a few times. What if I want to change all those instances of the phrase to SONAR 6.0 instead? Luckily, I'm using a word processing program on my computer, so all I would have to do is use the search and replace feature to have the program automatically make the changes for me. I mention this point because the Interpolate feature is similar to the search and replace feature you find in most word processing programs. The difference is that the Interpolate feature works with event properties, and in addition to simply searching and replacing, it can scale entire ranges of event properties from one set of values to another. This means that you can easily transpose notes, change key signatures, convert one type of controller message into another, and so on. It works like this:

1. Select the data you want to change.
2. Choose Process > Interpolate to open the Event Filter - Search dialog box. You learned about this dialog box and its parameters in Chapter 5.
3. Set all the available parameters so that SONAR can select the exact events you want to process.
4. Click OK to open the Event Filter - Replace dialog box (see Figure 8.21). This dialog box is almost the same as the Event Filter - Search dialog box. It has most of the same settings, except some of the settings are not available because here you need to enter only the values to which you want to change the original selected data. So enter the replacement values in the appropriate parameters.
5. Click OK.

SONAR will select all the events in your initial selection, according to the parameters you set in the Event Filter - Search dialog box. Then it will change the values of those events, according to the parameters you set in the Event Filter - Replace dialog box.

Interpolation Applications

You didn't think I was going to leave you high and dry, trying to figure out such a complicated feature, did you? The following sections describe some of the changes you can accomplish with this feature.

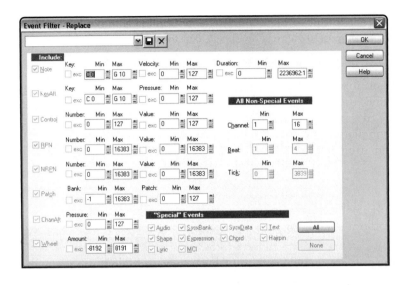

Figure 8.21 In the Event Filter - Replace dialog box, you can enter the replacement values only for the data you're trying to change.

Straight Replacement

If all you want to do is replace one value with another, setting up the parameters in both dialog boxes is fairly easy. Suppose that you want to change all the notes with a pitch of C#2 to notes with a pitch of D#7. To do so, set up the Event Filter - Search dialog box so that only the Note option is activated in the Include section. Then type C#2 for both the Key Min and Key Max parameters and click OK. In the Event Filter - Replace dialog box, type D#7 for the Key Min and Key Max parameters and click OK. All the C#2 notes will be changed to D#7 notes. Pretty easy, no? And you can use this approach with any of the data. Earlier, I mentioned changing one type of controller message to another. Just use the Control option along with the Number Min and Number Max parameters, as you did with the Note option and the Key Min and Key Max parameters.

> ### USING WILDCARDS
>
> You can also use wildcards when you're designating an octave number for the pitch of a note. With regard to the preceding example, suppose that you want to change all the C# notes to D notes, not just the ones in octave 2 to octave 7. Instead of using C#2, you can use C#?, and instead of using D#7, you can use D#?. The ? is the wildcard, which stands for any octave.

Scaling Values

When you're working with ranges of values, you can use the Interpolate feature to scale them from one range to another. This capability is useful for limiting certain values to keep them within a set of boundaries. For example, some of the note velocities in one of your MIDI tracks might be a bit high, and you might want to quiet them down a bit. Usually, quieting them would mean having to use the Piano Roll view to change them all one by one. Using the Interpolate feature, you can compress their range down in a couple of easy steps. To do so, set up the Event Filter - Search dialog box so that only the Note option is activated in the Include section. Then type 0 for Velocity Min and 127 for Velocity Max and click OK. In the Event Filter - Replace dialog box, type 0 for Velocity Min and 100 for Velocity Max and click OK. All the note velocities will be scaled down from a range of 0 to 127 to a range of 0 to 100. You can use this approach with any of the other value ranges, too.

Inverting Values

You also can invert any of the value ranges by reversing the Min and Max parameters. For example, what if you want to make all the loud volume controller messages soft and the soft volume controller messages loud? To do so, set up the Event Filter - Search dialog box so that only the Control option is activated in the Include section. Then type 7 (the number for volume controller messages) for both the Number Min and Number Max parameters. Also, type 0 for Value Min and 127 for Value Max and click OK. In the Event Filter - Replace dialog box, type 7 for both the Number Min and Number Max parameters. Also, type 127 for Value Min and 0 for Value Max and click OK. All the loud sections of your selected data will become soft and vice versa. Again, you can use this technique for any of the other value ranges.

As a matter of fact, you can change a whole bunch of different parameters at once by activating the appropriate parameters in the Event Filter - Search dialog box. (You can even mix straight replacement, scaling, and inverting.) For instance, you could easily set up all three of the preceding examples so that you would have to use the Interpolate feature only one time to process the same data. This feature is very powerful. You should experiment with it as much as possible because it can save you a lot of editing time in the long run.

> ❊ **OTHER INTERPOLATE APPLICATIONS**
>
> You can find some other Interpolate application ideas in the SONAR Help file under the Editing MIDI Events and Controllers > Searching for Events > Event Filters section.

The Length Feature

The Length feature is one of the very simple, but also very useful features, provided in SONAR. Using it, you can change the size of a clip or a group of selected data by specifying a percentage. It works like this:

1. Select the data you want to change.
2. Choose Process > Length to open the Length dialog box (see Figure 8.22).
3. Activate the Start Times or Durations options. Activating the Start Times option makes the Length feature change the start times of the selected events so the entire selection will change in size. Activating the Durations option makes the Length feature change the

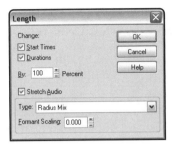

Figure 8.22 You can change the size of clips or selected groups of events by using the Length feature.

durations of the selected events. If you activate the Durations option without the Start Times option, the Length feature will change only the durations of the selected events. This feature can be useful if you want to create a staccato effect for your notes.

4. If you want the length of your audio data to be changed, you can activate the Stretch Audio option. If your audio consists of a single musical voice, choose Solo Instrument, Single Voice for the Type parameter. If your audio consists of a group of voices or instruments, choose Ensemble, Polyphonic for the Type parameter.

❄ **FORMANT SCALING**

Changing the length of audio data, can also affect its timbre or musical characteristics. If this happens, you can use the Formant Scaling parameter to correct the problem. The Formant Scaling parameter can be set anywhere from –2.000 to +2.000 octaves. If the audio data sounds like it is tuned too low, try entering a positive value. If the audio data sounds like it is tuned too high, try entering a negative value.

5. Enter a value for the By Percent parameter. A value of 100 percent doesn't make any changes at all. A value of 50 percent changes the selection to half its original length. A value of 200 percent changes the selection to twice its original length.

6. Click OK.

❄ **FIT TO TIME**

For a more intuitive way to change the length of your data (meaning you can enter a length using an actual time value instead of a percentage), use the Fit to Time feature.

The Retrograde Feature

The Retrograde feature works similarly to the Reverse feature. Instead of reversing the data in audio clips, the Retrograde feature reverses MIDI data. This means that you can have your

MIDI data play backward if you apply this feature. Just select the data you want to reverse and then select Process > Retrograde. SONAR will reverse the order of the selected events. In other words, if you were looking at the data via the Event view, the data would be changed so that this list essentially is flipped upside down.

The Transpose Feature

Transposition is a common occurrence when you're composing music, and SONAR's Transpose feature enables you to transpose quickly and easily. It works like this:

1. Select the data that you want to transpose.
2. Choose Process > Transpose to open the Transpose dialog box (see Figure 8.23).

Figure 8.23   By entering a number of steps, you can transpose the pitches of note events up or down using the Transpose feature.

3. You can use the Transpose feature to transpose the pitches of your note events either chromatically (so they can be changed by half steps) or diatonically (so they remain in the current key signature of your project). If you want to transpose chromatically, leave the Diatonic Math option deactivated. If you want to transpose diatonically, activate the Diatonic Math option.
4. If you have selected any audio data, you can opt to have its pitch changed. To do so, activate the Transpose Audio option. If your audio consists of a single musical voice, choose Solo Instrument, Single Voice for the Type parameter. If your audio consists of a group of voices or instruments, choose Ensemble, Polyphonic for the Type parameter.
5. Enter a value for the Amount parameter. A positive value transposes up, and a negative value transposes down. If you are transposing chromatically, this value corresponds to half steps. If you are transposing diatonically, the Transpose feature changes the pitches of your notes, according to the major scale of the current key signature. For example, if you enter a value of +1 and the key signature is D major, a D becomes an E, an E becomes an F#, and so on.
6. Click OK.

The Scale Velocity Feature

You learned about scaling the velocity values of events earlier in the description of the Interpolate feature. Using the Scale Velocity feature, you can do the same thing, but this feature has an extra option that scales the velocities by a percentage, rather than entering exact values or a range of values. It works like this:

1. Select the data you want to change.

2. Choose Process > Scale Velocity to open the Scale Velocity dialog box (see Figure 8.24).

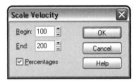

Figure 8.24   You can scale the velocities of note events by percentages if you use the Scale Velocity feature.

3. If you want to scale the velocities by percentages, activate the Percentages option. Otherwise, the values that you enter will be exact velocity values.

4. Enter values for the Begin and End parameters. For example, you can use the Scale Velocity feature to create crescendos and decrescendos. To create a crescendo, enter a small value (such as 0 or 50 percent) for the Begin parameter and a larger value (such as 127 or 150 percent) for the End parameter. Do the opposite for a decrescendo.

5. Click OK.

THE DRAW LINE TOOL

You can create crescendos and decrescendos with more precise control by drawing them with the Draw Line tool in the Controller pane of the Piano Roll view.

Fit to Time

The Fit to Time feature works similarly to the Length feature. Using it, you can change the size of clips and selected groups of data. But instead of having to use a percentage, you can specify an actual time (according to the Time Ruler) at which the data will end. For example, if you have a clip that begins at 1:01:000 and ends at 4:02:000, the start time of the clip will remain the same, but you can change the end time of the clip so that it stops playing at the exact moment you specify. This feature is great when you need to compose music to a precise length, such as for a radio commercial or a video. It works like this:

1. Select the data you want to change.

2. Choose Process > Fit to Time to open the Fit to Time dialog box (see Figure 8.25).

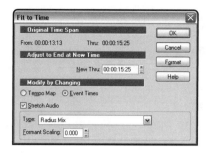

Figure 8.25   You can specify the exact length of clips or selected groups of events by using the Fit to Time feature.

3. The Original Time Span section shows the beginning and end times for the selected data. In the Adjust to End at New Time section, enter a new end time for the selected data. You can enter either hours, minutes, seconds, and frames or measures, beats, and ticks. To change the format, click the Format button.

4. In the Modify by Changing section, activate either the Tempo Map option or the Event Times option. If you want the actual data to be changed (meaning the start times of every event in the selection will be adjusted to accommodate the new end time), activate the Event Times option. If you would rather leave the data as it is and just have SONAR insert tempo changes into the project to accommodate the new end time, activate the Tempo Map option. The key difference here is that using the Tempo Map option affects the entire project, and all the data in all the tracks during the selected time will play at a different rate. If you want the data in only one track to be affected, you must use the Event Times option.

5. If you want to change the length of audio clips, you have to activate the Stretch Audio option. If your audio consists of a single musical voice, choose Solo Instrument, Single Voice for the Type parameter. If your audio consists of a group of voices or instruments, choose Ensemble, Polyphonic for the Type parameter.

6. Click OK.

Fit Improvisation

Having to play along with a metronome while recording in SONAR can be a nuisance sometimes. Depending on the type of music you are performing, using the metronome might not be conducive to your mood during the performance, which means you might end up with a less than acceptable recording. Some people just can't stand using a metronome. The problem is that if you don't use the metronome while recording in SONAR, your data will not line up correctly to the measure, beat, and tick values along the Time Ruler. Therefore, editing your music can be a lot more difficult.

If you are one of those people who hates metronomes, you're in luck. SONAR will record your MIDI tracks without using the metronome, but still lines up your data correctly after the fact by using the Fit Improvisation feature. This feature works by adding tempo changes to your project according to an additional reference track that you must record. This reference track gives SONAR an idea of the tempo at which you were playing when you were recording your MIDI track without the metronome. Here is a more detailed version of how this feature works:

1. Record a MIDI track without using the metronome. For the most accurate results, try to play using as steady a tempo as possible.

2. Choose Options > Global to open the Global Options dialog box. Click the MIDI tab. Be sure that only the Notes option in the Record section is activated. This filters out any extraneous events when you're recording your reference track so they don't mess up the timing. The more accurate your reference track, the better. After you're done recording your reference track, you can go back to the Global Options dialog box and change the options back to the way they were.

3. Record a reference MIDI track. To do so, simply tap out the tempo of your initial MIDI recording by hitting a key on your MIDI instrument for every beat. So if you recorded a track in 4/4 time, you would have to hit the key four times for every measure of music you recorded. Also, be sure that the first note in your reference track has a start time of 1:01:000, so it starts at the very beginning of the project. You can adjust it manually by using the Event view or Piano Roll view if you have to.

4. Select the reference track.

5. Choose Process > Fit Improvisation.

SONAR will scan your reference track, analyzing where the beats fall, and add tempo changes to your project so that the data in your recorded track lines up with the measure, beat, and tick values on the Time Ruler. Now you can edit your data just as you would any other data that was recorded along with the metronome.

Audio Snap

Expanding on the power provided by the previously mentioned time-based altering features, SONAR includes additional audio manipulation in the form of AudioSnap. A set of tools, AudioSnap changes the timing of audio data in a variety of ways. This includes changing tempo, groove, quantizing, and more.

Instead of rehashing the basic AudioSnap information included in the SONAR User's Guide, I will walk you through a number of practical uses. As such, I advise that you first read the AudioSnap section of the *User's Guide* before reading the rest of this chapter. In addition, take a good look at the AudioSnap palette picture on page 131 of the *Guide* because I'll be referring to that quite often.

AudioSnap Preparation

To get started with AudioSnap, there are a number of things you can do to set up your working environment to make the process easier. First, make the AudioSnap palette visible by choosing Process > AudioSnap Palette (or pressing Shift+A).

❄ **PALETTE OPACITY**

I like to position the AudioSnap palette at the bottom of the SONAR workspace and line up the bottom of the Track view with the top of the palette. That way I have complete access to the Track view and palette at the same time. You, however, might like to have the Track view fill the entire workspace. In that case, you can adjust the opacity of the palette so you can see through it but still access its functions. Right-click the title bar of the palette and choose Set Opacity.

Set up Snap to Grid

By default the Track view Snap to Grid is set up to snap to Musical Time and whole notes. Here are the snap settings I like to use while working with AudioSnap:

1. In the Track view, press Shift+N to open the Snap to Grid dialog box.
2. Keep the Musical Time option activated.
3. In the Standard Duration list, choose Sixteenth. If you're working with lower note values in your music, choose that value instead.
4. In the Landmarks list, activate the Audio Transients option.
5. Change the Mode option to Move To.
6. Change the Magnetic Strength option to Off.
7. Keep the Snap to Audio Zero Crossings option activated.

Set the Default Stretch

AudioSnap provides a number of different options for stretching audio. Some provide better quality than others, but also take up more processing power so they are only available when bouncing or exporting audio. You can set up the default stretching options by clicking the AudioSnap Options button in the palette to open the AudioSnap Options dialog box.

In the Default Stretch Algorithm section, choose options for Online and Offline Rendering. Online represents the sound you hear during playback of a project in real-time. If you are working with percussion material, choose the Percussion setting; otherwise, choose the Groove-Clip setting. For Offline Rendering, I've found the iZotope Radius Mix setting sounds quite nice, but this may be different depending on the material you are processing. The Offline Rendering option is used when you use the Bounce to Clip(s), Bounce to Track(s), and Export Audio features to create a permanent change to your processed audio.

Align the Time Ruler

One of the most common scenarios for using AudioSnap is when working with a live performance recording. In this case, when you import the audio, the beats will more than likely not line up with the measure lines in the Track view Time Ruler. Lining up the measure lines makes working with your data and composing additional music (with the live performance track as a reference) much easier.

Find the Default Tempo

If your audio recording already has accurate timing but just doesn't line up with the Time Ruler, you might be able to simply change the project tempo to the tempo of the recording. Here's an example:

1. Create a new blank project.

2. Choose File > Import >Audio. For this example, import the drums.wav file from the C:\Program Files\Cakewalk\SONAR 6 Producer Edition\Tutorials folder.

3. You'll notice that the beats and the end of the clip do not line up with the Time Ruler. Right-click the clip and choose Clip Properties. Click the Audio Stretching tab. In this tab, you can find the original tempo of the audio under the Stretch to Project Tempo option. In this case, the tempo is 105 (see Figure 8.26). Click Cancel to close the Clip Properties dialog box.

Figure 8.26   Find the original audio tempo under the Audio Stretching tab of the Clip Properties dialog box.

4. Use the Tempo toolbar or the Tempo view to change the project tempo to 105.

You'll notice that the audio beats now line up with the Time Ruler. Most of the time you probably won't be this lucky, but for most accurate performances, it should work.

Extract the Timing

Another way to line up accurate performances with the Time Ruler is to use the AudioSnap Extract Timing feature. Here's an example:

1. Create a new blank project.

2. Choose File > Import >Audio. For this example, import the drums.wav file from the C:\Program Files\Cakewalk\SONAR 6 Producer Edition\Tutorials folder.

3. Select the imported clip and click the AudioSnap Enable button in the palette.

4. Activate the Align Time Ruler option in the Task section of the palette.

5. In the Actions section of the palette, set the Expected Pulse Duration parameter to the lowest rhythmic value in your audio. In our example, you can hear the hi-hat playing eighth notes, This is the lowest rhythmic value being played, so set the parameter to Eighth.

6. You'll usually want to activate the Find a Steady Rhythm option. This option tells SONAR to look for a steady rhythm within the audio. For example, if you have a snare drum

track that has even hits on each beat but also has some syncopated hits between the beats, this option helps to ignore the syncopated hits and just pick up the steady rhythm values for an accurate analysis.

7. Click the Extract Timing button in the palette.

As with the last example, you'll notice that the audio beats now line up with the Time Ruler. SONAR accomplishes this by adding slight tempo changes to the project, which you can see using the Tempo view (Views > Tempo).

Set the Measure/Beat

The most accurate way to line up your audio with the Time Ruler is to set each individual measure/beat manually. Here's an example:

1. Create a new blank project.
2. Choose File > Import >Audio. For this example, import the drums.wav file from the C:\Program Files\Cakewalk\SONAR 6 Producer Edition\Tutorials folder.
3. Select the imported clip and click the AudioSnap Enable button in the palette.
4. Activate the Align Time Ruler option in the Task section of the palette.
5. Choose Go > Beginning to make sure the Now Time is set to the start of the project. Since the clip is already position at measure 1, beat 1, you don't need to worry about the first beat.
6. Click the AudioSnap Go to Next Transient Marker button in the palette twice to move the Now Time to the transient marker that represents the first beat in the audio. Transient markers represent every sound in the audio. If you'd like, you can try thinning them out using the Sensitivity and Threshold sliders in the palette to disable some of the extra transients, but you probably won't need to do this most of the time.
7. Click the Set Measure/Beat at Now button in the palette to open the Measure Beat/ Meter dialog box. Since we are on the second beat of the first measure, enter 1 for the Measure and 2 for the Beat. Click OK. You'll notice that the current transient is now lined up with the Time Ruler.
8. Click the AudioSnap Go to Next Transient Marker button three more times. Then click the Set Measure/Beat at Now button and enter 1 for the Measure and 3 for the Beat.
9. Click the AudioSnap Go to Next Transient Marker button three more times. Then click the Set Measure/Beat at Now button and enter 1 for the Measure and 4 for the Beat.
10. You'll notice that the end of the clip is slightly over the second measure line, but that is easily correctly with a quick slip-edit as shown in Figure 8.27.

❊ **SLIP-STRETCHING**

Hold down the Ctrl key while slip-editing a clip to slip-stretch the clip instead. This changes the actual length of the audio rather than simply hiding it.

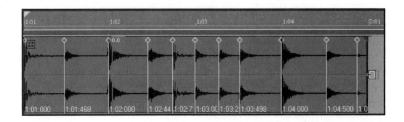

Figure 8.27 Use slip-editing for minor end-of-clip adjustments.

Using the manual method of aligning the Time Ruler can be tedious with long tracks, but it's the most accurate.

Fix and Regroove (Quantize)

Using AudioSnap to actually change your data is where the real fun and usefulness begins. You can use the quantize features to fix sloppy performances, change the groove of a performance, and synchronize one track with another.

Quantize

No longer the exclusive domain of MIDI data, you can now use SONAR's Quantize feature to fix your audio performances. The basic steps for fixing a sloppy performance are as follows:

1. Select the audio clip(s) you want to quantize and click the AudioSnap Enable button in the palette.
2. You may want to adjust the Sensitivity and Threshold sliders in the palette to disable some of the transient markers so that some of the audio data is not qualitized. This can be useful if you only want to alter the transients on each beat and leave the feel of the performance between each beat.

❋ MANUAL TRANSIENT EDITING

If the Sensitivity and Threshold sliders are disabling too many transients or not the right ones, you can leave them alone and edit the transients manually. Simply right-click a transient and choose an option from the menu. Choose Disable to turn a marker off. Choose Promote to lock a marker so it can't be changed.

---

3. Activate the Quantize option in the Task section of the palette and click the Quantize button to open the Quantize dialog box (see Figure 8.28).
4. Set the Duration parameter to the lowest rhythmic value in your audio.
5. Make sure the AudioSnap Beats option is activated.

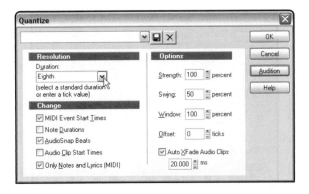

Figure 8.28 Use the AudioSnap Quantize feature to correct the timing of your audio performance.

6. Leave the Strength parameter set to 100, Swing to 50, Window to 100, and Offset to 0. These settings will give you exact quantization.

7. Click OK.

Your audio is quantized so that the transients fall perfectly on the beat. If you want to experiment with the feel a bit, try setting the Swing parameter to 30 or 70 to have the performance fall before or after the beat.

Groove Quantize

You can go even farther with feel experimentation using the AudioSnap Groove Quantize feature. The Groove Quantize feature applies preexisting rhythmic grooves to your data. Here's an example:

1. Create a new blank project.

2. Choose File > Import >Audio. For this example, import the drums.wav file from the C:\Program Files\Cakewalk\SONAR 6 Producer Edition\Tutorials folder.

3. Select the imported clip, click the AudioSnap Enable button in the palette, and use the Align Time Ruler option to align the beats in the clip.

4. Activate the Quantize button in the Task area of the palette and click the Groove Quantize button to open the Groove Quantize dialog box (see Figure 8.29).

5. Choose Cakewalk DNA Grooves.grv for the Groove File.

6. Choose a Groove Pattern.

7. For exact pattern matching, choose a Resolution set to the lowest rhythmic value in your audio. For this example, choose Eighth, since the hi-hat is playing eighth notes. For lining up the beat at measure boundaries, but keeping the general feel between measures, try using the Whole setting.

8. For exact pattern matching, use a Window Sensitivity of 100%. For lining up the beat at measure boundaries, try a setting of 25%.

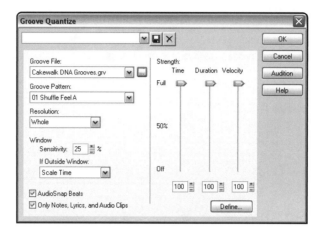

Figure 8.29 Use the AudioSnap Groove Quantize feature to apply a different rhythmic groove to your audio.

9. I usually use Do Not Change for the If Outside Window parameter, but when lining up the beat at measure boundaries, try using Scale Time.

10. Make sure the AudioSnap Beats option is activated.

11. Leave the Strength Time, Duration, and Velocity set to 100%. You can experiment with these (especially the Time parameter) by lowering them to keep more of the original rhythm, note durations, and note velocities intact.

12. Click the Audition button to preview the results while you experiment with the different Groove Patterns.

13. Click OK.

Groove Quantize is a great way to free up the feeling of a stiff groove.

The AudioSnap Pool

What about when you have multiple audio clips and you want to line them up to the same beat? The AudioSnap Pool feature will let you snap the groove of one audio clip to another. Here's an example:

1. Create a new blank project.

2. Choose File > Import >Audio. For this example, import the drums.wav file from the C:\Program Files\Cakewalk\SONAR 6 Producer Edition\Tutorials folder.

3. Select the imported clip, click the AudioSnap Enable button in the palette, and use the Align Time Ruler option to align the beats in the clip.

4. Click the AudioSnap Add Transients to Pool button in the palette.

5. Create a new audio track and import the Congas.wav file from the C:\Program Files \Cakewalk\SONAR 6 Producer Edition\Tutorials folder.

6. Select the conga clip and press Ctrl+L to remove the Groove-Clip Looping.

7. Slip-stretch (Ctrl + slip-edit) the end of the conga clip so that it lines up with the beginning of measure 2.

8. Click the AudioSnap Enable button in the palette to enable AudioSnap for the conga clip. If you play the project, you'll hear that the conga is not in time with the drums. You'll also see the transients are not lined up between the two clips as shown in Figure 8.30.

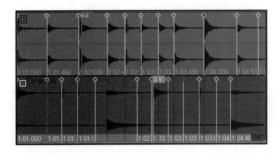

Figure 8.30 AudioSnap enables you to see the audio in multiple clips out of sync.

9. With the conga clip still selected, activate the Quantize to Pool option in the Task area of the palette.

10. In the Actions area of the palette, leave the Quantize Window and Quantize Strength parameters set to 100% because you want to sync the clips exactly with one another. If you wanted to leave some of the original feel of the conga clip, you could try reducing these parameters. A setting of 50% is a good start.

11. Set the Max Distance From Pool parameter to the lowest rhythmic value found in your reference audio. In this example, your reference audio is the drums clip and its lowest rhythmic value is eighth notes, so set this parameter to Eighth.

12. Click the Quantize to Pool button.

When you play the project, you'll hear that both clips are in sync with one another and playing with the same rhythmic groove. You can also see that all of the relevant transients are lined up.

Extract a Groove and Replace

What we did in the previous example was to extract the groove from the drums clip and use it to align the conga clip to the same groove using the AudioSnap Pool feature. We can also use that groove for other things.

Extract and Save

Using the AudioSnap Extract Groove feature, you can take a groove from selected audio data and save it as a groove pattern in a groove file for use with the Groove Quantize feature, as we did earlier. Here's how:

1. Select an audio clip.
2. Click the AudioSnap Enable button in the palette to enable AudioSnap for the clip.
3. Click the AudioSnap Add Transients to Pool button in the palette to add the clip's groove to the AudioSnap Pool.
4. Activate the Extract Groove option in the Task area of the palette.
5. Click the Save As Groove button in the Actions area of the palette to open the Define Groove dialog box.

After you save the groove using the Define Groove dialog box, the groove will be included in the Groove File and Groove Pattern parameters of the Groove Quantize dialog box and can be applied to any other audio clip.

Replace an Instrument

Using the AudioSnap Extract Groove feature, you can also convert a groove into MIDI notes. One of my favorite uses for this is to replace an instrument within a clip. For example, it becomes very easy to replace the snare drum in a drum clip as follows:

1. Create a new blank project.
2. Choose File > Import >Audio. For this example, import the drums.wav file from the C:\Program Files\Cakewalk\SONAR 6 Producer Edition\Tutorials folder.
3. Select the imported clip, click the AudioSnap Enable button in the palette, and use the Align Time Ruler option to align the beats in the clip.
4. Click the AudioSnap Add Transients to Pool button in the palette.
5. Right-click the clip and choose Envelopes > Create Track Envelope > Volume to add a volume envelope to the clip. We will use this to cut out the existing snare instrument.
6. Right-click the envelope and choose Add Nodes at Transient Markers.
7. Drag the node at beat 2 down to the bottom of the clip (see Figure 8.31).

Figure 8.31 Use an envelope to cut out the existing instrument with nodes aligned at transients.

8. Right-click each of the resulting diagonal envelope lines and choose Jump so the envelope will quickly lower and then raise the volume.
9. Do the same thing we did in steps 7 and 8 for beat 4 to cut out the other snare sound.
10. Now we want to disable all of the transient markers, except for the ones at beat 2 and 4 where the snare sound should be. As luck would have it, we can do this by selecting

the clip and moving the Threshold slider in the palette to the right so that it is set at 91%. Most of the time you would probably need to use a combination of sliders and manually disable the markers by right-clicking each one.

11. Activate the Extract Groove option in the Task section of the palette and click the Copy as MIDI Notes button.

12. Choose Insert > Soft Synths > Session Drummer 2.

13. In the Insert Soft Synth Options dialog box, make sure the MIDI Source, First Synth Audio Output, Synth Track Folder, and Synth Property Page options are activated and click OK.

14. In the Session Drummer 2 window, click the Prog button, choose Load Program, select the SL Groovy Kit Rock.prog file, and click Open to load a drum kit. Move the Session Drummer 2 window out of the way or close it.

15. Click the AudioSnap Options button in the palette to open the AudioSnap Options dialog box. In the MIDI Extraction section, set the Convert to MIDI Note parameter to D3 because that is the MIDI note you need to use to trigger the Session Drummer 2 snare drum instrument. Also, activate the Note Velocities Vary with Pulse Level option. This will take the loudness from each note in the extracted groove and use it for the MIDI trigger notes. This means the new snare instrument will be played with relatively the same loudness as the original. Click OK.

16. Choose Go > Beginning to make sure the Now Time is positioned at the start of the project.

17. Select the Session Drummer 2 MIDI track.

18. Choose Edit > Paste. In the Paste dialog box, make sure Starting at Time is 1:01:000, Repetitions is 1, and Destination Starting Track is 4. Click OK. Your project should look similar to what is shown in Figure 8.32.

Figure 8.32   You can use a soft synth to replace beats with AudioSnap.

19. Play the project.

The snare drum in the drum track is now being dynamically replaced in real-time as the project plays. That demonstrates the true power of the AudioSnap feature. Have fun!

9 Composing with Loops

In addition to creating music by recording and editing your MIDI and audio performances, SONAR allows you to compose music with *sample loops*. Sample loops are usually (though not always) short audio recordings that you can piece together to create entire musical performances. Using them is a great way to add some acoustic audio tracks to your project without actually having to do any recording or knowing how to play an instrument. For example, you can buy a CD full of sample loops that contain nothing but acoustic drum beats. Not only can you buy drum loops, but you can also get real guitar solos, vocal chorus recordings, orchestral recordings, and more. You can create an entire project just by using sample loops, and SONAR even provides you with the tools to create your own loops. This chapter will do the following:

* ❈ Explain loop based features.
* ❈ Explain Groove clips.
* ❈ Show you how to create and save Groove clips.
* ❈ Describe the Loop Construction view.
* ❈ Demonstrate how to work with Groove clips.
* ❈ Describe the Loop Explorer view.
* ❈ Explain project pitch and pitch markers.

Groove Clips

In SONAR, sample loops are known as *Groove clips*. If you're familiar with Sony's ACID software, you won't have any trouble with Groove clips because they are Cakewalk's equivalent to Sony's loops for ACID. Like loops for ACID, Groove clips automatically take care of the tedious chore of matching the playback tempo and pitch of each loop you use in a song. This is because Groove clips contain extra information that lets SONAR know their basic tempo, pitch, and playback properties. SONAR can accurately shift the tempo and pitch of the Groove clips so they match the tempo and pitch of the current project. Why is this important?

Because not all sample loops are recorded at the same tempo and pitch, and in order to use them in the same song, they have to "groove" with one another, so to speak. Before loops for ACID or Groove clips came along, a musician would have to match the tempo and pitch of multiple loops manually.

Of course, not all sample loops contain the extra information I mentioned earlier. Plain sample loops need to be converted into Groove clips before you can use them in a SONAR project.

Creating Groove Clips

There are two types of Groove clips: audio Groove clips and MIDI Groove clips. For the most part, both types of Groove clips are handled in the same way, but there are some subtle differences.

Creating Audio Groove Clips

You can easily convert any audio clip in SONAR into a Groove clip by following these steps:

1. Right-click an audio clip in the Clips pane of the Track view and choose Clip Properties to open the Clip Properties dialog box.
2. Click the Audio Stretching tab to display the Groove clips parameters (see Figure 9.1).
3. Activate the Enable Looping option. That's basically all you need to do, but there are some extra parameters that you need to deal with, if you want some extra control over how SONAR will handle your new Groove clip.

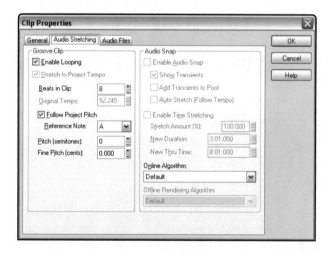

Figure 9.1 Use the Clip Properties dialog box to convert an audio clip into a Groove clip.

✳ QUICK GROOVE CLIP CREATION

Instead of opening the Clip Properties dialog box to enable looping for an audio clip, you can right-click the clip and choose Groove-Clip Looping. You also can select the clip (or multiple clips) and press Ctrl+L. These methods are quicker, but they don't give you access to the extra parameters.

4. When you activate the Enable Looping option for a clip, SONAR automatically activates the Stretch to Project Tempo parameter and makes a guess as to how many rhythmic beats are in the clip, as well as the original tempo of the clip. If the beats are inaccurate, you can change the number of beats for the clip by entering a new number in the Beats in Clip field. These parameters must be accurate for SONAR to be able to change the playback tempo of the clip to follow the tempo of your project.

5. In addition to changing the tempo of the clip, SONAR can change the pitch of the clip to follow the pitch of the project. This ensures that Groove clips stay in tune with one another in the same project. If you want SONAR to control the pitch of the clip, activate the Follow Project Pitch option.

✳ PERCUSSION GROOVE CLIPS

Not all Groove clips should follow the pitch of the project. Why? Well, if you have a Groove clip that contains percussive data like a drum instrument performance, you don't want the pitch of that clip to change because it will make the drum performance sound strange. For these types of Groove clips, only the Stretch to Project Tempo option should be activated. The Follow Project Pitch option should be activated only for clips containing pitch-related performances such as guitar, bass, woodwinds, horns, strings, vocals, and the like.

6. When you activate the Follow Project Pitch option, you have to tell SONAR the original pitch of the material in the clip. SONAR doesn't determine the pitch automatically for you. Choose a pitch from the Reference Note list. For example, if the notes played in the clip are based on a C chord, choose C. How do you know the original pitch of the clip? You have to figure it out by listening to it. Either that or sometimes when you purchase sample loops, the CD will include information about each loop file, including the original pitch.

7. If you want to transpose the pitch of the clip so that it plays differently from the project pitch, you can enter a value (measured in semitones) for the Pitch parameter. This parameter can come in handy if you are composing with orchestral instrument loops that need to be played in a different key.

8. If the pitch of the clip is slightly out of tune, you can adjust it by entering a value (measured in cents) for the Fine Pitch parameter.

9. Click OK.

SONAR will now treat your original audio clip as a Groove clip. If the tempo or pitch of the project changes, the Groove clip will be stretched and transposed accordingly. In addition, you'll notice that in the Track view, a regular audio clip is shown as a rectangle, but when a clip is converted into a Groove clip, it is shown as a rectangle with rounded corners (see Figure 9.2).

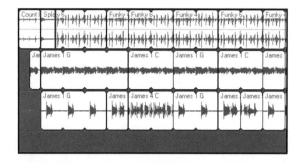

Figure 9.2 A Groove clip is indicated by a rectangle with rounded corners.

Creating MIDI Groove Clips

To create a MIDI Groove clip, you can follow the same procedures for creating audio Groove clips. The only difference is that MIDI Groove clips provide fewer parameters in the Clip Properties dialog box (see Figure 9.3).

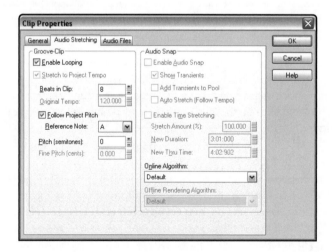

Figure 9.3 MIDI Groove clips provide fewer parameters in the Clip Properties dialog box.

The Clip Properties dialog box for a MIDI Groove clip only provides the Enable Looping option, the Beats in Clip parameter, the Follow Project Pitch option, and the Reference Note and Pitch parameters. These options and parameters work just like they do for audio Groove clips.

The Loop Construction View

There might be times when SONAR doesn't seem to stretch your audio Groove clips accurately. If this occurs, you'll hear slight anomalies in the audio when you change the tempo of your project. To correct this, you can try using the Loop Construction view to convert your audio clip by following these steps:

1. Right-click the audio clip in the Clips pane of the Track view and choose View > Loop Construction (or double-click the clip) to open the Loop Construction view (see Figure 9.4).

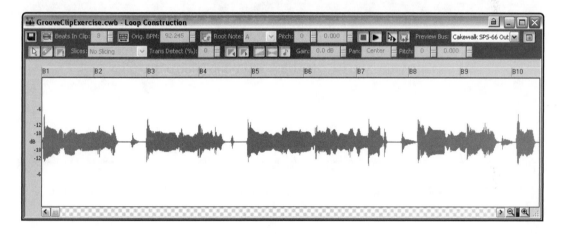

Figure 9.4 Instead of the Clip Properties dialog box, use the Loop Construction view to convert your clips.

2. Along the top of the view, you'll see a toolbar that contains all of the same parameters found in the Clip Properties dialog box. From left to right, the options are the Save Loop to WAV File function; the Enable Looping option; the Beats in Clip parameter; the Enable Stretching option (which is the same as the Stretch to Project Tempo option); the Orig. BPM parameter (which is the same as the Original Tempo parameter); the Follow Project Pitch option; the Root Note parameter (which is the same as the Reference Note parameter); and the Pitch parameters (which are the same as the Pitch and Fine Pitch parameters). You can set these parameters as I explained in the previous section.

3. The last five toolbar parameters are Stop Preview, Preview Loop, Enable Slice Auto-Preview, Slice Auto-Preview Loop, and Preview Bus. The Preview Loop and Stop Preview parameters let you listen to the loop currently displayed in the Loop Construction view.

The Preview Bus parameter lets you choose which bus (audio channel or sound card output) will be used to play the loop.

4. You'll also notice a second toolbar, as well as the audio waveform of the loop currently displayed in the Loop Construction view. Notice that when you activate the Enable Looping option, SONAR automatically adjusts two of the parameters in the second toolbar and adds vertical lines to the audio waveform (see Figure 9.5). These lines are *slicing markers*, which designate a specific place in a loop where the timing data needs to be preserved when the timing of the loop is being stretched to fit the project tempo. The slicing markers make it so that a loop can be stretched without having its pitch change at the same time.

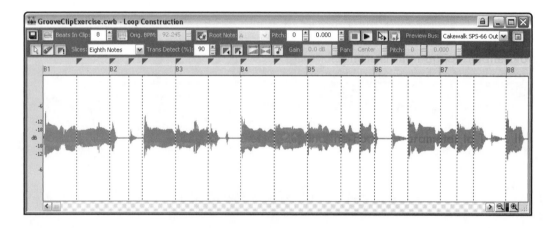

Figure 9.5 SONAR uses slicing markers to maintain the audio quality of a loop when it is stretched.

> ### EXPLANATION OF SLICING
>
> Normally, when you stretch (in other words, change the length of) audio data, the pitch is changed as well. Make the data shorter, and the pitch is raised. Make the data longer, and the pitch is lowered. By slicing the data into smaller pieces, you can stretch the data very accurately, preserving its original quality without changing its pitch. This slicing happens in real time during playback, and it's nondestructive (meaning the original data is not changed).

5. To control the way SONAR automatically adds slicing markers to your loop, you need to adjust the Slices and Trans Detect (short for *Transient Detection*) parameters, which are located on the second toolbar. The Slices parameter places slicing markers at specific rhythmic locations in the loop according to the Beats in Clip parameter (which I mentioned earlier). For example, if you set the Slices parameter to Eighth Notes, slicing markers will be placed at every eighth note location in your loop. If your loop contains four beats, it will have seven slicing markers. You would think there should be eight slicing

markers (since there are two eighth notes to every beat, and two multiplied by four is eight), but the beginning of a loop never needs a slicing marker, so there is one fewer than expected. When you adjust the Slices parameter, it's usually best to go with a note value equal to the smallest rhythmic value in your audio data performance. For example, if your loop contains sixteenth notes, try setting the Slices parameter to 16th Notes. You also can try a setting that is one value lower, which in this case would be eighth notes. Just be aware that too few or too many slicing markers will introduce unwanted artifacts into the audio when your loops are being stretched.

6. When you adjust the Trans Detect parameter, slicing markers are placed at the beginning of detected transients in the audio data of the loop. Transients are large spikes (big changes in volume) in the audio waveform. Because of this, the Trans Detect parameter works best with percussive material. A setting of about 90 percent usually works well. Usually, you'll want to use a combination of the Slices and Trans Detect parameters to get the optimum number of slicing markers set up in your loop.

7. If the Slices and Trans Detect parameters don't provide enough slicing markers, or if they provide the wrong placement, you can use the Select, Erase Marker, and Default All Markers tools to create, erase, and adjust the slicing markers manually. The first three buttons in the second toolbar correspond to the Select, Erase Marker, and Default All Markers tools, respectively. Use the Select tool to move existing slicing markers by clicking and dragging the marker triangles or marker lines in the audio waveform display (see Figure 9.6). You also can use the Select tool to create your own slicing markers by simply double-clicking in the marker area. Manually created or changed markers are shown with a purple triangle.

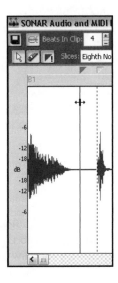

Figure 9.6 Use the Select tool to create or move slicing markers.

8. To erase a slicing marker, just choose the Erase Marker tool and click the triangle or line of the slicing marker that you want to erase.

9. If you moved any of the automatically created slicing markers and you want to put them back in their original positions, just click the Default All Markers button. If you created any slicing markers manually, those markers will remain untouched.

10. After you are finished adjusting all the parameters for your new Groove clip, close the Loop Construction view.

Usually, you can rely on the automatic settings that SONAR provides, but just in case, it's good to know that you have total control over how your Groove clips are handled.

Editing Individual Slices

In addition to manipulating the slicing markers themselves, SONAR lets you adjust the gain (volume), panning (stereo location), and pitch of the individual slices as follows:

1. Right-click the audio clip in the Clips pane of the Track view and choose View > Loop Construction (or double-click the clip) to open the Loop Construction view.

2. Use the Select tool to click between any two slicing markers to select that slice.

3. To hear what that slice sounds like, click the Enable Slice Auto-Preview button (or press A) and click the slice. If you would like to have the slice playback looped continuously, click the Slice Auto-Preview Loop button (or press Shift+A) and click the slice. To stop playback when looping, click the Stop Preview button (or press Ctrl+Shift+Space).

4. Using the last three parameters in the second toolbar, you can adjust the gain, panning, and pitch of each individual slice. Select a slice. To adjust the volume of that slice, double-click the Gain parameter and enter a new value. To adjust the panning of that slice, double-click the Pan parameter and enter a new value. To adjust the pitch of that slice, double-click one of the Pitch parameters (the first one is coarse and the other is fine) and enter a new value. For all the parameters, enter a positive number to increase the value and a negative number to decrease the value. You can also click the plus or minus spin controls next to each parameter for adjustment.

5. In the second toolbar after the Trans Detect parameter, you'll notice five buttons: Move to Previous Slice, Move to Next Slice, Show/Hide Gain Envelope, Show/Hide Pan Envelope, and Show/Hide Pitch Envelope. Use the Move to Previous Slice and Move to Next Slice buttons to quickly move to the previous or next slice from the currently selected slice. When you click any of the Show/Hide buttons, they toggle the Gain, Pan, and Pitch envelopes in the audio waveform. The envelopes adjust the gain, panning, and pitch of each slice just like the Gain, Pan, and Pitch parameters, but here you can do it graphically instead of numerically.

6. To adjust an envelope segment for a slice, just drag the part of the envelope located inside the slice you want to change (see Figure 9.7). To increase the value, drag up. To decrease the value, drag down. If you want to return the segment to its default position, double-click it.

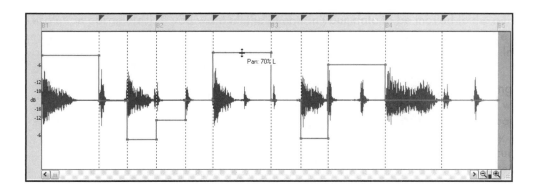

Figure 9.7 To adjust the Gain, Pan, or Pitch envelopes for a slice, drag the envelope segments up or down with your mouse.

7. Play the slice or the entire Groove clip to preview how it will sound.

8. After you are finished adjusting all the parameters for your new Groove clip, close the Loop Construction view.

With these new Groove clip parameters, you can get very creative with loop-based projects.

✺ **EDIT MIDI GROOVE CLIPS**

MIDI Groove clips don't rely on slicing, so you can't edit them with the Loop Construction view. Instead, you edit the data in MIDI Groove clips in the Piano Roll view, just like a regular MIDI clip. However, there are a couple unique aspects to editing MIDI Groove clips. First, you can edit data in any of the clip repetitions without affecting other repetitions. For example, if you delete a note in the first clip repetition, that note is not deleted in the other repetitions. Also, if you slip-edit a MIDI Groove clip to make it shorter, any edits you performed will be lost.

Saving Groove Clips

When you create Groove clips in a SONAR project, those clips are saved along with the project. But what if you want to use your Groove clips in another project? Or maybe you'd like to share the clips with your friends? This is where the Save Loop to WAV File function comes in handy. The Save Loop to WAV File function lets you save your Groove clips to disk as a special WAV file. Unlike most ordinary WAV files, which just contain audio data, the Groove clip WAV files contain all the special looping information I talked about earlier. Here's how it works:

1. With your Groove clip still open in the Loop Construction view, click the Save Loop to WAV File button (or press F) to open the Save As dialog box.

2. Use the Save In list to navigate to the location on your disk drive to which you want to save the file.

3. Type a name for the file in the File Name field.

4. Click Save.

Your Groove clip will be saved to disk as a WAV file that contains the audio data for the clip, plus all the looping information that you set, such as the Beats in Clip, Root Note, Pitch, and slicing markers. The next time you open the clip, this information will be loaded automatically.

Exporting MIDI Groove Clips

In addition to saving audio Groove clips, you can save (or export) MIDI Groove clips for later use in other projects. MIDI Groove clips are exported as standard MIDI files that can be imported later. To export a MIDI Groove clip, follow these steps:

1. Select the MIDI Groove clip and choose File > Export > MIDI Groove Clip to open the Export MIDI Groove Clip dialog box. (You can export only one clip at a time.)

2. Use the Save In list to navigate to the location on your disk drive to which you want to save the file.

3. Type a name for the file in the File Name field.

4. Click Save.

Your MIDI Groove clip will be saved as a MIDI (MID) file that contains the MIDI data for the clip, plus all the looping information you set, such as the Beats in Clip, Follow Project Pitch, and Reference Note parameters.

Working with Groove Clips

After you've created your Groove clips, you can use them to compose music in a current project or to create an entirely new project. Composing with Groove clips involves a combination of dragging and dropping to add clips to a project and slip-editing to make the clips conform to the music you are trying to create.

The Loop Explorer View

If you have some Groove clips stored on disk, you can use the Loop Explorer view to add them to your project. The Loop Explorer view lets you examine and preview your stored Groove clips, as well as add them to your project by dragging and dropping with your mouse. To use the Loop Explorer view, follow these steps:

1. Choose View > Loop Explorer (or press Alt + 1) to open the Loop Explorer view (see Figure 9.8). The Loop Explorer view is very similar to Windows Explorer.

2. In the Folders pane, navigate to the folder on your disk drive that contains your Groove clip files and then select the folder. Its contents will be displayed in the File pane.

3. You can display your Groove clip files as large or small icons, a list of file names, or a detailed list of file names. Use the Views list to choose your option (see Figure 9.9).

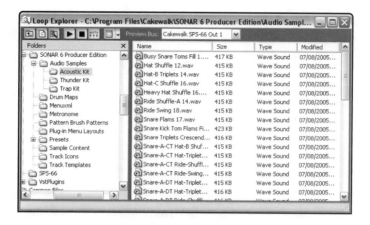

Figure 9.8 Use the Loop Explorer view to add existing Groove clips to your project.

Figure 9.9 Use the Views list to choose the Groove clip file display option.

4. To preview a Groove clip, select its file in the File pane and then click the Play button on the Loop Explorer view toolbar. To stop playback, click the Stop button. If you want a file to start playing automatically as soon as you select it, activate the Auto-Preview option (see Figure 9.10). As in the Loop Construction view, you can choose which bus to use for the loop playback.

5. To add a Groove clip to a project, just drag and drop the clip from the Loop Explorer view into the Clips pane of the Track view. If you drag the clip onto an existing track, the clip will be added to that track. If you drag the clip onto a blank area of the Clips pane, a new track containing the clip will be created for you. Also, depending on the horizontal position to which you drag and drop, the clip will be added to the track at the closest measure position in the track. For example, if you drag and drop the clip anywhere inside measure 2 in the track, the clip will be added to the track with its beginning at the start of measure 2.

6. You can keep the Loop Explorer view open for as long as you need to continue dragging and dropping Groove clips into your project.

Play
Stop
Auto-preview

Figure 9.10 Use the Play, Stop, and Auto-Preview options to preview a Groove clip file.

After you've added your Groove clips, you can slip-edit them to make them conform to the music you are trying to create. You can also add Groove clips to a project by using the Import Audio feature. slip-edit

Controlling Project Pitch

Controlling the pitch of the Groove clips in your project is extremely easy. The first thing you need to do is set the default pitch for the entire project. This is called the *project pitch*. To set the project pitch, follow these steps:

1. Make sure the Markers toolbar is visible by choosing Views > Toolbars. Activate the Markers option and click Close.

2. On the Markers toolbar, use the Default Groove-Clip Pitch list to set the initial pitch for your project (see Figure 9.11). For example, if you want the music in your project to start using a C chord, choose C.

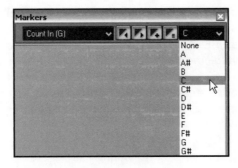

Figure 9.11 Use the Default Groove-Clip Pitch list to set the initial pitch of your project.

Pitch Markers

After you've set the initial pitch for your project, all the Groove clips automatically will be transposed to play using that pitch until you change it. To change the project pitch at specified points in your project, you need to use pitch markers. Although pitch markers work almost the same as regular markers, they do have a slight difference.

Creating Pitch Markers

Creating pitch markers is essentially the same as creating regular markers. You simply set the Now time to the measure, beat, and tick at which you want to place the marker in the project, activate the Marker dialog box, and type in a name. But you also have to designate a pitch setting for that marker, which tells SONAR to change the project pitch at that point in the project. To create a pitch marker, follow these steps:

1. Set the Now time to the measure, beat, and tick or the SMPTE time at which you want to place the marker in the object.

2. Choose Insert > Marker to open the Marker dialog box (see Figure 9.12). You can also open the Marker dialog box by pressing F11; holding the Ctrl key and clicking just above the Time Ruler (the Marker section) in the Track, Staff, or Piano Roll views; right-clicking in a Time Ruler; clicking on the Insert Marker button in the Markers toolbar; or clicking on the Insert Marker button in the Markers view.

Figure 9.12 Using the Marker dialog box, you can create a pitch marker.

3. Type a name for the marker.

4. If you want the marker to be assigned to a measure/beat/tick value, you don't need to do anything more.

5. If you want the marker to be assigned to an SMPTE time, activate the Lock to SMPTE (Real World) Time option.

❋ **LOCK TO SMPTE TIME**

If you use the Lock to SMPTE (Real World) Time value, your marker is assigned an exact hour/minute/second and frame value. It retains that value no matter what. Even if you change the tempo of the project, the marker keeps the same time value, although its measure/beat/tick location might change because of the tempo. This feature is especially handy when you're putting music and sound to video, and you need to have queues that always happen at an exact moment within the project.

By leaving a marker assigned to a measure/beat/tick value, you can be sure that it will always occur at that measure, beat, and tick even if you change the tempo of the project.

6. Assign a pitch to the marker using the Groove-Clip Pitch list.
7. Click OK.

When you're finished, your pitch marker (and its pitch) will be added to the marker section (just above the Time Ruler) in the Track, Staff, and Piano Roll views.

 ADD MARKERS DURING PLAYBACK

Usually, you add markers to a project while no real-time activity is going on, but you also can add markers while a project is playing. Simply press the F11 key, and SONAR will create a marker at the current Now time. The new marker will be assigned a temporary name automatically, which you can change later. You also need to add a pitch to each marker after you stop playback because SONAR will not assign pitches to markers automatically.

Changing Pitch Marker Names
To change the name of a pitch marker, follow these steps:

1. Right-click the marker in the Marker section of the Time Ruler in one of the views to open the Marker dialog box (or double-click the marker in the Markers view).
2. Type a new name for the marker.
3. Click OK.

Changing Pitch Marker Time
Follow these steps to change the time value of a pitch marker numerically:

1. Right-click the marker in the Marker section of the Time Ruler in one of the views to open the Marker dialog box (or double-click the marker in the Markers view).
2. Type a new measure/beat/tick value for the marker. If you want to use an SMPTE value, activate the Lock to SMPTE (Real World) Time option and then type a new hour/minute/second/frame value for the marker.
3. Click OK.

You also can change the time value of a pitch marker graphically by simply dragging the marker in the marker section of the Time Ruler in one of the views. Drag the marker to the left to decrease its time value, or drag it to the right to increase its time value. Simple, no?

Making a Copy of a Pitch Marker
To make a copy of a pitch marker, follow these steps:

1. Hold down the Ctrl key.
2. Click and drag a pitch marker to a new time location in the Marker section of the Time Ruler in one of the views.

3. Release the Ctrl key and mouse button. SONAR will display the Marker dialog box.

4. Enter a name for the marker. You can change the time by typing a new value if you want. The time value is initially set to the time corresponding to the location on the Time Ruler to which you dragged the marker.

5. Click OK.

Deleting a Pitch Marker

You can delete a marker in one of two ways—either directly in the Track, Staff, or Piano Roll views or via the Markers view. Here's the exact procedure:

1. If you want to use the Track, Staff, or Piano Roll views, click and hold the left mouse button on the marker you want to delete.

2. If you want to use the Markers view, select Views > Markers to open the Markers view. Then select the marker you want to delete from the list.

3. Press the Delete key.

A Groove Clip Exercise

Now that I've talked about how to create Groove clips and how to use them in a project, you can put that knowledge to practical use by working through a detailed exercise, so you can actually see Groove clips in action. Are you ready? Let's go:

❄ **GROOVE CLIP EXERCISE FILE**

To work on this exercise and listen to the finished version, please download the GrooveClipExercise.exe file from the *SONAR 6 Power!* book page on my Web site: www.garrigus.com/powerbooks.asp

After downloading, double-click the file to extract the contents to a folder on your Windows Desktop.

---

1. Start SONAR. A blank new project should open automatically. If not, then choose File > New and choose the Blank template from the New Project File dialog box to create one.

2. If there are any tracks in the project, delete them. You should now have a totally blank Track view.

3. Set the Default Project Pitch to C and set the tempo for the project to 114 bpm. Also activate the Snap to Grid feature and, in the Snap to Grid dialog box, choose the Musical Time: Measure options and Move To mode.

4. Choose View > Loop Explorer (or press Alt + 1) to open the Loop Explorer view. Navigate to the folder on your Windows Desktop that was created previously.

5. Drag and drop the file called *Count Off 1234.wav* into your new project. Drop it so that it will be positioned at the very beginning of the first track. You can also change the name of the first track to Drums if you'd like.

6. Drag and drop the file called *Funky 2.wav* into the first track. Drop it so that it will be positioned right after the first clip. Then slip-edit the Funky 2 clip so that it spans measures 2 through 11 (see Figure 9.13). Zoom in a bit so you can see the data in the clip.

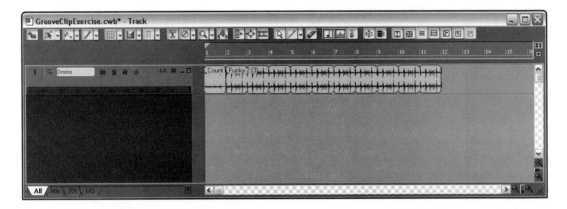

Figure 9.13 Start creating the Drum track for our project using the Count Off and Funky 2 Groove clips.

7. Drag and drop the file called *Funky Fill 1.wav* into the first track. Drop it so that it will be positioned to start at measure 12 (see Figure 9.14).

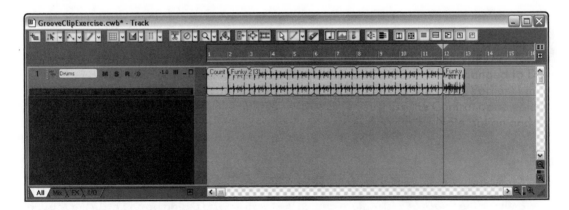

Figure 9.14 Drag and drop Funky Fill 1 into measure 12.

8. Drag and drop the file called *Pang Crash.wav* into the first track. Drop it so that it will be positioned to start at measure 13 (see Figure 9.15). Track 1 in our new project now contains all the drum parts. Play the project to hear what it sounds like so far. Also, save the project using the name Groove Clip Exercise.

266
✳ ✳ ✳

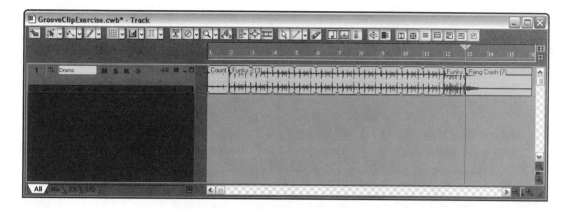

Figure 9.15 Track 1 contains all the drum parts for the project.

9. Drag and drop the *Shorty 1 C maj.wav* file from the Loop Explorer into your new project. Drop the clip somewhere underneath Track 1 in the new project so that SONAR will create a new track (track 2, Shorty 1). Position the start of the clip at measure 2. Widen the track so you can see the data in the clip.

10. Slip-edit the clip in Track 2 so that its end goes to the beginning of measure 13. Play the song. Sounds kind of dull, huh? OK, let's add some pitch markers.

11. Place pitch markers at the beginning of measures 2, 6, 8, 10, 11, and 12. Give these markers the following pitches respectively: C, F, C, G, F, C. Your project should now look like what is shown in Figure 9.16. Press Ctrl+S to save the project.

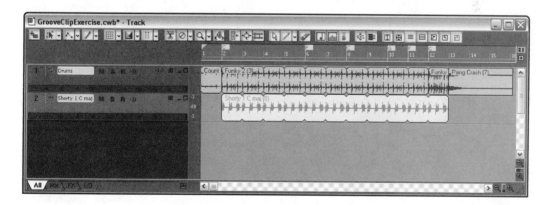

Figure 9.16 Place some pitch markers to make the project more interesting.

12. Play the project. Sounds better, right? The guitar doesn't sound quite right when it's transposed to G in measure 10, though, does it? SONAR seems to be transposing down

instead of up. Normally, there's no way around this by just using pitch markers. Instead, you need to create a Groove clip that is independent of the project pitch. Slip-edit the clip in Track 2 so that its end goes to the beginning of measure 10 rather than 13. Drag another copy of the *Shorty 1 C maj.wav* file from the Loop Explorer into Track 2, and position the start of the clip at measure 10. Now right-click the clip and choose Clip Properties > Groove-Clips. Deactivate the Follow Project Pitch option and enter a value of 7 for the Pitch parameter. This will transpose the clip up 7 semitones to G, and the project pitch won't affect it. Click OK.

13. Drag another copy of the *Shorty 1 C maj.wav* file from the Loop Explorer into Track 2 and position the start of the clip at measure 11. Then slip-edit the clip so that its end goes to the beginning of measure 13. Ah, now that sounds better.

14. Add a bass track by dragging the *Straight Slap 2 D.wav* file into your new project. Drop the clip somewhere underneath Track 2 so SONAR will create a new track (Track 3, Straight Slap). Position the start of the clip at measure 2. Widen the track so you can see the data in the clip.

15. Slip-edit the clip in Track 3 so that its end goes to the beginning of measure 13. Play the song. Cool! Now it's starting to sound like a real song. There's still one thing missing, though. It needs to be a little funkier.

16. Let's add another guitar track by dragging the *Wah Wah 3 A.wav* file into our new project. Drop the clip somewhere underneath Track 3 so SONAR will create a new track (Track 4, Wow Wah). Position the start of the clip at measure 6. Widen the track so you can see the data in the clip.

17. Drag another copy of *Wah Wah 3 A.wav* into Track 4 and position the start of the clip at measure 10 (see Figure 9.17).

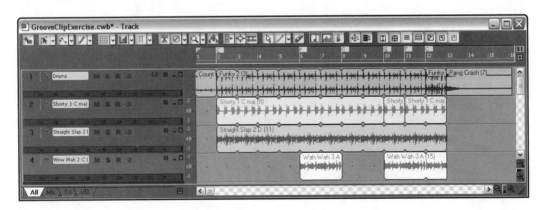

Figure 9.17 Create a new guitar track for a little more funk.

18. Open the Snap to Grid dialog box and set the Musical Time measurement to Quarter. Click OK.

19. Slip-edit the end of the second Wah Wah clip so that it ends a single quarter note into measure 13. You should see it snap into place as you are dragging the end of the clip. Press Ctrl+S to do a quick save.

20. The final version of your new project should look like Figure 9.18.

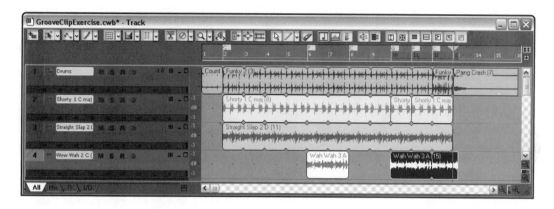

Figure 9.18 The final version of your example project should look like this.

21. Play the project. Sounds cool, no?

Now you have a good working knowledge of how to use Groove clips. You can add to this exercise by creating more tracks and inserting more clips. Don't forget that you can also change the mix by adjusting the volume and pan parameters for each track. Plus, because these are audio tracks, you can apply real-time effects as well.

❄ **ADJUST THE TEMPO**

Change the tempo of the example project to 120 bpm. Play the project. Isn't that great? SONAR automatically adjusts the Groove clips, so they will play at the correct speed whenever you change the tempo of the project.

10 } Software Synthesis

In Chapter 1, I talked about the differences between MIDI and digital audio. MIDI is simply performance data. MIDI data alone does not produce any sound. In order to have sound produced from your MIDI data, you need a MIDI instrument. Usually, a MIDI instrument comes in the form of a MIDI synthesizer keyboard or module. These are hardware-based synthesizers. Today, however, personal computers have become so powerful that it is now possible to simulate a MIDI synthesizer via a computer software program. This process is known as *software synthesis*, and basically it has the power to turn your computer into a full-fledged MIDI synthesizer module. SONAR has built-in software synthesis features. This chapter will do the following:

* Explain soft synths.
* Show you how to set up and play soft synths.
* Show you how to use the following soft synths: Cakewalk TTS-1, DreamStation, Cyclone, PSYN II, Pentagon I, Roland Groovesynth, the RXP Rex Player, and Session Drummer 2.
* Discuss the ReValver.
* Introduce SoundFonts and the sfz SoundFont Player.
* Explain the ReWire technology.

DX instruments (DXis for short) are a technology developed by Cakewalk that is based on Microsoft's DirectX technology. VST instruments (VSTis for short) are a technology developed by Steinberg. Cakewalk refers to DXis and VSTis as soft (short for software) synths. Soft synths come in the form of plug-ins that can simulate any kind of hardware-based synthesizer module. As a matter of fact, many soft synths have interfaces that look like on-screen versions of a hardware-based synth, with all kinds of knobs and switches that you can tweak with your mouse. Because soft synths are plug-ins, you can use them interchangeably with SONAR, just like effects plug-ins.

※ **WHAT IS A PLUG-IN?**

In basic terms, a *plug-in* is a small computer program that by itself does nothing, but when used with a larger application, it provides added functionality to the larger program. Therefore, you can use plug-ins to add new features easily to a program. In SONAR's case, plug-ins provide you with additional ways to produce music through the use of soft synths.

※ **INTRODUCTION TO SOFTWARE SYNTHESIZERS**

Before reading the rest of this chapter, you may want to learn a bit more about the background and basics of software synthesizers. Go to www.digifreq.com/digifreq/article.asp?ID=28 to read the Introduction to Software Synthesizers. Also, go to www.digifreq.com/digifreq/articles.asp for more information on this and other music technology topics.

Using Soft Synths

Using a soft synth to generate music is just like using a hardware-based synth, except that because a soft synth is software-based, it is run on your computer as an application from within SONAR. You control the settings of a soft synth by tweaking on-screen parameters. You can generate sound with a soft synth either in real time, as you perform on your MIDI keyboard, or by using data from a pre-existing MIDI track. To use a soft synth in your SONAR project, follow these steps:

1. Create a new project or open a pre-existing project.
2. Right-click in the Track pane of the Track view and choose Insert Audio Track to create a new audio track. Then widen the track to display its parameters.
3. Set the Input parameter to None and set the Output parameter to one of your sound card outputs.
4. Right-click in the Fx bin of the audio track and choose Soft Synths > [*name of the soft synth you want to use*] to set up a soft synth for that track (see Figure 10.1). If you ever want to remove a soft synth, just right-click its name in the Fx bin and choose Delete.

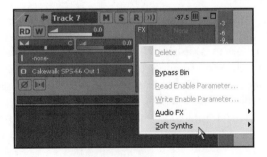

Figure 10.1   To use a soft synth, add it to the Fx bin of an audio track.

❋ **GENERATE SOUND**

Even though soft synths are software-based, they still need to use a sound card output (which is hardware) to generate sound. Adding a soft synth to an audio track allows the synth to use the output of the track to generate sound. You can also add soft synths to the audio bus Fx bins.

5. After you add a soft synth to the Fx bin of the audio track, the window for that soft synth will appear, showing the Property Page (or control interface) of the soft synth (see Figure 10.2). Using those controls, you can set up the soft synth's parameters, such as the sounds it will produce, and so on. After you've finished setting the soft synth's parameters, you can close the window to get it out of the way. If you need to access the soft synths controls again, double-click the name of the soft synth in the Fx bin of the audio track.

Figure 10.2 When a soft synth is added to the Fx bin, a window appears, showing all the controls available for the soft synth *that you chose.*

6. If you opened a pre-existing project that already contains MIDI tracks, you can skip this step. Otherwise, right-click in the Track pane of the Track view and choose Insert MIDI Track to create a new MIDI track. Then widen the track to display its parameters.

7. Set the Input parameter to the MIDI port and channel being used to receive data from your MIDI keyboard. Then click the Output parameter to display a list of available outputs. In addition to your MIDI interface outputs, the list will also show any soft synths you previously set up (see Figure 10.3). Choose the soft synth you want to use.

Figure 10.3   After you set up a soft synth, it will be displayed in the Output parameter list of your MIDI track.

8. Set the Channel, Bank, and Patch parameters for the MIDI track. The settings you choose for these parameters will depend on the soft synth you are using. For the Channel parameter, choose the same channel to which the soft synth is set. The Bank and Patch parameters automatically display different settings, depending on the soft synth. The parameters will show the sound presets available for the soft synth. Choose the bank and patch that correspond to the sound you want to use.

❋ **NO BANK AND PATCH INFO**

Some soft synths don't provide a bank and patch list that can be listed in the MIDI track parameters. In that case, use the soft synth's Property Page to choose the sound you want to use.

---

9. Either start performing some music on your MIDI keyboard or start playback of the project. Whichever action you choose, you should hear sound coming from the soft synth.

❋ **REAL-TIME PERFORMANCE**

When you use a soft synth in real time by performing on your MIDI keyboard, you might hear a delay between the time you press a key on your keyboard and the time it takes for the soft synth to produce sound. This is caused by sound card latency. To prevent this delay, you need to use ASIO or WDM drivers for your sound card, and you also need to adjust the Buffer Size slider in the Options > Audio > General dialog box to its lowest possible setting.

Those are the basic steps you need to use soft synths in your projects.

The Insert Soft Synths Function

There is actually an easier way to add a soft synth to a project, but I wanted to be sure you knew everything that was needed to add one manually. And it allowed me to explain the process in more detail. More often than not, however, you'll probably use the Insert Soft Synths function. This function automatically adds a soft synth to a project, along with the accompanying soft synth and MIDI tracks needed for the soft synth.

> ❄ **SOFT SYNTH TRACKS**
>
> When using the Insert Soft Synths function, special soft synth tracks are created (instead of regular audio tracks), which serve as audio outputs for the soft synth. The difference between an audio track and a soft synth track is that the soft synth track simply provides fewer parameters and can't be used to record audio. The soft synth track is simply an output track for the soft synth.

Here is how the Insert Soft Synths function works:

1. Create a new project or open a pre-existing project.
2. Choose Insert > Soft Synths > [*name of the soft synth you want to use*] to open the Insert Soft Synth Options dialog box (see Figure 10.4).

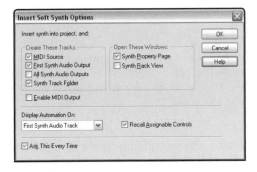

Figure 10.4 Use the Insert Soft Synths function as a quick way to add a soft synth to a project.

3. In the Create These Tracks section, activate the MIDI Source option if you want a MIDI track to be created automatically for your soft synth.
4. In the Create These Tracks section, activate either the First Synth Audio Output option or the All Synth Audio Outputs option to create the audio track(s) for your soft synth.

❋ MULTIPLE AUDIO OUTPUTS

Some soft synths provide multiple audio outputs, similar to some hardware-based synthesizers. This gives you more control over how the sounds of the soft synth are processed and routed. For example, if a soft synth can produce 16 different instrument sounds at the same time and has four outputs (like the Cakewalk TTS-1), you can group those 16 instruments into four different sections and send them to their own outputs. This means you could send all drum sounds to one output, all guitar sounds to another output, and so on. You could then apply different effects to each output (or group of sounds). Each output of a soft synth requires its own soft synth track. If you choose the All Synth Audio Outputs option in the Insert Soft Synth Options dialog box, and the soft synth provides four outputs, then four separate soft synth tracks will be created.

5. To keep things organized, you can have the MIDI and audio tracks associated with a soft synth stored in their own track folder. To do this, activate the Synth Track Folder option.

6. In the Open These Windows section, activate the Synth Property Page option if you want the soft synth's Property Page (or control interface) to be opened after the soft synth is added to the project.

7. In the Open These Windows section, activate the Synth Rack View option if you want the Synth Rack view to be opened after the soft synth is added to the project.

8. If you want to record the MIDI output from a soft synth, activate the Enable MIDI Output option.

❋ SOFT SYNTH MIDI OUTPUT

While all soft synths must provide at least one audio output so that you can hear and record their sounds, some also provide MIDI output. This output can come from a built-in arpeggiator (melody generator) or some other feature provided by the soft synth. By activating the Enable MIDI Output option, you can record the MIDI data from the soft synth into SONAR for editing.

9. Use the Display Automation On menu to choose where the automation data for the soft synth will be recorded. By default, automation data is recorded into the soft synth's audio track. To keep things organized, I usually leave this set to the default value.

❋ SOFT SYNTH AUTOMATION

In addition to recording soft synth audio and MIDI output, you can also record soft synth parameter changes over time. This means that you can dynamically change the sound currently being played by the soft synth. As you change the parameters in the soft synth's Property Page, those changes are recorded as data in SONAR and then played back as your project plays. This gives you total tonal control over the sound of the soft synth.

10. The Synth Rack view allows you to create on-screen controls to represent the various parameters of a soft synth. If you will be using multiple instances (copies) of the same soft synth in your project and you want each instance to have the same on-screen controls, activate the Recall Assignable Controls option.

11. Click OK. The soft synth you chose will be added to the project along with the MIDI track and soft synth track(s), depending on the options you activated in the Insert Soft Synth Options dialog box.

12. If you chose to have a MIDI track automatically created for you, you still need to set the track parameters. Set the Channel, Bank, and Patch parameters for the MIDI track.

13. Either start performing some music on your MIDI keyboard or start playback of the project. Whichever action you choose, you should hear sound coming from the soft synth.

Don't worry if the instructions in the last two sections seem a bit generic. I'll provide some more specific examples on how to use the soft synths that are included with SONAR a little later. Before we get to that, let me tell you about the Synth Rack view.

The Synth Rack View

When you add a soft synth to a project, the soft synth is listed as an entry in SONAR's Synth Rack view (see Figure 10.5). The Synth Rack view manages all the soft synths in a project by letting you add, remove, and change soft synths, as well as manipulate their properties.

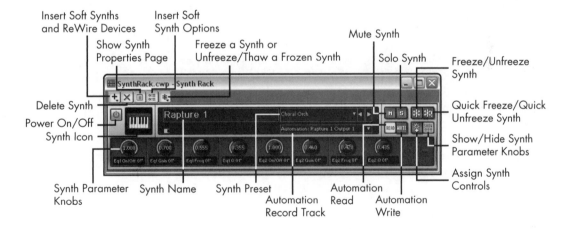

Figure 10.5 All soft synths in a project are listed in the Synth Rack view.

Adding a Soft Synth

To add a soft synth to a project using the Synth Rack view, just click the Insert Soft Synths and ReWire Devices button or press A. Then choose a soft synth from the menu. This will open the

Insert Soft Synth Options dialog box. From there, you can follow the same steps as shown in the previous section.

Removing a Soft Synth

To remove a soft synth from a project using the Synth Rack view, select the soft synth by clicking its icon. Then click the Delete button or press D.

DELETE ASSOCIATED TRACKS

If there are any MIDI, audio, or software synth tracks associated with the deleted soft synth, they will not be removed from the project. You have to delete those tracks manually if you no longer want them in the project.

Setting Soft Synth Properties

To access the Property Page (or control interface) of a soft synth via the Synth Rack view, select the soft synth by clicking its icon and then click the Properties button or press P. You can also just double-click the icon.

Synth Rack Parameters

When a soft synth is listed in the Synth Rack, it is shown using a graphical representation that has a number of control parameters you can use to manipulate certain aspects of the soft synth. These include turning the soft synth on or off, showing its name, displaying its current preset, muting or soloing the soft synth, and more.

Power On/Off

Just like a hardware-based synth, you can turn a soft synth on or off. To do so, click the soft synth's Power On/Off button in the Synth Rack. Internally, this changes the soft synth's connection to SONAR's audio engine. When the soft synth is on, it is connected to the audio engine, which means it produces sound and also takes up some of your computer's processing power. When the soft synth is off, it is not connected to the audio engine, which means it does not produce sound, and it doesn't use any of your computer's processing power. Using the Power On/Off button is an easy way to disable/enable a soft synth without having to keep adding or removing it (and its associated tracks) from a project.

CONNECTION METHODS

Sometimes, you might notice that the Power On/Off button is not available. This is because soft synths are "connected" to a project in two different ways. When you add a soft synth manually to a project by inserting it into the Fx bin of an audio track, the soft synth is treated like an effect, and it can't be disconnected from the SONAR audio engine without being removed completely from the project. When you add a soft synth via the Insert Soft Synths function, it is inserted into the input of the soft synth track, which means it can be disconnected from the SONAR audio engine without having to be removed from the project.

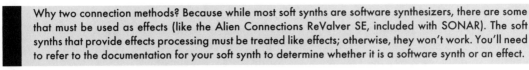

Why two connection methods? Because while most soft synths are software synthesizers, there are some that must be used as effects (like the Alien Connections ReValver SE, included with SONAR). The soft synths that provide effects processing must be treated like effects; otherwise, they won't work. You'll need to refer to the documentation for your soft synth to determine whether it is a software synth or an effect.

Presets

You can change the current synth preset (sound) of a soft synth in the Synth Rack by clicking the soft synth's Preset parameter. This displays a menu that chooses the preset you want to use. Unfortunately, this only works with SONAR presets, meaning the presets listed in the Presets menu of the Property Page of a soft synth. Many soft synths have their own method of storing presets, and some soft synths are multitimbral (they can produce more than one sound at the same time). For these soft synths, you need to access their Property Pages to change their presets. However, you can save your own presets using SONAR's Presets feature, and these presets will show up in the Synth Rack view.

Mute and Solo

You also can mute and solo soft synths in the Synth Rack by clicking their Mute and Solo buttons. This is just like muting and soloing tracks in the Track view. And just like muting a track, when you mute a soft synth, it no longer produces any sound, but it is still processed by your computer. Muting a soft synth doesn't disconnect it from the SONAR audio engine. If you want to mute and disconnect a soft synth, use the Power On/Off button instead.

Synth Icons

Each soft synth in the Synth Rack is provided with a synth icon. Synth icons are similar to Track icons. Synth icons can be used to help organize your soft synths and help you quickly identify the current sound of a synth. For example, if your synth is set to a guitar sound, you could assign a picture of a guitar to the synth. To manipulate the icon for a soft synth, right-click the icon and choose one of the following options:

- ❄ **Load Synth Icon.** Use this option to load a new icon for the synth. Simply select a new icon in the Open dialog box and click Open.
- ❄ **Reset Synth Icon.** Use this option to reset the icon to the default synth icon.
- ❄ **Set Icon as Synth Default.** Use this option to set the current icon as the default synth icon. Now when you use the Reset Synth Icon option, it will use the current icon as the default synth icon.
- ❄ **Show Synth Icons.** Remove the check mark from this option to hide all synth icons. To show all synth icons again, choose the SONAR menu item Options > Icons > Synth Rack > Show Large Icons.

Freeze/Unfreeze a Soft Synth

Another feature provided by the Synth Rack is the Freeze/Unfreeze Synth function. Depending on the power of your computer, using many different soft synths at the same time can start to bog down playback and recording in SONAR. The more soft synths you use, the more computer power is consumed. This can cause SONAR's performance to be affected, and you may experience audio skips or stuttering. SONAR may even stop playback altogether. In order to help with this situation, SONAR "freezes" soft synth tracks, which basically turns them into audio tracks and deactivates their associated soft synths. This relieves the strain on your computer, but still includes the soft synth performance in your project.

The Freeze/Unfreeze Synth function can be accessed in the Synth Rack by using the Freeze a Synth toolbar button or the Freeze/Unfreeze Synth button associated with a specific synth. If you use a synth's own Freeze/Unfreeze button, just click the button. If you use the toolbar button, first select the synth you want to work with and then choose one of the following options:

* **Freeze Synth.** Choose this option from the menu to freeze an active synth. The Freeze Synth option will automatically use SONAR's Bounce to Track function to take the audio output from the synth performance and place it in the synth's track. Then both the synth and its accompanying MIDI tracks are deactivated.

* **Unfreeze Synth.** After you have used the Freeze Synth function on a soft synth, you can "unfreeze" that synth by choosing this option. Choosing Unfreeze Synth will discard the bounced audio that was created with the Freeze Synth option, and it will reactivate both the synth and its accompanying MIDI tracks.

* **Quick Unfreeze Synth.** This option is similar to the Unfreeze Synth option, except that it doesn't discard the bounced audio.

❄ FREEZE SYNTH FROM THE TRACK VIEW

In addition to using the Synth Rack, you can also access the Freeze Synth function from the Track view. Simply right-click the soft synth track of the synth you want to freeze and choose Freeze > [one of the freeze options]. You can also choose Track > Freeze from SONAR's main menu.

Freeze Synth Options

There are several things you can do to alter the way the Freeze Synth function works. To access these settings, use the same methods described earlier, but choose Freeze Options to open the Freeze Options dialog box (see Figure 10.6).

Figure 10.6 Use the Freeze Options dialog box to alter the way the Freeze Synth function works.

The options in the Freeze Options dialog box work as follows:

❄ **Fast Bounce.** Having this option activated allows SONAR to bounce the audio output of a synth faster than real time, meaning it doesn't have to play through your entire project just to record the audio output of the synth. However, there are some soft synths on the market that require a real-time bounce. If you have trouble with a synth not having its audio output bounced correctly, then deactivating this option should solve the problem.

❄ **Hide MIDI Tracks.** Normally, when you freeze a synth, the MIDI tracks stay visible in the Track view. However, if you would like them to be hidden when you freeze a synth, then activate this option. This can come in handy when you're working with a lot of tracks, and you want to keep things organized.

❄ **Single Bounce Per Track.** Having this option activated tells SONAR to bounce the synth's audio output into a single, long audio clip. If you would rather have the audio bounced to multiple clips (corresponding to the times in the synth performance when only audio output is present), then deactivate this option.

❄ **Remove Silence.** This option uses SONAR's Remove Silence function to remove the silent sections of the single, long audio clip created when using the Single Bounce Per Track option, mentioned earlier.

❄ **Freeze Tail Duration.** If you have applied any effects to a synth, you may have noticed that the sound of the effect can sometimes continue playing even after the audio output from the synth has stopped. This is called an *effect tail*. In order to compensate for the effect tail, you need to count how many seconds the effect tail continues to play and then enter that value into the Freeze Tail Duration parameter. The default value for this parameter is five seconds. This should be sufficient in most cases, but there may be times when it needs an adjustment. If you freeze a synth, and you hear its playback cut off at the end of its performance, then you may need to increase the value for this parameter.

❄ **UNLOAD SYNTH AFTER FREEZE**

One last option provided by SONAR actually unloads a synth from your computer's memory when you freeze the synth. In a way, this can be a good thing because it will free up your computer's resources and may even give you a bit of a performance boost. However, if you decide to later unfreeze that same synth, it can take a lot longer because SONAR will then have to load that synth into memory again before unfreezing it. To access this option, choose Options > Global > General. Then either activate or deactivate the Unload Synth on Disconnect option.

Controlling Synth Parameters

In addition to giving you quick access to some of the global parameters of a synth, the Synth Rack allows you to assign on-screen knobs for easy access to specific synth parameters. Of course, you can simply open the Properties Page of a synth to access all its parameters, but the control knobs in the Synth Rack give you easy access to multiple parameters for multiples synths all in one window. To begin using control knobs in the synth rack, first activate the Show/Hide Synth Parameter button for the synth you want to work with. From here, you can create knobs for various synth parameters. Simply follow these steps:

1. Click the Assign Controls button for the synth you want to work with.
2. In the synth's Property Page, adjust each of the parameters for which you would like to create control knobs.
3. Close the synth's Property Page (this is optional).
4. Click the Assign Controls button again.
5. SONAR asks you if you are sure you want to assign the controls you adjusted. Click Yes.

The control knobs you created appear below the synth in the Synth Rack. You can now adjust these knobs and doing this will change the associated parameters in the synth.

ASSIGN CONTROLS MENU

Instead of using the Assign Controls button, you can simply right-click in the controls area beneath a synth and choose a parameter to create a control knob.

To edit a control knob, right-click the knob and choose one of the following options:

※ **Grouping.** You can group more than one knob together so that they can be adjusted simultaneously. To group knobs, choose Group > *Name of Group* to add a knob to a group. Add multiple knobs to the same group to group them together.

※ **Automation.** See the next section in this chapter, "Automating Synth Parameters."

※ **Remote Control.** The Remote Control feature allows you to use an external MIDI device to control on-screen parameter knobs.)

※ **Delete Control.** To remove a control knob from the synth in the Synth Rack, choose this option.

※ **Reassign Control.** To assign a different parameter to a control knob, choose Reassign Control > *Name of the Parameter* or choose Reassign Control > Assign Controls. If you use the Assign Controls method, adjust the parameter in the synths Property Page and click the Assign Controls button for the synth as described earlier.

Automating Synth Parameters

After you have created control knobs for a synth in the Synth Rack, you can automate the knobs so that a synth's parameters will change dynamically over time as a project plays. To automate a synth's control knobs in the Synth Rack, follow these steps:

1. In the Synth Rack, use the Automation Record Track parameter to specify in which track the automation data for the synth should be recorded. This defaults the synth's own synth track, and it's a good idea to leave it set this way for organizational purposes, but you can change it if you'd like.

2. Enable the synth's control knob(s) for automation recording. You can do this in two different ways. To enable only some of the control knobs, right-click each knob and choose Automation Write Enable from the menu. To enable all of a synth's control knobs, click the synth's Automation Write button.

3. Set the Now Time to the point in the project at which you would like to start recording automation.

4. Start project recording or playback. Automation can be recorded during either situation.

5. Adjust the control knob(s) for the synth in the Synth Rack.

6. When finished, stop project recording or playback.

7. Set the Now Time back to its original position and start project playback. If you don't like the automation that you recorded, go through steps 3 through 6 again.

8. If you like the recorded automation, click the synth's Automation Write button to disable automation recording for all the control knobs.

After you've recorded some automation for a synth, you'll notice that SONAR creates automation envelopes in the synth's synth track. The envelopes can be edited and adjusted in a variety of ways.

The Cakewalk TTS-1

SONAR ships with a number of soft synths, one of which is the Cakewalk TTS-1. This soft synth is multitimbral (meaning it can play more than one different sound at a time – up to 16 different sounds), has a polyphony of 128 voices (meaning it can play up to 128 notes at a time), and comes with 256 built-in sounds and nine different drum sets. You can also change the built-in sounds and save up to 512 user sounds and 128 user drum sets if you'd like.

TTS-1 Basics

If you examine the main interface for the TTS-1 (see Figure 10.7), you'll notice that it provides 16 parts—one part for each of the 16 available MIDI channels. Part 1 corresponds to MIDI channel 1, Part 2 to MIDI channel 2, and so on. Each part provides a number of adjustable parameters. These parameters include the instrument, volume, pan, reverb, and chorus.

Selecting Instruments

Instruments refers to the sounds, programs, or patches the TTS-1 provides. To assign an instrument to a part, click the name of the current patch located to the right of the volume fader for that part and choose an instrument (see Figure 10.8).

Figure 10.7 You can adjust the TTS-1 parameter settings using its main interface.

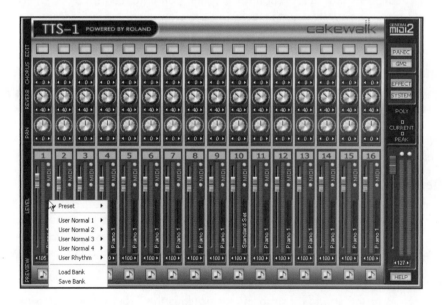

Figure 10.8 Click the name of the current patch to choose an instrument for a part.

To test the instrument and hear what it sounds like, click the Preview button for the part (see Figure 10.9). The button is located at the bottom of the part column and displays a musical note symbol.

Figure 10.9 To test the sound of the instrument, click the part's Preview button.

Adjusting Volume and Pan

To adjust the volume and pan parameters for each part, follow these steps:

1. Each part has a volume fader (slider). In the Level section, click and drag the fader up or down to increase or decrease the volume (see Figure 10.10). You can also double-click the numeric value, shown at the bottom of the fader, to type in a new volume level.

2. Each part also has a pan knob. Click and drag your mouse over the pan knob up or down to changing the panning for that part (see Figure 10.11). Drag up to pan right and down to pan left. You can also double-click the numeric value located just below the pan knob to type in a new panning value.

3. To set either the volume or pan for a part back to its default value, double-click the volume fader or pan knob, respectively.

Applying Effects

In addition, the TTS-1 provides effects that you can apply to each part individually. This gives you much more flexibility than if you were to apply SONAR's effects, because with the TTS-1 effects, you can apply a different amount of effect to each part. With SONAR's effects, you

Figure 10.10   Drag the part's fader up or down to change the volume for that part.

Figure 10.11   Drag the part's pan knob up or down to change the panning for that part.

would have to apply them to all the parts in the same amount because you would be assigning the effects to the soft synth track to which the TTS-1 was assigned.

Assigning effects to parts works in exactly the same way as adjusting the Pan parameter. To add reverb to a part, just click and drag up or down on the part's reverb knob (located in the Reverb section) to increase or decrease the reverb value, respectively. To add chorus to a part, just click and drag up or down on the part's chorus knob (located in the Chorus section) to increase or decrease the chorus value, respectively.

The only difference when adding effects is that each effect provides a number of variations. Each part cannot have its own effect variation; all parts use the same effect variation. To change the variation of an effect, just click the Effect button, which is located on the right side of the TTS-1 window (see Figure 10.12).

Figure 10.12   Choose effect variations by clicking the Effect button.

Clicking the Effect button opens the Effects window, as shown in Figure 10.13. This window chooses how the chorus and reverb effects will sound. You can choose a chorus and reverb type, as well as adjust various other parameters, to change the characteristics of the effects.

Figure 10.13   Adjust the parameters in the Effects window for different chorus and reverb variations.

❄ **SAVE INSTRUMENTATION PRESETS**

You can set some of the TTS-1 parameters by simply setting the corresponding MIDI track parameters. For instance, by changing the Volume, Pan, Bank, Patch, Chorus, and Reverb parameters of the MIDI track driving one of the TTS-1 parts, you can control the level, pan, instrument, chorus effect, and reverb effect parameters for that part. When you save your project, those parameters are stored along with it. But there is an advantage to adjusting parameters within the TTS-1 itself. You can save all the TTS-1 parameters as a preset using the Presets menu and Preset Save and Delete buttons located at the top of the TTS-1 window. By saving a number of parameter configurations as presets, you can switch quickly between configurations to test out different instrumentation for the project on which you are working.

Multiple Outputs

In the previous section, I mentioned that when you apply SONAR's effects to the TTS-1, you have to apply the same effect to all the parts because they share the same soft synth track. This isn't entirely true. The TTS-1 provides four separate audio outputs to which you can assign any of the 16 available parts. Each TTS-1 output gets its own soft synth track, so you could essentially separate the 16 parts into four different groups, each of which can use its own set of SONAR effects. This can come in handy if you want to apply one type of effect to your drum instruments, another type of effect to your guitar instruments, and so on.

Earlier I talked about how to set up a soft synth to use multiple outputs in a project, but you still need to set up the internal parameters of the synth, and this procedure is different for each synth. To designate the parts that are assigned to the four available outputs in the TTS-1, follow these steps:

1. In the TTS-1, click the System button (located on the right side of the window) to open the System Settings dialog box. Then click the Option button to open the Options dialog box (see Figure 10.14).

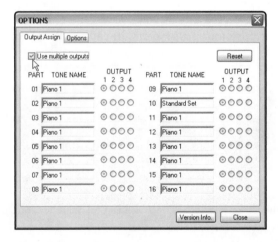

Figure 10.14   Use the System Settings dialog box to assign parts to different outputs.

2. Under the Output Assign tab, you'll see the part numbers listed in two columns and the output numbers shown to the right of each part. To assign a part to a specific output, line up your mouse with the part number and the output, and then click at that grid point to make the assignment.

3. If you want to reset all part assignments to output 1, click the Reset button.

4. You can turn on or off multiple outputs by using the Use Multiple Outputs option. This keeps your grid assignments intact if you want to send all parts to output 1 temporarily.

5. Click Close.

TTS-1 Exercise

Now that I've covered all the boring parameter basics, how about working through an exercise so that you can hear what the TTS-1 is really capable of doing? Try the following:

1. Choose File > Open and select the sample project called *Latin.cwp* that is included with SONAR. Click Open.

2. Click Cancel in the Auto-Send Sysx dialog box.

3. Close the File Info window and then delete Track 1. You won't need either of them.

4. Choose Insert > Soft Synths > Cakewalk TTS-1.

5. In the Insert Soft Synth Options dialog box, activate the All Synth Outputs, Synth Folder Track, and Synth Property Page options. Deactivate the MIDI Source option and click OK.

6. In the Track view, change the names of Tracks 11, 12, 13, and 14 to Drums, Bass, Piano, and Brass, respectively.

7. Select Tracks 1 through 10. Then choose Tracks > Property > Outputs and choose Cakewalk TTS-1 in the MIDI Outputs list. Click OK.

> ❋ **CHANGE MULTIPLE TRACK PARAMETERS**
>
> If you ever need to change the parameters for more than one track at a time, just select the tracks that you want to adjust and then use the Tracks > Property menu to change the properties for all of those tracks simultaneously.

8. Press the spacebar to start playback. Notice that in the TTS-1 window, all the MIDI tracks are being played by only four different parts—2, 3, 4, and 10. This works perfectly because the TTS-1 provides up to four separate audio outputs. You've already set up your soft synth tracks, but now you need to assign the TTS-1 parts to the different outputs.

9. In the TTS-1 window, click the System button to open the System Settings dialog box and then click the Option button. Under the Output Assign tab, assign Part 2 to Output 2 (Bass synth track), Part 3 to Output 3 (Piano synth track), Part 4 to Output 4 (Brass synth track), and Part 10 to Output 1 (Drums synth track), as shown in Figure 10.15. Then click OK.

10. Expand the four audio tracks in the Track view so you can see their playback meters and then play the project again. You should notice that the drum, bass, piano, and brass instruments are now playing through Tracks 11, 12, 13, and 14, respectively. This allows you to apply different SONAR audio effects to each separate group of instruments.

11. Right-click the Fx bin of Track 11 (Drums) and choose Audio FX > Cakewalk > FxReverb. In the Cakewalk FxReverb window, choose the Drum Room – Small, Warm preset, and then close the window. Now do the same for Track 13 (Piano).

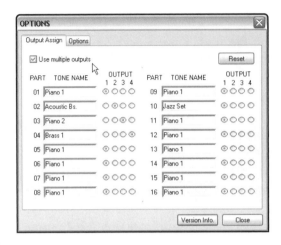

Figure 10.15   Assign Parts 2, 3, 4, and 10 to Outputs 2, 3, 4, and 1, respectively.

12. Right-click the Fx bin for Track 14 (Brass) and choose Audio FX > Cakewalk > FxChorus. In Cakewalk FxChorus window, choose the Big Stereo Spread preset and close the window.

13. Play the project one last time and then just sit back and listen.

Can you believe all of that sound is coming from one little software synthesizer? Of course, you can always try out different effects. Don't be afraid to experiment.

The DreamStation

Another of the software synths included with SONAR is the DreamStation, which simulates an analog modular synth (see Figure 10.16).

Figure 10.16   The DreamStation puts the power of analog synthesis in your hands.

The DreamStation provides three oscillator modules, an amplifier module, a filter module, an LFO (low frequency oscillator) module, an envelope module, vibrato and portamento features, and controls pertaining to synth output, such as volume and panning. By adjusting the controls provided by each of the modules, you can create your own unique synthesizer sounds, just like you would with a hardware-based analog synth.

> ❄ **INTRODUCTORY SYNTHESIS**
>
> Although I won't be going into the subjects of analog synthesis or how to create your own sounds with the DreamStation, check out the following articles for some good introductory synthesis information:
>
> * Introduction to Analog Synthesis
>
> www.digifreq.com/digifreq/article.asp?ID=29
>
> * The Basics of Synthesis and Sound Programming
>
> www.digifreq.com/digifreq/article.asp?ID=30
>
> Also, go to www.digifreq.com/digifreq/articles.asp for more information on these and other music technology topics.

> ❄ **RANDOM SOUND CREATION**
>
> There is one way you can create your own sounds with the DreamStation automatically and without having to know anything about analog synthesis. Just hold down the Shift key and click the CLR button at the top of the DreamStation window. This makes the DreamStation randomly set all of its parameters, thus automatically creating a new sound. Many of the sounds may not be usable, but click enough times, and you could come up with something very cool. Be sure to save it as a preset.

Loading and Saving Instruments

The DreamStation sounds are called *instruments*. You can save and load instruments for your own use, and you also can share instruments with others. To load and save instruments for your own use, follow these procedures:

- ❄ To load an instrument, choose an instrument name from the Preset menu at the top of the DreamStation window. The DreamStation comes with 95 pre-existing instruments.
- ❄ To save an instrument, type a name for the instrument in the Preset field and then click the Save button (the one with the picture of a floppy disk on it). Your new instrument will appear in the Preset menu.
- ❄ To delete an instrument from the Preset menu, select the instrument from the list and then click the Delete button (the one with the large red X on it).

In addition to saving and loading instruments for your own use, you can save and load instruments as DSI files to share with other SONAR and DreamStation users. To use DSI files, follow these procedures:

- ❄ To load a DSI file, click the Load button at the top of the DreamStation window. Choose your DSI file in the Open dialog box and then click Open.

✳ To save the current instrument as a DSI file, click the Save button. In the Save As dialog box, type a name for the DSI file and then click Save.

A DreamStation Exercise

To hear the DreamStation in action, try the following:

1. Choose File > Open and select the sample project file that comes included with SONAR called *Downtown.cwp*. Click Open.

2. Click Cancel in the Auto-Send Sysx dialog box.

3. Close the File Info window.

4. You'll use the TTS-1 to play your drum tracks. Choose Insert > Soft Synths > Cakewalk TTS-1. In the Insert Soft Synth Options dialog box, activate the First Synth Output option and make sure the other options are deactivated.

5. Select tracks 1, 2, and 3. Then choose Tracks > Property > Outputs and select Cakewalk TTS-1 in the MIDI Outputs menu of the Track Outputs dialog box. Click OK.

6. Choose Insert > Soft Synths > DreamStation DXi2. In the Insert Soft Synth Options dialog box, activate the First Synth Output and Synth Property Page options. Deactivate the MIDI Source and Synth Track Folder options. Click OK.

7. In the DreamStation window, choose Bass: 01-Soft Bass in the Preset drop-down list. Then close the window.

8. In the Track view, assign the Output of track 4 to DreamStation DXi2 1. Also adjust the Volume (Vol parameter) of track 4 to 75.

✳ **MULTIPLE INSTANCES**

One drawback to the DreamStation is that it is single timbral rather than multitimbral. This means that it can play only one kind of sound at a time. In addition, the DreamStation only provides one audio output. It doesn't have multiple outputs like the TTS-1. Luckily, the DreamStation doesn't take up much computer processing power, so you can set up multiple instances, each playing a unique sound.

---

9. Set up another instance of the DreamStation using the steps covered earlier. In the DreamStation window, choose Organ: 02-Jazz in the Preset drop-down list and close the window. Then set the Output of track 5 to DreamStation DXi2 2 and the Volume to 50.

10. Set up another instance of the DreamStation. In the DreamStation window, choose Synth: 09-Brass in the Preset list and close the window. Then set the Output parameters of tracks 6 and 7 to DreamStation DXi2 3 and the Volume parameters to 40.

11. Set up another instance of the DreamStation. In the DreamStation window, choose Synth: 21-Analogic 2 in the Preset list and close the window. Then set the Output of track 8 to DreamStation DXi2 4 and the Volume to 50.

12. Set up one last instance of the DreamStation. In the DreamStation window, choose Synth: 16-Rhodes in the Preset list and close the window. Then set the Output of track 9 to DreamStation DXi2 5 and the Volume to 80.

13. Play the project.

That's a cool sound, isn't it? Of course, you can liven things up even more by applying some effects. The nice thing about using multiple instances of the DreamStation is that each instance can have different effects applied to it.

The Roland GrooveSynth

Similar to the Cakewalk TTS-1, the Roland GrooveSynth (see Figure 10.17) is a soft synth that provides a large collection of preprogrammed sounds and drum sets. You can also change the built-in sounds and save them as presets for future use. The Roland GrooveSynth, however, is single timbral and can only play one synth sound or one drum set at a time. In this regard, it is similar to the DreamStation, where if you want to play more than one sound at the same time, you have to set up multiple instances of the synth.

Figure 10.17 The Roland GrooveSynth is similar to the TTS-1 in regards to the features it provides.

Working with Synth Sounds

The Roland GrooveSynth can be set up to provide either a single synth sound or a single drum kit for playback. To set up the GrooveSynth to provide a single synth sound for playback, do the following:

1. Click the Sound Name display and choose a sound from the menu (see Figure 10.18). This sets the synth sound that will be played by the GrooveSynth.

Figure 10.18 Use the Sound Name display to choose a synth sound.

2. To adjust the volume and panning for the sound, use the Level and Pan parameters shown on the right side of the GrooveSynth window. To change these parameters, either click and drag the knobs up and down with your mouse or double-click the numeric displays and enter a new value.

3. To adjust the characteristics of the sound and create a unique sound of your own, adjust the other available parameters shown in the GrooveSynth window.

4. To save your sound, type a name for the sound in the Presets field (at the top of the window) and click the Save button (the one with a floppy disk shown on it).

5. Use the Presets list to load your sound anytime you want to use it.

6. If you ever want to delete one of your sounds, just select it from the Presets menu and click the Delete button (the one with a red X shown on it).

The GrooveSynth is now ready to play the synth sound that you chose or created.

Working with Drum Kits

In addition to synth sounds, the GrooveSynth provides a number of drum kits. It can be used to play one kit at a time. You can adjust the overall sound of the entire kit, as well as the sound of each individual drum instrument in the kit. To set up the GrooveSynth to provide a single drum kit for playback, do the following:

1. Click the Sound Name display and choose a sound from the menu. In this case, move your mouse to the bottom of the menu and choose a kit from the Rhythm Set category. You'll notice that the GrooveSynth now displays its Rhythm Edit view.

2. To adjust the volume and panning for the entire drum kit, use the Level and Pan parameters shown on the right side of the window.

3. To adjust the characteristics of the entire drum kit, you can adjust the parameters in the Tone and Filter sections of the window.

4. To adjust the characteristics of a single drum sound in the kit, first choose the drum sound you would like to edit by clicking the Drum Name display in the center of the window and selecting a sound from the menu (see Figure 10.19). This menu will also show you the corresponding pitch for each of the drum sounds in the kit, so you will know what pitches to use when composing your drum tracks.

5. To adjust the characteristics of the individual drum sound (such as volume, panning, and tuning), adjust the parameters in the Voice and Tune section shown in the center of the GrooveSynth window. You can make these adjustments for each of the individual drum sounds in the kit, which gives you a lot of flexibility over the sound of your drum tracks.

6. To save your drum kit, type a name for the kit in the Presets field and click the Save button (the one with a floppy disk shown on it).

7. Use the Presets menu to load your kit anytime you want to use it.

8. If you ever want to delete a kit, just select it from the Presets menu and click the Delete button (the one with a red X shown on it).

Figure 10.19 Use the Drum Name display to choose a drum sound from the selected drum kit.

The GrooveSynth is now ready to play the drum kit that you chose or created.

A GrooveSynth Exercise

To hear the GrooveSynth in action, try the following:

1. Choose File > Open and select the sample project file that comes included with SONAR called *Latin.cwp*. Click Open.

2. Click Cancel in the Auto-Send Sysx dialog box.

3. Close the File Info window.

4. Choose Insert > Soft Synths > Roland GrooveSynth. In the Insert Soft Synth Options dialog box, activate the First Synth Output and Synth Property Page options and make sure that the other options are deactivated.

5. In the GrooveSynth window, choose Rhythm Set > Ethnic from the Sound Name menu. Then close the GrooveSynth window.

6. Select tracks 5 through 11. Then choose Tracks > Property > Outputs and select Roland GrooveSynth 1 in the MIDI Outputs drop-down menu of the Track Outputs dialog box. Click OK.

7. Set up another instance of the GrooveSynth using the steps covered earlier. In the GrooveSynth window, choose AC.Piano > Bright Piano from the Sound Name menu and close the window. Then set the Output of track 2 to Roland GrooveSynth 2.

8. Set up another instance of the GrooveSynth. In the GrooveSynth window, choose Bass > Ac.Bass 1 from the Sound Name menu and close the window. Then set the Output parameter of track 3 to Roland GrooveSynth 3.

9. Set up one last instance of the GrooveSynth. In the GrooveSynth window, choose AC.Brass > Bright Brass from the Sound Name menu and close the window. Then set the Output of track 4 to Roland GrooveSynth 4.

10. Play the project.

Can you feel that rhythm? Of course, you can make changes to the instruments or even add effects to the GrooveSynth tracks. And since the GrooveSynth requires multiple instances, you can assign different effects to each of the instruments in the song.

The Pentagon I

Another of the software synths included with SONAR is the Pentagon I. Like the DreamStation, the Pentagon I simulates an analog modular synth (see Figure 10.20). Also, like the Dream-Station, the Pentagon I can only play one sound at a time, which means to use more than one sound, you need to load multiple instances of the synth.

Figure 10.20 The Pentagon I puts the power of analog synthesis in your hands.

The Pentagon I provides four oscillator modules, two amplifier modules, two filter modules, four LFO (*low frequency oscillator*) modules, pitch and portamento features, built-in chorus, delay, and EQ effects, and controls pertaining to synth output, such as volume and panning. By adjusting the controls provided by each of the modules, you can create your own unique synthesizer sounds just like you would with a hardware-based analog synth.

Loading and Saving Programs

The Pentagon I sounds are called *programs*. You can save and load programs for your own use, and you also can share programs with others.

Loading Pentagon I Programs

To load programs for use in the Pentagon I, do the following:

1. To load a program, click one of the Bank buttons located at the top of the Pentagon I window. Programs are organized into six banks labeled A, B, C, D, E, and F (see Figure 10.21).

Figure 10.21   Use the Bank buttons to select a bank of programs from which to choose.

2. Click the up and down arrows in the Program area (located in the upper right corner of the window) to cycle through the programs in the selected bank.

> ❋ **QUICK PROGRAM SELECTION**
>
> An easier way to select a program from a bank is to right-click anywhere in the Pentagon I window and choose a program from the menu.

3. Audition the program by dragging your mouse in the dark-colored strip located at the bottom of the Pentagon I window. Click and hold your left mouse button and drag your mouse within the strip to hear how the current program sounds. Click in the left half of the strip to hear low notes played and click in the right half of the strip to hear high notes played.
4. You can also load programs from files on disk. To do so, left-click over the Pentagon I name and choose Program > Load Program from the menu (see Figure 10.22).
5. In the Load Program dialog box, choose a program file and click Open to load the program into the current program slot of the current bank.
6. You can also load entire banks of programs from files on disk. To do so, left-click the Pentagon I name and choose Program > Load Bank from the menu.
7. In the Load Program Bank dialog box, choose a bank file and click Open to load the bank file into the currently selected bank.

Figure 10.22   Use the Program menu to load programs from files on disk.

Saving Pentagon I Programs

To save programs for use in the Pentagon I, do the following:

1. Choose a bank in which you would like to save your new program.

2. Choose a program slot in the bank into which you would like to save your new program.

3. Create the new program by adjusting the synth parameters.

4. Name the new program by clicking in the Program area and typing a new name (see Figure 10.23). Press Enter to finish.

Figure 10.23   Name your new program by using the Program area in the Pentagon I window.

5. To save your new program as an individual file, left-click the Pentagon I name and choose Program > Save Program.

6. In the Save Program dialog box, type in a name for the program file and click Save.

7. To save your program as part of the currently selected bank, left-click the Pentagon I name and choose Program > Save Bank.

8. In the Save Program Bank dialog box, type a name for the bank file and click Save.

Using these procedures, you can create and save your own programs for future use, as well as share with other Pentagon I users.

A Pentagon I Exercise

To hear the Pentagon I in action, try the following:

1. Choose File > Open and select the sample project file that comes included with SONAR called *2-Part Invention #13 in A minor.cwp.* Click Open.

2. Close the File Info window.

3. Choose Insert > Soft Synths > Pentagon I. In the Insert Soft Synth Options dialog box, activate the First Synth Audio Output and the Synth Property Page options. Make sure that the other options are deactivated. Click OK.

4. Select tracks 1 and 2. Then choose Tracks > Property > Outputs and select Pentagon I 1 in the MIDI Outputs menu of the Track Outputs dialog box. Click OK.

5. In the Pentagon I window, select Bank A and choose the DX Organ program.

6. Play the project.

As the project plays, cycle through some of the provided programs. The Pentagon I includes a huge array of analog synth sounds that you are sure to find useful in your projects.

MORE PENTAGON I INFORMATION

For more information about the Pentagon I, go to the www.rgcaudio.com/pentagon_I.htm Web site.

The PSYN II

Another of the software synths included with SONAR is the PSYN II. Like the DreamStation, the PSYN II simulates an analog modular synth (see Figure 10.24). Also, like the DreamStation, the PSYN II can only play one sound at a time, which means to use more than one sound, you need to load multiple instances of the synth.

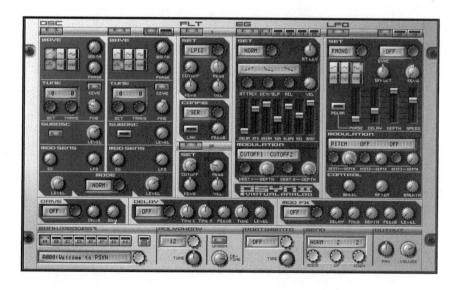

Figure 10.24 The PSYN II puts the power of analog synthesis in your hands.

The PSYN II provides four oscillator modules, a sub oscillator, two filter modules, three LFO (*low frequency oscillator*) modules, five envelope generators, pitch and portamento features, built-in drive, delay, and modulation effects, and controls pertaining to synth output, such as volume and panning. By adjusting the controls provided by each of the modules, you can create your own unique synthesizer sounds just like you would with a hardware-based analog synth.

Loading and Saving Programs

The PSYN II sounds are called *programs*. You can save and load programs for your own use, and you also can share programs with others.

Loading PSYN II Programs

To load programs for use in the PSYN II, do the following:

1. To load a program, click one of the Bank buttons located in the lower left corner of the PSYN II window. Programs are organized into eight banks labeled A, B, C, D, E, F, G, and H (see Figure 10.25).

Figure 10.25 Use the Bank buttons to select a bank of programs from which to choose.

2. Left-click or right-click the Program Name display (located just below the Bank buttons) to cycle through the programs in the selected bank.

❄ **QUICK PROGRAM SELECTION**

An easier way to select a program from a bank is to use the Presets menu in the upper left corner of the PSYN II window.

---

3. You can also load programs from files on disk. To do so, click the Disk button and choose Load Program from the menu (see Figure 10.26).
4. In the Load Program File dialog box, choose a program file and click Open to load the program into the current program slot of the current bank.
5. You can also load entire banks of programs from files on disk. To do so, click the Disk button and choose Load Bank.
6. In the Load Program Bank File dialog box, choose a bank file and click Open to load the bank file into the currently selected bank.

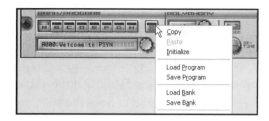

Figure 10.26 Use the Disk button menu to load programs from files on disk.

Saving PSYN II Programs

To save programs for use in the PSYN II, do the following:

1. Choose a bank in which you would like to save your new program.
2. Choose a program slot in the bank into which you would like to save your new program.
3. Create the new program by adjusting the synth parameters.
4. Name the new program by holding down the Shift key, clicking in the Program Name display, and typing a new name (see Figure 10.27). Press Tab to finish.

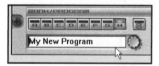

Figure 10.27 Name your new program by using the Program Name display in the PSYN II window.

5. To save your new program as an individual file, click the Disk button and choose Save Program.
6. In the Save Program File dialog box, type in a name for the program file and click Save.
7. To save your program as part of the currently selected bank, click the Disk button and choose Save Bank.
8. In the Save Program Bank File dialog box, type a name for the bank file and click Save.

Using these procedures, you can create and save your own programs for future use, as well as share with other PSYN II users.

A PSYN II Exercise

To hear the PSYN II in action, try the following:

1. Choose File > Open and select the sample project file that comes included with SONAR called *2-Part Invention #13 in A minor.cwp*. Click Open.
2. Close the File Info window.

3. Choose Insert > Soft Synths > PSYN II. In the Insert Soft Synth Options dialog box, activate the First Synth Audio Output and the Synth Property Page options. Make sure that the other options are deactivated. Click OK.

4. Select tracks 1 and 2. Then choose Tracks > Property > Outputs and select PSYN II 1 in the MIDI Outputs drop-down menu of the Track Outputs dialog box. Click OK.

5. In the PSYN II window, select Bank A and choose the Hit Organ program.

6. Play the project.

As the project plays, cycle through some of the provided programs. The PSYN II includes a huge array of analog synth sounds that you are sure to find useful in your projects.

 MORE PSYN II INFORMATION

For more information about the PSYN II, left-click once anywhere inside the PSYN II window and then press the F1 key to open the PSYN II Help file.

The Cyclone

The Cyclone is the equivalent of a very powerful MIDI sample playback device. Like the TTS-1, the Cyclone is multitimbral (meaning it can play more than one different sound at a time—up to 16), but instead of having built-in sounds, the Cyclone loads in your own sounds in the form of audio sample loops in the WAV file format.

Cyclone Basics

If you examine the main interface for the Cyclone (see Figure 10.28), you'll notice that it provides 16 parts (called *Pad Groups*), one Pad Group for each of the 16 available MIDI channels. Pad Group 1 for MIDI channel 1, Pad Group 2 for MIDI channel 2, and so on (although you can assign any MIDI channel to any Pad Group if you want).

Each Pad Group provides a number of adjustable parameters, which include Sample File Load, Volume, Pan, Sync, Loop, Mute, and Solo (see Figure 10.29).

Loading Sample Files

To load a sample file into a Pad Group, click the Load button. Then select a WAV file in the Open dialog box and click Open. If you want to remove a file from a Pad Group later, right-click the Pad Group and choose Clear Pad from the menu.

Loop Bin Loading

When you load a sample file into a Pad Group, the sample file is listed in the Loop Bin as well (see Figure 10.30).

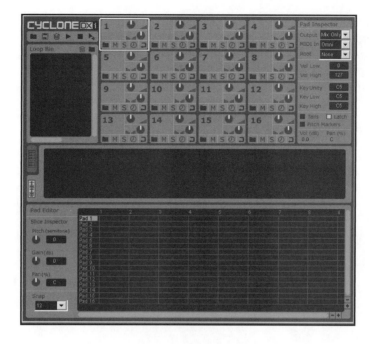

Figure 10.28 You can adjust the Cyclone parameters by using its main interface.

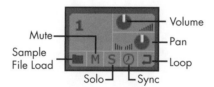

Figure 10.29 Each Pad Group provides some adjustable parameters.

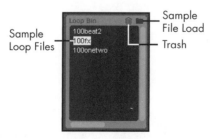

Figure 10.30 Sample files loaded into Pad Groups are also listed in the Loop Bin.

The Loop Bin lists all the sample files in the current Cyclone Sound Bank. You can load sample files into the Loop Bin separately and then apply them to Pad Groups later if you want. Just click the Loop Bin Load button, choose a sample file in the Open dialog box, and click Open. To apply a sample file from the Loop Bin to a Pad Group, drag and drop the file from the Loop Bin onto the Pad Group.

USE THE LOOP EXPLORER

You also can use the Loop Explorer view to apply sample files to Pad Groups. Just drag and drop files from the Loop Explorer onto the appropriate Pad Groups.

If you want to delete a file from the Loop Bin, select the file and click the Trash button.

DELETED FILES

If you delete a file that is being used by any of the Pad Groups from the Loop Bin, that file will be deleted from those Pad Groups as well.

Previewing Sample Files

To preview a sample file listed in the Loop Bin, just select the file and click the Preview button on the Cyclone toolbar (see Figure 10.31).

Figure 10.31 Preview sample files using the Preview button on the Cyclone toolbar.

To stop the sample file preview, click the Stop button. You also can preview a sample file that's already loaded into a Pad Group by clicking the number of the Pad Group. Click the number of the Pad Group a second time to stop playback.

Adjusting Pad Group Parameters

To adjust the Volume, Pan, Mute, Solo, Sync, and Loop parameters for each Pad Group, do the following:

* **Volume and Pan.** Click and hold your mouse on the on-screen knob; then drag your mouse up or down to raise or lower the value. If you want to reset the parameter to its default value, just double-click it.

* **Mute and Solo.** To mute or solo a Pad Group, just click the Mute or Solo buttons.

❊ **Sync.** Activating the Sync parameter will synchronize the playback tempo of the sample file loaded into the Pad Group with the playback tempo of the current SONAR project.

❊ **Loop.** Activating the Loop parameter will loop the playback of the sample file loaded into the Pad Group so that the file keeps repeating over and over again.

The Pad Inspector

Each Pad Group also provides a number of other adjustable parameters, which are accessed via the Pad Inspector (see Figure 10.32). To see the Pad Inspector parameter values for a Pad Group, just click the number of the Pad Group.

Figure 10.32 Use the Pad Inspector to adjust additional Pad Group parameters.

Output

Like the TTS-1, the Cyclone provides multiple audio outputs (up to 17–16 individual outputs and one mix output). Each Pad Group can be assigned to its own separate output using the Output parameter. If you choose the Mix Only option, the sound from the Pad Group will be sent only to the mix output, which contains a mix of all the sound coming from all the Pad Groups in Cyclone.

MIDI In

As I mentioned earlier, Cyclone can play up to 16 different sounds at once, each one assigned to its own MIDI channel. Use the MIDI In parameter to assign a MIDI input channel to a Pad Group. Then any MIDI data coming into that channel will be used to trigger playback of that Pad Group. If you choose the MIDI Omni option, then the Pad Group will receive MIDI data from all 16 MIDI channels.

Root

The Root parameter determines the original pitch of the sample file loaded into a Pad Group. If you load an ACID-compatible WAV file or a SONAR Groove Clip WAV file into a Pad Group, the Root parameter will be set for you automatically. If you load a regular WAV file into a Pad Group, you will have to determine the pitch of the file yourself and set the Root parameter manually.

Velocity and Key Map

When a Pad Group receives MIDI note messages via its assigned MIDI channel, those MIDI note messages trigger the playback of the sample file loaded into the Pad Group. You can limit the range of notes and their velocities that can be used to trigger the Pad Group by setting the Velocity and Key Map parameters as follows:

- **Velocity Low.** Set this to the lowest note velocity value that you want to trigger the Pad Group.
- **Velocity High.** Set this to the highest note velocity value that you want to trigger the Pad Group.
- **Key Map Unity.** Set this to the note value that will be used to play the sample file in the Pad Group at its Root pitch. Most of the time, you'll probably set this parameter to the same pitch value as the Root parameter.
- **Key Map Low.** Set this to the lowest note value that you want to trigger the Pad Group.
- **Key Map High.** Set this to the highest note value that you want to trigger the Pad Group.

Pitch Markers

I talked about pitch markers in Chapter 9. They are used to change the pitch of Groove Clips in a project. You also can use them to change the pitch of Pad Groups throughout a project. If your project uses pitch markers, and you want your Pad Groups to change pitch along with the markers, activate the Pitch Markers option for the Pad Groups in the Pad Inspector.

The Loop View

When you select a sample file listed in the Loop Bin, its audio waveform is displayed in the Loop view section of the Cyclone main interface (see Figure 10.33).

If the selected sample file is an ACID-compatible loop or a SONAR Groove Clip, then the Loop view will display any slices contained in the file as well; these slices are designated by vertical dotted lines shown on the audio waveform.

❋ SLICES IN CYCLONE

When you open a Groove Clip in the Loop Construction view, you'll notice that SONAR breaks the clip down into small sections. These sections are called *slices*. Slices are based on the beat values and audio waveform spikes (transients) in a clip. They allow SONAR to accurately change the tempo and pitch of a Groove Clip. In Cyclone, however, you can use slices to break sample files apart and create new sample files by combining the slices from several different files. This is where the Pad Editor comes into play.

The Pad Editor

When you load a sample file into a Pad Group, a track for that Pad Group is created in the Pad Editor (see Figure 10.34). This track contains green blocks, with each separate block representing a different slice in the sample file. At the end of the track is a white track handle that marks the point in the track at which the track will loop back to the beginning.

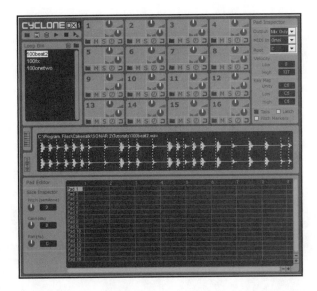

Figure 10.33 The Loop view displays sample file audio waveforms.

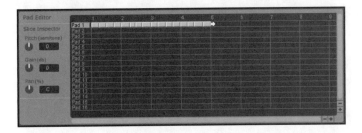

Figure 10.34 Examine and manipulate Pad Group sample file slices with the Pad Editor.

Using the Pad Editor, you can select, change, and edit slices to create entire compositions out of nothing but sample file slices if you want.

Selecting a Slice

To select a slice, just click its associated green block. If you want to select more than one slice, hold down the Shift key as you click the blocks. Also, to select all the slices in a track, double-click the track number.

The Slice Inspector

You can edit the parameters of a slice using the Slice Inspector. Each slice has adjustable pitch, gain (volume), and panning. Just select the slice you want to change and then click and drag your mouse over the parameter knobs. You also can change the settings by double-clicking the numerical values and typing in new values.

Changing Slices

You can change slices in a track by deleting them, moving them, or swapping them with slices from a different sample file. To delete a slice, just select it and press the Delete key.

You can move slices by clicking and dragging them with your mouse. To move a slice within the same track, click and drag the slice left or right. To move a slice to a different track, click and drag the slice up or down.

To swap a slice with another slice from a different file, first select a sample file in the Loop Bin so that its audio waveform is shown in the Loop view. Then click and drag a slice from the Loop view into the Pad Editor (see Figure 10.35).

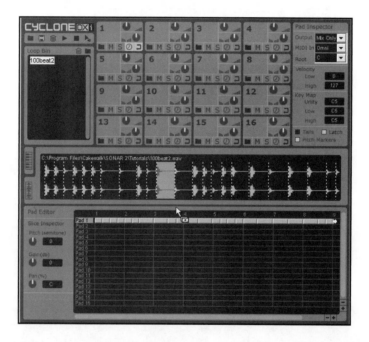

Figure 10.35   Click and drag slices from the Loop view to the Pad Editor to swap slices.

Cyclone Exercise

To hear what the Cyclone can do, try the following:

> ❀ **CYCLONE EXERCISE FILE**
>
> To work through this exercise or listen to the finished version, download the CycloneDXiExercise.exe file from the *SONAR 6 Power!* book page on my Web site: www.garrigus.com/powerbooks.asp

1. Choose File > New and select the Blank template in the New Project File dialog box to create a new project.
2. Choose Insert > Soft Synths > Cyclone to add an instance of the Cyclone to the project. In the Insert Soft Synth Options dialog box, activate the First Synth Output and Synth Property Page options while leaving the other options deactivated.
3. Download and run the CycloneDXiExercise.exe file mentioned earlier.
4. Choose View > Loop Explorer to open the Loop Explorer view and navigate to the folder created when you ran the CycloneDXiExercise.exe file.
5. Load the following file into Pad Group 1: Funky 2.wav.
6. Load the following file into Pad Group 2: Eighth G.wav.
7. Load the following file into Pad Group 3: Funk Junk 13 G.wav.
8. Load the following file into Pad Group 4: Claves 1.wav.
9. Click the numbers of Pad Groups 1 through 4 to start them playing. Sounds pretty good, huh? But it's also a little boring. I think we need to spice up this groove a bit.
10. Load the following file into the Loop Bin: Power Funky 2.wav. The file will be selected and shown in the Loop view.
11. Drag and drop the fifth slice in the Loop view onto the fifth slice in the Pad 1 track of the Pad Editor (see Figure 10.36).

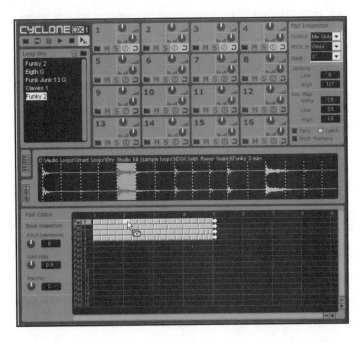

Figure 10.36 Drag and drop slices from the Loop view to the Pad Editor to replace slices (sounds) in a track.

12. Drag and drop the thirteenth slice in the Loop view onto the thirteenth slice in the Pad 1 track. Then click the Pad Group 1 number to hear it play. Click it again to stop playback.

✵ TAIL OPTION

You might have noticed when listening to Pad Group 1 that the new snare drum sound gets cut off. This can happen when you replace slices in a sample file because not all slices are exactly the same length. To remedy this, you can choose to have cut slices play through as if they weren't being cut off by having Cyclone allow the tail ends of the slices to play. To do this, select the Pad Group (by clicking its number) in which the slice resides, and then activate the Tails option for that Pad Group, which is located at the bottom of the Pad Inspector.

---

13. OK, the drums in Pad Group 1 sound pretty good, but the bass in Pad Group 2 is extremely boring. Load the following file into the Loop Bin: Marmalade 4 G.wav.

14. Drag and drop the first three slices from the Loop view onto the last three slices in the Pad 2 track of the Pad Editor. You'll notice that the track handle for that track has been moved out of position. You need to drag the track handle to the left so it lines up with the other track handles (see Figure 10.37). This will ensure that all the tracks loop at the same time. Play both Pad Groups 1 and 2 to hear what the groove sounds like so far.

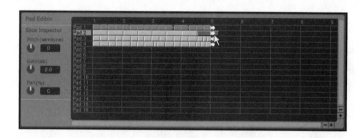

Figure 10.37 Move the Pad 2 track handle in the Pad Editor.

15. I think we'll leave the guitar in Pad Group 3 alone, but the percussion in Pad Group 4 needs some tweaking. Load the following file into the Loop Bin: Bongos Roll 1 (2 beats).wav.

16. Drag and drop the last four slices from the Loop view onto the last four slices in the Pad 4 track of the Pad Editor. Adjust the track handle so it lines up with the other track handles.

17. Click the numbers of Pad Groups 1 through 4 to hear the entire groove. Cool, no?

18. To save your current Cyclone setup as a file for later editing, click the Export Sound Bank button on the Cyclone toolbar (see Figure 10.38).

Figure 10.38   Use the Export Sound Bank function to save your current Cyclone setup as a Cyclone file.

That was just a small taste of what you can accomplish with Cyclone. This is one very powerful tool. In addition to creating entire compositions out of audio slices, you can use it for sample playback via MIDI tracks in a project, for live sample triggering via a MIDI keyboard, and for creating entirely new sample files. I'm sure you'll get a lot of creative use out of the Cyclone.

 MORE CYCLONE INFORMATION

For more information and tutorials concerning the Cyclone, be sure to read through the Cyclone section of the SONAR Help file.

I'll also provide additional Cyclone coverage in future issues of my DigiFreq music technology newsletter. Go to www.digifreq.com/digifreq/ to sign up for a free subscription.

RXP REX Player

Like the Cyclone, the RXP is also a MIDI sample playback device, but instead of loading ACID-compatible WAV files, it loads REX files. Another difference is that although the RXP can only load one file at a time, that doesn't mean it can only play one sound at a time. Instead of playing multiple files simultaneously, it plays multiple slices of a single file. In this capacity, it can be used as a drum machine, multiple sound generator, sound editor, and more.

❋ **REX FILES**

REX files are similar to ACID-compatible sample loops or Cakewalk Groove clips in that they are divided into slices, which allows their timing and pitch to be changed without degrading the audio data. This means that REX files can be played as loops, which are synced to the tempo of your project. In addition to loop playback, however, REX files provide slice playback. This is where a REX file is loaded into a player, and the individual slices within the file are triggered by MIDI notes. Using sliced playback, REX files provide dynamic sample playback options, including being able to trigger different instrument sounds (such as those in a drum kit).

RXP Basics

If you examine the main interface for the RXP (see Figure 10.39), you'll notice that it is divided into three sections—the Waveform and Slice Display, the Filter (EQ) and Amp (Volume/Pan) section, and the Pad section.

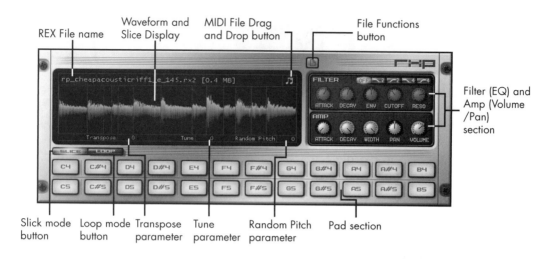

REX File name

Waveform and
Slice Display

MIDI File Drag
and Drop button

File Functions
button

Filter (EQ) and
Amp (Volume
/Pan)
section

Slice mode
button

Loop mode
button

Transpose
parameter

Tune
parameter

Random Pitch
parameter

Pad section

Figure 10.39   You can adjust the RXP parameters by using its main interface.

The Waveform and Slice Display shows the currently loaded REX file. The RXP can only load one file at a time, which means that in loop mode, you would need to use multiple instances of the RXP to play more than one file at a time. In slice mode, multiple slices from the one loaded file can be triggered simultaneously.

The Pad section allows you to play/preview the entire REX file in loop mode or individual slices in slice mode. I'll show you how this is done shortly.

Finally, the Filter and Amp section allows you to apply equalization and volume/pan changes to the entire REX file. You cannot make changes to individual slices.

Loading Sample Files

To load a sample file into RXP, click the File Functions button and choose Load from the menu. In the Load Multisample dialog box, select the file you want to load and click Open.

❋ **MULTIPLE FILE FORMATS**

You may have noticed in the Load Multisample dialog box that RXP supports many different audio file formats. REX files have a file extension of RX2. If you load something other than a REX file, it will be loaded and can be played as a loop in RXP, but slicing will not be supported. RXP will act as a simple audio loop player when loading files other than the REX format.

In addition to using the File Functions button, you can click the REX file name in the RXP window to open the Groove Browser (see Figure 10.40). The Groove Browser allows you to quickly and easily view the files you have stored in the C:\Program Files\Cakewalk\Shared Dxi\RXP\Contents folder on your hard drive. Click the plus sign next to a folder to open that folder. Double-click a file to load and preview that file in RXP automatically.

Figure 10.40   Use the Groove Browser to view your files and load them quickly into RXP.

❋ **USE WINDOWS EXPLORER**

You can also use the Windows Explorer to load files into RXP. Just drag and drop files from the Windows Explorer onto the Waveform and Slice Display in RXP.

Previewing Sample Files

Once loaded, you can preview and play files in two different modes: Loop and Slice. To preview a file, do the following:

1. Click the Loop or the Slice button to activate the appropriate mode.

2. In Loop mode, you'll notice that the pads in the Pad area are labeled with numbers. These are pitch transposition numbers. To play the file at its normal pitch, click the 0 pad. To play the file at a lower or higher pitch, click one of the negative or positive numbered pads, respectively. If you left-click a pad, you can control partial playback by holding down your mouse button and then letting it go to stop playback. Right-click a pad to play the entire file.

3. In Slice mode, you'll notice that the pads are labeled with musical note values. Each pad corresponds to an individual slice in the file. Left-click or right-click a pad to hear its associated slice played. This also shows you which MIDI note each slice will respond to when using a MIDI file to trigger slices.

4. To hear the file played at a different tempo, change the tempo of your Sonar project because the RXP follows the project tempo for all playback.

EASY SLICE PREVIEW

To preview a slice in either mode, just left-click the slice in the Waveform and Slice Display.

Editing, Saving, and Loading Programs

While the RXP doesn't allow you to edit and save REX files directly, you can edit and save the RXP settings, which are called *programs*. These settings include all of the Filter and Amp section parameters, as well as the slice positions and the Transpose, Tune, and Random Pitch parameters in the Waveform and Slice Display. All of these parameters affect the entire file rather than individual slices.

Editing Programs

The Filter and Amp parameters apply EQ and volume/panning to the file. To adjust a parameter in one of these sections, click and drag your mouse up or down over the graphic knob. To return a parameter to its default setting, double-click the graphic knob.

To transpose, tune, or apply random pitch changes to the file, use the appropriate parameters located in the bottom of the Waveform and Slice display. To adjust a parameter, click and drag your mouse up or down over the parameter value. To return a parameter to its default setting, double-click its value. The Transpose parameter transposes the file by +48 or –48 semitones. The Tune parameter fine-tunes the file by +100 or –100 cents. The Random Pitch parameter can be adjusted from 0 to 4800 cents and applies a random pitch change to each slice as the file is played.

In addition to editing the previously mentioned parameters, you can also change the position of slices in a file. Just click and drag a slice left or right to change its playback position in the file (see Figure 10.41). This is also the way to change a slice's assigned MIDI note trigger. If you start making a mess of things and want to return to the original slice positions, right-click in the display and choose Reset from the pop-up menu. You can also reverse or randomize the slice positions by right-clicking in the display and choosing the appropriate option from the menu.

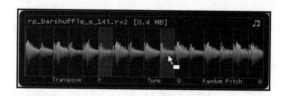

Figure 10.41   Drag and drop a slice to change its position.

To clear the current file and return all parameters to their default values, click the File Functions button and choose Initialize Program.

Saving and Loading Programs

Moving slices in a file or changing parameters doesn't actually change the file itself. This simply changes a pointer in the RXP program and when saved, the program saves these pointers to the original REX file. This means that even when you save a program, you still need to keep the original REX file on hand in order for the program to be of any use. It also means that you can create and save multiple programs for the same REX file without taking up much disk space, which provides a lot of flexibility.

To save a program, click the File Functions button and choose Save Program As from the menu. In the Save Program dialog box, type a name for your new program and then click Save. Programs are saved with a Prog file name extension. After having saved a new program, you can quickly save it again (after making parameter changes) by clicking the File Functions button and choosing Save Program. In addition, you can set a default program (one that will be loaded every time you open the RXP) by clicking the File Functions button and choosing Save Program Default.

To load a previously saved program, click the File Functions button and choose Load. In the Load Multisample dialog box, select the program you want to load and click Open. This will load the program parameters, as well as its associated REX file.

RXP Exercise

To see how the RXP can be used in a Sonar project, try the following:

> ❋ **RXP EXERCISE FILE**
>
> To listen to the finished version of this exercise, please download the RXPExercise.exe file from the *SONAR 6 Power!* book page on my Web site: www.garrigus.com/powerbooks.asp

1. Choose File > New and select the Blank template in the New Project File dialog box to create a new project. Click OK.
2. Choose Insert > Soft Synths > RXP to add an RXP instance to the project. In the Insert Soft Synth Options dialog box, activate the MIDI Source, First Synth Audio Output, and Synth Property Page options while leaving the others deactivated. Click OK.
3. Download the run the RXPExercise.exe file mentioned earlier.
3. In the RXP window, click the File Functions button and choose Load from the menu. In the Load Multisample dialog box, navigate to the folder created when you ran the downloaded file and select the following file: RP_SlinkyGroove_A_145.rx2. Click Open.
4. In the RXP window, click and drag the MIDI File Drag and Drop button into track 2 of the Sonar project and make sure the clip is positioned at the beginning of the project (see Figure 10.42). Then close the RXP window.

❋ REX FILE MIDI DATA

Most REX files have an accompanying MIDI file included within them. This MIDI file contains the MIDI notes used to trigger the individual slices of the REX file. To utilize this MIDI data, you simply drag and drop the MIDI File Drag and Drop button into your SONAR project. If you drag into an existing MIDI track, the MIDI data will show up as a new clip in that track. If you drag into an empty section of the Clips pane in the Track view, a new MIDI track will be created containing the MIDI data in a new clip.

Figure 10.42   Drag the SlinkGroove bass MIDI file into the Sonar project.

5. Select the clip in track 2 and press Ctrl + L to convert it into a Groove clip. Then slip-edit the clip so that it extends to the beginning of measure 5. Now copy the clip and paste a copy at the beginning of measure 7. Slip-edit this second clip so that it extends to the beginning of measure 13. Right-click the second clip and choose Insert Effect > MIDI Effects > Cakewalk FX > Arpeggiator. In the Arpeggiator window, choose Guitar Pick from the Presets list and close the window. Your bass part of the project is now complete.

6. Insert another instance of the RXP (using the same insert soft synth options) and load the following REX file: RP_NastyGroove3_A_145.rx2.

7. Click and drag the MIDI File Drag and Drop button into track 4 of the project and make sure that the clip is positioned at the beginning of measure 3. Close the RXP window.

8. Select the clip in track 4 and copy it. Paste one copy at the beginning of measure 9 and another copy at the beginning of measure 13. Now right-click in the Fx bin of track 4 and choose MIDI Plugins > Cakewalk FX > Echo Delay. In the Echo Delay window, choose 1/4 Note from the Presets list and close the window. Your guitar part of the project is now complete.

9. Insert another instance of the RXP (using the same insert soft synth options) and load the following REX file: RP_VaVaVoom_145.rx2.

10. Click and drag the MIDI File Drag and Drop button into track 6 of the project and make sure that the clip is positioned at the beginning of the project. Close the RXP window.

11. Select the clip in track 6 and press Ctrl + L to convert it into a Groove clip. Then slip-edit the clip so that it extends to the beginning of measure 13. Your drums part of the project is now complete.

12. Insert another instance of the RXP (using the same insert soft synth options) and load the following REX file: RP_MickeyLead1_E_145.rx2.

13. In the RXP window, set the Transpose parameter to –7 so that this REX file will play in the same key as the other REX files you are using.

14. Click and drag the MIDI File Drag and Drop button into track 8 of the project and make sure that the clip is positioned at the beginning of measure 5. Close the RXP window.

15. Select the clip in track 8 and copy it. Paste one copy at the beginning of measure 11 and another copy at the beginning of measure 13. Right-click the first copy and choose Insert Effect > MIDI Effects > Cakewalk FX > Arpeggiator. In the Arpeggiator window, choose Guitar Pick from the Presets list and close the window. Right-click the second copy and choose Insert Effect > MIDI Effects > Cakewalk FX > Arpeggiator. In the Arpeggiator window, choose Guitar Pick from the Presets list and close the window. Right-click the second copy again and choose Insert Effect > MIDI Effects > Cakewalk FX > Echo Delay. In the Echo Delay window, choose 1/4 Note from the Presets list and close the window. With the second clip copy still selected, choose Process > Retrograde from Sonar's main menu. Your synth part of the project is now complete.

16. The completed project should look similar to what is shown in Figure 10.43. Play the project.

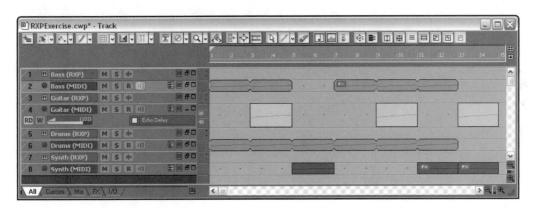

Figure 10.43 This figure shows the completed RXP exercise project.

Let me explain a little about what you are listening to as you play the project. The only data in this SONAR project being used within the tracks that you created is MIDI data. The individual MIDI notes in each clip are triggering the individual slices in each of the REX files being used. This entire project uses only four REX files for all of the sounds that you are hearing. The reason some of the copied clips sound different from the original clips is that you manipulated the MIDI data using MIDI effects. By simply doing this, you have created an entire (albeit short) song using only four sound files. Using these same four files, you could even create an entirely different song simply by changing the MIDI trigger notes in each track. This demonstrates how powerful using REX files in your SONAR projects can be.

❄ **MORE RXP INFORMATION**

For more information about the RXP, left-click once anywhere inside the RXP window and then press the F1 key to open the RXP Help file.

I'll also provide additional RXP coverage in future issues of my DigiFreq music technology newsletter. Go to www.digifreq.com/digifreq/ to sign up for a free subscription.

The ReValver

Unlike all the other software synths included with SONAR, the ReValver is actually an audio effect. You use it to apply amplifier simulation effects to your audio tracks.

The best way to describe the ReValver is to actually show it to you in action. To use the ReValver in a project, follow these steps:

1. Choose File > Open and select the sample project file that comes included with SONAR called *SONAR Audio and MIDI DEMO2.cwb*. Click Open.

2. If you'd like, you can delete all the tracks in the project except for the Guitar track. You won't need the others for this demonstration.

3. Right-click the FxReverb in the Fx bin of the Guitar track and delete it. Then right-click in the empty Fx bin and choose Soft Synths > Alien Connections ReValver SE to apply the ReValver to the track.

❄ **APPLY TO FX BIN**

As I mentioned earlier, the ReValver must be added to a project via the Fx bin of an audio track rather than through the Insert Soft Synth Options dialog box. Because the ReValver is an audio effect rather than a regular soft synth, it will not work if you apply it using the dialog box.

---

4. In the ReValver window, you'll see a virtual rack mount bay containing virtual rack mount modules used to virtually emulate preamplifiers, power amplifiers, speakers, and effects (see Figure 10.44). The first module in the rack is permanent and controls the ReValver. In the first module, adjust the In and Out parameters to control the input and output levels of the ReValver.

5. Click Bypass to temporarily turn off and on ReValver processing. This compares the audio signal with the ReValver applied and without it applied.

6. Click Clear to delete the current configuration of modules in the rack.

Figure 10.44   The main ReValver interface looks like a virtual rack mount bay.

7. Click Save to save the current configuration of modules in the rack as a ReValver preset file.
8. Click Load to open a ReValver preset file.

❄ REVALVER PRESETS

The ReValver includes a selection of preset files, which are located in the following folder on your hard drive: C:\Program Files\Cakewalk\Shared DXi\ReValver SE\presets.

---

9. By clicking a module, you can move, remove, replace, bypass, reset, as well as load and save individual presets for a module by choosing the appropriate option from the menu.
10. To add a new module to the rack, click in an empty rack space and choose Insert Module Here from the menu to open the Choose Module dialog box (see Figure 10.45).

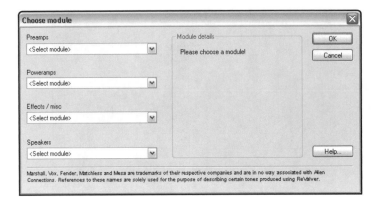

Figure 10.45   Use the Choose Module dialog box to insert a new module into the rack mount space.

11. To add a preamplifier module, choose one from the Preamps list. To add a power am-
    plifier, choose one from the Poweramps list. To add an effect, choose one from the
    Effects/Misc list. To choose a speaker simulator, choose one from the Speakers list. Then
    click OK.

12. If you play the project, you should hear the Guitar track being processed by the
    ReValver. The audio signal is processed starting with the first module in the rack and
    ending with the last module in the rack. This means that the order in which the modules
    appear in the rack makes a difference as to how the audio is processed and how it
    sounds.

13. You also can adjust the individual parameters of some of the modules to affect process-
    ing. Each module is different.

Those are the basic steps required for using the ReValver. For more in-depth information about
how the ReValver works and how to adjust the parameters of each individual module, you
should read the ReValver manual by clicking the Help button in the first ReValver module.

ReWire

In addition to DX and VST instruments, there are software-based synthesizers that run as
separate applications. This means that normally they cannot be connected in any way to a
sequencing application such as SONAR. If, however, the software synth application supports
a technology called *ReWire*, the synth can be used within SONAR, almost exactly like a soft
synth.

ReWire is a virtual connection technology that allows two different music applications to
connect to one another and share audio data, synchronize their internal clocks, and share
transport control. For example, Cakewalk's Project5 software synthesizer studio supports
ReWire. Project5 provides built-in synthesis and sequencing features. When ReWired with
SONAR, you can stream audio from Project5 to SONAR just like you would with a soft synth.

In addition, the sequencer aspects in both Project5 and SONAR are completely synchronized, meaning that the Now time in SONAR would correspond to the exact same sequencer time in Project5. And both applications share common transport functions, meaning that using the Play, Stop, Rewind, functions in one application trigger those same functions in the other application. The ReWire technology is very powerful and allows you to use SONAR with any other ReWire-compatible application on the market.

MORE PROJECT5 INFO

For more information about Project5, visit www.zzounds.com/a-303813/item-CAKPROJECT5

As far as using the ReWire functions in SONAR—to be honest, there really isn't much more I can say that isn't already covered in the SONAR Help file. Instead of just rehashing the same information, I recommend that you read through the ReWire information in the file. If you have questions, go to www.digifreq.com/digifreq/ and don't be afraid to post them in the discussion area of my DigiFreq music technology Web site.

MORE REWIRE INFO

For more information about the ReWire technology in general, be sure to visit www.propellerheads.se/technologies/rewire/index.cfm?fuseaction=mainframe

SoundFonts

Most modern MIDI instruments and sound cards use sample playback to produce sounds. Sample playback can produce some very realistic sounds. The reason for this realism lies in the fact that a sample playback device plays samples, which are actually audio recordings of real-life instruments and sounds. When the sample playback device receives a MIDI Note On message, instead of creating a sound electronically from scratch, it plays a digital sample, which can be anything from the sound of a piano note to the sound of a coyote howling.

A SoundFont is a special type of digital sample format that works only with a SoundFont-compatible sound card. Creative Labs, the makers of the ever-popular Sound Blaster line of sound cards, developed the SoundFont format. Most recent Sound Blaster sound cards are SoundFont compatible. For more information about Sound Blaster sound cards, check out www.soundblaster.com. For more information about SoundFonts, go to www.digifreq.com/digifreq/article.asp?ID=32 to read the article entitled *Using SoundFonts in Your Computer Music Studio*. And be sure to visit www.digifreq.com/digifreq/articles.asp for more great music technology articles.

Using the sfz SoundFont Player

If you don't have a sound card that supports SoundFonts, you can use the sfz SoundFont Player included with SONAR. To use the sfx, follow these steps:

1. Create a new project or open a pre-existing project.
2. Choose Insert > Soft Synths > VST sfx.
3. In the Insert Soft Synth Options dialog box, activate the First Synth Audio Output and Synth Property page options.
4. Click OK. The sfz window opens (see Figure 10.46).

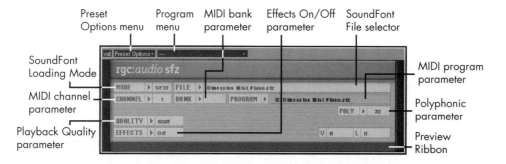

Figure 10.46   Use the sfz SoundFont Player to play SoundFonts within SONAR.

5. In the sfx window, click the arrow next to the SoundFont Loading Mode parameter and choose a loading mode from the menu.

SOUNDFONT LOADING MODES

For more information about SoundFont loading modes, go to www.rgcaudio.com/sfzfaq.htm to read the sfz FAQ (Frequently Asked Questions) page.

6. Click the SoundFont File Selector and choose the SoundFont you want to use. Click Open.
7. You can set up each of the MIDI channels with different bank, program, and polyphony settings. Use the MIDI Channel parameter to set the MIDI channel. Use the MIDI Bank parameter to set the bank for the channel. Use the MIDI Program parameter to set the program for the bank.
8. Use the Polyphonic parameter to set the polyphony for the MIDI channel. This parameter limits the number of voices that can be played simultaneously. The lowest setting is 1 and the highest setting is 256. If you experience playback problems, you might want to try lowering this parameter to take off some of the strain on your computer processor.

9. You can use the internal chorus and reverb effects (if the SoundFont is programmed to use them) by setting the Effects parameter to either on or off.

10. Use the Playback Quality parameter to both determine the quality of the sound and the amount of computer processing power consumed during playback. Setting this parameter to Draft provides the lowest quality of playback, but the least amount of strain on your computer processor.

11. Audition the SoundFont by dragging your mouse in the Preview Ribbon located at the bottom of the sfx window. Click and hold your left mouse button and drag your mouse within the strip to hear how the current program sounds. Click in the left half of the strip to hear low notes played and click in the right half of the strip to hear high notes played.

12. If you opened a pre-existing project that already contains MIDI tracks, you can skip this step. Otherwise, right-click in the Track pane of the Track view and choose Insert MIDI Track to create a new MIDI track. Then widen the track to display its parameters.

13. Set the Input parameter to the MIDI channel that is being used to receive data from your MIDI keyboard and set the Output parameter to VST sfz.

14. Set the Channel parameter to the same MIDI channel as your MIDI keyboard. Set the Bank parameter to the same bank that contains the SoundFont you want to use for this MIDI track. Set the Patch parameter to one of the patches available in the SoundFont.

15. Repeat steps 12 through 14 to set up any additional new or pre-existing MIDI tracks.

After you record some data in your MIDI tracks (or if the tracks already contained data), when you play the project, your MIDI tracks will drive the sfz, which in turn will play the appropriate sounds from the SoundFonts you have loaded.

❈ **MORE SFZ INFORMATION**

For more information about the sfz, go to the C:\Program Files\Cakewalk\VstPlugins\SFZ folder on your hard drive and double-click the file named sfz.chm to access the sfz Help file.

Using SoundFonts with a Compatible Sound Card

If you have a SoundFont-compatible sound card (like the Sound Blaster Live!), you can play SoundFonts with your sound card. The procedure for using a sound card to play SoundFonts is as follows:

1. Create a new project or open a pre-existing project.

2. Choose Options > SoundFonts to open the SoundFont Banks dialog box.

3. Select an empty bank and click the Attach button to open the SoundFont File dialog box.

4. Choose the SoundFont file you want to load and click Open. The SoundFont you chose will be loaded into the bank you selected.

5. Repeat Steps 3 and 4 to load any additional SoundFonts.

6. To remove a SoundFont from your project, just select it in the list and click Detach.

7. Click Close when you're finished loading SoundFonts.

8. If you opened a pre-existing project that already contains MIDI tracks, you can skip this step. Otherwise, right-click in the Track pane of the Track view and choose Insert MIDI Track to create a new MIDI track. Then widen the track to display its parameters.

9. Set the Input parameter to the MIDI channel that is being used to receive data from your MIDI keyboard and set the Output parameter to SoundFont Device.

10. Set the Channel parameter to the same MIDI channel as your MIDI keyboard. Set the Bank parameter to the same bank that contains the SoundFont you want to use for this MIDI track. Set the Patch parameter to one of the patches available in the SoundFont. You'll see a list of available patches.

11. Repeat Steps 8 through 10 to set up any additional new or pre-existing MIDI tracks.

After you record some data into your MIDI tracks (or if the tracks already contained data), when you play the project, your MIDI tracks will drive your SoundFont-compatible sound card, which in turn will play the appropriate sounds from the SoundFonts you have loaded.

Session Drummer 2

Like the Cyclone and RXP, Session Drummer 2 is a MIDI sample playback synth, but it is geared toward the playback of percussion instruments. Session Drummer 2 is multitimbral (meaning it can play more than one different sound at a time—up to 10) and instead of being limited to one-shot samples or sample loops, it can load multisamples, which provide very realistic playback.

Session Drummer 2 Basics

If you examine the Session Drummer 2 (SD2) main interface (see Figure 10.47), you'll notice that it is divided into three sections—the File Functions and MIDI Pattern section, the Instrument Pad section, and the Drum Mixer.

The File Functions and MIDI Pattern section allows you to load and save programs/MIDI patterns, kits, and instruments. You also use this section to control MIDI playback. The Instrument Pad section allows you to assign different instruments to each pad, preview instruments, and assign output channels to each pad. The Drum Mixer lets you adjust the volume, width, panning, and tuning for each pad, as well as set the main volume, width, panning, and tuning for all pads.

To begin working with SD2, you need to first load in some sounds, which come in the form of *instruments*. This is the name given to the sample files loaded into each pad. A group of 10 Instruments (corresponding to the 10 available pads) is called a *kit*. And a kit combined with Drum Mixer settings and 8 MIDI patterns (corresponding to the 8 available MIDI Pattern Pads) is called a *program*. You can load/save programs, kits, and instruments.

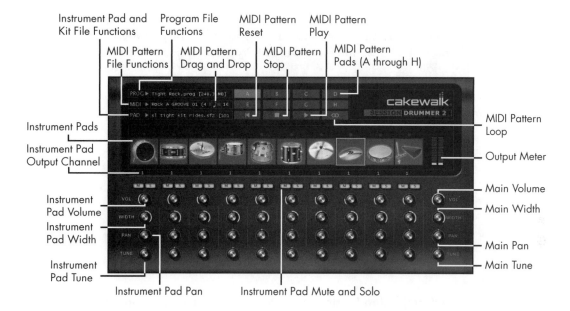

Figure 10.47 You can adjust the Session Drummer 2 parameters by using its main interface.

Working with Programs

A program stores all of the SD2 parameter settings including the currently loaded kit/ instruments, the 8 MIDI patterns associated with that kit, as well as all of the Drum Mixer parameter values. The quickest way to start working with SD2 is to simply load up an existing program. Click the Program File Functions button (PROG) to perform the following program-related tasks:

- ❄ **Initialize Program.** This option will clear all of SD2's parameter settings including the currently loaded kit/instruments and MIDI patterns.

- ❄ **Load Program.** Use this option to load an SD2 program. SONAR ships with a large number of predefined programs, which are located in the following hard drive folder: C:\Program Files\Cakewalk\Shared Dxi\Session Drummer 2\Contents\Programs. After choosing a program, SD2 will load up a drum kit (along with the associated instruments), MIDI patterns, and Drum Mixer settings.

- ❄ **Save Program or Save Program As.** If you make changes to a program (such as loading in different instruments or MIDI patterns, or changing Drum Mixer settings), you can save your changes using these options. Use Save Program to save your changes into the same program file that you loaded. This will overwrite the existing program file. To keep the original program file and create a different file, use the Save Program As option and use a new name for the program.

⁂ **Save Default Program.** Normally, when you load up SD2, it contains a blank program. If you would like a program to be automatically loaded every time you use SD2, then load a program and choose the Save Default Program option to save the current program as the default.

THE PROGRAM BROWSER

Click the program name (located to the right of the Program File Functions button) to open the Program Browser for a quick way to load an SD2 program.

Working with Kits

A kit keeps track of what instruments are loaded into each of the instrument pads. A kit does not contain any MIDI patterns or Drum Mixer settings. This allows you to keep your existing MIDI patterns and Drum Mixer settings loaded while experimenting with different drum kits. Click the Instrument Pad and Kit File Functions button (PAD) to perform the following kit-related tasks:

⁂ **Load Instrument and Unload Instrument.** Click an instrument pad and then use one of these options to load an instrument into the selected pad or unload the current pad instrument.

⁂ **Load Kit.** Use this option to load an SD2 kit. SONAR ships will four different drum kits, which are located in the following hard drive folder: C:\Program Files\Cakewalk\ Shared Dxi\Session Drummer 2\Contents\Kits. After choosing a kit, SD2 will load an instrument into each of the instrument pads. MIDI patterns and Drum Mixer settings remain unchanged.

⁂ **Save Kit or Save Kit As.** If you make changes to a kit (such as loading in different instruments), you can save your changes using these options. Use Save Kit to save your changes into the same kit file that you loaded. This will overwrite the existing kit file. To keep the original kit file and create a different file, use the Save Kit As option and use a new name for the kit.

Working with Instruments

SD2 can have up to 10 different instruments loaded at once, each represented by an instrument pad. An instrument is actually the SD2 name for sample file. An instrument can be any audio sample file in the following formats: WAV (Microsoft Windows Wav format), AIF or AIFF (Apple Interchange File Format), or OGG (Ogg-Vorbis format). In addition, instruments can be represented by SFZ files, which are not audio files but definition files that define how audio files should be loaded. SFZ files can be used to load multisamples into SD2.

❋ SFZ AND MULTISAMPLES

Multisamples are special instruments that have more than one audio sample file associated with them. An SFZ file defines a multisample that tells SD2 the multiple sample files that need to be loaded for a single instrument and pad. Why use multiple sample files for a single instrument? When a real, live, acoustic drum is played, it sounds different at various loudness levels. If you hit the drum hard or soft, not only does the volume of the instrument change, but so does the timbre. In order to provide a more realistic sound, multisamples include audio recordings of the same instrument at various playing levels. These different samples are triggered at different MIDI velocity levels so it sounds like you are playing a real drum. SD2 ships with a number of multisample instruments, and you can even create your own, but you'll need to learn the SFZ file format. You can find more information at: www.rgcaudio.com/sfzfaq.htm

To use SD2 instruments, follow these steps:

1. Right-click an instrument pad and choose Load Instrument to load a sample file or SFZ file. SONAR ships with a number of different instruments, which are located in the following hard drive folder: C:\Program Files\Cakewalk\Shared Dxi\Session Drummer 2\ Contents\Kits. In this folder, you'll find more folders for each of the various types of available instruments.

2. If you chose an SFZ file, you can skip this step. If you chose a regular audio file (like WAV, AIF, or OGG), you will also need to set a MIDI note number for the instrument pad. SFZ files contain all the information needed to set up an instrument pad, but regular audio sample files do not. After you have loaded a sample file, right-click the instrument pad again and choose a MIDI note number from the menu. This is the MIDI note number that must be used in your MIDI tracks to trigger the instrument pad and play the instrument.

3. To audition an instrument, click its pad.

4. To clear an instrument pad, right-click the pad and choose Unload Instrument.

5. You can also assign an audio output channel to each instrument pad. Click and drag your mouse on the pad's Output Channel number. Drag up or down to increase or decrease the number. Initially, each pad is set to channel 1, which means all instruments will use the first SD2 track, but each instrument can have its own channel/track. To use multiple channels, you must have selected the All Synth Audio Outputs option in the Insert Soft Synth Options dialog box. This will create 8 different output tracks for SD2.

❋ MULTIPLE OUTPUTS

Using multiple outputs allows you to process each drum instrument separately with different effects. For example, the bass drum is usually presented dry in an audio mix, but the snare drum usually has some reverb added to it. In addition, you can apply EQ effects to each drum instrument and make your kit sound unique, rather than have it sound the same as every other SONAR user.

Using the Drum Mixer

After you've loaded some instruments either individually or via a kit or program, you can manipulate them in various ways using the Drum Mixer. The Drum Mixer changes the volume, width, panning, and tuning of each instrument via on-screen knobs, which can be adjusted by clicking and dragging up (to increase the value) or down (to decrease the value) with the mouse. Double-click a knob to return it to its default value. Here are descriptions of each of the Drum Mixer controls:

* **Mute (M) and Solo (S).** Click the Mute and Solo buttons to mute or solo an instrument. Muting an instrument will silence it. Soloing an instrument will silence all other instruments while the soloed instrument continues to play. Use these options to audition different instrument combinations.

* **Volume (VOL).** Adjust the volume knob to increase or decrease the amplitude of an instrument. Volume is measured as a percentage: 0% (off) to 100% (full volume).

* **Width (Width).** Adjust the Width knob to alter the stereo spread of an instrument. The samples included with SD2 are in stereo. Using the Width knob, you can control the size of the stereo field of an instrument. Width is measured as follows: –100% to 0% to +100%. At –100%, an instrument sounds as if it is being played from an audience perspective. At +100%, an instrument sounds as if it is being played from the drummer's perspective. At 0%, a stereo instrument in converted into a mono instrument. The 0% setting can come in handy if you want to have full control over an instrument's position in the stereo field. Just set Width to 0% and use the Pan knob to control the exact position.

* **Pan (Pan).** Adjust the Pan knob to alter the position of an instrument in the stereo field. Pan is measured as follows: –100% (full left) to 0% (centered) to +100% (full right).

* **Tune (Tune).** Adjust the Tune knob to alter the pitch of an instrument. Tuning is measured in semitones as follows: –24 st (lowered 2 octaves) to 0 st (original sound) to +24 st (raised 2 octaves). Some creative uses of the Tune knob can be to alter instruments to the point where a drum kit sounds entirely different. For example, SONAR doesn't include any electronic drum kits, but if you increase the tuning to +24 st on all the instruments in a kit, you'll get an electronic type of sound.

In addition to the individual instrument pad controls, the Drum Mixer provides main controls, which can be used to adjust the volume, width, panning, and tuning of the entire drum kit.

Using MIDI Patterns

Along with instruments and Drum Mixer settings, a program loads in eight associated MIDI patterns. These patterns are specifically matched to the program that is loaded. This means the patterns automatically work well with the instruments/kit in the program. This makes it very easy to create a drum part with a particular drum kit. To work with the SD2 MIDI pattern features, do the following:

1. After loading a program, the eight MIDI Pattern Pads (A through H) will each be loaded with a different MIDI pattern. Click a Pattern Pad to select it. When you select a Pad, the

name of its MIDI pattern and the number of beats in that pattern are shown next to the MIDI Pattern File Functions button.

2. To play the Pad, click the MIDI Pattern Play button.

3. To stop Pad playback, click the MIDI Pattern Stop button.

4. To loop playback, activate the MIDI Pattern Loop button.

5. To reset playback of the Pad to the beginning of its pattern, click the MIDI Pattern Reset button.

6. To load a new pattern into the Pad independent of the current program, click the MIDI Pattern File Functions button and choose Load Pattern.

7. To clear the pattern in the Pad, click the MIDI Pattern File Functions button and choose Unload Pattern. You can also clear all patterns from all Pads by choosing Unload All Patterns.

Using those steps, you can quickly and easily audition the MIDI patterns in a program. To actually create a drum part for your project using the MIDI patterns requires some additional steps.

Creating a Drum Part with Session Drummer 2

Using the MIDI patterns in an SD2 program, you can create a drum part for your project in two ways. One method involves dragging and dropping the patterns from SD2 into the SD2 MIDI track. The other method involves leaving the patterns in SD2 and triggering their playback via special MIDI note numbers in the SD2 MIDI track.

Drag and Drop Drumming

To create a drum part by dragging and dropping MIDI patterns, follow this example:

1. For this example, create a new project. Set the project tempo to 100. Set the Track view Snap to Grid parameters to Musical Time – Quarter, Mode: Move To.

2. With a new or existing project already opened, choose Insert > Soft Synths > Session Drummer 2 to open the Insert Soft Synth Options dialog box.

3. Activate the MIDI Source, First Synth Audio Output, and Synth Property Page options. Disable the other options.

4. Tab the SD2 window. This step is optional.

> ❄ **TAB THE SD2 WINDOW**
>
> To make things easier, I like to tab the SD2 window so that it is placed inside the Track view. This provides easy access to both the SD2 MIDI Pattern parameters and the tracks in a project. To tab the SD2 window, click the left corner of the window's title bar and choose Enable Tabbed from the menu.

5. In SD2, click the Program File Functions button and choose Load Program. For this example, open the Rock folder and select the Room Rock.prog file and click Open.

6. In the MIDI Pattern Pad area, select Pad A. Then click and drag the MIDI Pattern Drag and Drop button from SD2 into the SD2 MIDI track (see Figure 10.48).

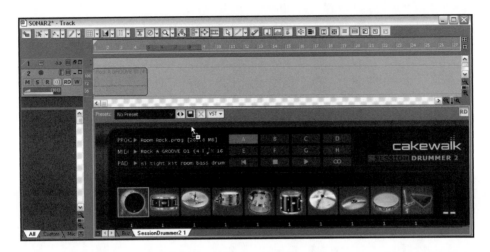

Figure 10.48   You can click and drag MIDI patterns from SD2 into a MIDI track for quick and easy drum part creation.

7. Now select and drag the following MIDI pad patterns in this order: B, C, C, H, G, D. Your new drum part should look similar to the one shown in Figure 10.49.

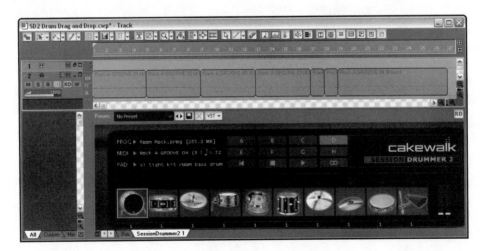

Figure 10.49   A SD2 drum part created by dragging and dropping MIDI patterns.

MIDI Pattern Triggering

Now let's create the same drum part as we did in the previous section, but this time instead of dragging and dropping MIDI patterns, we will keep the patterns inside SD2 and trigger their playback by using single MIDI notes added to the SD2 MIDI track.

1. Follow steps 1 through 5 in the previous exercise to create a new project and get SD2 up and running.
2. Open the SD2 MIDI track in the Piano Roll view.
3. Activate the Pencil tool and choose the Whole Note duration.
4. Place a note at the beginning of the track at note Eb2 on the keyboard and drag the end of the note out so that it stops at the beginning of measure 5 (see Figure 10.50). The reason we need to increase the duration of the note is because the MIDI pattern will only play while the MIDI note is sounding. In order to play the entire four-bar pattern, we need to make sure the MIDI note is four bars long.

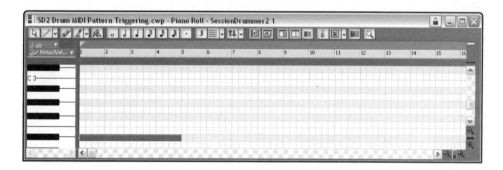

Figure 10.50   Add MIDI notes to the SD2 MIDI track to trigger the SD2 MIDI patterns.

❄ **MIDI PATTERN TRIGGER NOTES**

Each of the MIDI Pattern Pads in SD2 has a designated MIDI trigger note. The notes are as follows: Pad A = Eb2; Pad B = E2; Pad C = F2; Pad D = F#2; Pad E = G2; Pad F = G#2; Pad G = A2; Pad H = Bb2. You'll need to keep this information handy if you want to build drum tracks with SD2 via MIDI Pattern triggering.

---

5. Place a four-bar note at E2 starting at measure 5 and ending at measure 9 to trigger Pad B.
6. Place two four-bar notes at F2 starting at measure 9 and ending at measure 17 to trigger Pad C twice. The reason we don't use one long eight-bar note is because the MIDI pattern in Pad C is 4 bars long and we need to play it twice, which means it must be triggered twice.

7. Place a one-bar note at Bb2 starting at measure 17 and ending at measure 18 to trigger Pad H.

8. Place a one-bar note at A2 starting at measure 18 and ending at measure 19 to trigger Pad G.

9. Place an eight-bar note at F#2 starting at measure 19 and ending at measure 27 to trigger Pad D.

Your new drum part should look similar to the one shown in Figure 10.51.

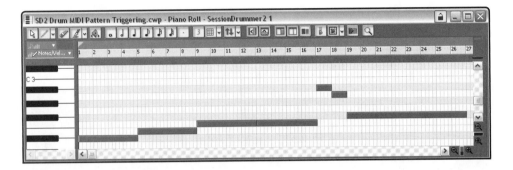

Figure 10.51   A SD2 drum part created by triggering MIDI patterns.

This drum part should sound the same as the drum part from the previous exercise. These exercises demonstrate the various ways you can create drum parts with Session Drummer 2. I've only just scratched the surface of what you can do with Session Drummer 2, but the information provided here should get you up and running and able to quickly and easily create your own great sounding drum parts.

11 } Exploring Effects

Just as adding spices to a recipe makes it taste better, adding effects to your music data makes it sound better. Effects can make the difference between a dull, lifeless recording and a recording that really rocks. For example, you can apply echoes and background ambience to give the illusion that your song was recorded in a certain environment, such as a concert hall. You also can use effects to make your vocals sound rich and full. And the list goes on. SONAR provides a number of different effects features that you can use to spice up both your MIDI and audio tracks. Although applying these effects to your data isn't overly complicated, understanding what they do and how to use them can sometimes be confusing. This chapter will do the following:

- ❊ Explain plug-ins.
- ❊ Discuss offline and real-time processing.
- ❊ Introduce audio effects, including chorus, equalization, reverb, delay, flanging, pitch shifting, time/pitch stretching, and more.
- ❊ Introduce MIDI effects, including quantization, delay, filtering, arpeggio, chord analyzing, transposition, and velocity.

Offline or Real-Time?

SONAR's Effects features are very similar to its editing features, but there are a couple of differences. Although the Effects features are included with SONAR, they are not actually part of the main application. Instead, they come in the form of plug-ins.

❊ **PLUG-INS**

In basic terms, a plug-in is a small computer program that by itself does nothing, but when used together with a larger application, provides added functionality to the larger program. You can use plug-ins to add new features to a program easily. In SONAR's case, plug-ins provide you with additional ways to process your MIDI and audio data. As a matter of fact, Cakewalk (and other manufacturers) have additional

---

plug-in products for sale so that you can add even more power to your copy of SONAR, which uses any plug-ins that are in the DirectX or VST formats.

Because the Effects features are plug-ins, not only do they add functionality to SONAR, but they also add more flexibility. Unlike the editing features, you can use the effects features to process your data in two different ways—offline and real-time.

Offline Processing

You already know what offline processing is because you used it when you learned about SONAR's editing features. With offline processing, the MIDI and audio data in your clips and tracks is permanently changed. Therefore, offline processing is also called *destructive processing* because it "destroys" the original data by modifying (or overwriting) it according to any processing you apply.

 UNDO OFFLINE PROCESSING

You can remove any offline processing done to your data by using SONAR's Undo feature. You also can load a saved copy of your project that contains the original data. But neither of these restoration methods is as convenient as using real-time processing.

The basic procedure for using effects in offline mode is essentially the same as when you use any of SONAR's editing features. You just follow these steps:

1. Select the data you want to change.
2. Choose the MIDI or audio effects feature you want to use by choosing either Process > Audio Fx or Process > MIDI Fx.
3. Make the appropriate parameter adjustments in the dialog box that appears.
4. Click the Audition button to test the current parameter settings. Make further adjustments, if necessary.
6. Click OK to close the dialog box.

SONAR will process the data by applying the effect, according to the parameter settings you specified.

Real-Time Processing

On the other hand, real-time processing doesn't change the actual data in your clips and tracks. Instead, the effects features are applied only during playback, which lets you hear the results while leaving your original data intact. Therefore, real-time processing is also called *nondestructive* because it doesn't apply any permanent changes to your data. By simply turning off the effects features, you can listen to your data as it was originally recorded.

The basic procedure for using effects in real-time mode isn't any more difficult than using them in offline mode, although it is a little different, as you can see here:

1. In the Track view, right-click in the Fx bin of the track to which you want to add an effect. A menu will appear.

 USE THE CONSOLE VIEW

You also can apply effects in real time by using the Console view.

2. Choose the effect you want to use from the menu. Depending on whether the track is for MIDI or audio, the list of effects will be different. The effect you choose will be added to the list in the Fx bin.

3. The corresponding window for the effect will be opened automatically. You also can open an effect window by double-clicking it in the Fx bin.

EFFECTS WINDOWS

In real-time mode, the parameters of an effect are displayed in a window instead of a dialog box. Therefore, you can access any of the other features in SONAR while still having access to the effect parameters. You also can use more than one effect at the same time.

4. Make the appropriate parameter adjustments.

5. Start playback of the project. You immediately will hear the results of the effect being applied to the data in the track. While the project plays, you can make further parameter adjustments, if necessary.

THE BYPASS BUTTON

If you want to make a quick comparison between how the original data sounds and how it sounds with the effect applied, some of the effects provide a Bypass button.

When you activate the button, it bypasses (or turns off) the effect so you can hear how the original data sounds. When you deactivate the button, you can hear how the data sounds with the effect applied. You also can bypass an effect by clicking on the green box next to the name of the effect in the Fx bin.

In addition, if you have many effects applied to the Fx bin of a track, you can quickly bypass all the effects at once by right-clicking the Fx bin and choosing Bypass Bin.

6. If you want to add another effect to the same track (or add some effects to different tracks), go back to step 1. You can leave the effects windows open or you can close them; it doesn't matter. You also can let the project continue to play as you add new

effects. As soon as you add an effect to the Fx bin, you will hear the results, according to the current parameter settings.

7. If you want to remove an effect, right-click the effect you want to remove and select Delete.

ORDER OF EFFECTS

If you apply more than one effect to a track, the order in which the effects appear in the Fx bin will determine the order in which they are applied to the data in the track. For example, if you have the Chorus and Reverb effects added (in that order) to the Fx bin of an audio track, SONAR will apply the Chorus effect to the data and then take the result of that application and apply the Reverb effect to it. This means that the order in which you apply effects to a track matters. If you apply effects in a different order, you will get different results. This makes for some interesting experimentation. To change the order of the effects listed in the Fx bin, simply drag the name of an effect up or down within the list.

You can continue using SONAR with the real-time effects in place. Remember that you will be aware of the results only during playback. The original data looks the same, even if you examine it in the various views. Also, editing your original data doesn't change how the effects are applied to it. For example, if you have a track set up with some effects applied, and you transpose the pitch of one of the clips within that track, during playback SONAR still will apply the effects to the track in the same way. When the Now time reaches the point in the track containing the transposed clip, you simply will hear the effect applied to the transposed data. This is one of the features that makes real-time effects so flexible.

APPLY EFFECTS DURING RECORDING

You also can apply real-time effects during recording. For example, this allows you to add some reverberation to a vocal part to make it sound more appealing to the performer while his part is being recorded. This helps a performer get more "in the groove," so to speak. To apply real-time effects during recording, you have to activate input monitoring.

Clip-based Effects

In addition to applying effects to entire tracks, you can apply effects to individual clips. Each clip in a SONAR project contains its own unique Fx bin. This feature gives you the flexibility to apply different effects to different parts of the same track, rather than being limited to applying effects to all the clips in that track.

To apply an effect to a clip, right-click the clip and choose Insert Effect. Once you apply an effect to a clip, a small FX button will appear in the upper left corner of the clip. To access the Fx bin for the clip, click on the FX button. From here, you can use the same procedures outlined in the last section for applying effects in real time.

CLIP FX BIN

You can also access the Fx bin for a clip by right-clicking the clip and choosing Clip Properties. Under the General tab in the Clip Properties dialog box, you'll see the Fx bin for the clip.

Advantages and Disadvantages to Real-Time Processing

You might be asking yourself, "Why don't I just use real-time processing all the time? It's so much more flexible?" Well, applying effects in real time is very flexible, but in a couple of instances you need to apply them offline. The first instance deals with your computer's processing power. Most of SONAR's effects need to perform complex mathematical calculations to achieve their results. Applying effects in real time means that not only does your computer have to deal with these calculations, but it also has to deal with SONAR playing back your MIDI and audio data. All these things going on at once can put a lot of strain on your computer's CPU. If you use too many effects in real time at once, your computer might not be able to keep up. You might hear skips in playback, or SONAR might stop playing altogether. If this ever happens, you need to apply some of the effects offline and keep only a few of them going in real time. You lose a bit of flexibility in terms of being able to make changes to your data, but there's no limit to the number of effects you can apply to your data offline.

Applying effects offline also comes in handy when you want to process some specifically selected data. For example, if you want to process a short segment of data within a track or clip, you have to do it offline. In real time, you can apply effects only to entire clips or tracks.

USE AUTOMATION

Actually, you can apply real-time effects to specific parts of a track by using automation, but it's a bit more complicated than simply applying an effect offline.

The Freeze Tracks Function

To make working with real-time effects even easier, SONAR provides the Freeze Tracks function. Depending on the power of your computer, using many different real-time effects at the same time can start to bog down playback and recording in SONAR. In order to help with this situation, SONAR "freezes" the real-time effects in audio tracks, which basically bounces the audio in the track to new audio clips and applies the real-time effects to the data. It also temporarily disables the Fx bin. This allows you to hear your effects, but takes the strain off your computer.

The Freeze Tracks function can be accessed by either right-clicking the number of an audio track and choosing one of the freeze options, or by selecting the audio track and choosing Tracks > Freeze from SONAR's main menu. To use the Freeze Tracks function, follow these procedures:

* **Freeze Track**. Choose this option from the menu to freeze an audio track. The Freeze Track option will automatically use SONAR's Bounce to Clip(s) function to take the audio output with the applied real-time effects from the audio track and combine it into a new clip (or set of clips) in the same track. Then the track's Fx bin (along with all the real-time effects) is deactivated.

* **Unfreeze Track**. After you have used the Freeze Track function on an audio track, you can "unfreeze" that track by choosing this option. Choosing Unfreeze Track will discard the bounced audio that was created with the Freeze Track option, restore the original audio, and it will reactivate the Fx bin along with any real-time effects it contains.

* **Quick Unfreeze Track**. This option is similar to the Unfreeze Track option, except that it doesn't discard the bounced audio. Instead, it simply hides and mutes the bounced audio so you can use the Quick Freeze Track option (which appears in place of the Freeze Track option) to quickly reveal the bounced audio again.

Freeze Track Options

There are several things you can do to alter the way the Freeze Track function works. To access these settings, use the same methods described earlier, but choose Freeze Options to open the Freeze Options dialog box.

The options in the Freeze Options dialog box work as follows:

* **Fast Bounce.** Having this option activated allows SONAR to bounce the audio output of a track faster than real time, meaning it doesn't have to play through your entire project just to record the audio output of the track. However, there are some real-time effects on the market that require a real-time bounce. If you have trouble with a track not having its audio output bounced correctly, deactivating this option should solve the problem.

* **Hide MIDI Tracks.** This option only applies to freezing software synthesizers.

* **Single Bounce Per Track.** Having this option activated tells SONAR to bounce the track's audio output into a single, long audio clip. If you would rather have the audio bounced to multiple clips (corresponding to the times in the audio performance when only audio output is present), then deactivate this option.

* **Remove Silence.** This option uses SONAR's Remove Silence function to remove the silent sections of the single, long audio clip created when using the Single Bounce Per Track option (see Chapter 8).

* **Freeze Tail Duration.** If you have applied any effects to a track (especially reverberation), you may have noticed that the sound of the effect can sometimes continue playing even after the audio output from the track has stopped. This is called an *effect tail*. In order to compensate for the effect tail, you need to count how many seconds the effect tail continues to play and then enter that value into the Freeze Tail Duration parameter. The default value for this parameter is 5 seconds. This should be sufficient in most cases, but there may be times when it needs an adjustment. If you freeze a track and you hear its playback cut off at the end of its performance, then you may need to increase the value for this parameter.

Audio Effects

SONAR provides more than 30 different audio effects. If you choose either Process > Audio Fx or Process > Audio Fx > Cakewalk, you'll notice that some of these effects cover the same type of processing. Why would Cakewalk include multiple effects that accomplish the same task?

Well, some of the effects are designed to work with mono audio signals, and others are designed to work with stereo audio. They include parameters for both the left and right stereo channels. In addition, some of the effects process audio with a lower level of quality, and they include fewer parameter settings. So why include them? Because they provide one advantage: They don't take up as much computer-processing power. This means that you can apply more of the lower-quality effects to your tracks in real time, especially if you have a slow computer system.

You also might have noticed that some of the effects mimic some of SONAR's editing features. They mimic these editing features so you can process your data with these features in real time. You can't use SONAR's editing features in real time because they aren't plug-ins. The Effects features, however, come with their own sets of parameters, so I'll go over them here step-by-step.

Equalization

You have a radio in your car, right? Maybe even a cassette or a CD player, too? If so, then you've probably used equalization without even knowing it. Adjusting the bass and treble controls on your car radio is a form of equalization. Equalization (EQ) enables you to adjust the tonal characteristics of an audio signal by increasing (boosting) or decreasing (cutting) the amplitude of different frequencies in the audio spectrum.

> ✳ **THE AUDIO SPECTRUM**
>
> When a musical object (such as a string) vibrates, it emits a sound. The speed at which the object vibrates is called the *frequency*, which is measured in vibrations (or cycles) per second. This measurement is also called *Hertz* (Hz). If an object vibrates 60 times per second, the frequency would be 60 Hz. The tricky point to remember here, though, is that most objects vibrate at a number of different frequencies at the same time. The combination of all these different vibrations makes up the distinct sound (or *timbre*) of a vibrating object. That's why a bell sounds like a bell, a horn sounds like a horn, and so on with all other types of sounds.
>
> We humans can't perceive some very slow and very fast vibrations. Technically, the range of human hearing resides between the frequencies of 20 Hz and 20 kHz (1 kHz is equal to 1,000 Hz). This range is known as the *audio spectrum*.
>
> Equalization enables you to manipulate the frequencies of the audio spectrum, and because sounds contain many of these frequencies, you can change their tonal characteristics (or timbre).

In other words, using EQ, you can bump up the bass, add more presence, reduce rumble, and sometimes eliminate noise in your audio material. Not only that, but you also can use EQ as an effect. You know how in some of the modern dance tunes, the vocals sound like they're coming out of a telephone receiver or an old radio? That's an effect done with EQ.

2-Band EQ

The 2-Band EQ effect uses parametric equalization. Parametric EQ allows you to specify an exact frequency to adjust, and you can cut or boost that frequency. You also can process a range of frequencies at the same time, such as cutting all frequencies above 10 kHz by 20 dB (which would reduce all the frequencies between 10 kHz and 20 kHz, but leave the frequencies between 20 Hz and 10 kHz alone). I can explain the 2-Band EQ feature a little better by showing you how it works:

1. Select the audio data you want to process.

2. Choose Process > Audio Fx > Cakewalk > 2-Band EQ to open the 2-Band EQ dialog box.

3. Activate one or both of the Active options to turn on each type of EQ. The 2-Band EQ effect applies two different types of EQ at the same time if you would like.

4. Choose one of the options in the Filter Type section—High-Pass, Low-Pass, Band-Pass (Peak), or Band-Stop (Notch). Then set the appropriate parameters in the Filter Parameters section. You can use the F1 and F2 parameters to set the frequencies you want to adjust. They work differently, depending on the type of filter you choose.
   The Cut parameter enables you to reduce the volume of the frequencies. To change this setting, just enter a negative number (such as −20) to cut by that number of decibels. The Gain parameter boosts the volume of the frequencies. To change this setting, just enter a positive number (such as +20) to boost by that number of decibels.
   If you select the High-Pass filter type, all the frequencies below the frequency that you set in the F1 parameter will be cut, and all the frequencies above it will be boosted, depending on how you set the Cut and Gain parameters. If you select the Low-Pass filter type, all the frequencies above the frequency that you set in the F1 parameter will be cut, and all the frequencies below it will be boosted, depending on how you set the Cut and Gain parameters.
   If you select either the Band-Pass (Peak) or Band-Stop (Notch) filter types, you have to set up a range of frequencies using both the F1 and F2 parameters. Use the F1 parameter to mark the beginning of the range and the F2 parameter to mark the end of the range. For the Band-Pass (Peak) filter type, any frequencies outside the range are cut, and frequencies within the range are boosted, depending on how you set the Cut and Gain parameters. For the Band-Stop (Notch) filter type, any frequencies outside the range are boosted and frequencies within the range are cut, depending on how you set the Cut and Gain parameters.

5. Click the Audition button to test the current parameter settings. Make further adjustments, if necessary.

6. If you want to use the current settings at a later time, save them as a preset.

7. Click OK.

Parametric EQ

Even though the Parametric EQ effect also provides parametric equalization, its parameters are a bit different from those previously mentioned. You use it like this:

1. Select the audio data you want to process.

2. Select Process > Audio Fx > Cakewalk > Parametric EQ to open the Parametric EQ dialog box.

3. In the Band section, select the number of the EQ band you want to modify. Like the 2-Band EQ effect, the Parametric EQ effect enables you to set up more than one equalization type at once. In this case, you can have up to four different equalization types set up to process your data at the same time.

4. You'll notice a couple of familiar parameters in the Band Data section—Gain and Q (same as Bandwidth). They work just as they do in all the other EQ effects. You can set the Gain from −24 to +24dB, and you can set the Q from 0.1 to 30. The Center Freq (short for frequency) parameter works a bit differently, depending on what type of equalization you choose in the Band Type section. Essentially, it determines the frequency below which other frequencies will be cut or boosted, above which other frequencies will be cut or boosted, or exactly where boosting or cutting will occur. You can set the Center Freq parameter from 16 to 22050 Hz. Choose the settings that you want to use for these parameters.

5. In the Band Type section, choose the type of equalization you want to use. If you choose the Low Shelf option, any frequencies below the Center Freq will be boosted or cut, depending on Gain. If you choose the High Shelf option, any frequencies above the Center Freq will be boosted or cut, depending Gain. If you choose the Peak option, the exact frequency designated by the Center Freq parameter will be boosted or cut, depending on Gain.

❄ **EQ GRAPH DISPLAY**

You've probably noticed that in addition to the parameter settings, the Parametric EQ dialog box contains a graph display. This graph shows the current equalization settings for all four types (bands). Along the left, it shows the amplitudes (gain), and along the bottom it shows the frequencies. The shape of the line drawn on the graph shows you what frequencies in the audio spectrum are either boosted or cut. Four colored points on the graph represent each EQ band. Red is for band 1, blue is for band 2, green is for band 3, and purple is for band 4. By clicking and dragging these points, you can change the Gain and Center Freq settings graphically for each of the EQ types (bands), essentially "drawing" the EQ settings. You still have to set the Band Type and Q settings manually, though.

---

6. If you want to set up more than one equalization type, go through steps 3 through 5 again.

7. Click the Audition button to test the current parameter settings. Make further adjustments, if necessary.

8. If you want to use the current settings at a later time, save them as a preset.

9. Click OK.

FxEq

Like Parametric EQ, the FxEq effect provides multiple EQ bands (with many of the same parameters) for you to adjust, but instead of four, you now have eight bands at your disposal, plus hi-shelf and lo-shelf filters. Here is how it works:

1. Select the audio data you want to process.

2. Choose Process > Audio Fx > Cakewalk > FxEq to open the FxEq dialog box.

3. In the Bands section, click the number of the EQ band you want to modify to select it. To turn a band on or off, click the green button located just above the band number.

4. When you select a band, you'll notice that the Voice section displays the name of the selected band, as well as the Gain setting for that band. To adjust the Gain, just drag the appropriate slider for the selected band up or down.

> ❋ **ADJUST THE AMPLITUDE RANGE**
>
> You can adjust the amplitude range for all the EQ bands by setting the dB Scale control, which is located just above the Monitor section. Setting the dB Scale control limits the Gain range for each of EQ bands. For example, setting the dB Scale to 15 dB means that the gain for each EQ band can only be adjusted from −15 dB to +15 dB.

5. Selecting a band also displays the Center Frequency and Bandwidth (Q) for that band in the sections of the same names. These parameters work the same as they do for the Parametric EQ effect.

6. If you want to set up more than one EQ band, go through steps 3 through 5 again.

7. You also can set up a hi-shelf or a lo-shelf filter using the controls in the Shelf section. These parameters work like the High Shelf and Low Shelf band types in the Parametric EQ effect.

8. To adjust the final output volume, use the Trim control.

9. You also can determine whether the FxEq effect will process the left, right, or both channels of a stereo signal by using the controls in the Monitor section.

10 . Click the Audition button to test the current parameter settings.

11. If you want to use the current settings at a later time, save them as a preset.

12. Click OK.

Sonitus:fx Equalizer (SONAR Producer Edition)

If you purchase the Producer Edition of SONAR, you'll have an additional EQ effect at your disposal. This is the Equalizer effect from the Sonitus:fx collection. Like the FxEq, the Equalizer provides multiple EQ bands for you to adjust; in this case, it's six bands. Here is how it works:

1. Select the audio data you want to process.
2. Choose Process > Audio Fx > Sonitus:fx > Equalizer to open the Equalizer dialog box.
3. In the lower section of the dialog box, there are six EQ bands. You need to activate bands in order for their parameters to be adjusted. To activate a band, click its number button. You also can turn the entire Equalizer effect on or off by clicking the Bypass button in the upper section of the dialog box.
4. To adjust the gain for a band, just drag its Gain slider left or right.

❊ **PRECISE ADJUSTMENTS**

To make precise parameter adjustments, double-click the Gain number parameter and enter a new value using your computer keyboard.

---

5. There are also Center Frequency (Freq) and Bandwidth (Q) parameters available for each band. These parameters work the same as they do for the Parametric EQ effect.
6. To set the type of equalization a band will use, click the Filter button. If you choose the Peak/Dip option, the exact frequency designated by the Freq parameter will be boosted or cut, depending on how you set the Gain parameter. If you choose the Shelving Low option, any frequencies below the Freq setting will be boosted or cut. If you choose the Shelving High option, any frequencies above the Freq setting will be boosted or cut. If you choose the Lowpass option, all the frequencies above the Freq setting will be cut, and all the frequencies below it will be boosted. If you choose the Highpass option, all the frequencies below the Freq setting will be cut, and all the frequencies above it will be boosted.
7. To reset a band to its default parameter values, right-click the band's number button and choose Set Band Defaults. You also can reset the parameters for all the bands by clicking the Reset button in the upper section of the dialog box.
8. If you want to set up more than one EQ band, repeat steps 3 through 7.

❊ **THE EQ GRAPH**

As with the Parametric EQ effect, you can adjust the Sonitus:fx Equalizer Gain and Frequency settings graphically by clicking and dragging the colored balls on the EQ graph.

---

9. To adjust the final output volume of the Equalizer effect, use the Output parameter in the lower section of the dialog box.
10. Click the Audition button to test the current parameter settings.
11. If you want to use the current settings at a later time, save them as a preset.
12. Click OK.

Delay

An echo is a repeating sound that mimics an initial sound. For example, if you yell the word *hello* in a large enclosed area (such as a concert hall or a canyon), you will hear that word repeated (or echoed) over and over until it fades away. This is exactly what the Delay effect does to your audio data. You can create echoes that vary in the number of repeats and the time between each repeat.

Delay/Echo (Mono)

The Delay/Echo (Mono) effect is pretty straightforward in terms of operation. This effect is intended to be used with monophonic audio rather than stereo. It works like this:

1. Select the audio data you want to process.
2. Select Process > Audio Fx > Cakewalk > Delay/Echo (Mono) to open the Delay/Echo (Mono) dialog box.
3. Set the Delay Time parameter. This parameter determines the time (in milliseconds) that occurs between each echo. You can set the Delay Time from 0.02 to 5000 milliseconds (which is equal to 5 seconds).

❋ **SYCHRONIZE ECHOES**

Many professional musicians use delay to synchronize the echoes with the music. For instance, you can have the echoes play in time with each quarter note, eighth note, sixteenth note, and so on. All that's required for this cool trick is a little simple math.

Begin by figuring the Delay Time needed to synchronize the echoes to each quarter note. To do so, simply divide 60,000 (the number of milliseconds in one minute) by the current tempo (measured in beats per minute) of your project. So, for a tempo of 120 bpm, you get 500 milliseconds. If you set the Delay Time to 500, the resulting echoes sound at the same time as each quarter note.

To figure out the Delay Time for other note values, you just need to divide or multiply. Because an eighth note is half the value of a quarter note, you simply divide 500 by 2 to get 250 milliseconds. A sixteenth note is half the value of an eighth note, so 250 divided by 2 is 125. See how it works? If you want to find out larger note values, just multiply by 2. Because a half note is twice as long as a quarter note, you multiply 500 by 2 to get 1,000 milliseconds, and so on.

4. Set the Dry Mix and Wet Mix parameters. When you apply an effect to your original data, you can determine how much of the effect and how much of the original data will

end up in the final sound. This way, you can add a certain amount of effect without drowning out all the original data. The Dry Mix parameter determines how much of the original data you will hear in the final signal, and the Wet Mix parameter determines how much of the effect you will hear. You can set both of these parameters anywhere from 0 to 100 percent.

5. Set the Feedback Mix parameter. With some effects, you can take their resulting signals and send them back through to have the effect applied multiple times. That's what the Feedback Mix parameter does. The resulting sound can differ, depending on the effect. For delay effects, the Feedback Mix controls the number of echoes that occurs. You can set it anywhere from 0 to 100 percent. The lower the value, the fewer the number of echoes; the higher the value, the more echoes.

6. Set the Mod Rate and Mod Depth parameters. These parameters are a bit difficult to describe. They enable you to add a "warble" type of effect to your audio data along with the echoes. The sound is also similar to that of the tremolo you hear on an electronic organ. To hear what I mean, check out the Fast Tremolo Delay preset. The Mod Rate determines the speed (in Hz or cycles per second) of the warble, and the Mod Depth determines how much your audio data will be affected by it.

7. Click the Audition button to test the current parameter settings.

8. If you want to use the current settings at a later time, save them as a preset.

9. Click OK.

Delay

Very similar to Delay/Echo (Mono), the Delay effect has most of the same parameters. Because it works with stereo audio, however, there are two sets, plus a few extras. It works like this:

1. Select the audio data that you want to process.

2. Select Process > Audio Fx > Cakewalk > Delay to open the Delay dialog box.

3. Set the Left Delay and Right Delay parameters. These parameters work the same way as the Delay Time parameter in the Delay/Echo (Mono) effect. In this case, separate controls are available for the left and right stereo channels. A Link option is also available. Activating this option links the Left Delay and Right Delay parameters together, so if you change the value of one, the other will be set to the same value. Most of the time, you should keep the Link option activated so that both stereo channels have the same amount of delay.

4. Set the Dry Mix and Wet Mix parameters. These parameters work the same way as their counterparts in the Delay/Echo (Mono) effect. Separate controls are not available for each stereo channel in this case, but a Link option is available. Activating this option links the Dry Mix and Wet Mix parameters together, so if you increase the value of the Wet Mix, the value of the Dry Mix will decrease and vice versa. This feature enables you to achieve a perfect balance between the original data and the effect.

5. Set the Left Feedback and Right Feedback parameters. These parameters work the same way as the Feedback Mix parameter in the Delay/Echo (Mono) effect. In this case, separate controls are available for the left and right stereo channels. A Cross Feedback parameter also is available. Using this parameter, you can take the resulting signal from the left channel and send it back through the right channel, and you can take the resulting signal from the right channel and send it back through the left channel. Essentially, this means that this parameter provides control over the number of echoes that will occur and, at the same time, helps to make the stereo field sound "fuller."

6. Set the LFO Depth and LFO Rate parameters. These parameters work the same way as the Mod Depth and Mod Rate parameters in the Delay/Echo (Mono) effect. In addition, two other options called *Triangular* and *Sinusoidal* are available. They determine the type of warble that will be applied. The Triangular option creates a coarse or sharp sound, and the Sinusoidal option creates a smooth or flowing sound.

7. Click the Audition button to test the current parameter settings.

8. If you want to use the current settings at a later time, save them as a preset.

9. Click OK.

FxDelay

The FxDelay effect creates very complex echo effects by letting you set up multiple delays at once, such as setting up multiple Delay/Echo (Mono) effects at the same time to process your audio data. Here is how the FxDelay effect works:

1. Select the audio data you want to process.

2. Choose Process > Audio Fx > Cakewalk > FxDelay to open the FxDelay dialog box.

3. Set the Mix Level parameter. This parameter works just like the Wet Dry Mix parameter in the Echo effect.

4. Set the On options for each of the Voice parameters (1, 2, 3, and 4). The On options let you determine how many different delays you want to set up in your effect. You can have up to four different delays.

5. Each Voice (delay) comes with its own Gain, Delay, Pan, and Feedback parameters. This means that you can control the initial volume, echo time, panning in the stereo field, and feedback (number of echoes) for each voice. To adjust the parameters for a voice, select the number of the voice via the Sel options. Then adjust the Gain, Delay, Feedback, and Pan parameters for that voice. You can do this for all four voices individually.

6. To adjust the gain for all four voices simultaneously, use the Global parameter.

7. Set the Output Level parameter, which controls the overall volume level of the effect output.

8. Click the Audition button to test the current parameter settings.

9. If you want to use the current settings at a later time, save them as a preset.

10. Click OK.

Sonitus:fx Delay (SONAR Producer Edition)

The Sonitus:fx Delay effect provides a single stereo delay with separate controls for both the left and right channels. It works like this:

1. Select the audio data you want to process.

2. Choose Process > Audio Fx > Sonitus:fx > Delay to open the Delay dialog box.

3. If you want specify a delay using a time value, set the Delay Time parameters for each channel. These parameters work the same way as the Delay Time parameter in the Delay/Echo (Mono) effect. In this case, separate controls are available for the left and right stereo channels. A Link option is also available. Activating this option links the Delay parameters together, so if you change the value of one, the other will be set to the same value.

4. If you want to specify a delay that will be synchronized to a specific musical tempo, activate the Tempo Sync option. If you choose Manual mode, you can type in a tempo. If you choose Host mode, the tempo of your current project will be used. Now instead of using the Delay Time parameters, set the Factor parameters for each channel. These parameters set the delay by using musical values based on the tempo. A Factor of 1 equals a quarter-note delay. A Factor of one-half equals an eighth-note delay, and so on.

5. Set the Mix parameters. A value of 0 percent equals a totally dry signal, a value of 50 percent equals a 50/50 mix of the dry and wet signal, and a value of 100 percent equals a totally wet signal.

6. Set the Feedback and Crossfeed parameters. These parameters work the same way as the Feedback Mix and Cross Feedback parameters of the Delay effect.

7. The Diffusion parameter simulates environments more precisely. Instead of hearing distinct echoes, you hear a large number of echoes that sound together very quickly, giving you the illusion of your audio being played in an irregularly shaped environment. The higher the Time value, the farther apart the echoes will sound, simulating a larger environment. The higher the Amount value, the more pronounced the effect will be.

8. If you want to apply some low-pass and high-pass EQ to your delay effect, use the High Filter and Low Filter functions. You can set frequency and Q for both functions. There's no gain control because they both simply cut out frequencies. Use High Filter to cut frequencies above its Frequency setting; use Low Filter to cut frequencies below its Frequency setting. Check out some of the supplied presets to see how you can use these functions to simulate different effects.

9. Click the Audition button to test the current parameter settings.

✳ **LISTEN MODE**

Click the Listen button to set it to either Mix or Delay. When it is set to Mix, you will hear both the original audio signal and the delay effect. When it is set to Delay, you will hear only the delay effect.

10. If you want to use the current settings at a later time, save them as a preset.

11. Click OK.

Chorus

SONAR's chorus effects have many of the same parameters as its delay effects. Why? Because technically, chorus is a form of delay. Chorus uses delay and detuning to achieve its results. You don't hear echoes when using chorus, though, because the delay is extremely short. Instead, chorus makes your audio data sound fatter or fuller. The name *chorus* comes from the fact that people singing in a chorus produce a full sound because each person sings slightly out of tune and out of time—not enough to make the music sound bad, but enough to actually make it sound better. You can use SONAR's chorus effects to achieve similar results with your audio data. The following sections describe how to use them.

Chorus (Mono)

The Chorus (Mono) effect is designed to work with monophonic audio rather than stereo. To apply the Chorus (Mono) effect, follow these steps:

1. Select the audio data you want to process.

2. Select Process > Audio Fx > Cakewalk > Chorus (Mono) to open the Chorus (Mono) dialog box.

3. Set the Delay Time parameter. The only difference between this Delay Time parameter and the same parameter in the Delay/Echo (Mono) effect is that this one has a range of only 20 to 80 milliseconds. If you set this parameter high enough, you actually can get some quick repeating echoes out of it. For adding chorus to your audio, though, you should keep it set somewhere between 20 and 35.

4. Set the Dry Mix and Wet Mix parameters (see Delay/Echo (Mono)).

5. Set the Feedback Mix parameter. Instead of setting the number echoes to occur (as in the Delay/Echo (Mono) effect), this parameter determines the thickness of the chorus. The higher the value, the thicker the chorus.

6. Set the Mod Rate and Mod Depth parameters. Instead of adding a warble to your audio (as in the Delay/Echo (Mono) effect), these parameters determine how detuning is added to the chorus. The Mod Rate determines how quickly the detuning occurs, and the Mod Depth determines the amount of detuning. A high Mod Depth setting makes your audio sound really out of tune (which isn't usually desirable), but a lower setting produces a nice chorusing.

7. Click the Audition button to test the current parameter settings.

8. If you want to use the current settings at a later time, save them as a preset.

9. Click OK.

Chorus

The Chorus effect is designed to work with stereo audio. To apply this effect, follow these steps:

1. Select the audio data you want to process.
2. Select Process > Audio Fx > Cakewalk > Chorus to open the Chorus dialog box.
3. Set the Left Delay and Right Delay parameters. They provide the same chorusing results as the Delay Time parameter in the Chorus (Mono) effect, but for the separate left and right stereo channels. You also can link these parameters by activating the Link option.
4. Set the Dry Mix and Wet Mix parameters (see Delay/Echo (Mono)).
5. Set the Left Feedback and Right Feedback parameters. They provide the same chorusing results as the Feedback Mix parameter in the Chorus (Mono) effect, but for the separate left and right stereo channels. Also, just as the Cross Feedback parameter in the Delay effect enhances the delay, this Cross Feedback parameter enhances the chorus.
6. Set the LFO Depth and LFO Rate parameters. They provide the same results as the Mod Depth and Mod Rate parameters in the Chorus (Mono) effect.
7. Click the Audition button to test the current parameter settings.
8. If you want to use the current settings at a later time, save them as a preset.
9. Click OK.

FxChorus

The FxChorus effect creates very complex chorus effects by letting you set up multiple choruses at once, such as setting up multiple Chorus (Mono) effects at the same time to process your audio data. Here is how the FxChorus effect works:

1. Select the audio data you want to process.
2. Choose Process > Audio Fx > Cakewalk > FxChorus to open the FxChorus dialog box.
3. Set the Mix Level parameter. This parameter works just like the Wet Dry Mix parameter in the Echo effect.
4. Set the On options for each of the Voice parameters (1, 2, 3, and 4). The On options let you determine the number of different choruses you want to set up in your effect. You can have up to four different choruses.
5. Each voice (chorus) comes with its own Gain, Delay, Pan, Mod Depth, and Mod Freq parameters. This means that you can control the initial volume, chorus strength, panning in the stereo field, and depth and speed of the warble for each voice. To adjust the parameters for a voice, select the number of the voice via the Sel options. Then adjust the Gain, Delay, Pan, Mod Depth, and Mod Freq parameters for that voice. You can do this for all four voices individually.
6. To adjust the Gain for all four voices simultaneously, use the Global parameter.
7. Set the Output Level parameter, which controls the overall volume level of the effect output.
8. Click the Audition button to test the current parameter settings.

9. If you want to use the current settings at a later time, save them as a preset.

10. Click OK.

Flanging

Guess what? As with SONAR's chorus effects, you'll find that the program's flanger effects have many of the same parameters as its delay effects because flanging is also a form of delay. Flanging produces a kind of spacey or whooshy type of sound by mixing a slightly delayed version of the original data with itself. As with the chorus, you don't hear echoes because the delay occurs so quickly. It's difficult to describe what flanging sounds like, so you'll have to hear it for yourself. You can apply SONAR's flanging effects, as described in the following sections.

Flanger (Mono)

The Flanger (Mono) effect is designed to work with monophonic audio, rather than stereo. To apply the Flanger (Mono) effect, follow these steps:

1. Select the audio data you want to process.

2. Select Process > Audio Fx > Cakewalk > Flanger (Mono) to open the Flanger (Mono) dialog box.

3. Set the Delay Time parameter. The only difference between this Delay Time parameter and the same parameter in the Delay/Echo (Mono) effect is that this one has a range of only 1 to 20 milliseconds. If you set this parameter high enough, you can actually get some chorusing out of it. To add flanging to your audio, you should keep it set somewhere between 1 and 11.

4. Set the Dry Mix and Wet Mix parameters (see Delay/Echo (Mono)).

5. Set the Feedback Mix parameter. Instead of setting the number of echoes to occur (as in the Delay/Echo (Mono) effect), this parameter determines the thickness of the flanging. The higher the value, the thicker the flanger.

6. Set the Mod Rate and Mod Depth parameters. Instead of adding a warble to your audio (as in the Delay/Echo (Mono) effect), these parameters determine the speed and amount of the flanging. The Mod Rate determines the speed at which the flanging occurs, and the Mod Depth determines the amount of flanging. Check out some of the included presets to get an idea of what values to use for these parameters.

7. Click the Audition button to test the current parameter settings.

8. If you want to use the current settings at a later time, save them as a preset.

9. Click OK.

Flanger

The Flanger effect is designed to work with stereo audio. To apply this effect, follow these steps:

1. Select the audio data you want to process.

2. Select Process > Audio Fx > Cakewalk > Flanger to open the Flanger dialog box.

3. Set the Left Delay and Right Delay parameters. They provide the same flanging results as the Delay Time parameter in the Flanger (Mono) effect, but for the separate left and right stereo channels. You also can link these parameters together by activating the Link option.

4. Set the Dry Mix and Wet Mix parameters (see Delay/Echo (Mono)).

5. Set the Left Feedback and Right Feedback parameters. They provide the same flanging results as the Feedback Mix parameter in the Flanger (Mono) effect, but for the separate left and right stereo channels. Also, just like the Cross Feedback parameter in the Delay effect enhances the delay, this Cross Feedback parameter enhances the flanging.

6. Set the LFO Depth and LFO Rate parameters. They provide the same results as the Mod Depth and Mod Rate parameters in the Flanger (Mono) effect.

7. Click the Audition button to test the current parameter settings.

8. If you want to use the current settings at a later time, save them as a preset.

9. Click OK.

FxFlange

The FxFlange effect creates complex flange effects by letting you set up multiple flanges at once, such as setting up multiple Flanger (Mono) effects at the same time to process your audio data. Here is how the FxFlange effect works:

1. Select the audio data you want to process.

2. Choose Process > Audio Fx > Cakewalk > FxFlange to open the FxFlange dialog box.

3. Set the Mix parameter. This parameter works just like the Wet Dry Mix parameter in the Echo effect.

4. Set the On options for each of the Voice parameters (1 and 2). The On options let you determine how many different flanges you want to set up in your effect. You can have up to two different flanges.

5. Each voice (flange) comes with its own Gain, Delay, Pan, Feedback, and Mod Freq parameters. This means you can control the initial volume, flanging strength, panning in the stereo field, and depth and speed of the flanging of each voice. To adjust the parameters for a voice, select the number of the voice via the Sel options. Then adjust the Gain, Delay, Pan, Feedback, and Mod Freq parameters for that voice. You can do this for both voices individually.

6. To adjust the gain for both voices simultaneously, use the Global parameter.

7. Set the Level parameter, which controls the overall volume level of the effect output.

8. Click the Audition button to test the current parameter settings.

9. If you want to use the current settings at a later time, save them as a preset.

10. Click OK.

Reverberation

Reverb (short for reverberation) is also a form of delay, but it's special because instead of distinct echoes, reverb adds a complex series of very small echoes that simulate artificial ambience. In other words, reverb produces a dense collection of echoes that are so close together that they create a wash of sound, making the original audio data sound like it's being played in another environment, such as a large concert hall. Using SONAR's reverb effects, you can make your music sound like it's being played in all kinds of different places, such as in an arena, a club, or even on a live stage.

Reverb (Mono)

The Reverb (Mono) effect is designed to work with monophonic audio, rather than stereo. To apply the Reverb (Mono) effect to your data, follow these steps:

1. Select the audio data you want to process.

2. Select Process > Audio Fx > Cakewalk > Reverb (Mono) to open the Reverb (Mono) dialog box.

3. Set the Decay Time parameter. When you're applying reverb to your data, you should imagine the type of environment you want to create. Doing so will help you set the effect parameters. Technically, the Decay Time determines how long it takes for the reverberation to fade away, but you can think of it as controlling how large the artificial environment will be. The lower the Decay Time, the smaller the environment; the higher the Decay Time, the larger the environment. You can set the Decay Time from 0.20 to 5 seconds. If you want to make your music sound like it's playing in a small room, a good Decay Time might be about 0.25. If you want to make your music sound like it's being played on a live stage, a good Decay Time might be about 1.50. Be sure to check out some of the included presets for more sample parameter settings.

4. Set the Dry Mix and Wet Mix parameters (see Delay/Echo (Mono)). One point you should note is that in the case of reverb, the Dry Mix and Wet Mix parameters also make a difference on how the effect sounds. If you set the Dry Mix high and the Wet Mix low, your audio data will sound like it's positioned closer to the front of the imaginary environment. If you set the Dry Mix low and the Wet Mix high, your audio data will sound like it's positioned farther away. For example, if you want to simulate what it sounds like to be seated in the very back row of a music concert, you can set the Dry Mix low and the Wet Mix high. You need to experiment to get the exact parameter settings.

5. In the Early Reflections section, choose one of the following options: None, Dense, or Sparse. When you make a sound in any enclosed environment, some very quick echoes always occur because of the reflective surfaces (such as walls) that you are standing next to. These echoes are known as *early reflections*. To make your reverb simulations sound more authentic, SONAR provides this parameter so you can control the density of the early reflections. If you select None, no early reflections are added to the effect. The Sparse option makes the reflections sound more like distinct echoes, and the Dense option makes the reverb effect sound thicker. Early reflections are more pronounced in larger spaces, so if you want to simulate a really large space, you'll probably want to

use the Sparse option. If you want to simulate a moderately sized space, you'll probably want to use the Dense option. And if you want to simulate a small space (such as a room), you should use the None option.

6. In the Frequency Cutoff section, set the High Pass and Low Pass parameters. If you think these parameters look like equalization settings, you're right. Using these parameters also helps to create more authentic environment simulations because smaller, closed environments tend to stifle some frequencies of the audio spectrum, and larger environments usually sound brighter, meaning they promote more of the frequencies. The High Pass and Low Pass parameters work just like the previous EQ effect parameters. If you activate the High Pass parameter and set its frequency (in Hz), any frequencies above that frequency will be allowed to pass and will be included in the Effect, and any frequencies below that frequency will be cut. If you activate the Low Pass parameter and set its frequency, any frequencies below that frequency will be allowed to pass, and any frequencies above that frequency will be cut. If you want to simulate a small room, you can leave the High Pass parameter deactivated, activate the Low Pass parameter, and set its frequency to around 8000 Hz. This setting would cut out any really high frequencies, making the room sound small and enclosed. For more examples on how to set these parameters, be sure to take a look at some of the included presets.

7. Click the Audition button to test the current parameter settings.

8. If you want to use the current settings at a later time, save them as a preset.

9. Click OK.

Reverb

The Reverb effect is designed to work with stereo audio. To apply this effect, follow these steps:

1. Select the audio data you want to process.

2. Select Process > Audio Fx > Cakewalk > Reverb to open the Reverb dialog box.

3. Set the Decay(s) parameter. It is exactly the same as the Decay Time parameter in the Reverb (Mono) effect, except that it controls both the left and right channels of the signal if your audio is in stereo.

4. Set the Dry Mix and Wet Mix parameters. They are exactly the same as the Dry Mix and Wet Mix parameters in the Reverb (Mono) effect, except that they control both the left and right channels of the signal if your audio is in stereo. A Link option is also available.

5. Choose an early reflections option. The No Echo, Dense Echo, and Sparse Echo options are exactly the same as the None, Dense, and Sparse options in the Reverb (Mono) effect, respectively.

6. Activate and set the frequency cutoff parameters. The LP Filter and HP Filter parameters are exactly the same as the Low Pass and High Pass filters in the Reverb (Mono) effect, respectively.

7. Click the Audition button to test the current parameter settings.

8. If you want to use the current settings at a later time, save them as a preset.

9. Click OK.

FxReverb

In contrast to the previously mentioned reverb effects, the FxReverb provides a high-quality sound, as well as more adjustable parameters. Here is how it works:

1. Select the audio data you want to process.

2. Choose Process > Audio Fx > Cakewalk > FxReverb to open the FxReverb dialog box.

3. Set the Room Size parameter. This parameter determines the size of the environment you are trying to simulate.

4. Set the Mix parameter. It is similar to the Wet Dry Mix parameter used in other effects. One point you should note is that in the case of reverb, the Mix parameter also makes a difference in how the effect sounds. If you set the Mix parameter low, your audio data will sound like it's positioned closer to the front of the imaginary environment. If you set the Mix parameter high, your audio data will sound like it's positioned farther away. For example, if you want to simulate what it sounds like to be seated in the very back row of a music concert, you can set the Mix parameter high. You need to experiment to get the exact parameter settings you desire.

5. Set the Decay Time parameter. When you're applying reverb to your data, you should imagine the type of environment you want to create. Doing so will help you set the parameters. Technically, the Decay Time determines how long it takes for the reverberation to fade away, but you can also think of it as controlling how large the artificial environment will be. It works in conjunction with the Room Size parameter. The lower the Decay Time, the smaller the environment, and vice versa. If you want to make your audio sound like it's playing in a small room, a good Decay Time might be about 0.5 seconds. If you want to make your audio sound like it's playing in a large area, a good Decay Time might be about 3 seconds.

6. Set the Pre Delay parameter. This parameter is similar to the Decay Time parameter, except that the Pre Delay determines the time between when your audio is first heard and when the reverb effect begins. This gives you even more control in determining your artificial environment. For small spaces, use a low setting (such as 1 millisecond). For large spaces, use a high setting (such as 70 milliseconds).

7. Set the High Frequency Rolloff and High Frequency Decay parameters. If you think these parameters look like equalization settings, you're right. Using these parameters also helps to create more authentic environment simulations because smaller, closed environments tend to stifle some frequencies of the audio spectrum, and larger environments usually sound brighter, meaning they promote more of the frequencies. When you set the High Frequency Rolloff parameter (in Hz), any frequencies below that frequency are allowed to pass, and any frequencies above that frequency are cut. Setting the High Frequency Decay parameter determines how quickly the high frequencies above the

High Frequency Rolloff are cut as the reverberation sounds. For examples on how to set these parameters, be sure to take a look at some of the included presets.

8. Set the Density parameter. This parameter determines the thickness of the reverberation. Experiment with it to hear what I mean.

9. Set the Motion Depth and Motion Rate parameters. In a real environment, reverberation is constantly changing as it sounds; it isn't static at all. The reverberant echoes actually move around the environment, which is what gives the environment a distinct sound. You can simulate this movement using the Motion Depth and Motion Rate parameters. The Motion Depth parameter determines how much movement there is, and the Motion Rate parameter determines the speed of that movement. For examples on how to set these parameters, be sure to take a look at some of the included presets.

10. Set the Level parameter, which controls the overall volume level of the effect output.

11. Click the Audition button to test the current parameter settings.

12. If you want to use the current settings at a later time, save them as a preset.

13. Click OK.

Sonitus:fx Reverb (SONAR Producer Edition)

If you purchased the Producer Edition of SONAR, you have access to an additional reverb effect called *Sonitus:fx Reverb*. Here is how it works:

1. Select the audio data you want to process.

2. Choose Process > Audio Fx > Sonitus:fx > Reverb to open the Reverb dialog box.

3. Set the Input parameter. This parameter lets you set the level of the signal coming into the Reverb effect.

4. Set the Low Cut and High Cut parameters. These are EQ parameters that define the frequencies for different types of environments. The Low Cut parameter cuts out low frequencies below the frequency you specify. The High Cut parameter cuts out frequencies above the frequency you specify.

5. Set the Predelay parameter. This parameter determines the time between when your audio is first heard and when the reverb effect begins. To simulate small spaces, use a low setting (such as 1 millisecond). For large spaces, use a higher setting (such as 45 to 70 milliseconds).

6. Set the Room Size parameter. This parameter determines the size of the environment you are trying to simulate. For small spaces, use a low value (such as 20). For large spaces, use a high value (such as 70).

7. Set the Diffusion parameter. This parameter determines the thickness of the reverberation. Experiment with it to hear what I mean.

8. Set the Decay Time parameter. When you're applying reverb to your data, you should imagine the type of environment you want to create. Doing so will help you set the parameters. Technically, the Decay Time determines how long it takes for the reverberation to fade away, but you can also think of it as controlling how large the environment

will be. It works in conjunction with the Room Size parameter. The lower the Decay Time, the smaller the environment, and vice versa.

9. Set the Crossover and Bass Multiplier parameters. There may be times when you want to simulate an environment that has more or less bass sound to it. The Bass Multiplier parameter specifies how much longer or shorter the Decay Time of the bass frequencies (as compared to the other frequencies) will last in your environment. Setting the Bass Multiplier higher than 1.0 makes the bass decay longer; setting it lower than 1.0 makes the bass decay shorter. The Crossover parameter determines the frequency below which other frequencies will have a longer or shorter decay. For example, if you want to simulate a bright-sounding room, you would want the bass frequencies to decay faster. So you might set the Crossover parameter to something like 500 Hz and the Bass Multiplier to something like 0.5.

10. Set the High Damping parameter. Using this parameter also helps to create a more authentic environment simulation because smaller, closed environments tend to stifle some frequencies, and larger environments usually sound brighter, meaning they promote more of the frequencies. When you set the High Damping parameter (in Hz), any frequencies above that frequency are slowly reduced (dampened) to simulate the same high-frequency reduction that happens as the reverb effect fades.

11. Set the Dry parameter. This parameter determines the level of the original nonaffected audio signal.

12. Set the E.R. parameter. This parameter determines the level of the early reflections in the reverb effect (see Reverb (Mono)).

13. Set the Reverb parameter. This parameter determines the level of the affected audio signal, also known as the *wet* signal. It works the same as the Wet Mix parameter (see Reverb (Mono)).

14. Set the Width parameter. This parameter adjusts the stereo width of the reverberation effect. Use a setting of 0 to create a monophonic signal; use a setting of 100 to create a regular stereo signal. Use a setting of more than 100 for a simulated wide stereo signal.

15. Click the Audition button to test the current parameter settings.

16. If you want to use the current settings at a later time, save them as a preset.

17. Click OK.

Lexicon Pantheon (SONAR Producer Edition)

In addition to the Sonitus:fx Reverb effect, SONAR Producer Edition users get a very high-quality reverb effect called the *Lexicon Pantheon*. Here is how it works:

1. Select the audio data you want to process.

2. Choose Process > Audio Fx > Lexicon > Pantheon to open the Lexicon Pantheon dialog box.

3. Set the Reverb Type parameter. This parameter determines the type of environment you are trying to simulate. The available options are self-explanatory.

4. Set the Mix and Level parameters. These parameters work the same as the Mix and Level parameters of the FxReverb effect.

5. Set the Pre-Delay parameter. This parameter works the same as the Pre Delay parameter for the FxReverb effect.

6. Set the Room Size parameter. This parameter works the same as the Room Size parameter for the FxReverb effect.

7. Set the RT 60 parameter. This parameter sets the reverberation time, and it works the same as the Decay Time parameter for the FxReverb effect.

8. Set the Damping parameter. This parameter works the same as the High Damping parameter for the Sonitus:fx Reverb effect.

9. Set the Density Regen and Delay parameters. These parameters work the same as the Density parameter for the FxReverb effect, except that here you have more control over the thickness of the reverberation. Lower Regen and Delay values provide a more natural reverb effect.

10. Set the Echo Level and Time values. Together, these parameters introduce echo effects into both the left and right stereo channels of your reverb effect. It's similar to applying a delay effect to your audio data and then applying a reverb effect after that.

11. Set the Bass Boost and Bass Freq parameters. These parameters work the same as the Bass Multiplier and Crossover parameters for the Sonitus:fx Reverb effect.

12. Set the Diffusion parameter. This parameter works the same as the Diffusion parameter for the Sonitus:fx Reverb effect.

13. Set the Spread parameter. This parameter works the same as the Width parameter for the Sonitus:fx Reverb effect.

14. Click the Audition button to test the current parameter settings.

15. If you want to use the current settings at a later time, save them as a preset.

16. Click OK.

Perfect Space Convolution Reverb (SONAR Producer Edition)

The highest-quality reverb effect provided by SONAR is the *Perfect Space Convolution Reverb*, which is only available to SONAR Producer Edition users. Like the other reverb effects, Perfect Space simulates environments, but it is much more sophisticated because the simulations are based on real-life environments. Here is how it works:

1. Select the audio data you want to process.

2. Choose Process > Audio Fx > PerfectSpace to open the PerfectSpace dialog box (see Figure 11.1).

3. Click the File Menu button to open the Select Wave File to Load dialog box and choose an Impulse file. Click Open. The Perfect Space effect bases its environment simulations on real-life environments by using what are called *Impulse* files. An Impulse file is similar

File Menu button

Envelope enable buttons

Envelope type buttons

Envelope

Impulse waveform display

Figure 11.1 Use the Perfect Space effect to apply complex environment simulation effects to your audio data.

to an actual recording of an acoustic space or signature. It models the characteristics of a real environment, such as a concert hall or even a kitchen in someone's home. SONAR ships with a large collection of Impulse files that you can use to make it seem as if your audio is playing in a variety of real environments. Perfect Space supports Impulse files in the WAV or AIF audio file format.

❋ CREATIVE IMPULSES

In addition to environments, Impulse files can be used to model the characteristics of different audio equipment. This includes guitar amps. What this means is that you can make it sound as if your audio was played through a certain type of amp using Perfect Space, even if you don't own that particular amp. Perfect Space ships with a number of amp-based Impulse files that you can use. The effect is pretty cool.

The Perfect Space effect also lets you use any ordinary WAV or AIF file as the basis for its processing. You can get some really weird effects using the effect in this manner. Sound effects work really well here. For example, try using a quick car horn sound and process your audio data with it. Your audio takes on the characteristics of the car horn.

---

4. Located just below the Impulse waveform display are the In-Mono, Left-Mono, Auto Gain, and Reverse parameters. You can turn these parameters on or off by clicking on them. If your original audio is monophonic (one channel), activate the In-Mono parameter so that Perfect Space will process the original audio as mono rather than stereo. If your original audio is in stereo (two channels), but you only want to process the left channel, activate the Left-Mono parameter. The Auto Gain parameter automatically adjusts the

volume of loaded Impulse files so that they are equal. This allows you to load different Impulse files without having to continuously adjust the Dry and Wet parameters to compensate. You'll usually want to keep the Auto Gain parameter activated. The Reverse parameter simply reverses the Impulse file to allow you to hear what it is like to have your audio processed by the Impulse file in reverse. This can provide some interesting effects, depending on the Impulse file being used.

5. Set the Dry, Wet, and Wet Pan parameters in the Output section. The Dry parameter controls the volume of the original audio signal. The Wet parameter controls the volume of the processed audio signal. For example, if you are processing a guitar part, the higher you set the Dry parameter, the more of the guitar part you will hear. And the higher you adjust the Wet parameter, the more of the reverb effect you will hear. The Wet Pan parameter controls the panning for the processed audio. For example, if your guitar part is panned to the center, you could use the Wet Pan parameter to pan the reverb effect to the left or right for some interesting effects. Personally, I like to keep the Dry and Wet parameters set to 0 dB and the Wet Pan parameter set to C (Center). This gives me a frame of reference when I'm adjusting the other parameters, and then afterwards I can come back and adjust these parameters again if they need some final tweaking.

6. The Offset, Length, and Delay parameters in the Impulse Adjust section determine how the Impulse file is used to process your audio. Change the Offset parameter to the starting point within the Impulse file at which your audio will begin to be processed. This allows you to use only part of the impulse file to process your audio. As you raise the Offset parameter, the beginning of the Impulse file is cropped so that less of the beginning of the file is used. You'll also notice that this changes the Length parameter. If you want to crop the end of the Impulse file rather than the beginning, you can set the Offset to 0 and lower the Length parameter. When using an environment-based Impulse file, either adjustment will make it sound like the environment is getting smaller. The Delay parameter is somewhat different, in that raising its value will cause you to hear the processed audio later than the original audio. It is sort of like introducing an echo into the effect, and it can be used to make an environment sound larger.

7. Like the parameters in the Impulse Adjust section, the Envelope Type buttons represent parameters that determine how the Impulse file is used to process your audio. These parameters adjust the volume, stereo width, panning, lo-pass EQ, hi-pass EQ, and overall EQ of the Impulse file over time using envelopes. To access and edit the envelope for each parameter, click the appropriate Envelope Type button. To enable or disable each parameter, click its associated Envelope Enable button. Adjust envelope nodes by clicking and dragging them. Parameter values are displayed on the right side of the Waveform display with time values being shown at the bottom (except for EQ, when frequencies are shown). Add envelope nodes by double-clicking anywhere on the envelope line. Delete nodes by double-clicking them.

You can also adjust the Waveform display by holding down the ALT key on your computer keyboard and then clicking and dragging your mouse to zoom in on a section. To zoom out, hold down ALT and double-click the display. While zoomed in, you can scroll the display by holding down the CTRL key and clicking and dragging your mouse left or right.

8. Adjust the Volume envelope. This parameter controls the volume of the Impulse file over time. When using an environment-based Impulse file, adjusting the Volume envelope essentially controls the start and stop points of the file, similar to the Offset and Length parameters. But using an envelope gives you much more control.

9. Adjust the Width envelope. This parameter controls the stereo width of the Impulse file over time. The lower you set the value, the narrower the stereo field will be. This means that the audio sounds more like it's being compressed between your two speakers. If you set the value to 0, you are basically converting the stereo signal to mono. Setting the value above 100, expands the stereo signal.

10. Adjust the Pan envelope. This parameter controls the panning of the Impulse file over time. It is essentially the same as the Wet Pan parameter (discussed earlier), except it gives you much more control.

11. Set the Lo Pass, Hi Pass, and EQ envelopes. These parameters apply low pass, high pass, and overall equalization to the Impulse file over time.

12. Click the Audition button to test the current parameter settings.

13. If you want to use the current settings at a later time, save them as a preset.

14. Click OK.

❋ MORE PERFECT SPACE INFO

In the Perfect Space window, click the Info button. Then click the Help button to access the Perfect Space help file for more information about this effect.

Dynamics

SONAR includes a number of effects that apply dynamic processing to your audio data, including compression and limiting. What does that mean? Well, one way to explain it would be to talk about taming vocal recordings. Suppose that you recorded this vocalist who can really belt out a tune, but doesn't have very good microphone technique. When he sings, he just stays in one place in front of the mike. Professional singers know that during the quiet parts of the song, they need to sing up close to the mike, and during the loud parts, they need to back away so that an even amplitude level is recorded. If a singer doesn't do this, the amplitude of the recorded audio will be very uneven. That's where compression and limiting come in. Compression squashes the audio signal so the amplitude levels are more even. Limiting stops the amplitude of the audio signal from rising past a certain level to prevent clipping. This can happen if the performer sings too loudly. I'll talk about each of the available effects one at a time.

FX Compressor/Gate

The FX Compressor/Gate effect applies compression to your audio data. Here is how it works:

1. Select the audio data you want to process.

2. Choose Process > Audio Fx > Cakewalk > FX Compressor/Gate to open the FX Compressor/Gate dialog box. The dialog box displays a graph. The right side of the graph shows output amplitude, and the bottom of the graph shows input amplitude. Inside the graph is a line representing the input amplitude and output amplitude as they relate to each other. Initially, the line is drawn diagonally, and you read it from left to right. This shows a 1:1 ratio between input and output amplitudes, meaning as the input level goes up 1 dB, the output level also goes up 1 dB.

3. Set the Compressor Thr (threshold) parameter. The FX Compressor/Gate effect uses a digital noise gate to identify the parts of your audio data that should be processed. The Compressor Thr parameter determines at what amplitude level your audio data will start being compressed. When the amplitude of your audio data reaches the Threshold level, processing will begin.

4. Set the Compressor Ratio parameter. This parameter determines how much processing is done to your audio data. A ratio of 1:1 means no processing is done. A ratio of 2:1 means that for every 2 dB increase in input amplitude, there is only a 1 dB increase in output amplitude. Thus, the amplitude is being compressed. If you set the Ratio parameter to its highest value (Inf:1), that causes limiting, so no matter how loud the input amplitude gets, it is limited to the level set by the Threshold parameter.

5. Set the Attack Time parameter. This parameter determines how quickly after the input level has reached the threshold that processing is applied. For example, if the input level reaches the threshold, it doesn't have to be compressed right away. A slow attack means the signal won't be compressed unless it lasts for a while. This is a good way to make sure fast, percussive parts are left alone, but long, drawn-out parts are compressed.

6. Set the Release Time parameter. This parameter determines how quickly after the input level goes below the threshold that processing is stopped (or the digital noise gate is closed). If you set the Release Time parameter too low, your audio could be cut off. A longer release allows processing to sound more natural. You'll have to experiment to get to the right setting.

7. In addition to being able to compress audio data, the FX Compressor/Gate effect can cut out noises using a special noise gate (hence the name Compressor/Gate). By setting the Gate Thr (threshold) parameter, you can remove any unwanted noises that have an amplitude level that falls below the threshold. This is great for removing bad notes or string noise on guitar parts, for instance. Setting the Expander Ratio determines how soft the amplitudes below the Gate Thr will be made. For example, if you set the Expander Ratio to 100:1, then any sounds that fall below the Gate Thr will be cut out completely.

8. Set the Detection Algorithm parameter. This parameter establishes how the FX Compressor/Gate effect will determine the amplitude level of the incoming audio signal. Choosing the Average option tells the effect to determine the average value of the input

signal and use that to apply compression appropriately. Choosing the RMS (root mean square) option tells the effect to determine the perceived loudness (as a listener would hear it over a period of time) of the input signal and use that to apply compression appropriately. The best method to use depends on the material being processed. You'll need to experiment to see which one works best.

9. Set the Stereo Interaction parameter. Choose the Maximum option to apply compression to both stereo channels equally. Choose the Side Chain option to apply compression only to the right channel of the stereo signal, while using the left channel signal to activate the threshold. You can use this option as a *ducking* effect, which can come in handy if you have music playing in the right channel and a voiceover playing in the left channel. As the voice comes in, the music will be lowered so that listeners can hear the voice over the background music. For most applications, you'll want to use the Maximum option.

10. Activate the Soft Knee option to give a smoother transition as the input signal starts to be compressed.

11. Set the Output Gain parameter. This parameter adjusts the overall amplitude of your audio after it is processed.

12. Click the Audition button to test the current parameter settings.

13. If you want to use the current settings at a later time, save them as a preset.

14. Click OK.

FX Expander/Gate

Like the special noise gate option in the FX Compressor/Gate effect, the FX Expander/Gate effect cuts out unwanted noises below a certain amplitude threshold. This effect takes less CPU processing power for those times when you don't need compression. Here is how it works:

1. Select the audio data you want to process.

2. Choose Process > Audio Fx > Cakewalk > FX Expander/Gate to open the FX Expander/Gate dialog box. The dialog box displays a graph, which is the same as the one in the FX Compressor/Gate effect.

3. Set the Expander Thr (threshold) parameter. This parameter works the same as the Gate Thr parameter in the FX Compressor/Gate effect.

4. Set the Expander Ratio parameter. This parameter works the same as the Expander Ratio parameter in the FX Compressor/Gate effect.

5. Set the Attack Time parameter. This parameter works the same as the Attack Time parameter in the FX Compressor/Gate effect.

6. Set the Release Time parameter. This parameter works the same as the Release Time parameter in the FX Compressor/Gate effect.

7. Set the Detection Algorithm parameter. This parameter works the same as the Detection Algorithm parameter in the FX Compressor/Gate effect, except there is one additional option. Choosing the Peak option tells the effect to determine the peak value of the input signal and use that to apply processing appropriately.

8. Set the Stereo Interaction parameter. This parameter works the same as the Stereo Interaction parameter in the FX Compressor/Gate effect.

9. Activate the Soft Knee option to give a smoother transition as the input signal starts to be processed.

10. Set the Output Gain parameter. This parameter adjusts the overall amplitude of your audio after it is processed.

11. Click the Audition button to test the current parameter settings.

12. If you want to use the current settings at a later time, save them as a preset.

13. Click OK.

FX Limiter

The FX Limiter effect stops an audio signal from getting any louder than a specified amplitude level. You can put this effect to good use during recording to prevent your input signal from getting too high and causing distortion or clipping. Here is how the effect works:

1. Select the audio you want to process.

2. Choose Process > Audio Fx > Cakewalk > FX Limiter to open the FX Limiter dialog box.

3. Set the Limiter Thr (threshold) parameter. This is the level above which you don't want your audio signal level to go. This means the amplitude of the audio won't be able to get any higher than this value.

4. Set the Stereo Interaction parameter. This parameter works the same as the Stereo Interaction parameter in the FX Compressor/Gate effect.

5. Set the Output Gain parameter. This parameter adjusts the overall amplitude of your audio after it is processed.

6. Click the Audition button to test the current parameter settings.

7. If you want to use the current settings at a later time, save them as a preset.

8. Click OK.

FX Dynamics Processor

The FX Dynamics Processor effect combines all of the features of the previous dynamics effects into one. This means that this one effect can perform all of the functions of the FX Compressor/Gate, FX Expander/Gate, and FX Limiter effects. It also has the same parameter settings, which were previously described. To access the effect, choose Process > Audio Fx > Cakewalk > FX Dynamics Processor.

Sonitus: fx Compressor (SONAR Producer Edition)

If you purchased the Producer Edition of SONAR, you'll have three additional dynamics effects at your disposal. The first is the Sonitus:fx Compressor, which provides pretty much the same functionality as FX Compressor/Gate effect. Here is how it works:

1. Select the audio data you want to process.
2. Choose Process > Audio Fx > Sonitus:fx > Compressor to open the Compressor dialog box.
3. To adjust the input signal level, just drag the Input slider up or down.
4. Set the Threshold parameter. This parameter works the same as the Threshold parameter for the FX Compressor/Gate effect.
5. Set the Ratio parameter. This parameter works the same as the Ratio parameter for the FX Compressor/Gate effect.
6. Set the Attack parameter. This parameter works the same as the Attack parameter for the FX Compressor/Gate effect.
7. Set the Release parameter. This parameter works the same as the Release parameter for the FX Compressor/Gate effect, with one exception. Just to the right of the Release parameter is a button labeled *TCR*. Activating this button tells the Compressor effect to try to determine the release time automatically during processing. This may or may not work well, depending on the material you are processing.
8. In addition to being able to compress audio data, the Compressor effect can apply limiting to your data. To turn limiting on or off, use the Limiter button located to the right of the Attack parameter.
9. Set the Type parameter by clicking the Type button. A setting of Normal provides the operation of a normal compressor effect. A setting of Vintage emulates the compression characteristics of a classic analog-based compressor like the Teletronix LA2A. This might give your audio data more warmth and punch.
10. Set the Knee parameter. Choosing a soft setting (10 dB or greater) will give you a warmer quality to the compression. Choosing a hard setting (below 10 dB) will give you a harsher quality to the compression.
11. Set the Gain parameter. This parameter works the same as the Output Gain parameter in the FX Compressor/Gate effect.
12. Click the Audition button to test the current parameter settings.
13. If you want to use the current settings at a later time, save them as a preset.
14. Click OK.

Sonitus:fx Gate

The second extra dynamics effect that you receive with the SONAR Producer Edition is the Sonitus:fx Gate effect. I've talked about digital noise gates before as they pertain to other functions, but you also can use digital noise gates independently to remove (or reduce the level of) parts of your audio data. For example, if you want the quiet sections in a vocal dialogue recording to be turned to silence, you can use a noise gate. The Sonitus:fx Gate effect can do this, and here is how it works:

1. Select the audio data you want to process.
2. Choose Process > Audio Fx > Sonitus:fx > Gate to open the Gate dialog box.
3. To adjust the input signal level, just drag the Input slider up or down.

4. Set the Threshold parameter. This parameter determines at what amplitude audio passes through the gate unaffected. Anything below the threshold will have its level reduced.

5. Set the Depth parameter. This parameter determines how soft the input signal level will be made after the gate is closed. Most of the time this parameter is set to -Inf, making the signal completely silent.

6. Set the Low Cut and High Cut parameters. These are EQ parameters that allow you to gate an audio signal according to frequency. Any frequencies below the Low Cut frequency are reduced; any frequencies above the High Cut frequency are reduced.

7. Set the Gate Mode parameter using the Gate Mode button (which is located below the High Cut parameter). Initially, the button displays a Normal setting. Click the button to toggle it to Duck mode and vice versa. In Duck mode, the gate is inverted so that signals below the threshold are allowed to pass and signals above the threshold are attenuated.

8. Set the Punch Mode, Punch Level, and Punch Tune parameters (which are located next to the Gate Mode button). The Punch feature adds gain to the signal as it starts to pass through the gate. This can be useful to add punch to percussion sounds. Setting the mode to Wide adds punch to a wide signal range. Setting the mode to Tuned adds punch to a specific frequency. The Level and Tune parameters let you specify the amount of gain added and the frequency used.

9. Set the Attack parameter. This parameter determines how quickly after the input level has reached the threshold that the noise gate opens and allows audio through. A low setting keeps any quick, percussive sound intact.

10. Set the Hold parameter. This parameter determines how long the gate stays open after the input signal has gone below the threshold.

11. Set the Release parameter. This parameter determines how quickly after the input level goes below the threshold and the hold time ends that the noise gate is closed. A low setting makes the noise gate close quickly. Again, this is good for percussive sounds.

12. Set the Look ahead parameter. Increasing this parameter allows the Gate effect to scan the input signal ahead of time. This can be useful if you have percussive sounds, but you want to use a longer attack time and not chop off part of the signal.

13. Set the Gain parameter. This parameter adjusts the overall amplitude of your audio after it is processed.

14. Click the Audition button to test the current parameter settings.

15. If you want to use the current settings at a later time, save them as a preset.

16. Click OK.

Sonitus:fx Multiband

Like the Sonitus:fx Compressor effect, the Multiband effect applies compression to your audio data. This effect has one important difference, though: it allows you to process different frequency ranges in your audio independently. Why is that important? Well, one way to explain it is to talk about *de-essing*. You might have noticed while doing vocal recordings that some singers produce a sort of hissing sound whenever they pronounce words with the letter "s" in them. That hissing sound is called *sibilance*, and you usually don't want it in your audio. The process of removing sibilance is called de-essing, and it is done by compressing certain frequencies in the audio spectrum. To use the Multiband effect, follow these steps:

1. Select the audio data you want to process.

2. Choose Process > Audio Fx > Sonitus:fx > Multiband to open the Multiband dialog box.

3. The Multiband effect actually provides five compression effects in one. It's basically like having five of the Sonitus:fx Compressor effects together in one effect. You'll find five sets of controls called *bands* in the upper-left section of the dialog box. You can turn each band on or off using the Byp (bypass) buttons, and you can solo a band using the Solo buttons. All the bands are identical.

4. To set the Threshold parameter for each band, use the vertical sliders or type in a value. The Threshold parameters work the same as for the Sonitus:fx Compressor effect.

5. In the lower-right section of the dialog box, you'll find a tabbed area. Clicking a numbered tab displays the compression settings for each band.

6. Set the Ratio, Knee, Type, Gain, Attack, and Release parameters for each band. All of these parameters work the same as the corresponding parameters for the Sonitus:fx Compressor effect.

7. Clicking the Common tab displays all the band settings in a grid, as well as some global effect settings.

8. Set the TCR, Limit, and Out parameters. These also work the same as they do for the Sonitus:fx Compressor effect.

9. The lower-left portion of the dialog box contains the frequency graph. This graph displays the frequency ranges for each band. You can adjust the ranges by clicking and dragging the four separators on the graph, or you can type in new values for the Low, LowMid, HighMid, and High parameters. These parameters determine the range of frequencies that will be affected by each band.

10. There is also a global Q parameter that affects all the bands located in the Common panel. The Q parameter works the same as the previously mentioned Q parameter in the "Equalization" section of this chapter.

11. Click the Audition button to test the current parameter settings.

12. If you want to use the current settings at a later time, save them as a preset.

13. Click OK.

MASTERING

In addition to regular compression/limiting tasks, the high quality of the Multiband effect allows you to use it for mastering. *Mastering* is the procedure during which the final mixed-down stereo audio for a song is processed with various effects (such as EQ, compression, and limiting), to give the song that final professional touch before it is burned to CD. There have been entire books written on the topic of mastering, but check out the following articles for some good information:

> ❋ Audio Mastering Basics—An Introduction to Mastering—
> www.digifreq.com/digifreq/article.asp?ID=33
>
> ❋ Audio Mastering Advice from Professional Engineers—
> www.digifreq.com/digifreq/article.asp?ID=34
>
> ❋ Audio Mastering—A Step-by-Step Guide to Mastering Your Recordings—
> www.digifreq.com/digifreq/article.asp?ID=35
>
> Also, go to www.digifreq.com/digifreq/articles.asp for more information on these and other music tech-
> nology topics. And be sure to get my free DigiFreq music technology newsletter so you don't miss the
> mastering information I will be providing in future issues. Go to www.digifreq.com/digifreq/ to sign up.

Changing Time and Pitch

In addition to the Length and Transpose editing features, SONAR provides the Pitch Shifter and Time/Pitch Stretch effects, which you also can use to change the length and pitch of your audio data. The effects, however, are more powerful and flexible. This is especially true of the Time/Pitch Stretch effect. SONAR Producer users also get a very powerful vocal processing effect called V-Vocal.

Pitch Shifter

The Pitch Shifter effect provides low quality, but it doesn't take up as much CPU processing power. If you want to try out the Cakewalk FX Pitch Shifter, here's how it works:

1. Select the audio data you want to process.

2. Select Process > Audio Fx > Cakewalk > Pitch Shifter to open the Pitch Shifter dialog box.

3. Set the Pitch Shift parameter. It is exactly the same as the Amount parameter in the Transpose editing function. You can use it to transpose the pitch of your audio data from −12 to +12 semitones (an entire octave down or up).

> ❋ **UNWANTED ARTIFACTS**
>
> Normally, when you change the pitch of audio data, the length is altered, too. Raise the pitch, and the data gets shorter; lower the pitch, and the data gets longer. When this happens, the processed audio no longer plays in sync with the other data in your project. Luckily, you can use SONAR's pitch-shifting effects to change pitch without changing the length of the audio data. The only problem to be leery of is that pitch shifting can produce unwanted artifacts if you use too great an interval. The famous Alvin & the Chipmunks were a product of this phenomenon. It's best to stay within an interval of a major third (four semitones) up or down, if possible.

4. Set the Dry Mix and Wet Mix parameters. You should almost always keep the Dry Mix set to 0 percent and the Wet Mix set to 100 percent.

5. As far as the Feedback Mix, Delay Time, and Mod Depth parameters are concerned, they don't seem to have anything to do with the Cakewalk FX Pitch Shifter effect. Changing these parameters only introduces unwanted artifacts into the sound. My advice is

simply to leave them set at their default values: Feedback Mix = 0, Delay Time = 0, and Mod Depth = 35.

6. Click the Audition button to test the current parameter settings.

7. If you want to use the current settings at a later time, save them as a preset.

8. Click OK.

Time/Pitch Stretch 2

The Time/Pitch Stretch 2 effect is much more advanced and flexible, and it provides better quality than the Pitch Shifter effect. However, that doesn't mean it's difficult to use. Some of the more advanced parameters can be a bit confusing, but I'll go over them one at a time. The effect works like this:

1. Select the audio data you want to process.

2. Select Process > Audio Fx > Cakewalk > Time/Pitch Stretch 2 to open the Time/Pitch Stretch 2 dialog box.

3. Set the Time parameter. Using the Time parameter, you can change the length of your audio data as a percentage. If you want to make the data shorter, set the Time parameter to a percentage less than 100. For example, to make the data half of its original length, use a setting of 50 percent. If you want to make the data longer, set the Time parameter to a percentage greater than 100. If you want to make data the twice its original length, use a setting of 200 percent. To change the Time parameter, just type a value or use the horizontal slider.

STAY WITHIN 10 PERCENT

When you're transposing audio, it's best to stay within a major third (four semitones) up or down, if possible, because audio doesn't react well to higher values. The same concept applies when you're changing the length of audio data. You should try to stay within 10 percent longer or shorter, if possible; otherwise, the results might not sound very good.

4. Set the Pitch parameter. Using the Pitch parameter, you can transpose your audio data up or down one octave (in semitones). To change the Pitch parameter, just type a value or use the vertical slider.

TIME/PITCH GRAPH

Notice that a graph is shown in the Time/Pitch Stretch dialog box. Using this graph, you can change the Time and Pitch parameters by dragging the small blue square. Drag the square up or down to change the Pitch parameter. Drag the square left or right to change the Time parameter. If you hold down the Shift key on your computer keyboard at the same time, the square automatically will snap to the exact grid points on the graph.

5. To get the best quality, make sure the MPEX option under the Advanced tab is activated. Processing will probably be a bit slower, but the audio will sound better. Also, choose a setting for the Quality parameter. If you are processing a single instrument, choose one of the single instrument options.

6. Click the Audition button to test the current parameter settings.

7. If you want to use the current settings at a later time, save them as a preset.

8. Click OK.

V-Vocal Voice Processor

V-Vocal is an accurate and powerful vocal processing effect that adjusts the pitch, timing, loudness, and timbre of monophonic vocal audio recordings.

V-Vocal Basics

V-Vocal is not applied in the same way as all the other audio effects in SONAR. When you apply V-Vocal to a selected region of audio data or a selected clip, a new V-Vocal clip is created. This new clip overlaps the original audio data, which still exists below the V-Vocal data, but is muted. The steps to start using V-Vocal to process your audio are as follows:

1. Either select a region of audio and choose Edit > Create V-Vocal Clip or simply right-click a clip and choose V-Vocal > Create V-Vocal Clip. A new V-Vocal clip is created (displaying the V-Vocal logo in the upper left corner), and the V-Vocal window is automatically opened (see Figure 11.2).

2. The V-Vocal window displays the V-Vocal clip in its entirety within a Waveform display. Along the top of the Waveform display is the Timeline (which is the same Time Ruler in the Track view). Along the left of the Waveform display are values, which differ, depending on the editing mode you are using. I will talk about editing modes shortly. Along the bottom and right of the Waveform display are the Horizontal and Vertical Scroll bars and arrows. Use these controls to scroll the Waveform display. You can also click and drag with the Hand tool directly within the display to scroll.

❊ **WAVEFORM DISPLAY SIZE**

To make the Waveform display larger or smaller, click the Edit Area button to hide or show some of the V-Vocal parameters. You can also change the size of the V-Vocal window itself to create a larger display.

---

3. For zooming, use the Zoom control and Zoom tool. Click the up and down arrows on the Zoom control to zoom out and in vertically. Click the left and right arrows on the Zoom control to zoom out and in horizontally. To zoom out all the way both vertically and horizontally (thus fitting the entire clip within the display), double-click the center of the Zoom control. To zoom in on a specific area, use the Zoom tool to make a rectangular selection in the Waveform display.

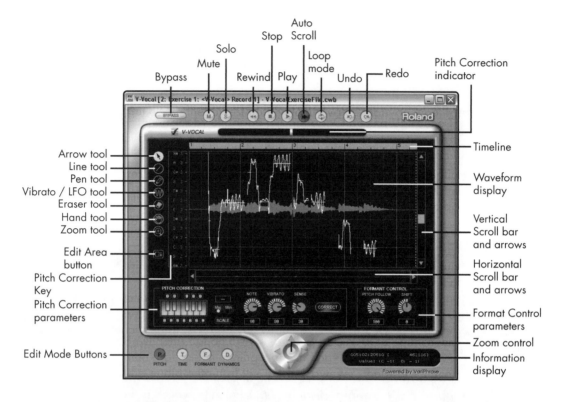

Figure 11.2 Use the V-Vocal window to access the V-Vocal effect parameters.

4. Without a data selection, V-Vocal parameters make changes to the entire audio wave-form. To edit only a portion of the waveform, use the Arrow tool and click and drag within the Waveform display to make a selection.

5. Use the Line, Pen, Vibrato/LFO, and Eraser tools to edit your data.

6. Use the Undo and Redo buttons to remove mistakes that you've made during editing. You can also right-click the Waveform display and choose Undo or Redo from the pop-up menu, or you can press Ctrl + Z (Undo) or Ctrl + Shift + Z (Redo).

7. Use the Rewind, Stop, and Play buttons to control playback of the clip. These buttons are the same as the regular transport buttons in SONAR. During playback, you'll notice a cursor moving across the Waveform display. This cursor is the same as the Now Time cursor in the Track view.

8. If you are zoomed in, you can have the Waveform display automatically scroll during playback by clicking the Auto Scroll button.

9. You can also loop playback (just like in the Track view) by clicking the Loop Mode button. If you've made a data selection, only that selection will be played and looped; otherwise, the entire clip is played and looped.

10. Click the Bypass button to temporarily turn off all V-Vocal processing. This allows you to compare the original audio to the V-Vocal processed audio.

11. Use the Mute and Solo buttons to mute or solo the track upon which the V-Vocal clip resides. This enables you to hear the clip alone or along with the other audio in your project.

12. When you're finished, close the V-Vocal window. When you play your project, the V-Vocal processing will be played as well.

13. To open the V-Vocal window and make additional changes, just double-click the clip.

14. To permanently remove any V-Vocal changes, right-click the clip and choose V-Vocal > Remove V-Vocal.

Automatically Adjusting Vocal Pitch

When adjusting the pitch of a vocal part, the first thing you'll want to do is let V-Vocal try and make the corrections automatically. The results can be very accurate if the vocal part isn't too far off pitch to begin with. Here are the steps for using V-Vocal's automatic pitch correction features:

1. With the V-Vocal clip created and the window open, click the Pitch Edit Mode button.

2. To have the audio waveform shown under the V-Vocal waveform markings, right-click the Waveform display and choose View > Waveform. This will give you a better idea of the vocal part section you are editing.

3. Make sure that the Pitch Follow parameter in the Formant Control section is set to 0. This ensures that the timbral characteristics of your vocal will not change when you change the pitch. If you set the Pitch Follow parameter above zero, it will give you a munchkin sounding type of vocal. If you set the Pitch Follow parameter below zero, it will give you a strange low voice type of vocal.

4. To correct only the pitch of one section of the clip, choose the Arrow tool and make a data selection. Otherwise, V-Vocal will pitch correct the entire clip.

5. In the Pitch Correction section, adjust the Note, Vibrato, and Sense parameters. The Note parameter controls how close the notes in your audio will be moved to the correct pitches. You would think you'd want them moved all the way, but depending on how far off your notes are to begin with, moving them too much can cause artifacts to be introduced into the audio. I've found the best setting for the Note parameter is between 70 and 90, but if your original audio isn't too far off, a setting of 100 could work. The Vibrato parameter controls how much of the original vibrato you want to keep. Most of the time, I keep this set to 100 because when I start lowering it too much to try and remove vibrato, the vocal ends up sounding artificial. The Sense parameter controls the amount of pitch correction applied. The higher the value, the closer your audio is changed to fit an exact pitch. I've found the default value of 30 to work nicely most of the time. If you set the Sense parameter too high, it will make the vocal sound very artificial.

6. Click the Correct button to apply the pitch correction. If you don't like the results, undo them and try again.

> **ARTIFICIAL VOCALS EFFECT**
>
> Remember that Cher song called "Believe" where she had those strange sounding vocals? Well, you can get the same effect with V-Vocal. Just set the Note parameter to 100, the Vibrato parameter to 0, and the Sense parameter to 100. Click the Correct button. Voilà! Instant artificial vocals.

7. V-Vocal can also automatically conform your audio to a musical scale. Click the Scale button to activate the Scale feature. Choose either the Maj or Min option to choose a major or minor musical scale. Then click a key on the tiny keyboard display to choose the root note for the scale. If you want to define your own scale, you can click the notes to include (blue color), exclude (gray color), or bypass them (red color). Click the Correct button. To set the scale feature back to its default values, double-click the Maj or Min option.

> **NOTE SELECTION**
>
> Click the note names in the Pitch Correction Key (shown on the left of the Waveform display) to include, exclude, or bypass notes.

8. Close the V-Vocal window when you're finished.

Manually Adjusting Vocal Pitch

Instead of relying on the automatic adjustments provided by V-Vocal, you can make pitch adjustments manually by doing the following:

1. With the V-Vocal clip created and the window open, click the Pitch Edit Mode button.

2. To have the audio waveform shown under the V-Vocal waveform markings, right-click the Waveform display and choose View > Waveform. This will give you a better idea of the vocal part section you are editing.

3. Make sure that the Pitch Follow parameter in the Formant Control section is set to 0. This ensures that the timbral characteristics of your vocal will not change when you change the pitch. If you set the Pitch Follow parameter above zero, it will give you a munchkin sounding type of vocal. If you set the Pitch Follow parameter below zero, it will give you a strange low voice type of vocal.

4. Looking at the Waveform display, you'll notice the yellow curved lines representing the different pitches in your audio. These are called *Pitch Curves*. To edit a Pitch Curve, select the Arrow tool. Then hover the Arrow tool over the center line of the Pitch Curve and click and drag the curve up or down to change its pitch (see Figure 11.3). After you move a Pitch Curve, you'll notice the original pitch curve is also displayed in red. This gives you a reference for your edits. You can also change multiple Pitch Curves at once by first making a selection with the Arrow tool.

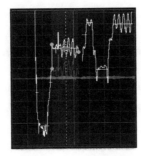

Figure 11.3   Drag the yellow Pitch Curves up or down to change the pitch of your audio data.

✳ **SNAP TO PITCH**

While dragging a curve up or down, hold down the Ctrl key to snap the curve to the nearest pitch value. Hold down the Shift key to snap to the nearest 100 cent increment.

5. You can also change multiple Pitch Curves at once or parts of a curve by first making a selection with the Arrow tool. You'll notice a number of green nodes that appear on the curve. Click and drag the nodes up or down to make changes to the curve.

6. In addition to changing the curves, you can draw your own curve by using the Line and Pen tools. To draw straight lines, use the Line tool. To draw freehand (any shape curve you would like), use the Pen tool.

7. To remove specific edits that you've done, select the Eraser tool and draw your mouse over the edits to return the curves to their original values.

8. Finally, using the Vibrato/LFO tool, you can adjust the vibrato of the vocal parts. To add vibrato, place your mouse at the point on the curve where you want to start drawing. The mouse will turn into a pen with a vibrato icon attached to it. Click and drag to draw vibrato. To edit vibrato, place your mouse over the vibrato portion of the curve. The mouse will turn into a double-arrow icon. Click and drag up and down to edit amplitude, or left and right to edit frequency. To fade in a vibrato section, move your mouse to the beginning of the vibrato to see another double-arrow icon. Then click and drag to the right to create a vibrato fade-in.

Adjusting Vocal Timing

To adjust the timing of your vocal parts, do the following:

1. With the V-Vocal clip created and the window open, click the Time Edit Mode button. You'll notice that the Waveform display now shows only your audio data waveform.

2. Select the Arrow tool.

3. Move your mouse to the center of the display over a point in the waveform that you would like to edit. Your mouse will turn into a double-pointed arrow icon.

4. Double-click to add a green line to the display.

5. Click and drag the green line left or right to change the timing of the audio data. You can also click and drag over the audio data between the green lines to change the timing.

6. Add more green lines and edit them. While editing, hold down the Ctrl key to move all the green lines the same amount of distance simultaneously.

7. To remove any edit lines, choose the Eraser tool and drag your mouse over the lines.

What I like to do is separate the words in my vocal part by placing edit lines between each word (see Figure 11.4). Then I can easily adjust the timing of each word in the vocal.

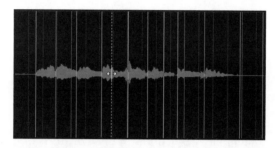

Figure 11.4   Separate each word in the vocal part for more efficient editing.

Adjusting Vocal Dynamics (Loudness)

To adjust the dynamics (loudness) of your vocal parts, do the following:

1. With the V-Vocal clip created and the window open, click the Dynamics Mode button. You'll notice that the Waveform display now shows only your audio data waveform. You'll also notice a yellow line across the center of the waveform and the display. This is the amplitude envelope. You can adjust the envelope in a number of ways.

2. Using the Arrow tool, you can grab the envelope and move it up or down to increase or decrease the amplitude of the audio. You can also double-click the envelope to add nodes. You can then drag these nodes up and down to create your own envelope shape, thus changing the amplitude of the audio (see Figure 11.5).

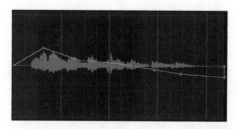

Figure 11.5   Use the Arrow tool to adjust the amplitude envelope.

3. If you want to get really creative, you can use the Line and Pen tools to draw your own unique envelope. Just select a tool and click and drag your mouse over the display to draw an envelope.

4. You can also use the Vibrato/LFO tool to draw an amplitude modulation envelope. This is where the waveform moves up and down in a pattern. In this case, it can be a sine wave or a square wave. Right-click the Waveform display and choose LFO Type > *type of wave you want to use*.

5. To remove any envelope nodes, choose the Eraser tool and drag your mouse over the nodes.

I like to use the Arrow tool to select a single word and then drag the envelope segment inside the selection up or down to change the amplitude of the word (see Figure 11.6). This way I can easily adjust the amplitude of each word in the vocal without affecting the others at the same time.

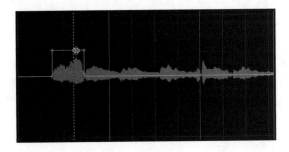

Figure 11.6   Use the Arrow tool to select a word and drag the envelope segment to change the amplitude of only that word.

Adjusting Vocal Formants (Timbre)

Last, but not least, V-Vocal edits the timbre of your vocal data using its Formant features. You can do this either automatically for an entire clip or manually for individual parts of a clip.

To adjust the timbre of an entire clip, adjust the Shift parameter in the Formant Control section. If you adjust it too high, you'll get a munchkin type of vocal sound. If you adjust it too low, you'll get a really creepy low vocal sound. Useful settings are anywhere from −10 to +10. I've found that anything beyond that just doesn't sound right.

Adjust the timbre manually just like you adjusted the amplitude back in the Adjusting Vocal Dynamics (Loudness) section. You can follow those same steps. Just keep the envelope values between –10 and +10, and you should get some good results.

Amplifier Simulation

For all you electric guitar players out there, SONAR provides the Amp Sim effect. Using this effect, you can simulate the sound of real-life guitar amplifiers, making your recorded guitar audio data sound like it's being played through different kinds of amps. To achieve this sound, the effect uses technology called *physical modeling*. In this technology, the characteristics of a real instrument or device are converted into a mathematical algorithm (called a *model*). You can use the model to apply those same characteristics to your audio data to achieve more authentic-sounding recordings. This explanation of the process is simplified, but that's the gist of it. The Amp Sim effect works like this:

1. Select the audio data you want to process.

> ❈ **USEFUL FOR VOCALS**
>
> Even though the Amp Sim effect was designed for guitar amplifiers, that doesn't mean you can't use it on other types of data. The distorted sounds the effect produces also work well on vocals, especially if you're looking for that hard rock sound. Check out some of the music by Kid Rock to hear what I mean.

2. Select Process > Audio Fx > Cakewalk > Amp Sim to open the Amp Sim dialog box.

3. In the Amp Model section, select the type of guitar amplifier you want to simulate. An additional parameter called *Bright* also is available in this section. It is similar to the Brightness switch found on many guitar amplifiers. It makes the effect sound brighter by boosting the high frequencies (everything above 500 Hz) of the audio spectrum.

4. In the Cabinet Enclosure section, select the type of cabinet you want to use for your virtual guitar amplifier. By setting this parameter, you can simulate different types of speaker enclosures. You have five options to choose from - No Speaker, 1×12, 2×12, 4×10, and 4×12. If you choose the No Speaker option, the effect will sound as though you plugged your guitar directly into the output of the amplifier and recorded the sound without using a microphone or the amplifier speakers. If you choose any of the other options, the effect will sound as though you played your guitar through an amplifier that has a certain number of speakers of a certain size and recorded the output by placing a microphone in front of the amp. For example, if you choose 4×12, the simulated amp will contain four speakers each at 12 inches in size. Also, when you select the other options, two other parameters become available—Open Back and Off-Axis. Activating the Open Back parameter makes the effect simulate a guitar amplifier that has a cabinet enclosure with an open (rather than a closed) back. Activating the Off-Axis parameter makes the effect sound as though you placed the virtual microphone off to the side of the amplifier speaker, rather than directly in front of it.

5. In the Tremolo section, set the Rate and Depth parameters. Setting these parameters adds a warble type of sound to the effect. The Rate parameter controls the speed of the tremolo, and the Depth parameter controls the amount of tremolo added. There is also a bias control (like that found on most guitar amps) that lets you determine whether the tremolo will add to or subtract from the volume level of the effect. In addition, by activating the Mono option, the tremolo will produce a mono output rather than stereo.

6. Set the Bass, Mid, and Treb parameters in the EQ section. These parameters act similarly to the parameters in SONAR's Graphic EQ editing feature. Each parameter cuts or boosts a specific frequency by −10 or +10dB. The Bass parameter is set to 60 Hz, the Mid parameter is set to 600 kHz, and the Treb parameter is set to 6000 kHz.

7. Set the Drive parameter. This parameter basically controls the amount of distortion added to the audio data being processing.

8. Set the Presence parameter. This parameter acts like a high-pass EQ with a permanent frequency of 750 Hz. You can use it to boost some of the higher frequencies of the effect, giving it more presence.

9. Set the Volume parameter. This parameter controls the overall volume of the effect. No Dry Mix or Wet Mix parameters are available for this effect, so you hear only the totally processed signal through this one.

10. Click the Audition button to test the current parameter settings.

11. If you want to use the current settings at a later time, save them as a preset.

12. Click OK.

Analog Tape Simulation

Similar to the Amp Sim effect, the FX2 Tape Sim effect uses physical modeling to simulate a realistic audio situation. But instead of simulating the sound of a guitar amplifier, the FX2 Tape Sim effect simulates the sound of your audio data being played off an analog tape deck. Why would you want to simulate old recording technology, especially when you have the clean and crisp sound of digital recording? Well, analog tape recording provides a sort of warm sound that can't be produced with digital recording, and you can use that sound to create authentic jazz or blues recordings. And some musicians just prefer the warm sound of analog, as opposed to the crisp sound of digital. The FX2 Tape Sim effect lets you achieve that warm sound, and here is how it works:

1. Select the audio data you want to process.

2. Choose Process > Audio Fx > Cakewalk > FX2 Tape Sim to open the FX2 Tape Sim dialog box.

3. Choose the type of tape machine you want to simulate by setting the Tape Speed and Eq Curve parameters. An additional parameter called *LF Boost* adds a small increase to the lower frequencies of the audio data, giving it an even warmer sound.

4. Set the Input Gain parameter. This parameter controls the volume of the input signal into the effect. Usually, you'll just want to keep it set at 0 dB.

5. Set the Rec (short for Record) Level parameter. This parameter controls the level of the audio that would be recorded in an actual tape-recording situation. Setting this parameter too high will cause distortion.

6. Set the Warmth parameter. This parameter controls that warmth sound.

7. Set the Hiss parameter. As in an actual tape-recording situation, you usually get tape hiss. If you want to be totally authentic in your simulation, you can use this parameter to add hiss to your audio data. A setting of 0 will turn off the Hiss parameter.

8. Set the Output Gain parameter. This parameter controls the overall volume of the effect. No Dry Mix or Wet Mix parameters are available for this effect, so you hear only the totally processed signal through this one.

9. Click the Audition button to test the current parameter settings.

10. If you want to use the current settings at a later time, save them as a preset.

11. Click OK.

Other Effects

SONAR users also have seven additional effects (six of which are only available in the Producer Edition)—Sonitus:fx Phase, Sonitus:fx Modulator, Sonitus:fx Wahwah, Sonitus:fx Surround, SpectraFX, Vintage Channel, and Analyst. These effects didn't fit into the previously mentioned categories, so I will cover them separately here.

Sonitus:fx Phase (SONAR Producer Edition)

When you mix certain sound files together, phase cancellation can occur. Phase cancellation occurs when one audio waveform increases in volume and the other decreases in volume at exactly the same time and by the same amount. Because of this phenomenon, they cancel each other out, making the mixed audio sound hollow. You can use the Sonitus:fx Phase effect to change the phase of audio data either for correction or for many different kinds of effects. Here is how it works:

1. Select the audio data you want to process.

2. Choose Process > Audio Fx > Sonitus:fx > Phase to open the Phase dialog box.

3. Set the Filter parameter. Use the IIR (*Infinite Impulse Response*) filter type for more accurate phase shift of low-frequency material. Use the FIR (*Finite Impulse Response*) filter type for more accurate phase shift of high-frequency material.

4. Set the Mode parameter. The LR Phase mode adjusts the phase of the left and right channels of a stereo signal. The MS Phase mode adjusts the phase of the middle (mono) and side (stereo difference) signals. The CS Encode mode adjusts the phase of a stereo signal by placing the center part of the signal in the left channel and the surrounding material in the right channel. The SC Encode mode adjusts the phase of a stereo signal by placing the center part of the signal in the right channel and the surrounding material in the left channel.

5. Set the Phase parameter. This parameter specifies the amount of phase shift that will occur. A value of 0 means no phase shift. To make the left and right channels of a stereo

signal completely out of phase with one another, you can use a value of −180 degrees or +180 degrees.

6. Set the Width parameter. This parameter controls the width of the stereo signal. A value of 100 percent means no change to the incoming stereo signal. A value of 0 percent converts the stereo signal into a mono signal. A value of 200 percent makes it sound like the stereo signal is spread beyond the positions of your stereo speakers.

7. Set the Output parameter. This parameter adjusts the overall amplitude of your audio after it is processed.

8. Click the Audition button to test the current parameter settings.

9. If you want to use the current settings at a later time, save them as a preset.

10. Click OK.

Be sure to check out the presets supplied with the Phase effect. This effect has many uses, including converting a mono signal to a stereo signal, widening a stereo signal, and even removing vocals from a song.

Sonitus:fx Modulator (SONAR Producer Edition)

The Modulator effect is actually a number of different effects rolled into one. It provides flanging, phasing, and chorus effects. I've already talked about all these effects in previous sections of this chapter, and you'll find most of the parameters for the Modulator effect to be familiar. To access the Modulator effect choose Process > Audio Fx > Sonitus:fx > Modulator.

The main differences are the Mode and Tape parameters. The Mode parameter sets the type of effect you want to use. The Flanger setting creates a flanging effect. The Ensemble setting creates a chorus effect . The String Phaser, Phaser 6, and Phaser 12 settings create phasing effects. Phasing effects let you change the phase of stereo data in real time for some very interesting sounds. The Tremolo setting creates warble effects by modulating the amplitude of your audio data, similar to the tremolo effect you hear on an electronic organ. Use the Tape parameter to create an effect similar to the old type of analog tape-recorder flanging. This effect ships with a large number of presets. Be sure to try them out for demonstrations of what they can do.

Sonitus:fx Wahwah (SONAR Producer Edition)

The Sonitus:fx Wahwah effect simulates the classic guitar wahwah stomp box effect. Here is how it works:

1. Select the audio data you want to process.

2. Choose Process > Audio Fx > Sonitus:fx > Wahwah to open the Wahwah dialog box.

3. Set the Mode parameter. The Wahwah effect uses the up and down movement of an envelope to apply itself to your audio data. The Mode parameter determines how that envelope is controlled. Use the Auto mode to control the up and down speed of the envelope using a tempo setting. Use the Triggered mode to control the envelope using a threshold setting. Use the Manual mode to control the envelope manually using the Wah slider.

4. Set the Wah parameter. If you chose the Auto mode, the Wah parameter will determine the starting point of the envelope as it's applied to the audio. If you chose the Triggered mode, the Wah parameter will determine the range of the envelope and thus how much of the effect will be applied to the audio after the amplitude of the audio goes above the threshold. If you chose the Manual mode, you can use the Wah parameter slider to control the up and down motion of the envelope.

5. If you chose the Auto mode, set the Tempo parameter. This parameter determines the cycling speed (meaning the speed of one up-and-down motion) of the envelope and thus the wah effect.

6. If you chose the Triggered mode, set the Threshold parameter. If the level of your audio stays below the threshold, the wah effect will not be applied. If the level of your audio goes above the threshold, the wah effect will be applied, and the amount above the threshold determines how the amount of the effect applied.

7. If you chose the Triggered mode, also set the Attack and Release parameters. These parameters determine the up and down speed of the envelope, respectively.

8. You also can apply some EQ to the effect using the High and Low Freq, Q, and Gain parameters. These parameters work just like all the other similarly named EQ parameters I've described.

9. Set the Mix parameter to determine how much of the original audio signal and how much of the affected signal will be heard.

10. Set the Output parameter to determine the overall volume level of the effect output.

11. Click the Audition button to test the current parameter settings.

12. If you want to use the current settings at a later time, save them as a preset.

13. Click OK.

Sonitus:fx Surround (SONAR Producer Edition)

The Sonitus:fx Surround effect creates surround sound panning for your audio data. To get the full effect, you need to have a surround sound decoder and speaker system, but even with only a pair of stereo speakers, you can hear some of the effect. Here is how it works:

1. Select the audio data you want to process.

2. Choose Process > Audio Fx > Sonitus:fx > Surround to open the Surround dialog box.

3. In the left portion of the dialog box, you will see a graph with four speaker icons and a crosshair icon. The four speakers represent the locations of the Left, Center, Right, and Surround speakers, thus designating the listening field. The crosshair icon represents the position of your audio data being played in the listening field. You can click and drag the crosshair to move the playing position of your audio data.

4. If you want to move your audio data position outside of the listening field (so it sounds like the audio is being played from a point beyond the speaker positions), use the Zoom parameter. A setting of 1 designates a normal listening field. Settings of 3 or 5 designate larger listening fields outside of the speaker range.

5. Set the Input parameter. Choose Mono to process your audio as a mono signal. Choose stereo to process your audio as a stereo signal. Choose Left to process the left channel of a stereo signal. Choose Right to process the right channel of a stereo signal.

6. Set the Focal Point parameter to On or Off. If you turn the parameter on, a yellow cross will appear on the graph, designating the position of a virtual listener in the listening field. You can click and drag the cross to change the position of the virtual listener. This creates attenuation and Doppler shift effects.

7. If you turn the Focal Point parameter on, you also need to set the Attenuation and Doppler parameters. The Attenuation parameter determines how soft your audio data will get when its position is moved away from the virtual listener. This creates more realistic surround effects because as audio moves away from a listener in real life, its volume gets lower. The Doppler parameter determines how much of a pitch change will be applied to your audio data as it gets closer or farther away from the virtual listener. In real life, a sound seems to get higher in pitch as it moves toward you and lower in pitch as it moves away from you. The Doppler parameter lets you simulate that effect.

8. In addition to manually setting the playing position of your audio data in the listening field, you can have the playing position move in real time, according to a path that you draw on the listening field. To create this automatic panning effect, set the Path parameter to On. When you do this, the crosshair icon will turn into a white square, designating the starting position of the path. Click the white square and drag your mouse to a new position. This will drag the first line in the path. To create additional lines, double-click anywhere on the path to create a node. You can drag this node to another position. You can keep creating nodes and dragging them to new positions to create a complex path.

9. With the Path parameter on, you also can determine whether the path will be open or closed by setting the Closed Path parameter.

10. With the Path parameter on, use the Path Time parameter to determine how long it will take for the audio position to move along the path.

11. If you have the Path parameter off, you can control the audio position using a joystick. Set the Joystick parameter to On to use the joystick to control the audio panning position.

12. Click the Audition button to test the current parameter settings.

13. If you want to use the current settings at a later time, save them as a preset.

14. Click OK.

SpectraFX

The SpectraFX effect is actually a number of different effects rolled into one. It provides chorus, wah, flanging, distortion, delay, and compression effects. The unique aspects of the SpectraFX effect are that it is very easy to use and provides an X-Y control interface for quick automation of parameters. Here is how it works:

1. Select the audio data you want to process.

2. Choose Process > Audio Fx > Cakewalk > SpectraFX to open the SpectraFX dialog box (see Figure 11.7).

Figure 11.7 Create many different effects using the SpectraFX multi-effects processor.

3. Choose the effect you want to use by making a selection in the FX Presets list. There are 39 different effects from which to choose, and each provides different parameters for automation.

❋ ASSIGNABLE FX

If you find that you have some favorite effects you like to work with from the FX Presets list, you can assign them to the FX buttons in the Assignable FX section. This saves you from having to keep searching through the list of effects. These buttons do not save any parameter settings. You'll have to use the Preset feature for that.

4. In the center of the SpectraFX interface, you'll see the X-Y Control area. You use this area to change the parameter settings of the selected effect. Each effect provided by SpectraFX has two parameters. The parameters themselves are preset and can not be changed—only their values can be changed. Unfortunately, there is no list as to what the parameters are for each effect, so you will have to experiment by listening in order to get the effect you desire. To change the parameter values for the selected effect, click and drag the Locus (the blue circle in the center of the X-Y Control area) with your mouse. Dragging the Locus along the X axis (left and right) changes the value of one parameter (dragging left lowers the value and dragging right raises the value). Dragging the Locus along the Y axis (up and down) changes the value of the other parameter (dragging down lowers the value and dragging right raises the value). You can also drag the Locus diagonally, which changes both parameter values at once. In addition, if you want to move the Locus in a precise manner, use the X and Y sliders located at the right and bottom of the X-Y Control area, respectively.

❋ RESETTING THE LOCUS

To reset the Locus to its default position either vertically or horizontally, double-click the Y and X sliders, respectively.

5. In addition to changing the effect parameters manually, you can automate them by using the LFO function. This function automates the effect parameters in a repeating pattern that you create graphically in the X-Y Control area. To activate the LFO function, click either the Beats button or Meas button in the LFO area. This determines the repeat rate of the automation pattern. If you want the pattern to repeat over a specified number of beats, click the Beats button. To specify a repetition of measures, click the Meas button. In addition, the Rate parameter sets the number of beats or measures over which the pattern will repeat. Click the + or – buttons to raise or lower the Rate value, respectively. The speed of the automation pattern will follow the current SONAR project tempo.

6. After activating the LFO function, you can further define how the effect parameters will be automated by manipulating the graphical ellipse shown in the X-Y Control area. In the center of the ellipse is small circle (the Position node). Click and drag the Position node to change the position of the entire ellipse. To change the shape of the ellipse, click and drag the Shape node (see Figure 11.8).

Figure 11.8   Drag the Shape node to change the shape of the ellipse.

To change the size or angle of the ellipse, drag one of the Orb nodes (see Figure 11.9).

Figure 11.9   Drag one of the Orb nodes to change the size or angle of the ellipse.

7. Set the Mix Level parameter to determine how much of the original audio signal and how much of the affected signal will be heard. To change this parameter, click and drag the Mix Level knob up or down to increase or decrease its value, respectively.

8. Set the Gain parameter located in the Input section to determine the level of the audio signal that is fed into the SpectraFX. To change this parameter, click and drag the Gain knob up or down to increase or decrease its value, respectively.

9. Click the Audition button to test the current parameter settings. Notice that if you activate the LFO function, the Locus in the X-Y Control area will follow the automation pattern that you set, and this will automatically change the current effect parameter values.

10. If you want to use the current settings at a later time, save them as a preset.

11. Click OK.

 ADDITIONAL SPECTRAFX HELP

For additional help using the SpectraFX effect, right-click anywhere inside the SpectraFX interface and choose Help.

Vintage Channel (SONAR Producer Edition)

Vintage Channel is a multi-effects plug-in that can be used to process individual tracks or entire mixes. You can even use it for mastering. Vintage Channel provides dual-EQs, dual-compressors, gating, and de-essing. Other than the fact that all these processes are provided in one plug-in, Vintage Channel is special because it provides high-end processing. More importantly, it allows you to route an audio signal internally through the different effects in a variety of ways to provide superior output. The Vintage Channel is accessed by choosing Process > Audio Fx > Vintage Channel.

Master, De-Esser, and Gate

Vintage Channel is divided into three vertical sections. The Master, De-Esser, and Gate controls are located in the left area of the interface (see Figure 11.10). To utilize these controls, do the following:

1. Activate Master Power button. This button toggles the entire Vintage Channel on/off. You can use the Master Power button as a bypass button to quickly test your audio with or without the Vintage Channel processing.

2. Right-click inside the Routings area and choose an effect routing from the menu. Choosing a routing allows you to determine how your audio signal will be sent through each of the effects in the Vintage Channel. In the Routings area, you'll see a small graphic representing the effects routing. The audio signal (represented by a line) flows left to right in the graphic and each box represents a different effect. The effect abbreviations are as follows: NG (Gate), DE (De-Esser), E1 (Equalizer 1), E2 (Equalizer 2), C1 (Compressor 1), C2 (Compressor 2). For example, if you choose the Instrument Setup routing, your audio signal will flow through the effects in the following order: Gate, De-Esser, Equalizer 1, Compressor 1, Equalizer 2, and Compressor 2.

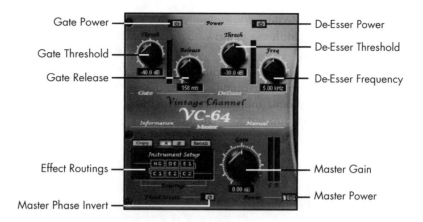

Gate Power — De-Esser Power
Gate Threshold — De-Esser Threshold
Gate Release — De-Esser Frequency

Effect Routings — Master Gain
Master Phase Invert — Master Power

Figure 11.10 Utilize the Master, De-Esser and Gate controls to begin working with the Vintage Channel.

❄ **ROUTING NOT PROCESSING**

Just because you choose a specific routing that shows your audio signal will flow through all the effects in the Vintage Channel does not mean your audio will definitely be processed by all the effects. You can choose whether or not an effect will be used by toggling its individual Power button.

---

3. Adjust the Master Gain. The Master Gain parameter determines the final amplitude level of the audio signal coming out of the Vintage Channel. At this point, you can leave it set to the default value, but you will probably have to adjust it after you have finished adjusting the other effect parameters because they will change the signal level.

4. Toggle the Master Phase Invert button. Use this button to invert the phase of the final audio signal output. When you mix certain sound files together, phase cancellation can occur. Phase cancellation occurs when one audio waveform increases in volume and the other decreases in volume at exactly the same time and by the same amount. Because of this phenomenon, they cancel each other out, making the mixed audio sound hollow. You can use the Phase parameter to change the phase of the audio data either for correction or even for different kinds of processing.

5. If you want to use the Gate effect, activate the Gate Power button.

6. Adjust the Gate Threshold. The Gate effect uses a digital noise gate to identify the parts of your audio data that should be processed. The Gate Threshold parameter determines at what amplitude level your audio data will start being compressed. When the amplitude of your audio data reaches the Threshold level, processing will begin. Gating is usually used to remove noise. Start by setting the Threshold to its lowest value (-80dB) and gradually raise it to the point where you hear the noise being reduced but your audio quality isn't being compromised.

7. Adjust the Gate Release. This parameter determines how quickly after the input level goes below the threshold that processing is stopped (or the digital noise gate is closed). If you set the Release Time parameter too low, your audio could be cut off. A longer release allows processing to sound more natural. Start off with a value of around 900ms. If your audio is being cut off, try slowly increasing the Release value or if you hear noise, try slowly decreasing the value.

8. If you want to use the De-Esser effect, activate the De-Esser Power button.

> **❄ DE-ESSING WITH VINTAGE CHANNEL**
>
> You may have noticed while doing vocal recordings that some singers produce a sort of "hissing" sound whenever they pronounce words with the letter "s" in them. That "hissing" sound is called *sibilance*, and you usually don't want it in your audio. The process or removing sibilance is called *de-essing*, which is done by compressing certain audio frequencies. When de-essing with the Vintage Channel, it's best to process a single track (with the vocal on its own) rather than a mix that has both the music and vocal mixed together already.

9. Adjust the De-Esser Threshold. The Threshold parameter determines at what amplitude level de-essing will begin. Start with a high setting and gradually decrease the value until you hear "hissing" sounds being reduced.

10. Adjust the De-Esser Freq (Frequency). Any audio frequencies above this setting will be processed. A good starting point is 5 kHz. At and above this frequency is where most "hissing" noises occur.

Compressors

The Vintage Channel provides two Compressor effects with identical parameters. The controls for both compressors are located in the center of the interface (see Figure 11.11). To utilize the Compressor effects, do the following:

1. To adjust the parameters for Compressor 1 or 2, click the C1 or C2 buttons, respectively.

2. Turn the Compressor on using the Compressor Power button.

3. You can adjust the phase of the audio signal using the Compressor Phase button.

4. Use the Input Meter, Output Meter, and Gain Reduction Meter buttons to change how the signal of the VU Meter will display. Click IN to show the level of the signal entering the Compressor. Click OUT to show the level of the signal leaving the Compressor. Click GR to show how much the Compressor is reducing the signal level.

5. Set the Gain In parameter. This controls the level of the audio signal entering the Compressor. You'll usually want to keep this set at 0 dB, which keeps the audio at its original level.

6. Set the Threshold. The Threshold determines at what amplitude level your audio data will start being compressed. When the amplitude of your audio data reaches the Threshold level, processing will begin.

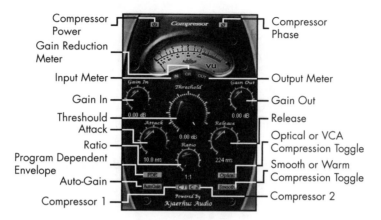

Compressor Power — Compressor Phase
Gain Reduction Meter
Input Meter — Output Meter
Gain In — Gain Out
Threshould — Release
Attack
Ratio — Optical or VCA Compression Toggle
Program Dependent Envelope — Smooth or Warm Compression Toggle
Auto-Gain
Compressor 1 — Compressor 2

Figure 11.11 Adjust the Compressor effects with the controls located in the center of the Vintage Channel interface.

7. Set the Ratio parameter. This parameter determines how much processing is done to your audio data. A ratio of 1:1 means no processing is done. A ratio of 2:1 means that for every 2 dB increase in input amplitude, there is only a 1 dB increase in output amplitude. Thus, the amplitude is being compressed. If you set the Ratio parameter to its highest value (Inf:1), that causes limiting, so no matter how loud the input amplitude gets, it is limited to the level set by the Threshold parameter.

8. Set the Attack parameter. This parameter determines how quickly after the input level has reached the threshold that processing is applied. For example, if the input level reaches the threshold, it doesn't have to be compressed right away. A slow attack means the signal won't be compressed unless it lasts for a while. This is a good way to make sure fast, percussive parts are left alone, but long, drawn-out parts are compressed.

9. Set the Release parameter. This parameter determines how quickly after the input level goes below the threshold that processing is stopped. If you set the Release too low, your audio could be cut off. A longer release allows processing to sound more natural. You'll have to experiment to get to the right setting.

10. When you set a medium to long release time, you can sometimes get what is called a "pumping" sound in your audio. This is where you can hear the compressor trying to compress the audio, but it is out of time with the music and sounds strange. Activating the Program Dependent Envelope feature while using a medium to long release time can help minimize pumping. Click the PDE button to toggle this feature on/off.

11. Click the Optical button to choose between Optical compression and VCA compression. Basically, Optical compression simulates an older type of compression that relied on imprecise optical components to produce a distinct sound of its own. In part, this means that the parameter settings are not taken to be exact (such as the Threshold). VCA

compression provides a more precise means of processing; for example, you can rely on the Threshold values that you set.

12. Click the Smooth button to choose between a smooth (clean) sound and a warm sound. This parameter is a matter of taste, and you'll need to try it to hear which setting works best with the material you are processing.

13. After compression the audio signal, the level will obviously be lower. To bring the overall level back up, you can activate the Auto-Gain option and adjust the Gain Out parameter.

Equalizers

The Vintage Channel provides two Equalizer effects with identical parameters. The controls for both EQs are located in the right area of the interface (see Figure 11.12). To utilize the EQ effects, do the following:

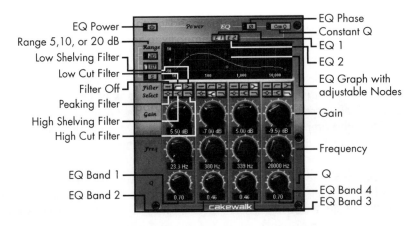

Figure 11.12 Adjust the EQ effects with the controls located on the right in the Vintage Channel interface.

1. To adjust the parameters for EQ 1 or 2, click the E1 or E2 buttons, respectively.
2. Turn the EQ on using the EQ Power button.
3. You can adjust the phase of the audio signal using the EQ Phase button.
4. Each EQ in the Vintage Channel provides up to four bands, which means you can have up to four different types of simultaneous EQ processing for each EQ. Use the Filter Select area to choose the type of EQ you want to use for each band. Click the Filter Off button to turn a band off. Click one of the other Filter buttons to turn a band on and select an EQ type. If you choose Peaking, the exact frequency designated by the Freq parameter will be boosted or cut, depending on how you set the Gain parameter. If you choose Low Shelving, any frequencies below the Freq setting will be boosted or cut, depending on how you set the Gain parameter. If you choose High Shelving, any frequencies above the Freq setting will be boosted or cut, depending on how you set the Gain parameter.

If you choose High Cut, all the frequencies above the Freq setting will be cut. If you choose Low Cut, all the frequencies below the Freq setting will be cut.

5. Adjust the Freq (frequency) parameter for each EQ band. This parameter works a bit differently, depending on what type of equalization you choose. Essentially, it determines the frequency below which other frequencies will be cut or boosted, above which other frequencies will be cut or boosted, or exactly where boosting or cutting will occur.

6. Adjust the Gain parameter for each EQ band. This parameter boosts or cuts the amplitude of the frequencies you set with the EQ type and Freq parameters.

7. Adjust the Q parameter for each EQ band. Also known as bandwidth, this parameter influences how many other frequencies around the Freq you set will be affected. A low value means few frequencies will be affected. A high value means more frequencies will be affected. For example, if you are trying to get rid of a precise frequency (like the 60Hz hum you sometimes get from electrical interference), you should set the Q to a low value in order to cut that one frequency and no others. In addition to Q, there is the Constant Q option. For a more musical sounding EQ, turn the Constant Q option off. For surgical equalization tasks, turn the Constant Q option on.

❄ **EQ GRAPH DISPLAY**

You've probably noticed that in addition to the parameter settings, the EQ area contains a graph display. This graph shows all the current equalization settings for all four types (bands). Along the left, it shows the amplitudes (gain) and along the bottom it shows the frequencies. The amplitude range of the graph can be adjusted using the Range buttons (this setting only affects the display and not actual Gain range). The shape of the line drawn on the graph shows you what frequencies in the audio spectrum are either boosted or cut, but that's not all. Four colored points on the graph represent each EQ band. Red is for band 1, yellow is for band 2, green is for band 3, and blue is for band 4. By clicking and dragging these points, you can change the Gain and Freq settings graphically for each of the EQ types (bands), essentially "drawing" the EQ settings. You still have to set the EQ type and Q settings manually, though.

The Vintage Channel is an extremely powerful effect that can be used for a multitude of tasks on single tracks and entire mixes. Be sure to check out some of the presets for starting points. And for more info, click the Help button or press F1 on your computer keyboard to access the Vintage Channel help file.

Analyst –Spectrum Analyzer

In Chapter 8, I talked about frequencies, the audio spectrum, and how different sounds are created via multiple, simultaneous vibrations at different frequencies. I also talked about how you can alter the tonal characteristics (or timbre) of a sound by using equalization. But in order to know what frequencies should be boosted or cut to get the changes you want, you have to know which frequencies (and their amplitudes) are present within a sound. That's where spectrum analysis comes in.

If you happen to have a boom box or a stereo component that has an animated graph feature, which changes as music is played, then you've had some experience with spectrum analysis. That animated graph shows the amplitudes of different frequencies within the music as it is played. It can tell you if there is too much bass or too much treble and allow you to make the appropriate adjustments so that the music sound better. SONAR's Analyst lets you do this, too, but with a much higher degree of accuracy.

You can use Analyst to analyze the frequency content in your audio and determine which frequencies are loud or soft. Then you can use the equalization features to make changes. The best way to use Analyst is in real time. Here is how Analyst works:

1. Right-click in the Fx bin of an audio track or bus and choose Audio FX > Cakewalk > Analyst to open the Analyst window (see Figure 11.13). The window displays a graph showing frequency values along the bottom and amplitude values along the left side. This lets you look at the graph, pick out a frequency, and find the amplitude of that frequency within your audio data.

Figure 11.13   Use Analyst to analyze the frequency content in your audio.

2. When you first open the window, the amplitude scale will show 0 to –70 dB and the frequency scale will show 20Hz to 20 kHz, but these scales can be changed. To change the range of the amplitude scale, hover your mouse over the bottom edge of the graph until it turns into a double-arrow. Then click and drag up or down. To change the range of the frequency scale, click and drag over the right edge of the graph.

3. You can also zoom in or out on the graph vertically (for more detailed amplitude readings) or horizontally (for more detailed frequency readings). To zoom vertically, click

and drag over the top edge of the graph. To zoom horizontally, click and drag over the left edge of the graph.

4. To return the range or zoom of any part of the graph to its default value, double-click the appropriate edge of the graph.

5. To the right of the graph is a small area separated into five sections. The first two sections provide specific amplitude and frequency information. As you move your mouse within the graph, you'll see the amplitude of the current mouse position shown in the first section. The second section displays the frequency and pitch. By aligning the cursor to the top of a frequency bar in the graph, you can get a reading of the amplitude and pitch of that frequency.

6. The third section controls the grid display. Click this to toggle the graph background grid on/off.

7. The fourth section controls the accuracy (or Resolution) of the analysis. The Lo setting provides faster graph updates while Analyst is analyzing your data in real time, but it is the least accurate. If your computer can handle it, you will get the best results using the Hi setting.

8. When you start project playback, Analyst displays its data in real time. In addition to the individual frequency bars, you can choose to have an average value shown as a small square at the top of each bar. Click the AVG button to toggle this on/off.

9. You can also have the minimum and maximum values of each frequency shown as line graphs by clicking the Min and Max buttons to toggle these options. To have the values reevaluated at a specific time during playback, click the Reset button.

10. Initially, Analyst runs in Spectrum mode, but it also provides the Sonograph mode. Click the Sonograph button to activate this mode (see 11.14).

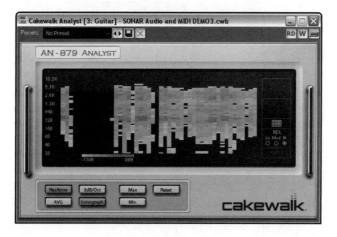

Figure 11.14   In addition to Spectrum mode, Analyst provides the Sonograph mode.

11. In the Sonograph mode, Analyst provides a color-coded display of your audio data over time. During playback, the display scrolls from right to the left with the right edge of the graph representing the current Now time. The left side of the graph shows the frequency scale. The bottom of the graph shows the color key so you can get a basic idea of the amplitude of each frequency. Like Spectrum mode, you can adjust the accuracy of the graph using the Resolution options to the right of the graph. None of the other options is available in this mode.

12. As in the Spectrum mode, you can move your mouse over the graph, but here you only get frequency and pitch information.

13. When you're finished with Analyst, close its window and remove it from the Fx bin.

Analyst Automation

As I mentioned earlier, Analyst provides an automation function. This function splits up the audio spectrum into four bands and records the amplitude of these bands over time as four automation envelopes. (A fifth envelope records the overall amplitude of the entire spectrum.) You can then assign these envelopes to other functions (such as EQ) to achieve some interesting effects based on the spectrum information of your audio. Here is how the Analyst automation function works:

1. With Analyst already set up in the Fx bin of an audio track or bus, click the Auto option located to the right of the graph.

2. In the upper right corner of the Analyst window, click the W button to activate the Automation Write option for Analyst.

3. Right-click Analyst in the Fx bin and choose Write Enable Parameter to open the Cakewalk Analyst dialog box (see Figure 11.15).

Figure 11.15 Use the Cakewalk Analyst dialog box to set up automation parameters for Analyst.

4. Activate the Analyst frequency bands for which you would like to record automation. Click Enable All or Disable All to activate or deactivate all bands. You can also select each band one at a time and assign an envelope color using the Choose Color button. Click OK.

5. Set the Now time to the point in the project where you would like to begin recording automation and start playback.

6. Stop project playback when you're done. Sonar will display the automation in the track as envelopes representing each band: Below 500 Hz, 500 Hz to 1 kHz, 1 kHz to 5 kHz, Above 5 kHz, and Full (the entire spectrum).

7. In the Analyst window, click the W button to deactivate the Automation Write option.

8. Add another effect plug-in to the Fx bin.

9. Right-click each envelope and choose Assign Envelope > *parameter you would like to automate.*

By reassigning the envelopes to control other effect parameters, you can control various effects using the audio spectrum analysis output from Analyst.

MIDI Effects

SONAR provides a set of seven MIDI effects, one of which (Chord Analyzer) is not really an effect. Like the audio effects, some of the MIDI effects mimic some of SONAR's editing features. Again, they have this capability so that you can process your data with these features in real time. You cannot use SONAR's editing features in real time because they aren't plug-ins. In addition, the effects provide more power and flexibility, and they include additional parameters not found in the editing features, so I'll go over them here step-by-step.

 BASIC OFFLINE STEPS

As I mentioned earlier, because I've already covered how to apply effects offline and in real time, I'm just going to include the basic offline steps (along with parameter descriptions) in each of the following explanations. For detailed step-by-step procedures for applying effects offline and in real time, refer to the previous sections in this chapter.

Automatic Arpeggios

In music, you can play the notes of a chord in a number of different ways. Most often, the notes are played all at once. You also can play them one at a time in sequence; this is called an *arpeggio.* SONAR's Arpeggiator effect automatically creates arpeggios for each note or chord in your selected MIDI data. Depending on how you set the parameters, you can achieve some very strange and interesting "melodies." This feature works as follows:

1. Select the MIDI data you want to process.

2. Choose Process > MIDI Fx > Cakewalk FX > Arpeggiator to open the Arpeggiator dialog box.

3. Set the Swing parameter. This parameter works the same as the Swing parameter in the Quantize editing feature. The only difference is that 50 percent is the normal setting (meaning no swing is applied); in this case, 0 percent is the normal setting. And you can set this Swing parameter from −100 to +100 percent. More often than not, you'll want to keep it set to 0 percent.

4. Set the Rate and Units parameters. These two parameters work together. The Rate parameter determines the amount of time between each note in the arpeggio, and the Units parameter determines what units you want to use to set the Rate parameter. You can set the Rate parameter in notes, ticks, or milliseconds. By setting the Units parameter to Notes, you can easily synchronize the notes in the arpeggio to a certain note value so that you know they will play in sync with the rest of the music in your project.

5. Set the Legato parameter. This parameter determines the duration of the notes in the arpeggio. If you set the Legato parameter to 1 percent (the lowest value), the notes in the arpeggio will be played with a very short duration (as in a staccato fashion, in which the note is played and let go very quickly). If you set the Legato parameter to 99 percent (the highest value), the notes in the arpeggio will be played with a very long duration. To be exact, each note plays until the start of the next note in the arpeggio.

6. Set the Path parameter. This parameter determines the direction in which the notes in the arpeggio will be played. If you select Up, Up, the notes in the arpeggio will go up consecutively in pitch. If you select Up, Down, the notes in the arpeggio will go up in pitch first, and then come back down. If you select Down, Down, the notes in the arpeggio will go down consecutively in pitch. If you select Down, Up, the notes in the arpeggio will go down in pitch first, and then come back up.

7. Set the Play Through option. If you activate the Play Through option, your original data will remain intact and play along with the new arpeggio data. If you deactivate the Play Through option, only the arpeggio data will remain, and your original data will be removed.

8. Set the Output option and parameters. If you activate the Output option, additional notes will be added so the arpeggio will play smoothly over each octave in the range you specify. Otherwise, only your original will be used to create the arpeggio. The Lowest Note parameter (located near the bottom of the Output option) determines the lowest note that will be included in the arpeggio. The Highest Note parameter (located near the top of the Output option) determines the highest note that will be included in the arpeggio.

9. Set the Chord option and parameters. If you activate the Chord option, the Arpeggiator effect will analyze the original data that falls in the range you specify, and then guess at what chord is being played. If you use the effect in real-time mode, the name of the chord that is guessed will be shown in the Recognized Chord field. The effect uses the

recognized chord to create the notes for the arpeggio (meaning the notes in the arpeggio are based on the recognized chord).

10. Click the Audition button to test the current parameter settings.

11. If you want to use the current settings at a later time, save them as a preset.

12. Click OK.

I know the parameter settings for the Arpeggiator effect can be a bit confusing. Sometimes, it's difficult to tell what the results will be after you apply the effect. Basically, they'll be different, depending on the data you process. This effect usually works best on slow, chord-based data.

Chord Analysis

As I mentioned earlier, the Chord Analyzer isn't really an effect. It doesn't do anything to your data, meaning it doesn't make any changes. The Chord Analyzer simply looks at your data and guesses what kind of chord is being played. Here is how it works:

BEST IN REAL-TIME

Although you can use the Chord Analyzer effect offline, it works best in real time as your project is playing. Therefore, I'll go through the real-time procedure here instead of the offline procedure.

1. In the Track view, right-click in the Fx bin of the track to which you want to add an effect.

2. Choose MIDI Fx > Cakewalk FX > Chord Analyzer to add the Chord Analyzer to the list.

3. The Chord Analyzer window will open.

4. Set the Analysis Window parameter. Using this parameter, you can control how often the Chord Analyzer effect analyzes your data. The lower the number, the more accurate it is at guessing the names of the chords being played. This feature also requires more processing power from your computer, but I've never had any problems keeping this parameter set at 1 (the lowest setting). Unless you have trouble with playback, I recommend that you just leave this setting at its default value.

5. Start playback of the project. As the project plays, the effect will analyze your data and display the name of the chord it thinks is being played, along with how the chord looks in music notation and on a piano keyboard.

This effect can be useful as a learning tool because it displays the chords being played on a piano keyboard and as music notation. Plus, it lists (in the Chord Recognized section) some possible alternatives you might want to try in place of the chord you are currently using.

Echo Delay

Just as the delay effects add echoes to your audio data, the Echo Delay effect adds echoes to your MIDI data. But because this effect works on MIDI data, some of the parameters are different, and some additional parameters are available as well. This feature works as follows:

1. Select the MIDI data you want to process.
2. Choose Process > MIDI Fx > Cakewalk FX > Echo Delay to open the Echo Delay dialog box.
3. Set the Delay and Delay Units parameters. These two parameters work together. The Delay parameter determines the amount of time between each echo. The Delay Units parameter (located below the Delay parameter) determines the units you want to use to set the Delay parameter. You can set the Delay parameter in notes, ticks, and milliseconds. By setting the Delay Units parameter to Notes, you can easily synchronize the echoes to a certain note value so you know they will play in sync with the rest of the music in your project.

❄ **THE TAP BUTTON**

You also can set the Delay parameter by clicking the Tap button in the Echo Delay dialog box. Clicking the button at a certain tempo sets the Delay parameter to that tempo.

4. Set the Decay parameter by double-clicking the numerical value or moving the crosshair in the graphic display. This parameter determines whether the echoes get softer or louder (and by how much). If you set the Decay parameter to a value below 100 percent, the echoes will get softer. If you set the Decay parameter to a value above 100 percent, the echoes will get louder.
5. Set the Echoes parameter by double-clicking the numerical value or moving the crosshair in the graphic display. This parameter determines how many echoes you will have.
6. Set the Swing parameter. This parameter works the same way as the Swing parameter in the Quantize editing feature. The only difference is that 50 percent is the normal setting (meaning no swing is applied); 0 percent is the normal setting. And you can set this Swing parameter from −100 to +100 percent. In general, you'll want to keep it set to 0 percent.
7. Set the Pitch parameter. If you want, you can have each echo transposed to a different pitch value, which creates some interesting sounds. You can set the Pitch parameter from −12 to +12 steps. You determine the types of steps by choosing either the Diatonic (the pitches follow the diatonic musical scale) or Chromatic (the pitches follow the chromatic musical scale) options.
8. Click the Audition button to test the current parameter settings.
9. If you want to use the current settings at a later time, save them as a preset.
10 Click OK.

10. Click OK.

The Echo Delay effect is fairly easy to use, but just to give you a quick idea of what you can do with it, try the following example:

1. Select File > Open, select the file called 2-Part Invention #13 in A minor.cwp and click Open to open that sample project.
2. Close all the windows except for the Track view.
3. Play the project to hear what the original data sounds like.
4. Select Track 1.
5. Choose Process > MIDI Fx > Cakewalk FX > Echo Delay.
6. Choose the preset called 16th Note.
7. Click OK.
8. Play the project again.

Hear that echo? You can achieve some pretty cool sounds by using this effect.

MIDI Event Filter

The MIDI Event Filter effect works almost the same as the Select by Filter editing feature. The only difference is that instead of simply selecting the specified events, it deletes them. This feature gives you a quick way to remove specific kinds of MIDI data from your clips or tracks. It works like this:

1. Select the MIDI data you want to process.
2. Choose Process > MIDI Fx > Cakewalk FX > MIDI Event Filter to open the MIDI Event Filter dialog box.
3. Set the appropriate parameters for the types of MIDI data you want to remove. These settings are the same as the settings for the Event Filter - Select Some dialog box (see Chapter 8).
4. Click the Audition button to test the current parameter settings.
5. If you want to use the current settings at a later time, save them as a preset.
6. Click OK.

Quantize

The Quantize effect works almost exactly the same as the Quantize editing feature. The only difference is that the effect provides a couple of additional parameters. It works like this:

1. Select the MIDI data you want to process.
2. Choose Process > MIDI Fx > Cakewalk FX > Quantize to open the Quantize dialog box.
3. Set the Quantize parameter by activating/deactivating the Start Times and Durations options. These settings simply tell SONAR whether you want to quantize the start times or durations of each selected MIDI event.

4. Set the Resolution parameter. This parameter works exactly the same as the Resolution parameter in the Quantize editing feature (see Chapter 8).

5. Set the Tuplet option. Using this option, you can further define the Resolution parameter. For example, if you want to quantize your data according to an odd note value, activate the Tuplet option and set its related parameters to 5 and 4 (which would mean you want to quantize your data to the value of five notes occurring in the time of four notes).

6. Set the Strength, Swing, Window, and Offset parameters. These parameters work exactly the same as the Strength, Swing, Window, and Offset parameters in the Quantize editing feature.

7. Set the Random option. If you activate this option, a random time offset will be applied to the timing of each quantized event. You can use this option to achieve some very strange sounds. Do a little experimenting to hear what I mean.

8. Click the Audition button to test the current parameter settings.

9. If you want to use the current settings at a later time, save them as a preset.

10. Click OK.

Transpose

Like the Transpose editing feature, the Transpose effect transposes your MIDI note data up or down by a number of half-steps, either chromatically or diatonically. However, the Transpose effect also provides some more advanced transposition methods. It works like this:

1. Select the MIDI data you want to process.

2. Choose Process > MIDI Fx > Cakewalk FX > Transpose to open the Transpose dialog box.

3. If you want to transpose your data by a simple musical interval, choose the Interval option for the Transposition Method parameter. Then enter the number of half steps (−127 to +127) into the Offset parameter by which you want to transpose the data.

4. If you want to transpose your data diatonically so that the notes are changed according to degrees of a certain musical scale, choose the Diatonic option for the Transposition Method parameter. Then enter the number of scale degrees (-24 to +24) into the Offset parameter by which you want to transpose the data. Also, choose the musical scale you want to use by setting the To parameter.

❋ **CONSTRAIN TO SCALE**

If you want any of the notes in your data that don't fit within the chosen musical scale to be transposed so they will fit, activate the Constrain to Scale option. This feature works well for pop music. For something like jazz, though, in which many different nonscale notes are used in the music, it's best to keep this option deactivated. This option works for both the Diatonic and Key/Scale Transposition Methods.

---

5. If you want to transpose your data from one musical key and scale to another, choose the Key/Scale option for the Transposition Method parameter. In the From and To parameters, choose the musical keys and scales by which you want to transpose your data. You also can transpose the data up or down by a number of octaves at the same time by setting the Offset parameter.

6. To specify exactly how each note in the musical scale will be transposed, choose the Custom Map option for the Transposition Method parameter. Using this option, you can define your own transposition map. This means you can set the note to which each note in the musical scale will be transposed. To change the transposition value of a note in the musical scale, double-click the note in the From column of the Transposition Map and then type in a new note value to transpose that note up or down. This option is pretty tedious, but it gives you precise control over every musical note.

✳ **PITCH OR NOTE NUMBER**

You can view notes in the Transposition Map either by note name or by MIDI note number. Simply select the appropriate option (Pitch or Notes).

---

7. Click the Audition button to test the current parameter settings.

8. If you want to use the current settings at a later time, save them as a preset.

9. Click OK.

Velocity

I'm tempted to compare the Velocity effect to the Scale Velocity editing feature, but the effect not only enables you to scale MIDI velocity data, but it also enables you to change it in many more advanced ways. As a matter of fact, you'll probably stop using the Scale Velocity editing feature when you get the hang of the Velocity effect, because you can use this effect as an editing tool as well. It works like this:

1. Select the MIDI data you want to process.

2. Choose Process > MIDI Fx > Cakewalk FX > Velocity to open the Velocity dialog box.

3. To change all MIDI velocity values to an exact number, choose the Set To option and then designate the value (1 to 127) you want to use.

4. To add or subtract a certain amount from each MIDI velocity in your selected data, choose the Change option and designate the value (−127 to +127) you want to use.

5. To scale all MIDI velocity values by a certain percentage, choose the Scale option and designate the value (1 to 900 percent) that you want to use.

6. If you choose the Limit option, all the MIDI velocities in your selected data will be changed to fit within the range of velocity values (1 to 127) you specify.

7. The next two options also scale MIDI velocities, but from one value to another. If you choose the first Change Gradually option, you can scale MIDI velocities by exact values

(1 to 127). If you choose the second Change Gradually option, you can scale MIDI velocities by a percentage (1 to 900 percent).

8. In addition to choosing one of the previous options, you can choose the Velocity effect's Randomize option, which works in tandem with the others. By activating this option, you can add or subtract a random offset to or from each MIDI velocity in your selected data. You can enter a maximum value (1 to 127) to be used (by adjusting the Amount parameter), and you can give priority over whether the random offset will be lower or higher (−10 to +10) than the maximum value that you specify (by adjusting the Tendency parameter).

9. Click the Audition button to test the current parameter settings.

10. If you want to use the current settings at a later time, save them as a preset.

11. Click OK.

And that will do it for this chapter. You should now have a good working knowledge of all the effects that SONAR provides. Remember to have fun and don't be afraid to experiment!

12 } **Mixing It Down**

After you've recorded, edited, and added effects to your MIDI and audio data, it's time to mix down your project. This is called the *mixdown process* because you are taking all the MIDI and audio tracks in your project and mixing them together into a single stereo audio track. From there, you can put your music on CD, distribute it over the Internet, or record it onto tape. SONAR provides a number of different features that make the mixdown process as simple and intuitive as possible. This chapter will do the following:

* Show you how to use the Console view and Track view for mixing.
* Explain the Module and Track Managers.
* Demonstrate how to take a Snapshot.
* Show you how to record and edit automation.
* Explain grouping.
* Demonstrate working with envelopes.

The Console View

For mixing down the MIDI and audio tracks in your project, you can use either the Console view or the Track view. I've already covered many of the Track view features in earlier chapters, so in this chapter I'll tell you about the Console view and also let you know how the Track view fits into the mixdown process.

The Console view adjusts the main parameters for each track in your project via on-screen buttons, knobs, sliders, and faders (vertical sliders). Similar in appearance to a hardware-based mixing board found in most recording studios, the Console view displays tracks as a collection of modules, each with its own set of adjustable controls.

More precisely, the Console view consists of four major sections (starting from left to right): the toolbar (containing some of the view's related controls); the MIDI and audio track modules (displaying the controls for each MIDI and audio track in the project); the buses (containing additional mixing controls, which I'll explain later); and the mains (also containing additional mixing controls, which I'll explain later).

Opening the Console View

To open the Console view, simply choose Views > Console (or press ALT + 3). The Console view will open, displaying modules for every track in the current project. To see how it works, follow these steps:

1. Choose File > Open. In the Open dialog box that appears, select one of the project files that ships with SONAR and click Open.
2. Choose Views > Console.

The Console view should look similar to Figure 12.1.

Figure 12.1 When you open the Console view, it automatically displays a module for every track in the current project.

The MIDI Track Modules

Each MIDI track module contains a number of different controls that manipulate many of its corresponding track parameters (see Figure 12.2).

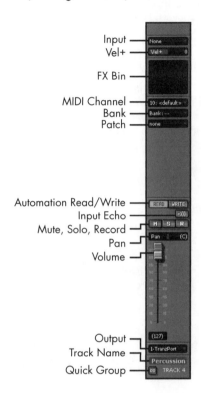

Input
Vel+
FX Bin
MIDI Channel
Bank
Patch

Automation Read/Write
Input Echo
Mute, Solo, Record
Pan
Volume

Output
Track Name
Quick Group

Figure 12.2 A MIDI track module contains controls for adjusting the parameters of its corresponding track.

As matter of fact, all the controls are the equivalent of the track parameters shown in the Track pane of the Track view. This means that if you change the value of a control in the Console view, the equivalent track parameter is also changed in the Track view. From top to bottom, the controls in a MIDI track module correspond to the controls described in the following sections.

Input

The Input parameter sets the MIDI input of the track. It is the equivalent of the Input parameter in the Track view. You can change the input by clicking the control and selecting a new input from the menu.

Vel+

The Vel+ parameter raises or lowers the MIDI velocity of each note in a track by adding or subtracting a number from -127 to +127. It is the equivalent of the Velocity Trim parameter in the Track view. You can change the Vel+ parameter by clicking and dragging your mouse over the parameter. Click and drag left or right to decrease or increase the value.

> ❄ **SET DEFAULT VALUES**
>
> When you're adjusting sliders, knobs, or faders in the Console view or parameters in the Track view, a quick way to return them to their original positions is to double-click them. When you do, the control snaps back to its default value. You also can change the default value for a control. To do so, set the control to the value you want to use as its default. Then right-click the control and choose Value > Set Snap-To = Current.

Fx Bin

You can use the Fx bin to assign effects to the track. These effects are applied only in real time. The Fx bin works exactly the same as the Fx bin in the Track view.

Channel

The Channel parameter sets the MIDI channel of the track. It is the equivalent of the Channel parameter in the Track view. You can change the channel by clicking the parameter and selecting a new MIDI channel.

Bank

You can use the Bank parameter to set the MIDI patch bank of the track. It is the equivalent of the Bank parameter in the Track view. You can change the bank by clicking the parameter and selecting a new MIDI patch bank.

Patch

You can use the Patch parameter to set the MIDI patch of the track. It is the equivalent of the Patch parameter in the Track view. You can change the patch by clicking the parameter and selecting a new MIDI patch.

Input Echo

You can use the Input Echo parameter to turn MIDI echo on or off for the track. It is the equivalent of the Input Echo parameter in the Track view. Just click the button to change the parameter.

Mute, Solo, and Record

The Mute, Solo, and Record parameters turn the mute, solo, and record (for recording) options on or off for the track. They are the equivalents of the Mute, Solo, and Record options in the Track view. Toggle these options on and off by clicking them.

CONSOLE VIEW RECORDING

The Record parameter is available in the Console view because you can actually use the view during recording instead of the Track view if you want. You can even create new tracks in the Console view. To do so, right-click in any blank space and choose Insert Audio Track or Insert MIDI Track. A new MIDI or audio track module will be added to the Console and Track views.

Pan

You can use the Pan parameter to set the MIDI panning of the track. It is the equivalent of the Pan parameter in the Track view. You can change the pan by clicking and dragging the slider left or right.

Volume

Using the Volume parameter, you can set the MIDI volume of the track. It is the equivalent of the Volume parameter in the Track view. You can change the volume by clicking and dragging the fader (vertical slider) up or down. As you drag the fader, the number box located below the slider will display the current value of the parameter. The value can range from 0 (the lowest volume level) to 127 (the highest volume level).

Output

Using the Output parameter, you can set the MIDI output of the track. It is the equivalent of the Output parameter in the Track view. You can change the output by clicking the parameter and selecting a new MIDI port.

Name

The Name parameter displays the name of the track. It is the equivalent of the Name parameter in the Track view. You can change the name by double-clicking the parameter, typing some new text, and pressing the Enter key.

Quick Group

Clicking this button activates the Quick Group option and quickly groups all controls in the MIDI track module to all other controls in any other track modules that have their Quick Group option activated. Hold down the CTRL key and click the Quick Group buttons for the track modules you would like to group. Click one of the activated Quick Group buttons to ungroup the track modules.

The Audio Track Modules

Like the MIDI track modules, the audio track modules contain a number of different controls you can use to manipulate their corresponding track parameters (see Figure 12.3).

Many of the controls are the same as those on the MIDI track modules. Included are the Input, Fx Bin, Mute, Solo, Record Arm, Pan, Volume, Name, Quick Group parameters. They all work in exactly the same manner as they do on the MIDI track modules, except, they are controlling audio data instead of MIDI data. The one difference is the Volume control. Instead of displaying its value as a MIDI volume controller number, its value is shown as decibels (dB).

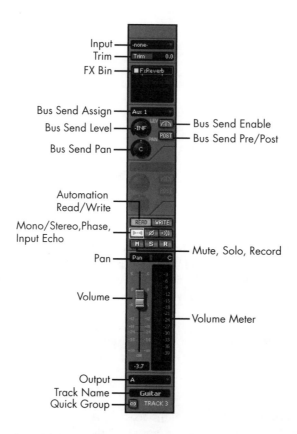

Input
Trim
FX Bin

Bus Send Assign
Bus Send Level —— Bus Send Enable
—— Bus Send Pre/Post
Bus Send Pan

Automation
Read/Write
Mono/Stereo,Phase,
Input Echo
—— Mute, Solo, Record
Pan
Volume
—— Volume Meter

Output
Track Name
Quick Group

Figure 12.3 The audio track modules are similar to the MIDI track modules in terms of the controls they provide.

Some of the parameters, however, are unique to audio track modules.

Trim

The Trim parameter adjusts the volume of a track before the signal gets to the regular Volume parameter. This can be helpful for adjusting the relative volume of one track to another without having to change the final mix positions of your Volume parameters. It is the equivalent of the Volume Trim parameter in the Track view. Click and drag your mouse left or right over the parameter to adjust it.

EQ Parameters (SONAR Producer Edition)

This section of the audio track module is not shown, but is normally located below the Trim parameter and above the FX bin. The EQ provides built-in EQ effects that you can apply to your tracks. It provides four bands of EQ, each with several parameters: EQ Graph, Frequency, Gain, Q, Type, and Enable (Bypass). To adjust a certain band, use the EQ Band parameter. This EQ effect provides the same parameters as the Sonitus:fx Equalizer. To display the Equalizer dialog box, double-click the EQ Graph.

Phase

Sometimes, phase cancellation can occur between the audio data of two different tracks. Phase cancellation occurs when one audio waveform increases in volume and the other decreases in volume at exactly the same time and by the same amount. Because of this phenomenon, they cancel each other out, making the mixed audio sound hollow. The Phase parameter inverts the audio waveform of the data in an audio track around the zero axis. This can sometimes help eliminate phase cancellation. To invert the data in an audio track, just click the Phase button in the Console view. The Phase parameter is the equivalent of the Phase parameter in the Track view.

Mono/Stereo

There might be times when you want to hear a stereo track play in mono (via one channel) or a mono track play in stereo (if stereo effects are applied). Using the Mono/Stereo parameter in the Console view or the Track view, you can determine how the data in a track will be played. To adjust the parameter, just click the Mono/Stereo button. A single left-speaker symbol means mono and a double-speaker symbol means stereo.

Input Echo

When you record an audio track, you usually want to listen to your performance as it's being recorded. In the past, due to the limitations of sound card drivers, you were able to listen only to the "dry" version of your performance. This means you had to listen to your performance without any effects applied. With the input monitoring feature, SONAR allows you to listen to your performance with effects applied as it's being recorded. This can be especially useful, for example, when you are recording vocals, when it's customary to let the singer hear a little echo or reverberation during the performance. Similar to MIDI tracks, audio tracks provide an Input Echo button. This button can be turned on or off, and it activates or deactivates the input monitoring feature.

Output

The Output parameter routes the data from the track represented by the audio track module to one of the available buses or mains. This parameter is the equivalent of the Output parameter in the Track view. You can change the output by clicking the parameter and selecting a new bus or main.

Bus Send Parameters

The Bus Send parameters route (send) the audio data from the track represented by the audio track module to one of the available buses or mains. You can have as many sends as you want for each audio track module. Each send has a number, which corresponds to the number of the bus to which its data will be sent (although you can change this, too). Each send also has four controls within it—an on/off button (Bus Send Enable), a level knob (Bus Send Level), a pan knob (Bus Send Pan), and a pre/post button (Bus Send Pre/Post).

To toggle a send on or off, just click its Bus Send Enable button. The Bus Send Level knob controls the volume (or level) of the audio data that will be sent to the bus. To adjust the knob, simply drag it up or down. If you drag the knob down, the value gets lower. If you drag the knob up, the value gets higher. You can adjust the send level from -INF (infinity, the lowest level setting) to +6 dB (the highest level setting). The Bus Send Pan knob controls the panning of the audio data that will be sent to the bus. Adjust it the same way as the Bus Send Level slider. The Bus Send Pre/Post button determines from what point in the audio track module the audio data will be taken and sent to the bus. You can toggle the Bus Send Pre/Post button by clicking it. Initially, the button is set to Pre. When you click the button, it changes its name to Post. When you click it again, it changes its name back to Pre.

❊ AUDIO SIGNAL FLOW

As SONAR plays a project, it reads the data for each audio track from your hard drive. It then routes the data through the appropriate sections of the Console view, until it is finally sent to your sound card and then to your speakers so you can hear it. The routing works as follows: The data for an audio track is read from your hard drive and routed through the corresponding audio track module. Within the module, the data first passes through the Fx bin, where any assigned effects are applied. The data is then sent through the Volume parameter (where its level can be adjusted), then the Pan parameter, and finally to the Output parameter. From here, it is sent out of the module and into the assigned bus or main.

During this routing process, the data can be sent to a bus either before or after it reaches the Volume parameter. If the Bus Send Pre/Post button is set to Pre, the data is routed to the bus after it goes through the Fx bin but before it reaches the Volume parameter. This means that the Volume parameter will have no effect on the level of the signal being sent to the bus. If the Bus Send Pre/Post button is set to Post, the data is routed to the bus after it goes through the Volume parameter. This means that the Volume parameter does affect the level of the signal being sent to the bus. For a graphical view of how audio signals are routed in SONAR, take a look at the following topic in the SONAR Help file: Mixing > Signal Flow.

The Buses

The buses provide additional mixing control for your audio signals (see Figure 12.4). Buses provide most of the same parameters as the audio track modules, including Input, EQ Parameters, Fx Bin, Mono/Stereo button, Mute, Solo, Pan, Volume, Output, and Name. A bus provides one parameter not found in an audio track module, which is Input Pan. This parameter adjusts the panning of the single coming into the bus.

You can also access the buses in the Track view by clicking the Show/Hide Bus Pane button located at the bottom of the Track view (see Figure 12.5).

What Are the Buses Good For?

One good use for the buses is to add the same effects to a number of different tracks. For example, suppose that you have four audio tracks (1, 2, 3, and 4) containing the background vocals for your project, and you want to add some nice chorus to them. Without using a bus, you would have to set up a Chorus effect in the Fx bin of each of the audio track modules for tracks 1, 2, 3, and 4 (each with identical parameter settings). Not only is this approach cumbersome and tedious, but it also puts extra strain on your computer because it has to process each of the four effects at the same time.

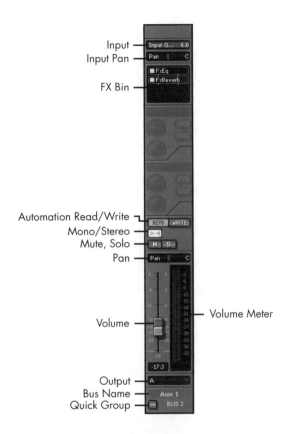

Input
Input Pan

FX Bin

Automation Read/Write
Mono/Stereo
Mute, Solo
Pan

Volume — Volume Meter

Output
Bus Name
Quick Group

Figure 12.4 Shown here in the Console view; the buses provide some of the same controls as the audio track modules.

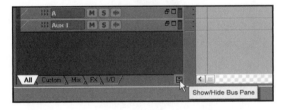

Figure 12.5 Access the buses in the Track view by clicking the Show/Hide Bus Pane button.

Using a bus, however, the process becomes much more streamlined. First, you create a send in track 1 by right-clicking in track 1 and choosing Insert Send > New Stereo Bus from the drop-down menu. This creates a new send in track 1 and also a new bus in the Bus pane (call it *Bus 1* for this example). Then you create new sends for tracks 2, 3, and 4. But this time instead of choosing Insert Send > New Stereo Bus, you choose Insert Send > Bus 1. This ensures that each send in each track is set to Bus 1. Also make sure to click the Bus Enable button for each send, since it is off by default. Then you set the Bus Send Level for each of the sends. In the Fx bin for Bus 1, you set up the Chorus effect. You only need to set up one effect because all four tracks are being sent to the bus. You then set the Input Gain, Input Pan, Output Gain, and Output Pan parameters for Bus 1. Finally, you set the Bus Send Pre/Post buttons to Pre or Post. If you set the buttons to Pre, the data in each audio track module is sent to the bus before it's routed through each Volume parameter. This means you can control the level of the effect (with the Bus Send Levels) and the level of the original data (with the Volume parameter) independently. If you set the buttons to Post, the level of the effect goes up and down with the level of the original data via the Volume parameters.

> ※ **SURROUND SOUND**
>
> There is another special kind of bus provided by SONAR, which creates surround sound mixes for your projects. I will cover all surround sound related information in Chapter 13, however, please finish reading this chapter to learn about mixing stereo projects first. You will need this knowledge in order to understand the additional information presented in Chapter 13.

The Mains

For every output on your sound card, a main will be displayed in the Console view (see Figure 12.6).

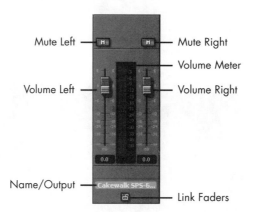

Figure 12.6 A main looks similar to an audio track module.

If your sound card has only one output, only one main is displayed, and all the audio data from the audio track modules and buses is sent to it. If your sound card has more than one output, more than one main is shown, and you can choose to which main the data from each audio track module and bus will be sent.

A main provides six different parameters: Mute (Left and Right), Volume (Left and Right), Link Faders, and Name/Output. These parameters all work the same way as the same parameters in an audio track module. The only differences are the Name/Output and Link Faders parameters. The Name/Output parameter simply displays the name of the sound card output assigned to that main. It cannot be changed. The Link Faders button links the two volume faders together so that you can change the volume of both the left and right sides of the stereo output simultaneously.

Configuring the Console and Track Views

Earlier, I mentioned that you could change the number of buses shown in the Console view. Along with these changes, you can customize how the Console view looks and works in many other ways. These methods are described in the following sections.

Number of Buses

To add a new bus, simply right-click a blank area of the Bus pane in the Console view and choose New Stereo Bus or New Surround Bus (see Figure 12.7).

Figure 12.7 You can adjust the number of buses by right-clicking in the Bus pane.

To delete a bus, right-click a blank part of the bus and choose Delete Bus. When you adjust the number of buses, it also affects the number of buses displayed in the Bus pane of the Track view.

The Track Managers

SONAR provides Track Managers for both the Console view and the Track view, which hides modules, buses, and mains. What might be a bit confusing is that the Track Managers in the Console view and Track view work independently of one another. This means that if you hide a track in the Track view, its corresponding track module in the Console view will *not* be hidden. Instead, you would have to hide the track module by using the Track Manager in the Console view. In a way, this might seem a bit awkward at first, but it provides you with the flexibility to have the Track view and Console view set up differently.

The Track Managers work as follows:

1. To open the Track view Track Manager, make sure that the Track view is the active window and then press the M key.
2. To open the Console view Track Manager, make sure that the Console view is the active window and then press the M key.
3. The Track Manager dialog box will open (see Figure 12.8). The Track Managers are identical, so the remaining instructions apply to both.

Figure 12.8 The Track Managers are identical in both the Track and Console views.

4. To hide an individual component, click to remove the check mark next to that component in the list and then click OK.
5. To hide a group of components (such as all the MIDI track modules, all the audio track modules, or all the buses), click the appropriate button in the Toggle section—Audio, MIDI, or Bus—to select the appropriate group and then press the spacebar to remove the check marks. There are also buttons for synth, muted, archived, and frozen tracks. Finally, click OK.

You also can make the components reappear by doing the opposite of the preceding procedures. These changes to the Console view and Track view are in appearance only; they don't affect what you hear during playback. For example, if you hide an audio track module that outputs data during playback, you still hear that data even if you hide the module. Hiding components of the Console view or Track view can come in handy when you want to work only on a certain group of tracks, and you don't want to be distracted or overwhelmed by the number of controls displayed.

Show/Hide Console Components

In addition to configuring the visibility of the tracks, buses and mains in the Console view, you can also show/hide all tracks, buses or mains or the individual module components using the toolbar located on the left side of the Console view window (see Figure 12.9).

Figure 12.9 Show/Hide individual module components with the Console view toolbar.

Here is a list of descriptions for each of the toolbar buttons in the order they are shown:

- ✳ **Tracks.** Show/hide all track modules.
- ✳ **Buses.** Show/hide all bus modules.
- ✳ **Mains.** Show/hide all main modules.
- ✳ **Narrow/Widen Strips.** Narrow or widen the horizontal size of all modules.
- ✳ **Input.** Show/hide all input components.
- ✳ **EQ Plot (SONAR Producer Edition).** Show/hide all EQ graph components.
- ✳ **EQ (SONAR Producer Edition).** Show/hide all EQ control components.
- ✳ **FX.** Show/hide all FX bins.
- ✳ **Send.** Show/hide all bus components.

✻ **M/S/R.** Show/hide all of the following module buttons: automation read/write, stereo/mono, phase, input echo, mute, solo, and record.

✻ **Vol.** Show/hide all pan, volume, and meter components.

✻ **Icon.** Show/hide all module icons.

✻ **Output.** Show/hide all output components.

Changing the Meters

You can also change how the volume meters in the Console and Track views behave. Use the Vol button to turn all meters on or off in the Console view. Or use the down arrow to the right of the Vol button to turn groups of meters on and off using the Track Record Meters, Track Playback Meters, Bus Meters, and Mains Meters options.

In the Track view, click the down arrow next to the Show/Hide All Meters button to access the meter options (see Figure 12.10).

Figure 12.10 Access meter options in the Track view by using the Show/Hide All Meters down arrow.

✻ **METER INDEPENDENCE**

Like the Track Managers, the meters in the Console view and Track view work independently. For instance, if you turn off the record meters in the Track view, the record meters in the Console view are *not* turned off and vice versa.

✻ **METER PERFORMANCE**

If you ever need to lighten the load on your computer during recording or playback, you might want to try turning off some or all of the meters. The meters can take up quite a bit of your computer's processing power and affect SONAR's performance.

In addition to being able to turn the meters on and off, you can set various options to determine how the meters will work. If you click the down arrow in the Console view or the Track view, you'll see a menu with a number of options available. These options let you set the way the meters will display the audio signal, the audio signal measurement, the range of measurement, and various cosmetic options, such as whether or not the decibel markings are shown. For detailed descriptions of each option, take a look at the following section of the SONAR Help file: Mixing > Metering > Changing the Meters' Display.

Waveform Preview

In addition to the normal metering options, SONAR provides the Waveform Preview feature that allows you to see a real-time display of the audio waveform being produced by buses and synth tracks. Not only does this feature let you to see the waveform, but it also provides a quick way to determine where your audio may be clipping. To turn the Waveform Preview feature on/off for a bus or synth track, click the Waveform Preview button, which is located next to the Solo button (see Figure 12.11).

Figure 12.11   Use the Waveform Preview feature to view a real-time waveform display for buses and synth tracks.

When you play back your project, SONAR displays the audio waveform in the Clips pane. By default, the waveform is green, but when clipping occurs, the waveform is shown as red.

Peak Markers

SONAR provides one more convenient feature for identifying clipping called *Peak Markers*. Each bus, audio, and synth track has its own Peak Marker, which can be activated by simply right-clicking the bus or track and choosing Show Peak Marker. You can also activate Peak Markers for all buses or tracks by using the down arrow next to the Show/Hide All Meters button. The options available from that menu are Show Track Peak Markers and Show Bus Peak Markers. When you activate the Peak Marker for a track or bus, SONAR will display a marker that follows the Now Time cursor during playback. The marker briefly indicates the current audio level and shows red when clipping occurs (see Figure 12.12).

Figure 12.12   Use the Peak Markers feature to identify clipping during audio playback.

After you stop playback, you can also move the Now Time cursor to the current Peak Marker by right-clicking the peak display of the track or bus and choosing Go to Peak (see Figure 12.13).

Figure 12.13 Quickly move the Now Time cursor to the current Peak Marker by right-clicking the peak display.

Taking Snapshots

SONAR provides a number of different methods of mixdown, one of which is called *Snapshots*. Using Snapshots, you can take a "picture" of all the current control values in the Console and Track views and then store those values in your project at a specified Now time. For example, if your project is a pop song with a number of different sections (such as the intro, verse, chorus, and so on), you might want to change the mix each time a new section is reached by the Now time during playback. You can do so easily by creating a different Snapshot at the beginning of each section of the song. During playback, as the Now time passes a point in the project where a Snapshot is stored, the values for all the recorded controls are changed to reflect the Snapshot automatically.

> ❋ **LINKED AUTOMATION**
>
> For automation purposes, the controls in the Console view and the parameters in the Track view work together rather than independently. This means that if you automate a control in the Console view, its corresponding parameter in the Track view will be automated as well and vice versa.

To create a Snapshot, just follow these steps:

1. Set the Now time to the point in the project where you want the Snapshot to be stored.
2. Adjust the controls in the Console or Track view to the values at which you want them to be set during that part of the project.
3. Right-click each control you adjusted and choose Automation Write Enable.

> ❋ **MULTIPLE ARMING**
>
> Instead of arming each control one-by-one, you can arm all the controls in a track by first selecting the track (click the track number to select it) and then choosing Tracks > Automation Write Enable, or you can click the W button in that track. You also can arm the controls in multiple tracks at once. Just select all the tracks whose controls you want to arm (use CTRL-click to select more than one track) and again choose Tracks > Automation Write Enable.

ARMING UNAVAILABLE

You'll notice that not all the parameters can be automated. If a parameter cannot be automated, the Automation Write Enable option in the menu will be grayed out. Also, after a parameter in the Track view is armed for automation, it will have a red outline displayed around it.

4. Make sure that the Automation toolbar is visible by choosing Views > Toolbars, activating the Automation option, and clicking Close. The Automation toolbar will be displayed (see Figure 12.14).

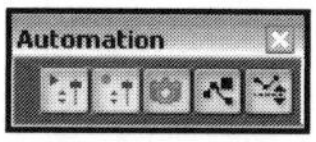

Figure 12.14 Use the Automation toolbar to take Snapshots.

5. Click the Automation Snapshot button (the third button from left to right) on the Automation toolbar.
6. Repeat steps 1 through 5 until you've created all the Snapshots you need for your project.
7. When you're finished, click the Clear All Automation Write Enables button (the fourth button from left to right) on the Automation toolbar to disarm all of the previously armed parameters.

When you play your project, you'll notice that the Snapshots take effect as the Now time passes each Snapshot point.

QUICK SNAPSHOTS

If you want to quickly take a snapshot of a single (or just a few parameters), you can set the Now Time, right-click the parameter, and choose Automation Snapshot.

ENABLE/DISABLE AUTOMATION

If you want to disable automation temporarily without changing or deleting any of the Snapshots in your project, click the Enable/Disable Automation Playback button (the first button from left to right) on the Automation toolbar.

Snapshot control values for each of the MIDI and audio track modules, as well as the buses, are stored as nodes on individual envelopes in the individual tracks represented by those modules. These envelope nodes can be edited, allowing you to change your recorded Snapshot data.

Automating the Mix

Snapshots are great if you need quick control for changing values at certain points in your project, but most of the time you'll want the controls to change smoothly over time as the project plays. To achieve this effect, you need to use SONAR's Write Automation feature. Using Write Automation, you can record the movements of any of the parameters in the Console or Track views. You do so in real time during project playback or recording.

You can record the values of the parameters in the Console and Track views into your project by activating the Write Automation feature and manipulating the controls with your mouse as the project plays. This feature works as follows:

1. Make sure the Automation toolbar is visible by choosing Views > Toolbars and then activate the Automation option and click Close. Also, make sure the Enable/Disable Automation Recording button (the second button from left to right) is activated.

2. Right-click each track and bus parameter you want to automate and choose Automation Write Enable. You can arm multiple parameters at the same time, as explained in the previous section.

3. Set the Now time to just before the point in the project where you want to start recording control changes.

4. Choose Transport > Play (spacebar) or Transport > Record (R key) to start project playback or recording and to start recording automation data.

5. When the Now time gets to the point in the project at which you want to begin recording parameter changes, adjust the parameters with your mouse.

6. When you're finished, choose Transport > Stop (spacebar) to stop playback.

7. Because you're manipulating on-screen parameters with your mouse, you can make only one change at a time. What if you want to have two different controls change at the same time? For every parameter that you want to change in the same time frame, you must repeat steps 2 through 6.

> ❈ **LOOP RECORDING**
>
> Instead of starting and stopping playback each time you want to record additional control changes, try setting up a loop, so SONAR will play the project (or the section of the project) over and over again.

10. After you've finished recording all the control changes you need for your mix, click the Clear All Automation Write Enables button (the fourth button from left to right) in the Automation toolbar to disarm all of the previously armed controls/parameters.

When you play your project, you'll notice the automation taking effect as the Now time passes the sections in which you recorded data.

Just as with Snapshots, the parameter values for each of the MIDI and audio track modules (as well as the buses) are stored as envelopes in the individual tracks represented by those modules. These envelopes can be edited, allowing you to change your recorded automation data.

Grouping

As I mentioned earlier, to change more than one parameter at the same time while you're recording automation data, you have to play through your project several times. To make things easier, you can connect a number of parameters together so if you move one, the others will move with it. You do so by using SONAR's Grouping feature. With the Grouping feature, you can create groups of parameters whose changes are linked to one another.

Quick Groups

The easiest way to group parameters in SONAR is to use the Quick Group feature. A Quick Group is a temporary group of all the controls on a bus or track to one or more buses or tracks. In other words, when multiple tracks are part of a Quick Group, all of their volume parameters are grouped, all of their pan parameters are grouped, and so on.

Creating a Quick Group

To create a Quick Group, you simply hold down the Ctrl key and click the strip selectors (the small triangles located to the left of the track numbers) of each track or bus you would like to group (see Figure 12.15) in the track view. In the Console view, use the Quick Group buttons at the bottom of each module.

Figure 12.15 Create a Quick Group by Ctrl-clicking on the track or bus strip selectors.

By the way, you can't group tracks and buses together, but you can create one Quick Group for tracks and another Quick Group for buses.

> ❊ **REALLY QUICK GROUPING**
>
> If the tracks or buses you want to Quick Group are adjacent to one another, you can click the first strip selector and then hold down the Shift key and click the last strip selector. In addition, you can Quick Group all tracks or all buses by double-clicking one of the strip selectors in your project.

Clearing a Quick Group

To clear a Quick Group, click one of the strip selectors in your project. You can also right-click one of the parameters in the group and choose Clear Group. Or to ungroup a single parameter type, choose Remove from Group.

Creating Permanent Groups

In addition to Quick Groups, SONAR creates Permanent Groups that can be saved. The number of parameters that can belong to a group is unlimited, and you can group different types of parameters to one another instead of having to group like parameters, as with Quick Groups. Permanent Groups use names and colors to designate themselves from one another. SONAR provides 24 default group names and colors, but you can also define your own. To create a Permanent Group, follow these steps:

1. Right-click a parameter in the Console view or the Track view and choose Group > A-X or choose Group > New. Depending on what letter you choose, that parameter takes on the associated color.

2. If you chose one of the default groups, that parameter is assigned to the group and takes on the associated color. If you chose to create a new group, the Group Attributes dialog box appears (see Figure 12.16).

Figure 12.16 Use the Group Attributes dialog box to create a new group.

3. Type in a name for the new group. Then click the Choose Color button to choose a color for the group from the Color dialog box.

4. Click OK to close the Color dialog box. Click OK to close the Group Attributes dialog box. The parameter is assigned to the new group and takes on the chosen color.

5. Right-click another parameter and assign it to a group. This time, choose the same group for this parameter as you did for the previous parameter. This other parameter will take on the same color.

6. Continue to add as many other parameters to the group as you want. You can even create other groups. However, the same parameter cannot belong to more than one group.

Now if you change the first parameter, the second parameter will change as well and vice versa. The values of both of these parameters will be recorded if you have them grouped while you are recording automation data.

❄ QUICK PERMANENT GROUPS

You can create a Permanent Group quickly, by converting a Quick Group to a Permanent Group. This makes it easy to group all selected track volume parameters, for example. First, create a Quick Group as described in the previous section. Then right-click one of the parameter types you would like to permanently group (such as the Volume parameters) and choose Group > Save. Choose a name and color for the group and click OK.

Ungrouping and Deleting Groups

To remove a parameter from a group, right-click the parameter and select Remove from Group. The color of the parameter will return to normal.

If you want to remove all parameters from a group while keeping the group itself intact for future use, just right-click one of the parameters in the group and choose Clear Group.

To delete a group, right-click one of the group parameters and choose Group Manager. Select the group you want to delete from the menu at the top of the dialog box. Then click the Delete button located to the right of the menu (with the picture of a big, red X on it). Click OK.

Group Properties

In addition to simple groups, in which you link different parameters so they change identically, you can create some advanced parameter groups by manipulating the properties of a group. To change the properties of a group, right-click one of the parameters in the group and select Group Manager to open the Group Manager dialog box (see Figure 12.17).

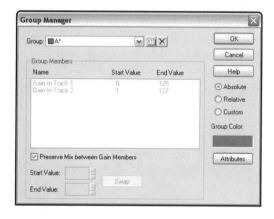

Figure 12.17 You can use the Group Manager dialog box to change the properties of a group.

By changing the properties of a group, you can change the way the parameters in the group are related to one another in terms of the way they change. Parameters in groups can be related absolutely, relatively, or via a custom definition.

Absolute To makes the parameters in a group related absolutely, select the Absolute option (which is the default setting when you create a new group) in the Group Manager dialog box and click OK. Parameters in a group that are related absolutely have the same range of change. This means that if you change one parameter in the group, the others will change by the same amount. This is true even if one parameter starts at one value and another parameter starts at a different value. For example, suppose that you have two Volume parameters on two different MIDI track modules linked together, and one of the Volume parameters has a value of 10 and the other has a value of 20. If you increase the value of the first parameter by 10, the other parameter value will increase by 10, too. Now the first parameter has a value of 20 and the second parameter has a value of 30.

Relative

To link the parameters in a group relatively, select the Relative option in the Group Manager dialog box and click OK. Parameters in a group that are linked relatively do not have the same range of change. This means that if you change one parameter in the group, the others can change by different amounts. For example, suppose that you have two Pan parameters linked, and one has a value of 100% Left and the other has a value of C (centered in the middle). If you change the first parameter so it has a value of C (centered in the middle), the other will change so that it has a value of 100% Right. Now if you change the first parameter to a value of 100% Right, the second parameter will remain at 100% Right. The second parameter can't go any higher so it stays at that value, while the first parameter continues to increase in value. I know this concept is a bit confusing, but if you try it for a while you'll begin to understand it.

Custom

To relate the parameters in a group, according to your own custom definition, select the Custom option in the Group Manager dialog box. All the parameters in the group will be listed in the dialog box (see Figure 12.18).

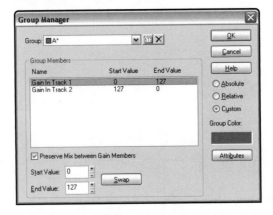

Figure 12.18   You can create complex relationships between parameters in a group by using the Custom option.

Along with the names of each parameter, the Start and End values are also listed. By changing the Start and End values for each parameter, you can define some complex value changes. For example, one good use of the Custom option is to create a crossfade between two Volume parameters. Suppose that you have one Volume parameter in a group with a Start value of 0 and an End value of 127, and another Volume parameter in the same group with a Start value of 127 and an End value of 0. As you increase the value of the first parameter, the second parameter value will decrease and vice versa. You also can set up more complex relationships simply by assigning different Start and End values to each parameter in a group.

To change the Start or End value of a parameter in the list in the Group Manager dialog box, select the parameter and then type a value for either the Start Value or End Value parameter located at the bottom of the box. If you want to exchange the current Start and End values, click the Swap button. After you've finished creating your custom definition, click OK.

❊ **QUICKLY SET START AND END**

You also can change the Start and End values of a parameter without opening the Group Manager dialog box. Just set the parameter to the value you want to set as the start or end, right-click the parameter, and select either Value > Set Start = Current or Value > Set End = Current.

Remote Control

Even with grouping, you still might find it cumbersome to adjust on-screen parameters with your mouse. To remedy this situation, SONAR provides a Remote Control feature. With the Remote Control feature, you can use an external MIDI device to control the changes to the on-screen parameters in the Console view or Track view. For example, if you have a MIDI keyboard, you can use a key on the keyboard to manipulate one of the button parameters. Or if you have a pitch bend wheel on your keyboard, you can use it to manipulate one of the knob or slider parameters.

By assigning different types of MIDI controller messages to the parameters in the Console view or Track view, you no longer have to use your mouse to change the value of the parameters; you can use the actual buttons and keys or levers and sliders on your MIDI instrument or device. To activate the Remote Control feature for a parameter, follow these steps:

1. Right-click the parameter and select Remote Control to open the Remote Control dialog box (see Figure 12.19).

2. If you want to use a key on your MIDI keyboard to manipulate this parameter, select either the Note On option or the Note On/Off option and then enter the pitch of the key that you want to use. If you choose Note On, the value of the parameter will be toggled on or off (for a button parameter) or set to minimum or maximum value (for knobs and sliders) each time you press the key. If you select the Note On/Off option, the value of the parameter will be toggled on when you press the key and off when you release the key.

3. If you want to use a lever or slider on your MIDI keyboard to manipulate this parameter, select the Controller option and then enter the value of the MIDI controller you want to use. You can use this option only to manipulate knob and slider parameters.

4. If you want to use the pitch bend wheel on your MIDI keyboard to manipulate this parameter, select the Wheel option.

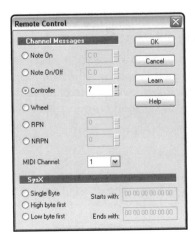

Figure 12.19 You can use the Remote Control dialog box to assign MIDI controller messages to parameters in the Console view so they can be changed via an external MIDI device.

5. If you want to use the special registered parameter number or nonregistered parameter number MIDI messages to manipulate this parameter, choose either the RPN or NRPN option and then enter the number of the RPN or NRPN that you want to use.

6. If you want to use a Sysx message to manipulate this parameter, choose a byte option. If the message contains a single byte of data that changes while the rest of bytes in the message remain static, choose the Single Byte option. If the changing data contains two bytes, with the first being the high byte, choose the High Byte First option. If the changing data contains two bytes with the first being the low byte, choose the Low Byte First option. Then enter into the Starts With field the bytes in the Sysx message that come before the changing data and enter into the Ends With field the bytes in the Sysx message that come after the changing data.

7. Set the MIDI channel your MIDI keyboard or device is using to transmit data.

8. Click OK.

THE LEARN FEATURE

Instead of having to figure out how you need to set the parameters for Remote Control, you can use the Learn feature to have it done for you automatically. First, move a control on your external MIDI device. Right-click the parameter in SONAR that you want to manipulate and choose Remote Control; then click the Learn button. The Remote Control parameters will be set up for you automatically. Click OK.

Now you can manipulate the parameter from your MIDI keyboard or device even while you are recording automation. To stop using Remote Control for a parameter, right-click the parameter and choose Disable Remote Control.

Global Remote Control Support

The Remote Control feature is fine for quick uses, but even though your Remote Control settings are saved with a project, they can't be transferred to other projects. This means you have to set up Remote Control for parameters with each new project. To remedy this, SONAR provides global remote control features that can be used with any project. These features come in the form of support for dedicated control surface devices. These devices provide hardware-based knobs, sliders, and buttons, which (when manipulated) transmit MIDI messages that can be used to control on-screen parameters. Some of the latest MIDI keyboards also provide built-in control surface hardware.

Control Surface Setup

SONAR provides special support for many of the control surfaces available today. To find out if your control surface is supported and to set it up, do the following:

1. Choose Options > Controllers/Surfaces to open the Controllers/Surfaces dialog box (see Figure 12.20).

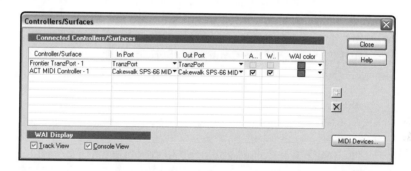

Figure 12.20 Use the Controllers/Surfaces dialog box to set up your MIDI control surface.

2. Click the Add New Controller/Surface button (shown with the yellow star) to open the Controller/Surface Settings dialog box.
3. Choose the name/model of control surface that you have from the Controller/Surface list.
4. Choose the MIDI in port to which your control surface is connected from the Input Port list.
5. Choose the MIDI out port to which your control surface is connected from the Output Port list.
6. Click OK.
7. Click Close.

You can now access the properties window for your control surface by choosing it from the bottom of SONAR's Tools menu. From here you are on your own in configuring the surface because each device is different. Please refer to the documentation that came with your device.

The Active Controller Technology (ACT) MIDI Controller

What about those of us who have an older or unsupported control surface? For this situation, SONAR provides the ACT MIDI Controller, which can be set up to work with just about any control surface you may have. For example, I have an old Kenton Control Freak Live that still works well and I like to use. What's also great about the ACT MIDI Controller is that not only can you control track, bus, and SONAR transport functions, but you can also control effect and soft synth plug-in parameters. In addition, as you switch from one plug-in to another, the ACT MIDI Controller remembers your parameter configurations so that your control surface is automatically set up to control the different plug-in parameters.

Set Up the ACT MIDI Controller

As with all control surfaces, you must first set up the ACT MIDI Controller as follows:

1. Choose Options > Controllers/Surfaces to open the Controllers/Surfaces dialog box.
2. Click the Add New Controller/Surface button to open the Controller/Surface Settings dialog box.
3. Choose ACT MIDI Controller in the Controller/Surface list.
4. Use the Input and Output Port lists to set the MIDI input and output ports for your surface. Click OK.
5. Click Close.

Create an ACT Preset

After setting up the ACT MIDI Controller, you need to create an ACT preset for your control surface. This procedure involves "telling" SONAR the MIDI messages that are transmitted by all of the buttons, knobs, and sliders on your control surface. SONAR can then translate these messages into on-screen parameter changes. To set up an ACT preset, do the following:

1. Set up your control surface to use one of the factory presets that came with the device. Most control surfaces are programmable and provide factory presets so that you can start using them right away. You should base your ACT preset on one of the factory presets to prevent problems in case you reprogram your control surface in the future.
2. Choose Tools > ACT MIDI Controller to open the ACT MIDI Controller properties window (see Figure 12.21). The ACT MIDI Controller provides support for up to four banks of eight knobs, sliders, and buttons. Each bank shares the same knob, slider, and button MIDI messages, but can be assigned to different SONAR functions. Displayed are four rows of control assignments with the first row representing knobs (or rotaries), the second row representing sliders, and the third and fourth row representing buttons. Each row has eight cells representing the eight knobs, eight sliders, and eight buttons (with an extra row for shifted buttons).

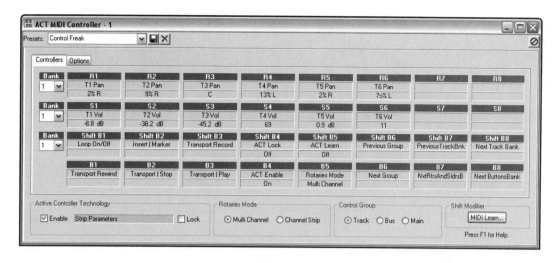

Figure 12.21 Use the ACT MIDI Controller properties window to set up an ACT preset for your control surface.

3. You can change the name of each cell by clicking the cell label and typing a new name into the Edit Label dialog box (see Figure 12.22).

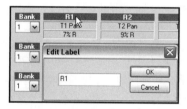

Figure 12.22 Use the Edit Label dialog box to edit the name of a control cell.

4. To assign a MIDI message to a cell, click the green area of the cell so that it displays the words "MIDI Learn" and then move the associated knob, slider, or button on your control surface (see Figure 12.23). Do this for every knob, slider, and button on your surface (up to eight each). For example, click in cell R1 in the ACT window and then move knob 1 on your control surface. Do this for all eight knobs. Then click in cell S1 and move slider 1 on your control surface. Do this for all eight sliders. Then click in cell B1 or Shift B1 (they share the same button) and push button 1 on your control surface. Do this for all eight buttons.

✳ KNOBS AND SLIDERS

Because knobs and sliders transmit the same type of MIDI messages, they look the same to SONAR. So if your control surface has all knobs and no sliders, you can assign control surface knobs to the slider cells in the ACT window and they will work just fine.

Figure 12.23   Click each cell in the ACT window to assign MIDI messages.

5. Because there are two rows representing buttons in the ACT window, we need to set up a Shift key that when pressed will access the shifted row of buttons. Even though you only have eight regular buttons on your control surface, there is usually a Shift key (button) provided that allows you to use the buttons for two different tasks. When the Shift key is not pressed, the buttons each access one program function. When the Shift key is pressed, the buttons each access a different program function. To assign a Shift key MIDI message, click the MIDI Learn button in the Shift Modifier section of the ACT window and then press the Shift key (button) on your control surface.

6. In the Active Controller Technology section of the ACT window, make sure the Enable option is activated. This turns ACT on so that it will work with effect and soft synth plug-ins. If ACT is off, the ACT MIDI Controller will only work on regular SONAR functions.

7. In the Rotaries Mode, make sure the Multi Channel option is activated. This controls multiple track and parameter controls, whereas the Channel Strip mode only works on one track at a time (the currently active or selected track).

8. Click the Options tab to access the Options area of the ACT window (see Figure 12.24). Here is where you can assign different SONAR functions to the knob, slider, and button cells shown in the Controllers area of the window. Each bank of knobs and sliders must share the same function. For example, if you choose Bank 1 and Pan for the Rotaries parameters, then all knobs in Bank 1 will control track panning. Each button in each bank, however, can be assigned a unique function. You can do this using the Button parameters—first choose a bank, then a button, and then a function from each of the lists.

9. When ACT is enabled, it allows you to control parameters in effect and soft synth windows. When one of these windows has focus, the ACT cells take on different functions. Normally, this means you would no longer be able to control SONAR functions like Stop, Play, etc. But you can exclude buttons from being "taken over" while working in an effect or soft synth window. When assigning button functions, activate the Exclude This Button from ACT option so that the button will retain its original function assignment.

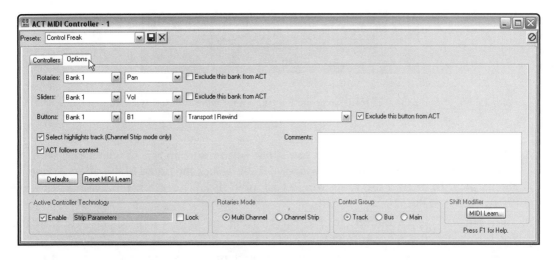

Figure 12.24 Use the Options area of the ACT window to assign knob, slider, and button functions.

10. If you want a track to be highlighted in Channel Strip mode so that you know what track you're working with, activate the Select Highlights Track option.

11. Make sure the ACT Follow Context option is activated. Having this option turned on allows SONAR to automatically change knob, slider, and button assignments when you switch between different effect and soft synth windows.

12. Type some notes for this preset in the Comments section. It's a good idea to include info about what control surface and factory preset you used here.

13. Use the Preset parameters at the top of the window to type a new name for the preset and save it.

You can now close the ACT window and move on to creating knob, slider, and button assignments for the effects and soft synths with which you want to work.

Create an ACT Map

Although you have already created basic SONAR function assignments for the knobs, sliders, and buttons on your control surface in the ACT properties window, you still need to create assignments for each of the parameters in the each of the effect and soft synth windows that you use. Do the following:

1. Make sure the Controllers/Surfaces toolbar is visible by choosing Views > Toolbars and putting a check mark next to Controllers/Surfaces in the Toolbars dialog box.

2. In the Controllers/Surfaces toolbar, make sure the ACT MIDI Controller is selected in the Controller/Surface list (see Figure 12.25).

Figure 12.25 Activate the ACT MIDI Controller to prepare for effect and soft synth parameter control
assignments.

3. Open the window for the effect or soft synth whose parameters to which you want to assign controls. To open an effect window, double-click the name of the effect in one of the FX bins. To open a soft synth window, double-click the synth in the Synth Rack view (Views > Synth Rack).

4. Click the ACT Learn button (second button from the left) in the Controllers/Surfaces toolbar to activate ACT Learn mode.

5. Change one of the on-screen parameters with your mouse. For example, in the Cakewalk FxEq window, move the Band 1 slider.

6. Move the first slider on your control surface.

7. Click the ACT Learn button again. SONAR will tell you how many parameters and controls were touched and ask you if you want to keep the assignments. Click Yes to save the assignments.

8. Repeat steps 4 through 7 to assign all controls.

> **MULTIPLE ASSIGNMENTS**
>
> Instead of clicking the ACT Learn button for each single parameter you want to assign, simply click the button and then adjust each of the on-screen parameters you want to assign in the order you want to assign them. Then move the control surface knobs, sliders, and buttons in the same order. Click the ACT Learn button again and all assignments will be made in the order that you chose.

Make parameter assignments for all of the effects and soft synths you want to use with your control surface. When you're finished, you can simply switch from one window to the other, and SONAR will automatically remember your parameter assignments. For example, if you are controlling slider 1 in the Cakewalk FxEq with slider 1 on your surface and then you click in the Track view to make that the focus, slider 1 will now control track volume 1 (or whatever track parameter you assigned) instead.

Where Am I (WAI)?

As you use your control surface, SONAR provides you with feedback as to which tracks and buses are being controlled by your surface using the WAI (Where Am I) feature. WAI displays a set of colored markers for each control surface you are using. These markers are shown to the left of the track numbers in the Track view (see Figure 12.26) and the bottom of the modules in the Console view.

WAI Markers

Figure 12.26 WAI markers show you which tracks and buses are being controlled by your surface.

To use the WAI feature with your control surface, do the following:

1. Choose Options > Options Controllers/Surfaces to open the Controllers/Surfaces dialog box.

2. Put a check mark in the WAI column for your control surface.

3. Select a color for your surface in the WAI Color column.

4. To display WAI markers in the Track or Console view, activate the Track View and Console View options in the WAI Display section of the box. Click Close.

5. Once the WAI markers are visible, you can click and drag them to change which tracks are being controlled by your surface. You can also right-click the markers and choose *Move-name of control surface* from the menu.

6. Double-click the markers to open the properties window for the associated control surface.

Working with Envelopes

In addition to the Snapshot and Record Automation features, SONAR provides one more method of automating its parameters: the Envelope feature. Using this feature, you can "draw" parameter changes into individual clips or entire tracks in the Track view. In the following sections, I'll cover how to create and edit parameter changes using the Envelope feature.

Creating and Editing Envelopes

Earlier, I mentioned that whenever you use the Snapshot or Record Automation features, SONAR stores the automation data as envelopes in the Track view. Well, you can also create (as well as edit) envelopes manually using the Envelope tools and your mouse.

Audio Envelopes

SONAR creates envelopes for both audio and MIDI tracks, as well as the buses in the Track view. Since the buses deal with audio data, you automate them by using audio envelopes. MIDI and audio envelopes are basically the same, but they have enough differences to require separate step-by-step procedures. To create or edit an audio envelope, follow these steps:

1. Activate the Envelope tool by clicking the Envelope Tool button or pressing E on your computer keyboard while the Track view is active.

2. If you want to create an envelope for an individual clip, right-click that clip and choose Envelopes > Create Clip Envelope > [*name of the parameter you want to automate*]. For individual clips, you can automate the gain (volume) or panning.

3. If you want to create an envelope for an entire track (including the buses), right-click that track in the Clips pane and choose Envelopes > Create Track Envelope (or Create Bus Envelopes) > [*name of the parameter you want to automate*]. For tracks, you can automate the Mute, Volume, Pan, Bus Send Level/Pan, and EQ parameters. The buses provide different parameters for automation (see the list in the menu).

❋ MERGED ENVELOPES

If you create an envelope for a clip inside a track that already has an envelope for the same parameter, the clip envelope will be merged into the track envelope.

4. Initially, the envelope is shown as a straight line that runs from left to right in the clip or track. If it's a clip envelope, it will stop at the end of the clip. If it's a track envelope, it will continue past the right side of the Track view (see Figure 12.27). The vertical position of the envelope inside the clip or track indicates the current value for its associated parameter. For example, if you're automating the Volume parameter and its current value is -INF, the envelope will be shown at the very bottom of the clip or track. If the Volume parameter value is +6dB, the envelope will be shown at the very top of the clip or track. Other values will be shown somewhere between the top and bottom of the clip or track.

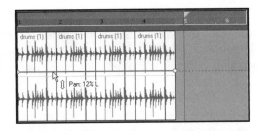

Figure 12.27 A straight line in a clip or track represents a new envelope.

❋ SHOW/HIDE ENVELOPES

You can show and hide envelopes for easier editing. If you don't see your new envelope, click the down arrow next to the Envelope Tool button and choose one of the options (such as Show All Envelopes) from the menu (see Figure 12.28).

Figure 12.28 Use the Envelope Tool menu to show/hide envelopes.

5. At the beginning of the envelope is a small circle (called a *node*). To change the value of the envelope, click and drag the node up or down. As you drag the node, you will see the value of the parameter represented by an envelope displayed alongside your mouse cursor.

6. To make things more interesting, you can add more nodes to the envelope either by double-clicking anywhere on the envelope or by right-clicking on the envelope and selecting Add Node. You can add as many nodes as you need, which enables you to create some very complex parameter value changes. In addition to dragging them up or down, you can also drag nodes left or right (to change their time/location within the project), so you can create any envelope shape you want (see Figure 12.29). You also can change the time and value of a node more precisely by right-clicking it, choosing Properties, and then entering the new values in the Edit Node dialog box.

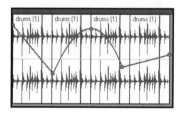

Figure 12.29 You can create complex envelopes by adding more nodes.

7. To make things even more interesting, you can change the shape of the line segments between two nodes. Right-click a line segment and choose one of the following options: Jump, Linear, Fast Curve, or Slow Curve. If you want abrupt changes in the parameter values, choose Jump. For straight changes in the values, choose Linear. For fast but smooth changes in the values, choose Fast Curve. For slow and smooth changes in the values, choose Slow Curve. Depending on the option you choose, the shape of the line segment will change accordingly.

8. If you need to delete a node, right-click it and select Delete Node. To delete all nodes, just right-click the envelope and select Clear All.

9. If you need to reset a node to its original position, right-click it and select Reset Node.

10. If you want to delete an entire envelope, right-click it and select Delete Envelope.

11. If you want to change an envelope assignment so it controls a different parameter, right-click the envelope and choose Assign Envelope > [*name of the new parameter to automate*].

MIDI Envelopes

To create or edit a MIDI envelope, follow these steps:

1. Activate the Envelope tool by clicking the Envelope Tool button or pressing E on your computer keyboard in the Track view.

2. If you want to create an envelope for an individual clip, right-click that clip and choose Envelopes > Create Clip Envelope > [*name of the parameter you want to automate*]. For individual MIDI clips, you can automate the velocity.

3. If you want to create an envelope for an entire track, right-click that track in the Clips pane and choose Envelopes > Create Track Envelope > [*name of the parameter you want to automate*]. For MIDI tracks, you can automate the Mute, Volume, Pan, Chorus, and Reverb parameters. In addition, you can automate any other MIDI controller messages by choosing the Envelopes > Create Track Envelope > MIDI option, which opens the MIDI Envelope dialog box (see Figure 12.30). In the dialog box, choose the type of controller, the value of that controller, and the MIDI channel you want to use for the controller. Then click OK to create the new envelope.

Figure 12.30 For MIDI tracks, you can create envelopes for any kind of MIDI controller messages.

CONVERT MIDI TO SHAPES

If you think the parameters in the MIDI Envelope dialog box look familiar, you're right. They are the same parameters found in the MIDI Event Type dialog box, which is accessed in the Piano Roll view when editing MIDI controllers in the Controller pane. If a track contains MIDI controller messages and you create an envelope for that track with the same controller, they will contradict one another. In this case, you should select the track and choose Edit > Convert MIDI to Shapes. You'll see the Convert MIDI to Shapes dialog box, which is exactly the same as the MIDI Envelope dialog box. Choose the controller you want to convert and click OK. The controller messages in that track will be converted to envelopes.

4. Initially, the envelope is shown as a straight line that runs from left to right in the clip or track. If it's a clip envelope, it will stop at the end of the clip. If it's a track envelope, it will continue past the right side of the Track view. The vertical position of the envelope inside the clip or track indicates the current value for its associated parameter. For example, if you're automating the Volume parameter and its current value is 0, the envelope will be shown at the very bottom of the clip or track. If the Volume parameter value is 127, the envelope will be shown at the very top of the clip or track. And other values will be shown somewhere between the top and bottom of the clip or track.

5. At the beginning of the envelope is a small circle (called a *node*). To change the value of the envelope, click and drag the node up or down. As you drag the node, you will see the value of the parameter represented by the envelope displayed alongside your mouse cursor.

6. To make things more interesting, you can add more nodes to the envelope, either by double-clicking anywhere on the envelope or by right-clicking on the envelope and selecting Add Node. You can add as many nodes as you need, which enables you to create some very complex parameter value changes. In addition to dragging them up or down, you can also drag nodes left or right (to change their time/location within the project), so you can create any envelope shape you want. You also can change the time and value of a node more precisely by right-clicking it, choosing Properties, and then entering the new values in the Edit Node dialog box.

7. To make things even more interesting, you can change the shape of the line segments between two nodes. Right-click a line segment and choose one of the following options from the menu: Jump, Linear, Fast Curve, or Slow Curve. If you want abrupt changes in the parameter values, choose Jump. For straight changes in the values, choose Linear. For fast but smooth changes in the values, choose Fast Curve. For slow and smooth changes in the values, choose Slow Curve. Depending on the option you choose, the shape of the line segment will change accordingly.

8. If you need to delete a node, right-click it and select Delete Node. To delete all nodes, just right-click the envelope and select Clear All.

9. If you need to reset a node to its original position, right-click it and select Reset Node.

10. If you want to delete an entire envelope, right-click it and select Delete Envelope.

11. If you want to change an envelope assignment so it controls a different parameter, right-click the envelope and choose Assign Envelope > [*name of the new parameter to automate*].

Now when you play your project, the parameter values you edited will follow the shape of the envelopes.

❄ **ENABLE/DISABLE ENVELOPES**

If you want to temporarily turn off all envelopes in your tracks to hear how your project sounds without the automation, click the Enable/Disable Automation Playback button on the Automation toolbar.

※ **ENVELOPE/OFFSET MODE**

Normally during playback, if you have an envelope assigned to a track parameter, you cannot change that parameter because the envelope is controlling it. But SONAR provides a special mode in which you can add an offset to envelope values by changing parameters during playback. This is called *Offset mode*, and you can activate it by choosing Offset mode from the Envelope Tool menu. Click the arrow to the right of the Envelope Tool button to access this menu. This option toggles between Envelope mode and Offset mode. Also be aware that when you return to Envelope mode, your last parameter offset settings are still in effect. So if you change a parameter in Offset mode and leave it, the parameter will still be offset even if you return to Envelope mode. A good use for this feature is when you have an envelope that's just about perfect, but you want to make an adjustment to the entire envelope without having to change all the nodes in it.

Additional Envelope Editing

Even though I've covered most of the editing procedures for envelopes in the previous sections, there are some additional ways in which you can edit envelopes.

The Envelope Draw Tool

In addition to the Envelope tool, SONAR provides the Envelope Draw tool, which allows you to literally draw any envelope shape that you would like to create. Once you've created an initial envelope, you can use the Envelope Draw tool to alter the shape of the envelope by simply drawing on the screen with your mouse. Here is how the Envelope Draw tool works:

1. Click the Envelope Draw tool button to activate the Envelope Draw tool (see Figure 12.31).

Figure 12.31   Use the Envelope Draw tool to create any envelope shape you would like by simply drawing with your mouse.

2. Click the downward arrow next to the Envelope Draw tool to choose the envelope shape you would like to use while drawing. Freehand allows you to simply draw any type of envelope shape you would like. Sine, Triangle, Square, and Saw mimic basic audio waveform shapes. Random creates a totally random envelope shape.

3. Click the envelope you would like to edit to select it.

4. Hover your mouse over the point at which you would like to start "drawing." Then click and hold the left mouse button. If you chose the Freehand shape, you can simply move your mouse anywhere over the track or clip and draw in any envelope shape. If you chose one of the waveform shapes, drag your mouse from left to right (as well as up and down, depending on how much parameter value change you want to occur) to create that waveform shape (see Figure 12.32).

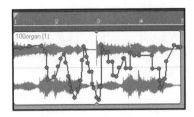

Figure 12.32 Complex envelope shapes are easy to create with the Envelope Draw tool.

5. If you don't like the new envelope shape, simply draw over it. You can also choose Edit > Undo (or press Ctrl + Z) to change the envelope back to its original shape.

Now when you play your project, the parameter values you edited will follow the shape of the envelopes.

Deleting Envelopes

Earlier, I mentioned that to delete an envelope, you just need to right-click it and choose Delete Envelope. But if you want to delete more than one envelope or only part of an envelope, the procedure is a bit different.

1. Make sure that the Select tool is activated by pressing T on your computer keyboard.
2. Select the data containing the envelope data you want to delete. This can be a single clip, an entire track, multiple tracks, or even part of a clip or track.
3. Choose Edit > Delete to open the Delete dialog box.
4. Depending on the data you selected in step 2, either the Track/Bus Automation option or the Clip Automation option will be available (or maybe both). Activate one or both options.

❄ **ENVELOPES ONLY**

If you don't want to delete any other data along with the envelope data, make sure to deactivate all other options in the Delete dialog box.

---

5. Click OK.

SONAR will delete your selected envelope/automation data.

Copying and Pasting Envelopes

You can also copy and paste an envelope (or part of an envelope) from one track to another. Why would you want to do that? Well, you might want the volume of one instrument in your project to follow the volume of another instrument. You can do this by copying and pasting the volume envelope from the first instrument track to the other. Here is how it works:

1. Make sure the Select tool is activated by pressing T.
2. Select the data containing the envelope data you want to copy. This can be a single clip, an entire track, multiple tracks, or even part of a clip or track.

> ❈ **SELECT TRACK ENVELOPES OPTION**
>
> If you are selecting clips in the Clips pane and you want to select the track envelope data for the track in which the clips reside, be sure to choose Edit > Select > Select Track Envelopes with Selected Clips.

3. Choose Edit > Copy to open the Copy dialog box.
4. Depending on the data you selected in step 2, either the Track/Bus Automation option or the Clip Automation option will be available (or maybe both). Activate one or both options.

> ❈ **ENVELOPES ONLY**
>
> If you don't want to copy any other data along with the envelope data, make sure to deactivate all other options in the Copy dialog box.

5. Click OK.
6. Select the tracks and change the Now time to the position in the project at which you want to paste the envelope data.
7. Choose Edit > Paste to open the Paste dialog box. Then click the Advanced button to expand the Paste dialog box to its full size.
8. Make sure the Blend Old and New option is activated in the What to Do with Existing Material section.
9. Make sure the Track/Bus Automation or Clip Automation options are activated in the What to Paste section.
10. Click OK.

SONAR will copy your selected envelope data and paste it at the new location in the project.

Automating Effects and Soft Synths

In addition to automating track parameters, SONAR automates individual audio effect and software synthesizer parameters. The procedures for automating audio effects and soft synths are essentially the same as for track parameters, but arming the parameters is a bit different.

Automating Effects Parameters

To automate effects parameters, you can follow the same procedures outlined in the "Taking Snapshots" and "Automating the Mix" sections of this chapter. But when you get to the part of the procedure where you need to arm the parameter that you want to automate, follow these steps instead:

1. Right-click the Fx bin of the audio track to which you want to apply the real-time effect and choose Audio Effects > [*the name of the effect you want to use*].
2. After the window for the effect appears, right-click the name of the effect in the Fx bin and choose Arm Parameter. Or if you want to automate all the parameters, click the W button located in the upper right corner of the effect window.
3. If you use the right-click method, a dialog box appears. Put a check mark next to each of the parameters you want to automate in the Param Armed list.
4. Click OK.

Now just follow the procedures in the "Taking Snapshots" or "Automating the Mix" sections of this chapter to record automation for your effect parameters.

As with track parameters, you can use envelopes to automate effects parameters. The procedure is basically the same as outlined in the "Audio Envelopes" section. But you can use only track envelopes to automate effects parameters, and the procedure for initially creating the envelope is a bit different. To create an envelope to automate an effect parameter, follow these steps:

1. Right-click the Fx bin of the audio track to which you want to apply the real-time effect and choose Audio Effects > [*the name of the effect you want to use*].
2. When the window for the effect appears, close it. Then right-click the Clips pane of the track to which you applied the effect and choose Envelopes > Create Track Envelope > [*the name of the effect to be automated*].
3. In the dialog box that appears, put a check mark next to each of the parameters you want to automate in the Envelope Exists list.
4. Click OK.

Now just follow the procedures in the "Audio Envelopes" section of this chapter to finish creating the envelopes for your effect parameters.

Automating Soft Synth Parameters

Unlike effects, some soft synths can be automated only by using envelopes. It depends on the soft synth. In addition, the procedure for recording soft synth parameter movements is different from what I described earlier, so I'll go through each procedure step by step.

Recording Parameter Movements

If you want to record automation for a soft synth by directly manipulating its on-screen parameters, follow these steps:

1. If you haven't done so already, set up a soft synth in the Track view of your project. Be sure to keep the soft synth's window open. Also, if you are using an older soft synth like the Cakewalk TTS-1, make sure to activate the Enable MIDI Output option in the Insert Soft Synth Options dialog box.

2. If you are using an older soft synth, arm the MIDI track for recording (by clicking the track's Record button) to which you want to record the automation data. If you are using a new soft synth like the PSYN II, you can record automation during either recording or playback.

3. If you're using an older soft synth, choose Transport > Record Options to set the recording mode. I explained this feature in Chapter 6; it works the same way here. More than likely, you'll want to keep the recording mode set to Sound on Sound. This will record new data to the track without overwriting any of the existing data.

4. Set up the soft synth to enable automation recording. This procedure is different for every soft synth, so you will have to refer to the soft synth's documentation for instructions. Most synths don't need any preparation because their controls already have automation values assigned to them.

5. For newer soft synths, be sure to activate the W (Automation Write) button in the upper right corner of the synth's property page window. You can also do this in the Synth Rack view.

6. Set the Now time to the point in the project at which you want to start recording automation.

7. If you're using an older soft synth, choose Transport > Record (or press the R key) to start recording. For newer soft synths, you can just start project playback.

8. Move the soft synth's controls to record their movements.

9. Choose Transport > Stop (or press the spacebar) to stop recording.

10. If you want to record more automation, repeat steps 6 through 9.

❄ **CONVERT MIDI TO SHAPES**

When you record automation data from an older soft synth, it is saved to the MIDI track as MIDI controller data. There's nothing wrong with this. You can edit the data easily by using the Controller pane in the Piano Roll view. But if you would rather edit the data as envelopes in the Track view, use the Edit > Convert MIDI to Shapes feature to convert the MIDI controller data to envelopes. Newer soft synths have their data recorded to the synth track as an envelope.

Using Envelopes

You'll find that using envelopes to automate soft synth parameters is more accurate, since you can actually draw the control movements. To use envelopes to automate soft synth parameters, follow these steps:

1. Set up a soft synth in the Track view of your project.

2. If you're using an older soft synth, in the MIDI track that drives the soft synth, right-click in the Clips pane and choose Envelopes > Create Track Envelope > MIDI to open the MIDI Envelope dialog box. If you're using a newer soft synth, right-click in the synth track and choose Envelopes > Create Track Envelope > [name of the soft synth].

3. If you're using an older soft synth, in the MIDI Envelope dialog box use the Type list to choose from the Control, RPN, or NRPN options. The Value list will show all of the parameters that the soft synth offers for automation. Choose a parameter from the list. Use the Channel list to choose the MIDI channel of the current patch (program) being used in the soft synth.

4. If you're using a new soft synth, a dialog box for the synth appears. In the box, put check marks next to the parameters you want to automate in the Envelope Exist section. You can also choose a different color to represent each parameter by using the Choose Color button.

5. Click OK.

Now follow the procedures in the "MIDI Envelopes" section of this chapter to automate the soft synth parameters.

The Next Steps

After you've finished mixing all the data in your tracks at just the right settings, it's time to create a final stereo track, which you can use to burn your project onto CD or get it ready for distribution in a multimedia project or on the Internet. Of course, if you're working on a surround sound project, there's still more to learn. Check out the next chapter for surround sound information.

13 } Surround Sound

In addition to creating a stereo mix of your project, you may also want to create a surround sound mix. Surround sound is extensively used in movie soundtracks as well as soundtracks for games. And these days, it is being used more and more for audio-only projects. You can create your own surround sound music with the special surround mixing tools provided by SONAR. From there, you can burn your music to CD or DVD and share it with others for playback on any home theater system. In this chapter, you will learn the following:

* How to find the equipment you need for surround sound.
* How to set up your studio for surround sound.
* How to set up a SONAR surround sound project.
* How to use the Surround Panner.
* How to add effects to a surround sound mix.
* How to export your surround project to an audio file.

❋ **SURROUND SOUND BACKGROUND**

Before reading the rest of this chapter, you may want to read some background and overview information about surround sound. Check out the following resources:

Introduction to Surround Sound: www.digifreq.com/digifreq/article.asp?ID=21

Setting Up Your Studio for Surround Sound: www.digifreq.com/digifreq/article.asp?ID=22

Surround Sound Mixing Techniques: www.digifreq.com/digifreq/article.asp?ID=23

More Audio and Surround Articles: www.digifreq.com/digifreq/articles.asp

Setting Up Your Studio

Working with surround sound isn't just a simple matter of changing a few settings in SONAR and like magic, having a surround sound mix of your project. There are certain steps you need to take in order to start working with surround sound. The first step will be to invest your money in some new studio equipment, including a new sound card and new monitors (speakers).

Surround Sound Cards

I'm going to assume you'll be working with a format of surround sound known as *5.1 Surround Sound*. There are many different surround sound formats, but 5.1 is the most common and is used in audio for DVDs and video games, as well as DVD-A (DVD Audio) discs (special music-only DVDs). As such, you will need a sound card that provides six separate mono audio outputs (or three stereo outputs). If your card already provides this number of outputs or more, then you're all set in the sound card department.

If your card doesn't provide at least six outputs, you'll need to invest in a new card. You can get both professional and prosumer cards from a number of different manufacturers. I usually recommend either Echo Audio (www.echoaudio.com) or M-Audio (www.m-audio.com). M-Audio also sells a line of consumer-based cards that provide great sound. One such card is the Revolution 7.1. This is a great card to use when you're starting out with surround sound, and I'll be using it to demonstrate how to use SONAR's surround features.

> **REVOLUTION REVIEW**
>
> You can read my review of the Revolution 7.1 surround sound card from M-Audio by going to:
>
> www.digifreq.com/digifreq/reviewdetails.asp?ProdReviewID=24

Surround Sound Monitors

In addition to a multi-output sound card, you'll need five matched monitors and a subwoofer (a special monitor for playing low frequency audio, often called the *Low Frequency Effects monitor*) to work in the 5.1 surround format. By matched monitors, I mean they should all be identical. For example, I have two KRK V4 monitors for creating stereo mixes in my studio. In order to expand that for 5.1 surround, I would have to purchase three more V4 monitors. This is the best way to go for a professional setup, but it can get very expensive.

If you're like me, you may want to ease your way into surround and get a prosumer monitor set up instead. I'm currently using the Z-5500 Digital 5.1 5-Piece Speaker System from Logitech. The cost of the system is about $250, and it provides everything you need to monitor in 5.1 surround. By everything, I mean five monitors plus a subwoofer, six analog inputs, two digital inputs, a computerized controller, and even a nifty remote control. On top of all that, it provides built-in Dolby and DTS decoding. Go to www.digifreq.com/digifreq/newsinfo.asp?NewsID=2567 for more information about the Logitech System.

Surround Monitor Setup

Once you have your monitoring equipment, you'll need to set it up. If you're thinking you can simply plop the speakers around your studio and get a good surround listening image, think again. The five monitors need to be placed in a certain pattern around the room with equal distance from your listening position; otherwise, you won't get a clear indication of where the musical elements are located in your mix during playback. Here's how to do it:

1. Place the center channel monitor dead center behind your mixing console or on top of your computer monitor. When you sit down to mix your tracks, you should see the center channel monitor centered right in front of you.

2. Get a microphone stand and place it in the same position where you will be sitting when mixing your audio.

3. Use a tape measure to measure the distance from the microphone stand to the center channel monitor.

4. Get a roll of string and tie the free end of the string to the microphone stand. Unroll the string, starting at the microphone stand and ending at the location of the center channel monitor. Then cut the string. This marks the distance you will use to position all of the other monitors.

5. Get a compass (one that includes degree markings). At the microphone stand position, point the compass at the center channel monitor. Then turn left so that the compass reading changes 30 degrees.

6. Extend the string in that 30-degree direction and now you have the location for your left channel monitor.

7. Reposition the compass so that it points at the center channel monitor again. Then turn 30 degrees to the right and find the location for your right channel monitor.

8. To find the locations for the right and left surround monitors, follow the same procedure with the compass and the string. This time, however, move 120 degrees to the left and right to find the left and right surround monitor locations, respectively.

When you're done positioning the monitors, they should be placed at precise locations along an imaginary circle, as shown in Figure 13.1. This is the standard 5.1 monitor positioning, according to the SMPTE (Society of Motion Picture and Television Engineers) and ITU (International Telecommunication Union) organizations. Since low frequencies are not directional, you can place the LFE monitor anywhere on the floor. Mine is placed on the floor to one side of my DAW (Digital Audio Workstation) desk.

Surround Monitor Calibration

Even after you've placed your monitors correctly, you're still not quite finished with setting them up. You also have to calibrate them. This means that you need to make sure they are all set to the same volume level so that when you are mixing, you don't get misled by how loud an audio track may be playing when you pan it around the surround sound field.

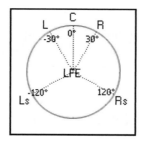

Figure 13.1 This is the standard 5.1 surround monitor positioning according to SMPTE and ITU.

You'll need two things to calibrate your monitors: a pink noise source and an SPL (Sound Pressure Level) meter. For pink noise, you can use a test tone CD, a tone generator, or even an audio editor (like Sony's Sound Forge) that includes a built-in noise generator. If you don't have any of these, you can download a pink noise audio file from www.5dot1.com/down-loads/pink_noise_44-1k.zip. For the SPL meter, you'll have to spend a few bucks, but you don't need anything expensive. Many audio engineers (even some professionals) use basic meters that can be bought for about $50. Go to www.zzounds.com/a–303813/item–GXYCM130 to check out the Galaxy Audio CM130 Checkmate Sound Level SPL Meter. Once you have these two items, you can calibrate your monitors by doing the following:

❄ **MONITOR CONNECTIONS**

Before you can calibrate your monitors, you need to connect them to your sound card. Since there are many different sound cards and monitoring systems on the market, I cannot walk you through this process. Read the documentation that came with your sound card and monitors. These documents should provide you with all the information you need to properly connect your monitors to your sound card.

1. Set your sound card output levels to 0dB. For example, if you are using the M-Audio Revolution, open its control panel. Then in the Output Mixer section of the panel, set all the outputs to a volume level of 0dB (see Figure 13.2). In addition, if your sound card has a surround sound configuration option, be sure to set that as well. For this example, set up your card for 5.1 surround sound.

2. Change the settings on your SPL meter to Slow Scale and C weighting. Refer to the documentation that came with your meter for explanations of these settings if you need them.

3. Play pink noise through the left-front monitor.

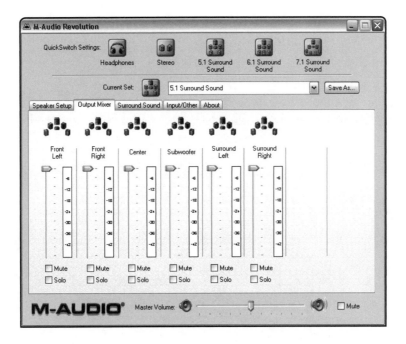

Figure 13.2 Set your sound card output levels to 0dB.

❄ **LOGITECH TEST NOISE**

If you're using the Logitech Z-5500 Digital 5.1 5-Piece Speaker System I mentioned earlier, you can use the built-in noise generator. Just press the Test button on your remote control. The Logitech system will cycle noise through each of the monitors automatically.

---

4. While sitting at your mix position, raise the SPL meter to ear level and point it at the left-front monitor.
5. Adjust the monitor volume so that the SPL meter reads 85dB.
6. Repeat Steps 3 through 5 for each of the remaining monitors, except for the LFE monitor.
7. Point the SPL meter at the LFE monitor and adjust the volume of the monitor so that the meter reads 90dB. The reading needs to be slightly higher because most SPL meters don't register low frequencies very well. The higher adjustment compensates for this shortcoming.

Setting Up SONAR for Surround

When your studio configuration is complete, you're ready to start working with surround sound in SONAR. The first step in creating a surround sound project is to either open an existing project file or create a new project. SONAR's surround sound settings need to be configured for each individual project that you create, but you can save your settings for use in multiple projects if you'd like.

Surround Project Options

After you've either created a new project or opened an existing one, choose Options > Project > Surround to open the Project Options – Surround dialog box (see Figure 13.3).

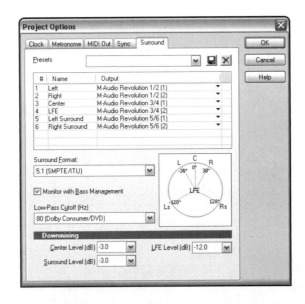

Figure 13.3 Use the Project Options – Surround dialog box to adjust your project's surround settings.

This dialog box is used to adjust the initial surround settings for your project. These settings include the surround format, sound card outputs, bass management, and downmixing.

Surround Format

Even though I've been primarily talking about the 5.1 surround sound format, there are actually many different formats available—even different 5.1 formats. SONAR provides support for these multiple formats and includes preset options from which you can choose. When you choose a surround format, what you are actually doing is specifying the number of monitors that are in use, the position of those monitors, and how they are connected to your sound card. With the Project Options – Surround dialog already open, use the Surround Format list to choose a format (see Figure 13.4).

Notice that as you choose different formats, the diagram (shown to the right of the Surround Format drop-down list) changes as well. This diagram displays the number of monitors required for the chosen format. It also shows how those monitors should be positioned around your mixing location. For demonstration purposes, I'll be using the default format – 5.1 (SMPTE/ITU).

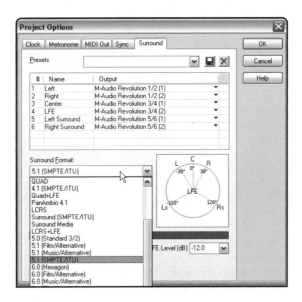

Figure 13.4 Use the Surround Format drop-down list to choose a surround format for your project.

Surround Sound Card Outputs

After you've chosen a format, you also need to configure your sound card outputs so that SONAR knows where to send the appropriate audio data to the monitors in your surround setup. You do this by using the sound card output list in the top half of the Project Options – Surround dialog box. This section of the box will list all of the monitors required to support the surround format that you have chosen. For example, with the 5.1 (SMPTE/ITU) format chosen, you'll see six monitors listed by number (#) and name. To the right of each monitor is shown a sound card output. To change the output for a monitor, click the down arrow to the right of the output and choose a new one from the list (see Figure 13.5).

When using a sound card such as the M-Audio Revolution (that provides multiple stereo outputs with individual left/right settings), you'll see the same sound card output listed twice, but each will have a different number in parenthesis next to it. For example, M-Audio Revolution 1/2 (1) means that you are choosing the left channel of the first stereo output of the sound card. The number in parenthesis tells you if you're choosing the left (1) or right (2) channel.

Bass Management

When your surround sound project is played on a home theater system, all the frequencies below a certain point are routed to the LFE monitor (subwoofer). This is because the smaller monitors that take care of the rest of the surround field are not large enough to reproduce very low frequencies. Because of this, you need to listen to your project in the same way. The bass management option provided by SONAR emulates the low frequency playback of a home theater system.

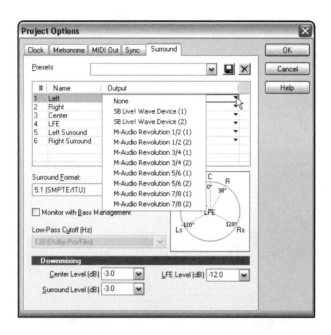

Figure 13.5 Configure your sound card outputs in the Project Options – Surround dialog box.

To activate bass management for your project, put a check mark next to the Monitor with Bass Management option in the Project Options – Surround dialog box. Then choose a cutoff point (the point below which frequencies will be routed to the LFE sound card channel) from the Low-Pass Cutoff drop-down list. The standard for playback on a home theater system is 80 Hz, but there are other options available if you need them, as shown in Figure 13.6.

Surround Sound Bussing

One last thing you need to do before you can start mixing your project in surround sound is to add at least one surround bus to your project. There are a number of different ways to add a surround bus.

The Insert Menu

To add a surround bus to your project using the Insert menu, choose Insert > Surround Bus (see Figure 13.7).

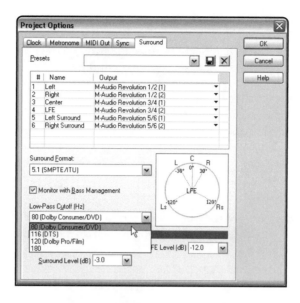

Figure 13.6 You should monitor your project with bass management, so you can hear what it will sound like when played by consumers.

Figure 13.7 You can use the Insert menu to add a surround bus.

The Bus Pane

You can also use the Bus pane in the Track view to add a new surround bus to your project. In the Bus pane, right-click and choose Insert Surround Bus (see Figure 13.8).

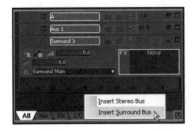

Figure 13.8 You can also add a surround bus via the Bus pane in the Track view.

Insert Send

An indirect way of adding a new surround bus to a project is to do it at the same time you are inserting a new send into an existing track. Right-click an existing audio track and choose Insert Send > New Surround Bus (see Figure 13.9).

Figure 13.9 Add a new surround bus at the same time you add a new audio track send.

Track Output

One last way to add a new surround bus to a project is simply to assign the output of an audio track to a new bus. SONAR creates the new bus automatically. Just click the Output parameter of the audio track and choose New Surround Bus (see Figure 13.10).

> **❋ TRACK ASSIGNMENT**
>
> If you don't use the track output method of creating a new surround bus, then you will have to manually assign the output of your audio tracks to the new bus or create a new bus for each track. You can also assign the output of your tracks to the Surround Main, which is a virtual main output dedicated to surround sound in Sonar. The Surround Main simply routes your audio directly to your sound card outputs as they were assigned in the Project Options – Surround dialog box. The drawback to this method is that you won't be able to assign any surround effects to your tracks. You need to use a surround bus to utilize surround effects.

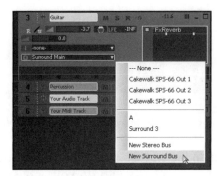

Figure 13.10 Assign the output of an audio track to a new surround bus.

Surround Sound Mixing

After you've created one or more surround buses for your project, you need to assign the outputs of your audio tracks to those buses, if you haven't done so already. When you assign the output of an audio track to a surround bus, you'll notice a number of changes made to the track. One change is the display of the output meters. Instead of two channel meters, you'll see multiple channel meters. The number of meters depends on the surround format you've chosen and how many channels exist in that format. For example, for the 5.1 (SMPTE/ITU) format, you will have a six-channel meter, as shown in Figure 13.11.

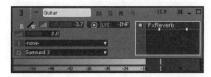

Figure 13.11 SONAR provides multichannel output meters for audio tracks when mixing in surround.

Surround Sound Panning

Another change made to the audio track is the replacement of the usual pan parameter with the Surround Panner. Instead of simply panning between two stereo speakers, you can now pan your audio track around a circular sound field between multiple speakers (the number of which depends on the surround format you are using). The Surround Panner comes in a variety of sizes, depending on where it is being accessed within Sonar.

The Micro Surround Panner

When working in surround, the normal pan parameter of an audio track becomes the Micro Surround Panner (see Figure 13.12).

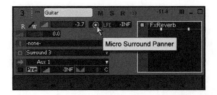

Figure 13.12 The normal pan parameter of an audio track transforms into the Micro Surround Panner.

By clicking and dragging within the Micro Surround Panner, you can change the surround panning location of your audio track. As you drag your mouse, you'll notice the Surround Pan Angle and Focus parameters being displayed and changed.

To the right of the Micro Surround Panner, you'll see the LFE Send parameter. This parameter determines how much of the signal from the current audio track you would like to send to the LFE channel. This can come in handy if you want to dedicate an audio track for effects that contain low frequency content like thunder claps, etc.

The Small Surround Panner

If you add an aux send to an audio track that is routed to a surround bus, the send will provide a Small Surround Panner, as shown in Figure 13.13. This works in a similar fashion as the Micro Surround Panner and provides an LFE send, as well as a bus send level and pre/post parameter like normal aux sends.

Figure 13.13 The Small Surround Panner is displayed on an aux send that is routed to a surround bus.

The Medium Surround Panner

As with the Micro Surround Panner, the Medium Surround Panner also replaces the normal pan parameter on an audio track, but, in this case, the Medium Surround Panner is displayed in the Track Inspector of the Track view and the audio channel strip for that track in the Console view (see Figure 13.14).

The Medium Surround Panner works the same way as the previous Panners. Click and drag within the Panner to pan your audio track in the surround field. The Medium Surround Panner also provides an LFE send like the other Panner. One additional feature of the Medium Surround Panner is the ability to mute individual monitors (speakers) in the surround field. You will see these monitors represented within the Panner as small white boxes (see Figure 13.15). Just click a box to mute that monitor. Click the box again to unmute the monitor.

Figure 13.14 The Medium Surround Panner is displayed in the Track and Console views.

Figure 13.15 Mute monitors by clicking the small white boxes in the Medium Surround Panner.

❉ **MUTING MONITORS**

You can also mute monitors by right-clicking in the Panner and choosing Mute [Name of Monitor]. This technique will also work with all the other Panners mentioned.

The Large Surround Panner

To give you the most detailed access to the surround parameters for an audio track, SONAR provides the Large Surround Panner (see Figure 13.16). To access the Large Surround Panner, just double-click one of the other Panners or right-click one of the other Panners and choose Open Surround Panner.

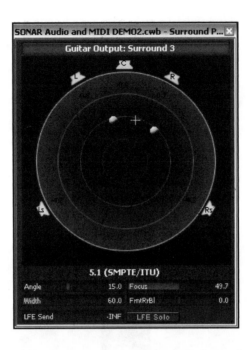

Figure 13.16 The Large Surround Panner gives you detailed access to an audio track's surround parameters.

❄ **CHANGING TRACKS**

Once open, you can change the track assignment for the Large Surround Panner by clicking the track name bar located at the top of the window.

In the top portion of the Large Surround Panner window, you will see a circular graphic representation of the surround sound field. Around this field, all the monitors are shown as small white speaker symbols and positioned according to the surround format you have chosen. You can click the speaker symbols to mute and unmute the appropriate monitors just like with the Medium Surround Panner.

Inside the surround field, a small crosshair icon represents the pan position of the current track in the surround sound field. As with the other Panners, you can simply click and drag your mouse within the field to change the pan position. As you do this, you will see the crosshair move, and you will also see the numerical values change in front of each monitor. These values represent the volume (in dB) of the audio track within each of the monitors.

In addition to the volume changes, you'll notice some other parameters changing in the bottom portion of the Large Surround Panner window. To change any of these parameters, just click and drag your mouse over the appropriate slider. Drag left or right to make a change.

Double-click a parameter to return it to its default value. You can also type a new value by selecting the parameter and pressing the Enter key.

These parameters represent the pan position of your audio track in the surround field, the stereo width of your track, and the volume balance between the front and rear monitors of the surround field. You'll also find an LFE send parameter (just like with the other Panners) and an LFE solo button, so you can quickly check only the sound coming from the LFE monitor.

Angle and Focus

The Angle and Focus parameters work together to designate the pan position of the audio track in the surround field. This is the reason both parameters change when you drag the crosshair around in the surround field. The Angle parameter designates the circular position of the audio track panning within the surround field. You can set the Angle parameter from –180 to 0 to +180 degrees. Notice that when you change the Angle parameter, the crosshair moves around in a circle within the surround field.

The Focus parameter designates how close the pan position of the audio track will be to the center of the surround field. You can set the Focus parameter from 0 to 100. A setting of 0 will put the pan position at the exact center of the surround field. A setting of 100 will put the pan position at the outer edge of the surround field (closest to the surrounding monitors).

Width

The Width parameter designates the width of the stereo audio track within the surround field. In surround field graphic, the width is represented by two green dots—one for the left channel and one for the right channel of stereo track. You can set the Width parameter from 0 to 360 degrees. The larger the value, the farther apart the stereo channels sound from one another. The smaller the value, the closer they sound. For example, a value of 0 will essentially make the track sound like a mono track because the stereo channels are right next to each other. Using a value of zero, you can make the pan position of the track sound like it's coming from a single focused point in the surround field.

Front/Rear Balance (FrntRrBl)

There may be times when you've found just the right pan position for an audio track in the surround field, but you would like to change its overall volume, as it pertains to the front and rear monitors. This is where the Front/Rear Balance parameter (abbreviated as FrntRrBl in the Panner window) can be used. The value for this parameter ranges from –100 to 0 to +100. The lower the value, the lower the volume of the front monitors. The higher the value, the lower the value of the rear monitors. A value of 0 makes the front/rear volumes equal.

Surround Panning Scenarios

Just to give you a few examples of how you can position an audio track within the surround field, I'll go through a few scenarios and show you what settings you need to achieve them.

Exact Center

To place your audio track in the exact center of the surround field, set the Angle, Focus, Width, and FrntRrBl parameters to 0.

Pinpoint Location

To place your audio track in at an exact pinpoint location in the surround field, set the Width and FrntRrBl parameters to 0. Now adjust the pan position by either changing the Angle and Focus parameters manually or clicking and dragging your mouse in the surround field graphic. This scenario also lets you make your audio track sound like it is coming directly from one of the monitors in the surround field. To do this, set the Focus parameter to 100 and then adjust the Angle parameter so that the pan position is exactly in front of the monitor from which you want the audio track to be heard.

Front and Rear Stereo

To make your audio track sound like an ordinary stereo track coming from the front monitors (see Figure 13.17), set the Angle parameter to 0, the Focus parameter to 100, and the FrntRrBl parameter to 0. Then adjust the Width parameter so that the two green dots line up with the front left and right monitors. To do this with the rear monitors, just change the Angle parameter to 180. Then adjust the Width so that the green dots line up with the rear left and right monitors.

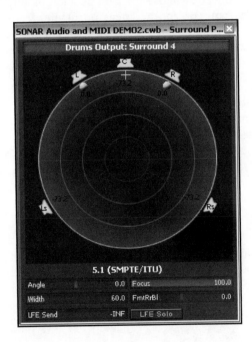

Figure 13.17 Creating an ordinary stereo sound for your audio track in the surround field.

Side Stereo

To make a stereo audio track sound like its being played in stereo on the side of the surround field (see Figure 13.18), set the Angle parameter to 90 to place the track on the right of the field or set the parameter to -90 to place the track on the left side of the field. Set the Focus parameter to 100 and the FrntRrBl parameter to 0. Then adjust the Width parameter to your liking (a good setting is about 60).

Figure 13.18 Create a left or right stereo sound for your audio track in the surround field.

❋ **SURROUND AUTOMATION AND GROUPING**

Automation and grouping for surround parameters work the same as for any other parameter. Just right-click the parameter and choose Automation Write Enable to designate the movements of that parameter for recording. Then follow the steps outlined in Chapter 12 for recording automation. In addition, you can arm all parameters for the Surround Panner at the same time by right-clicking the surround field graphic.

For grouping, just right-click the parameter and choose Group > [group letter] to group that parameter. Then follow the instructions provided in Chapter 12 covering how to use SONAR's grouping features.

Surround Sound Effects

Working with effects in surround is similar to that in stereo, except in surround you're dealing with multiple channels rather than just two. You can apply effects evenly to all surround channels, or you can apply an effect to a single surround channel. The only caveat is that you must apply surround effects to a surround bus. Surround effects cannot be applied to an audio track without using a surround bus. Because of this, there will probably be many times where you will want to assign a new surround bus to each of your audio tracks so that you can apply different effects to each track.

To apply an effect to a surround bus, you simply follow the same procedure as applying an effect to a stereo bus. Just right-click in the Fx bin of the surround bus and choose the effect you would like to apply.

Dedicated Surround Effects

SONAR provides two dedicated surround effects for use in your projects: the Sonitus Surround Compressor and the Lexicon Pantheon Surround Reverb. Both of these effects are actually based on their stereo versions. Be sure to read through that material in order to learn how to use these effects. There are a few basic differences, though, and I will explain those here.

Sonitus Surround Compressor

The Sonitus Surround Compressor provides four separate compressor effects in one. Each effect provides the same parameters. The difference between the Surround and the Stereo version comes into play when you are assigning the surround channels to each of the four compressor effects provided. When you open the Surround Compressor, you will see four compressor select buttons located at the top of the dialog box (see Figure 13.19). Initially, all the surround channels are assigned to the same compressor. You can leave them this way if you want. This will let you apply the same compression effect to all the surround channels.

Figure 13.19 The Sonitus Surround Compressor provides four compression effects.

To assign a surround channel to a different compressor effect, click the down arrow next to one of the effects and choose the surround channel(s) you want to use (see Figure 13.20).

You'll notice that each effect is given its own color. From left to right there is red, blue, green, and orange. When you assign a surround channel to a different effect, its input controls and its compression graph take on those colors. This lets you tell at a glance to what effect your surround channels are assigned.

Other than those differences, the Sonitus Surround Compressor works the same way as the stereo version. The surround version provides some presets from which you can learn. Just click the Presets button at the top of the dialog box and choose a preset from the list.

Lexicon Pantheon Surround Reverb

Like the Sonitus Surround Compressor, the Lexicon Pantheon Surround Reverb (see Figure 13.21) works in almost the same way as the Lexicon Pantheon Stereo Reverb. There are a few exceptions when it comes to the number of adjustable parameters provided.

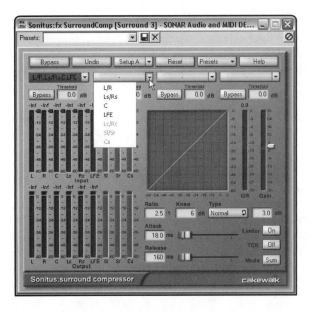

Figure 13.20 Use the down arrow next to an effect to assign its surround channels.

Figure 13.21 The Lexicon Pantheon Surround Reverb provides additional parameters for controlling reverberation in a surround environment.

The Surround Reverb provides Front Level and Rear Level parameters, which let you control the volume of the effect in the front and rear monitors independently. There are also F (Front) Rolloff and R (Rear) Rolloff parameters. In addition, there are echo sections in the Reverb dialog box for both the front and rear.

Using Stereo Effects in Surround

If SONAR simply provided two surround effects out of its entire arsenal, it wouldn't provide much power now would it? Even though there are only two dedicated surround effects included with SONAR, you can actually use all of SONAR's effects in your surround projects using some special built-in features.

When you assign a stereo effect (mono effects work too) to a surround bus, SONAR automatically creates multiple instances of that effect for each of the surround channels you are using. For example, when using the 5.1 surround format, SONAR will assign the front left and right channels to the left and right channels of the first stereo effect, the rear left and right channels to the left and right channels of the second stereo effect, then center channel to the left channel of the third stereo effect, and the LFE channel to the left channel of the fourth stereo effect. All of these controls are available in a single effect window, as shown in Figure 13.22.

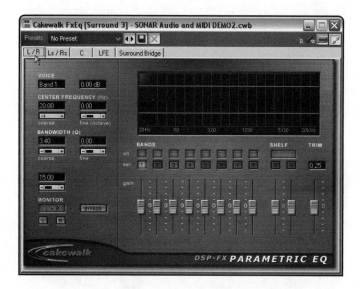

Figure 13.22 One effect window holds multiple instances of the effect to provide for all the surround channels.

Each effect instance can be accessed by clicking the appropriate tab at the top of the effect window. All the controls for each instance are identical, and the effect works just like its stereo version. In addition, all of the parameters for each instance are linked by default. This means that if you change a parameter on one instance, that same parameter will change on all the other instances. Having the parameters linked makes it easy to be sure the effect sounds the same on all the surround channels.

If you want to have the effect sound different on certain surround channels, you can unlink the parameters for each instance. First, click the tab for the effect instance you would like to change; then click the Unlink Automation Controls button at the top-right of the effect window (see Figure 13.23). Now the parameters for that instance can be changed, and the equivalent parameters in the other instances will remain the same.

Figure 13.23 Click the Unlink Controls button to change the parameters for one instance and not the others.

As far as the effect parameters themselves, they work exactly the same as their stereo versions.

The Surround Bridge

One other thing that makes using stereo effects in a surround project unique is SONAR's Surround Bridge feature. This is actually the feature that uses stereo effects in surround and automatically creates the multiple effects instances when you apply an effect to a surround bus. But there may be times when you want to change the order of the effect instances and assign the instances to different surround channels. You can do this by clicking the Surround Bride tab in the effect window (see Figure 13.24).

Under the Surround Bridge tab, you'll see the Plug-in Instance Configuration section showing how each of the effect instances is configured. The number of the instance is shown in the first column. The second column shows which surround channel is assigned to the left input of the instance. The third column shows which surround channel is assigned to the right input of the instance. To change a channel assignment, just click the down arrow next to the channel and make a new choice (see Figure 13.25). For example, you may want each surround channel to have its own effect instance. You would simply click the left channel input of a blank effect instance and assign it to a surround channel. This would remove the surround channel's current instance assignment and create a new instance tab at the top of the window for the new surround channel assignment.

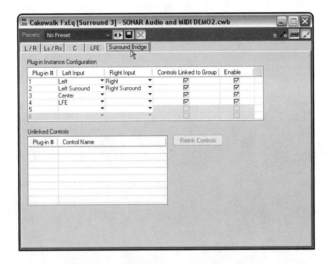

Figure 13.24   Click the Surround Bridge tab to access the Surround Bridge settings.

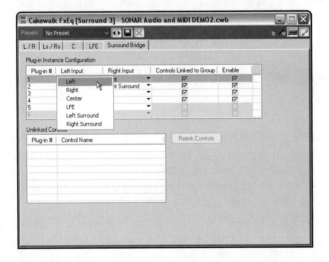

Figure 13.25   Change surround channel effect instance assignments with a simple click.

You can also quickly link or unlink all the controls in an effect instance by adding or removing its check mark in the column labeled Controls Linked to Group. In addition, if you want to disable an effect instance, just remove its check mark in the Enable column. Add the check mark to enable the instance again.

One last feature of the Surround Bridge is the Unlinked Controls section. When you select an effect instance in the Plug-in Instance Configuration section, the Unlinked Controls section lists all unlinked controls for that instance. You can relink any of the listed controls by clicking the control to select it and then clicking the Relink Controls button.

Exporting Your Surround Project

After you've added effects and mixed your tracks into a superb, surround masterpiece, you can use SONAR's export features to save your project as a multichannel audio file, which can then be burned to CD or DVD. Before exporting, however, be sure to check the downmix of your project.

Downmixing

When mixing a project in surround sound, you should always keep in the back of your mind the fact that your surround mix might be heard in stereo at one time or another. The reason for this is that a listener could select the stereo mode on their home theater system when playing your music. If they do this, the home theater system automatically mixes the six surround channels (in a 5.1 surround mix) down to the two stereo channels. The center surround channel is added to the left and right stereo channels equally. The left and right surround channels are also added to the left and right stereo channels. And the LFE channel is either added or in some instances, just removed. Because of this, you should always listen to your surround mix in stereo when you're finished. Here's how to check the downmix of your surround project:

1. If you don't have one, insert a stereo bus into your project by right-clicking in the Bus pane and choosing Insert Stereo Bus.

2. For every surround bus that you have in your project, assign its output to the new stereo bus.

3. Choose Options > Project > Surround to open the Project Options – Surround dialog box (see Figure 13.26.

4. In the Downmixing section, choose the volume levels (in dB) at which you want the center channel, surround channels, and LFE channel mixed into the left and right stereo channels. The default settings usually work well, but every project is different, so you'll have to try the different settings to see which ones work with your project.

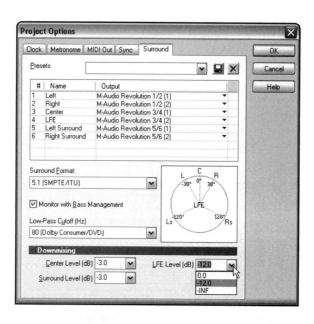

Figure 13.26 Use the Project Options – Surround dialog box to set your project's downmixing parameters.

❀ CONFIGURABLE DOWNMIXING SETTINGS

Even though SONAR provides a number of default downmixing values from which to choose, you can actually type in any dB level into the downmixing parameters that you would like. Just click inside a parameter and type in a new value.

---

5. Click OK.

6. Listen to your project through the new stereo bus. If it doesn't sound quite right, either adjust your mix or adjust the downmixing settings.

7. When you've got the right mix, you can export your project to a stereo file if you'd like, and SONAR will take into account your downmixing settings.

After you've finished downmixing, you can set your surround bus outputs back to their original values.

Exporting to Multichannel WAV or WMA

To let others hear your surround project, SONAR exports your project to a multichannel WAV file or Windows Media File. Here is how it's done:

1. Choose File > Export > Audio to open the Export Audio dialog box (see Figure 13.27).

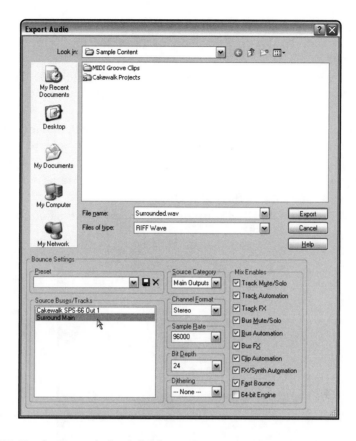

Figure 13.27 Use the Export Audio dialog box to save your project as a multichannel audio file.

2. Set the Look In parameter to the folder on your hard drive in which you would like to save your file.

3. Type in a File Name for the file.

4. Select a Files of Type for your file. If you plan on burning your project to DVD in the DVD-Audio or DVD-Video formats, export it as a WAV file by choosing the RIFF Wave format. If your project will be played using the Windows Media Player, you can export it as a Windows Media File by choosing the Windows Media Advanced Streaming Format.

5. More than likely, you have your surround buses all being output to the Surround Main (otherwise you wouldn't be able to mix in surround). So set the Source Category to Main Outputs.

6. Select Surround Main in the Source Buses/Tracks list.

7. Choose Multichannel for the Channel Format.

8. Depending on what you used for your project sampling rate, set the Sampling Rate to that same value here. You can use a sampling rate up to 96,000 for 5.1 surround in the DVD-Audio format.

9. Depending on what you used for your project bit depth, set the Bit Depth to that same value here. You can use a bit depth up to 24-bit for 5.1 surround in the DVD-Audio format.

10. In order to make sure all your automation and effects get included in your exported file, be sure to put check marks next to all the options in the Mix Enables section.

11. Click Export. If you chose the RIFF Wave format for your file, then SONAR will export the file, and you are now finished. If you chose the Windows Media Advanced Streaming Format file, there are some additional steps.

12. After you click Export, SONAR will display the Windows Media Format Encode Options dialog box (see Figure 13.28).

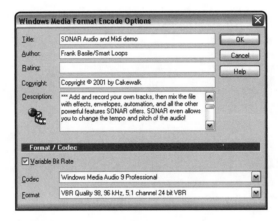

Figure 13.28 Use the Windows Media Format Encode Options dialog box to save your surround project as a Windows Media File.

13. Enter the information for your project in the Title, Author, Rating, Copyright, and Description fields. The Windows Media Player will display this information for your listeners.

14. Add or remove the check mark next to the Variable Bit Rate option. Activating this option tells SONAR to vary the bit rate during the encoding process. Sometimes, this can yield a higher quality sound and a smaller file size, but it depends on the material you are encoding. In addition, activating this option affects the selections available from the Codec and Format parameters.

15. With the Variable Bit Rate option activated, you can choose between Windows Media Audio 9 Professional and Windows Media Audio 9 Lossless for the Codec parameter.

The Lossless option means that there will be no quality loss in your encoded file, but choosing this option only gives you one choice for the Format parameter.

16. With the Variable Bit Rate option activated, you can choose three different options for the Format parameter. Each option begins with the text VBR Quality. The higher the quality number, the higher the quality of your encoded audio, but the larger the file will be. With the Variable Bit Rate option deactivated, you can choose from a large variety of options for the Format parameter. The higher the kbps rating you choose, the higher the quality of your encoded audio, but the larger the file will be.

17. Click OK.

After SONAR encodes your file, you can take it and burn it to CD or DVD for sharing with others.

Encoding and Burning

The two most common forms of distributing a 5.1 surround mix are on DVD in either the DVD-A (DVD-Audio) format or the DVD-V (DVD-Video) format. Unfortunately, SONAR doesn't provide the features for creating DVD-A or DVD-V discs. There's a reason for this—it would add a lot of extra cost to the software and with so many different choices on the market, users are better off being able to make their own choice as to what they need for DVD-A or DVD-V software.

I'm not going to go into the encoding process because each product is different, and there's no way to cover them all. However, you can find more information about creating DVD-A and DVD-V discs at the following resources:

❋ Encoding and Recording Your Surround Sound Mix to Disc—www.digifreq.com/digifreq/article.asp?ID=24

❋ More Audio and Surround Sound Articles—www.digifreq.com/digifreq/articles.asp

❋ 5dot1.com—www.5dot1.com/

❋ Everything You Wanted to Know about DVD-Audio—www.discwelder.com/pdfs/dvdAudioWhitepaper.pdf

❋ DVD Authoring—www.discwelder.com/pdfs/dvdr_whitepaper.pdf

❋ Dolby Digital Guidelines—www.minnetonkaaudio.com/pdfs/Dolby%20Digital%20Guidelines.pdf

Good luck in creating your very own surround sound projects using SONAR! Remember to experiment since mixing in surround gives you so much more flexibility than mixing in plain old stereo.

14 } Taking Your SONAR 6 Project to CD

Congratulations! Your project has been recorded, edited, and mixed, and now you can share it with the rest of the world. To be able to share it, you need to create your very own CD. This chapter will cover the basics of creating a custom audio CD and will do the following:

* Show you how to prepare your project for CD audio.
* Explain how to use Cakewalk's Pyro 5 CD-burning software.
* Demonstrate how to use the built-in Windows XP CD burning functions.

Preparing a Project for CD Audio

A project can't be laid down as audio tracks on a CD as is. Instead, you have to convert all your MIDI tracks in a project to audio tracks. Then you have to export those audio tracks to a WAV file, so that your CD recording software can write the file to your CD. To do so, you need to follow a number of steps, which the following sections will detail.

Converting Your MIDI Tracks

If you happen to have a consumer-level sound card that provides a built-in synthesizer, and you used that sound card synth for some of your MIDI tracks, the first step is to convert any MIDI tracks that use your sound card's built-in synthesizer for playback to audio tracks as follows:

1. Insert a new audio track and assign the input for the track to your sound card's stereo input. For instance, if you have a Sound Blaster Live! card, set the track to the Stereo SB Live Wave Device input. Also, activate the Record option for the track.
2. Mute all the tracks in your project, except the one you just created, and the MIDI tracks you're going to convert.
3. Open your sound card's mixer controls (see Figure 14.1) by double-clicking the small speaker icon in the Windows Taskbar.

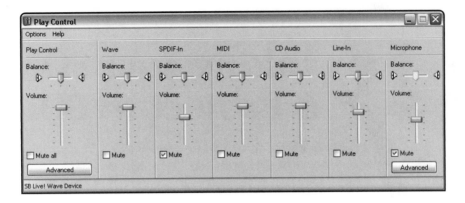

Figure 14.1   This window shows the sound card mixer controls for the Sound Blaster Live! sound card.

4. Choose Options > Properties and click Recording in the Adjust Volume For section of the resulting Properties dialog box. Then click OK to bring up the recording mixer controls, as shown in Figure 14.2.

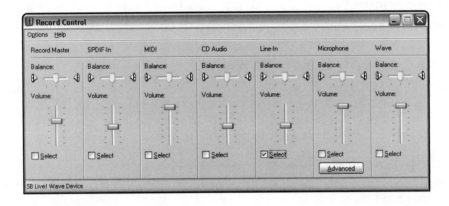

Figure 14.2   This window shows the recording mixer controls for the Sound Blaster Live! sound card.

5. Activate the recording source for your sound card's synth by clicking the appropriate Select option (see Figure 14.3).
6. Click the Record button on the toolbar in SONAR, and your MIDI tracks will be recorded to the stereo audio track.

Next you need to convert any MIDI tracks that use external MIDI instruments for playback to audio tracks, as shown in the following steps. If you don't have any MIDI tracks of this kind, you can skip this section.

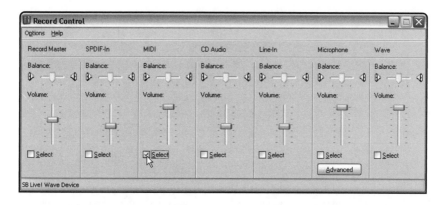

Figure 14.3 You need to activate your sound card's synth before you can record its output.

1. Insert a new audio track and assign the input for the track to your sound card's stereo input. For instance, if you have a Sound Blaster Live! card, set the track to the Stereo SB Live Wave Device input. Also, activate the Record option for the track.

2. Mute all the tracks in your project, except the one you just created and the MIDI tracks you're going to convert.

3. Open your sound card's mixer controls by double-clicking the small speaker icon in the Windows Taskbar.

4. Choose Options > Properties and then click Recording in the Adjust Volume For section of the resulting Properties dialog box. Then click OK to bring up the recording mixer controls.

5. Activate the recording source for your sound card's line input(s) by clicking the appropriate Select option (see Figure 14.4).

6. Be sure the audio outputs from your external MIDI instrument are connected to the line inputs of your sound card. If you have more than one MIDI instrument, and you're using a mixing board, connect the stereo outputs of your mixing board to the line inputs of your sound card.

7. Click the Rewind button on the toolbar in SONAR so that recording will start at the beginning of the song. Then click the Record button on the toolbar in SONAR, and your MIDI tracks will be recorded to the stereo audio track.

After you're finished, you should have two new audio tracks, representing your sound card's built-in synthesizer and your external MIDI instruments.

❈ ONVERTING SOFTWARE SYNTH TRACKS

 have any MIDI tracks in your project that use software synths, you do not need to do anything with racks when exporting. They will be exported just like regular audio tracks.

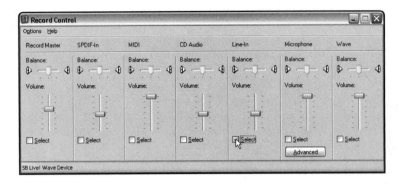

Figure 14.4   You need to activate your sound card's line input(s) before you can record any external MIDI instruments.

Converting Your Audio Tracks

After all your sound card and external MIDI tracks are converted to audio tracks, you need to mix and export all your audio tracks down to a WAV file. SONAR provides a very convenient feature expressly for this purpose, called *Export Audio*. This feature takes any number of original audio tracks (preserving their volume, pan, and effects settings) and mixes them into a single stereo WAV file. Here's how to use it:

1. Mute any of the MIDI tracks in your project and any audio tracks that you don't want included in the exported WAV file.
2. Choose File > Export > Audio to open the Export Audio dialog box, as shown in Figure 14.5.
3. From the Look In list, select the folder into which you want to save the WAV file. Then type a name for the file in the File Name field.
4. Choose the file type from the Files of Type list. In this case, use the RIFF Wave option.
5. Select the Channel Format you want to use. You can mix your audio tracks to a single stereo file, two mono files (that, when combined, create a stereo file), or a single mono file. You can also set the bit depth and sampling rate by using the Bit Depth and Sample Rate parameters.

❋ **BURNING TO CD**

If you plan to burn your project to CD, then choose the Stereo option for the Channel Format parameter, the 16-Bit option for the Bit Depth parameter, and the 44100 option for the Sample Rate parameter. This will give you a single stereo WAV file with a bit depth of 16 and a sampling rate of 44.1 kHz, w what you need for audio CD burning.

Figure 14.5 You use the Export Audio dialog box to mix and export your tracks.

6. For the Source Category parameter, choose the Entire Mix option.

7. If the original bit-depth of your project is 16-bit, then set the Dithering parameter to None. If the original bit-depth is higher than 16-bit, you need to choose a Dithering method. Why? Because converting audio from a high bit depth down to a lower bit depth can introduce harmonic distortion, making the sound less desirable. Dithering applies special mathematical processes to the data and smoothes out this noise so that it can't be heard. In this case, I would choose the Pow-r 3 option because it provides the most accurate processing. Pow-r 3 also requires the most computing power, so if it overtaxes your PC, try using Pow-r 2 or Pow-r 1.

8. Leave all the Mix Enables options activated to ensure that your new WAV file will sound exactly the same when played back as the original audio tracks. One exception might be the 64-bit Engine option. If your PC can handle it, I recommend activating the option because it will provide the most accurate processing, but if your PC gets overtaxed, deactivate the option.

9. Click the Export button, and SONAR will mix all your audio tracks down to a new WAV file.

When you're done, you should have a WAV file that you can use, along with your CD-recording software to create an audio CD.

Using Cakewalk Pyro 5

To burn your WAV file to an audio CD, you'll need a CD-burning application, such as Cakewalk's Pyro 5. Pyro 5 is very easy to use and provides a number of useful CD-burning features. To burn an audio WAV file to CD using Pyro 5, follow these basic steps:

1. Start Pyro 5 and click the Make Audio CD tab to display the audio CD burning screen, as shown in Figure 14.6. The top half of the screen shows all of the resources available on your PC. This includes your Windows desktop, the hard drives, and all the files stored on your computer. The left pane is the Folders view, and the right pane is the Files view. The bottom half of the screen represents your new audio CD. Initially you'll see only blank white space.

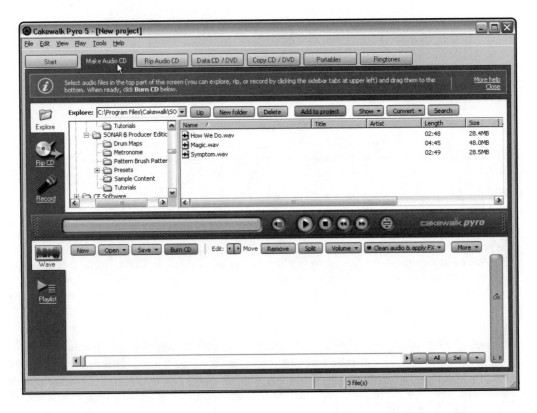

Figure 14.6   Click the Make Audio CD tab to access the audio CD functions.

2. In the Folders view, choose the resource or disk drive containing the audio files you want to burn to CD. For example, if you have some files on your Windows desktop that you want to burn, click Desktop in the Folders view. The Files view will then display a list of all the folders and files available on the desktop.

3. In the Files view, select the audio files you want to burn to CD. To select multiple files, hold down the CTRL key, as you click the files with your mouse.

4. Click the Add to Project button in the top half of the screen to add the selected files to your audio CD project. The files will be added to the audio CD project area, as shown in Figure 14.7.

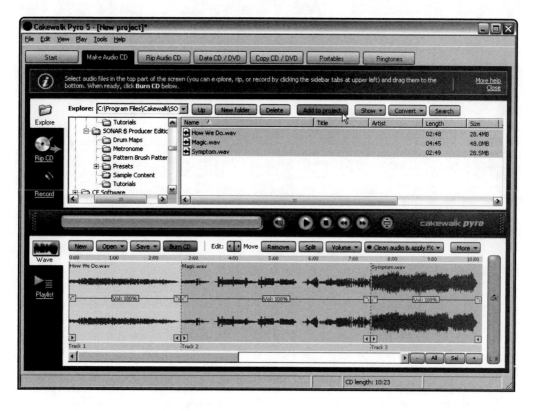

Figure 14.7   Click the Add to Project button to add files to your audio CD project.

5. To delete a file from the audio CD project, click it to select it and then click the Remove button.

❄ **LIST VIEW**

You can also view the tracks on your audio CD project as a list by clicking the View button, located on the far left of the audio CD project area (see Figure 14.8).

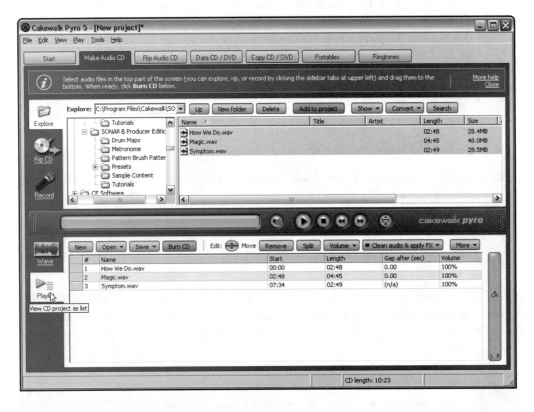

Figure 14.8 Click the View button to show the audio CD project as a list.

6. To move a file to a different track location in the audio CD project, click the file to select it and then use the Move buttons to move the file left or right in the project (left being toward the beginning of the CD and right being toward the end of the CD).

7. Repeat Steps 2 through 6 until you've finished adding all your files to the project.

8. Put a blank CD-R disc in your CD burner and then click the Burn CD button to display the CD Burning Options dialog box (see Figure 14.9).

9. Choose the drive you want to use from the Select a Drive for Burning drop-down list. If you have only one CD burner attached to your computer, it should be chosen automatically.

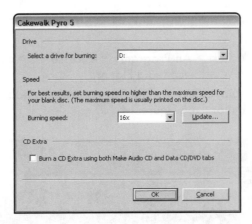

Figure 14.9 Use the CD Burning Options dialog box to choose the drive and the burning speed.

10. Choose the burning speed you want to use from the Burning Speed drop-down list. If the list doesn't look accurate, you can have Pyro 5 scan your drive by clicking the Update button.

❀ **CD BURNING SPEEDS**

When choosing a burning speed, be sure to read the label on the blank disc you are using to determine its maximum speed rating. Some CDs are created to withstand high burning speeds and some are not. If you choose a speed that is higher than what your disc can withstand, it might not burn correctly.

11. Click OK. Pyro 5 will show you its progress as it burns your new audio CD.

❀ **AVOIDING GLITCHES**

To avoid glitches in the burning process—especially for audio CDs—you should leave your computer alone until the process is complete. If it gets bogged down while burning, you could end up with a ruined CD. Of course, you can just go ahead and burn another one, but then you'll be wasting both your time and money.

Burning CDs with Windows XP

If you are running SONAR under Windows XP, then you don't need any third-party CD burning software because Windows XP provides built-in burning capabilities. By utilizing the

Windows Media Player (included with Windows XP), you can burn audio CDs by following these steps.

1. In Windows XP, click Start > All Programs > Accessories > Entertainment > Windows Media Player to open Windows Media Player.
2. If the Player is not displayed in full mode (as a normal window with a menu bar), click the Show Menu Bar button (see Figure 14.10).

Figure 14.10   Click the Show Menu Bar button to display Windows Media Player in a full window.

3. Click the Media Library button (located on the left side of the Player window) to display the Media Library (see Figure 14.11).
4. In the list on the left side of the Media Library, select All Audio.
5. Choose File > Add to Media Library > Add File to display the Open dialog box.
6. In the Look In list, choose the location of the WAV files you want to burn to CD.
7. In the file list below the Look In list, select the WAV files you want to burn to CD. To select multiple files, hold down the CTRL key, as you select files with your mouse.
8. When you are finished selecting files, click Open. Your selected files will be displayed as a list on the right side of the Media Library.
9. If you want to remove a file from the list, right-click the file and choose Delete from Library.

Figure 14.11   Access the Media Library by using the Media Library button.

10. To change the title of a file, right-click the file and choose Properties to open the Properties dialog box (see Figure 14.12). In addition to the title, you can also specify the file's artist, author, album, and genre. Click OK.

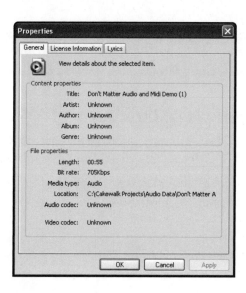

Figure 14.12   Use the Properties dialog box to specify a title, artist, and other attributes for your files.

11. Click the Copy to CD or Device button (located on the left side of the Player window) to display the CD Copier (see Figure 14.13).

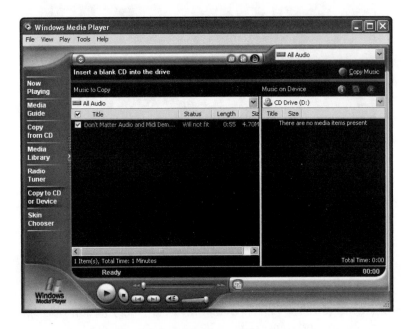

Figure 14.13   Use the CD Copier to burn your audio to CD.

12. Insert a blank CD-R disc into your CD-R drive. The CD Copier will recognize the blank disc and display the message Copy "All Audio" to "CD Drive."

13. To burn your CD, click the Copy Music button (located on the top right of the CD Copier).

ADDITIONAL CHAPTERS AVAILABLE ON WEB SITE

You may find additional SONAR 6·Power! Chapters 15-18 and Appendices A-B for download at http://www.courseptr.com/downloads. Please visit our site for further information on SONAR 6.

} Index

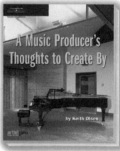

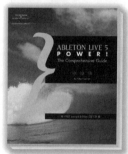

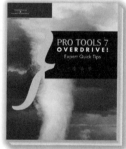